MANAGERIAL COMMUNICATION
A Finger on the Pulse

MANAGERIAL COMMUNICATION
A Finger on the Pulse

Paul R. Timm

School of Management
Brigham Young University

Prentice-Hall, Inc.
Englewood Cliffs, New Jersey   07632

Library of Congress Cataloging in Publication Data

Timm, Paul R
  Managerial communication.

  Includes bibliographies and index.
  1. Communication in management.   I. Title.
HF5718.T55   658.4'5   79-9528
ISBN 0-13-549824-4

Cover illustration from *Japanese Design Motifs:*
4260 Illustrations of Heraldic Crests. Dover
Publications Inc., New York, N.Y., 1972.

Printed in the United States of America

10   9   8   7   6   5   4

PRENTICE-HALL INTERNATIONAL, INC., *London*
PRENTICE-HALL OF AUSTRALIA PTY. LIMITED, *Sydney*
PRENTICE-HALL OF CANADA, LTD., *Toronto*
PRENTICE-HALL OF INDIA PRIVATE LIMITED, *New Delhi*
PRENTICE-HALL OF JAPAN, INC., *Tokyo*
PRENTICE-HALL OF SOUTHEAST ASIA PTE. LTD., *Singapore*
WHITEHALL BOOKS LIMITED, *Wellington, New Zealand*

PREFACE

Communication is what managers *do*. It breathes life into planning, organizing, motivating and controlling. It is the way we get meaningful work accomplished by coordinating the efforts of other individuals and groups. It consumes 90% of a manager's workday. Yet most college programs leading to degrees in management and much organization-sponsored management training fail to develop adequately the basic communication skills that managers need. This book is an attempt to bridge the gap between what has typically been taught and what we need.

In the following eleven chapters, we will look at some important ideas about managerial communication. Many of these are not systematically studied in academic programs ostensibly designed to train people for administrative management responsibilities. Some areas are covered in the traditional curriculum, albeit from a narrower "business communication"—letters and report writing—perspective. Many of these chapters are likely to be new to you unless you've had extensive interdisciplinary training. A few chapters may serve as concise reviews of material you've already covered. The chart on the following page indicates where the theme for each chapter tends to be covered (if at all) in the traditional university curriculum.

What I'm saying here is that the book you are now holding cuts through the maze of the traditional academic structure and attempts to provide the kinds of basic communication skills we all need. And I stress the *we*.

Chapter and Theme	Business Curriculum Coverage	Other Disciplines' Coverage
1. Definition of communication and its role in management	Some discussion of communication role in organizational behavior courses	Communication theory offered through speech curriculum
2. Communication climate	Not systematically covered	Seldom covered in other disciplines
3. Communication process and flow within organizations	Sometimes covered in information systems courses but seldom applied to human interactions	Seldom covered in other disciplines
4. Communication media and tools	May be covered briefly in business communications courses	Studied in journalism and advertising programs but seldom applied to internal organizational processes
5. One-with-one communication skills (interviewing, instruction giving, conversation, etc.)	Seldom specifically covered except for employment interviewing (for the job applicant) in business communication courses	Studied in interpersonal communication course but not focused on employer-employee situations; covered in some psychology courses
6. Interactional communication: meetings and conference skills	Some coverage in organizational behavior; also discussed in preparation for case analysis activities	A popular area of study in speech communication but seldom concentrates on managerial problems
7. Speaking before groups; briefings and presentations	May be covered briefly in business communication course; usually considered secondary to written skills training	A popular area of study in speech communication although emphasis tends to be more toward public speaking
8. Listening	Seldom covered	Sometimes available in speech communication or psychology curriculum
9. Business letters and memos	Normally covered in business communication courses	Seldom covered in other disciplines
10. Business report writing	Normally covered in business communication courses	Occasionally covered in English courses
11. Personal communication style	Seldom covered	Sometimes covered in speech communication curriculum under "interpersonal," "nonverbal," or "general semantics" courses

While I was finishing the manuscript of this book, one of my students, a production manager at a local packaging company, leafed through the final draft and said, "Wow, I know lots of people who need this." Sensing an early sale and eventual giant royalties, I asked, "How about you? Don't you think you need a few copies?" His answer surprised me a bit. He paused and said, "I don't know how to break this to you, Dr. Timm, but I, personally, don't have any communication problems. You see, I have studied language and have become something of a 'wordsmith.' In fact, I'm your basic 'silver-tongued fox.' I carefully fashion my messages so that there can be no misunderstanding. When I talk, people listen. So I don't really need this book, but maybe I'll get a copy for my boss—he has lots of communication problems—or for my wife—Lord knows, I'll never understand women. Or better yet I'll get copies for that group of clowns who work for me. They have yet to communicate a decent idea that would do the company any good."

Be honest: have you ever felt that communication is something *other people* don't do very well? Isn't it exasperating to see how often they foul up perfectly simple instructions or fail to make any sense at all? I certainly feel that way sometimes.

Well, this book is about communication problems caused by other people. But it's also about communication problems caused by *me* and *you*. Now hold it a minute before you get defensive. It's a fact of life that it takes two (or more) to create a communication problem. And it ain't always the other guy.

Most of you are managers or people training to become managers. Now I don't mean that you necessarily work in an office or supervise a group of assembly line workers. What I do mean is that you are (or soon will be) involved in the process of getting productive work done *with and through the efforts of other individuals and groups.* A homemaker is a manager when she gets the kids to help wash dishes; a basketball coach is a manager when she develops teamwork among her players; the officer in a college fraternity is a manager when he leads his brothers in pulling off a successful toga party; and a teacher or trainer is a manager when students have grown under his or her direction. I am, of course, using the term *management* in a broad sense, essentially synonymous with *leadership.*

If you find yourself fitting such a definition of a manager, this book was written for you. Its focus is on practical ideas and their immediate application in your leadership role. I'm willing to bet that you'll find some new ways of behaving that will have a real impact on your communication skills and managerial effectiveness. All of this presupposes, of course, that you are willing to change the ways you do things if you can be shown a better way. I'll try to show you some better ways. But this book will be of no value to you unless you are willing to try on some new behaviors—some different ways of doing things. I ask only that you read with an open mind.

Any book is the product of countless learning episodes. My academic studies and teaching in management and communication are tempered by seven years in the "real world" with Bell Telephone and Xerox Corporation. The experiences there—both productive and destructive—helped form the mental filters through which I see the world. To list all the people who have significantly affected my understanding would be impossible. One great teacher, however, deserves special mention: to Dr. Clarence Edney of Florida State University, my repeated thanks. I appreciate, too, the many business people and students who have taught me as I attempted to teach them. Included among these are the folks in my advanced communication classes at the University of North Carolina at Charlotte who critiqued my manuscript as it developed. Gail Erb, Dave Smith, Bob Blackwelder, Guy Wilkerson, Rob Williford, Brenda Rhen, and Doris Cauble provided especially helpful comments. My thanks also to Sherry Templeton and Mark Martinez for their original cartoons and photos and to Drs. Elliott A. Pood and Ethel Glenn for their work in developing the instructor's guide. To my colleagues at UNCC who wondered what the hermit in the corner office has been up to: here 'tis.

I reserve my most sincere appreciation for my wife and family who have supported me 100 percent in this effort throughout the last two years. And finally, to my dad, Roy C. Timm, who never gave up on me, though I gave him plenty of reasons to, I dedicate this book.

CONTENTS

PART IV
OUR PERSONAL COMMUNICATION STYLES

11   OUR PERSONAL STYLE
The Way We Word, 353

EPILOGUE, 377

INDEX, 379

PART I

THE BIG PICTURE

CHAPTER 1

MANAGERIAL COMMUNICATION
Creating Understanding in a World of Organizations

In our modern world we all spend a majority of our lives in some sort of organized activity. At birth we are introduced to an organization called the hospital staff. Within a few days we actively join an organization called a family. For the rest of our days our needs and wants will be fulfilled directly or indirectly by organizations. Manufacturing, farming, mining, and distribution organizations bring us products to satisfy our material needs. Schools, churches, clubs, and informal social groups serve our needs for information, understanding, personal growth, and affiliation. Governments are organized to provide essential services for the public good.

It's been estimated that 90 percent of us who work for a living do so in organizations. In contemporary society there are very few legitimate hermits. Being a recluse from organizational life is becoming ever more difficult.

When we think about organizations we tend to picture the physical aspects like buildings, office space, machines and tools, or capital assets as described in an annual report. But organizations can exist without any of these things so long as we have people assembled (physically or figuratively) for some purpose. The key ingredient is that we have some sustained patterns of coordinated action among people. These sustained patterns lead to the development of relationships so long as there is *communication*.

Leaders in an organization can have a tremendous impact on communication effectiveness. Indeed the role of managers—those who get things done through the efforts of others—is essentially one of organizing and communicating. The communicating breathes life into the organizing.

A Back-to-Basics View of Communication

Textbook writers can and typically do offer a number of definitions of communication. Indeed the term *communication* is widely used in at least three contexts. In one sense it has to do with the sending and receiving of messages. People "communicate" when they talk together or write to each other. In another sense, communication is used as a noun—"your recent communication"—describing the actual message. In a third, and broader sense, communication involves the whole process of sharing meanings. It involves complex mental processes as well as outward behaviors. Some people talk to each other, thereby sending "communications," but seldom seem to "communicate"—seldom establish an authentic understanding of each other's feelings, ideas, or values.

I will use the term *communication* in all of these ways in this book. But I would like to establish a conceptual framework for viewing the most important kinds of communication that occur in most organizations. In considering this it might be useful to take a "back-to-basics" stance, and simply consider the term's Latin root word, *communicare*, which means "to make common." When you have in your head the idea that I have in my head, we have communicated—we have made common our understanding. Our accuracy is determined by the degree of commonality we share.

Simple, right? Well, actually, no. In fact, human communication may well be one of the most complex and difficult processes we can ever study. There are a couple of reasons for this.

First, the "making common" of meanings—or, more often, the failure to achieve desired levels of understanding—comes about in many, often unpredictable ways. The numerous variables that affect communication can sometimes lead to surprising results. While these results can be disappointing, or worse, these same variables also provide us with "strings to pull" to improve our probability for effectiveness. Much of this book will deal with recognizing these strings and pulling them for better communication.

A second thing that makes communication analysis kind of tricky is the notion that when we study communication we are studying something that is exceedingly hard to examine objectively. We are studying *ourselves*. The closer we get to something, the harder it is to evaluate it fairly.

While others come to know us by our behaviors, often our behaviors are so automatic or unconscious that we don't recognize the way we come across to others. We tend to have a form of personal pride in the ways we, as individuals or as organizations, have been doing or saying things all along. We resist changes in behavior. It's usually more comfortable going on as we have been and instead getting *others* to change the ways *they* do things.

We are inextricably linked to our communication behavior. The ways we attempt to communicate are expressions of personality, the sum total of our psychological makeup. From our habits of thought, our attitudes and our values, we draw conclusions about reality. We learn how to respond to our world and we learn how others "should" respond. We assume that others see the world pretty much as it *is* (to us) and that they should be able to relate rather easily to what we are saying to them.

In fact, people not only do not *see* the world in the same way because of their different experiences and perceptions, but in a fairly literal sense, people don't even *live in* the same psychological world. Each of us have unique lives. From day one, we each have individual experiences which are never exactly like anything any other person experiences. These experiences, packed into our memory bank, shape the way we attach meanings to the things of our world. Each message we receive is evaluated in terms of what we already know to determine if it makes sense.

It is this complexity and closeness to ourselves that foils many people's understanding of communication. To cope, we oversimplify the communication process to picture it like a machine: "X does something to Y" or "Mr. A. transmits a message to Mrs. B." We get preoccupied with the mechanics and techniques for perking up our speaking or writing skills, and ignore many other important dimensions of the communication situation. We begin to think that because our message sounds better and better to us, that it must be getting better for our listeners.

A simple sender-does-something-to-a-receiver model may be adequate when we are talking about the conveying of simple directives or orders. But most of the things we communicate in real organizations—ideas, impressions, and feelings—are a lot more complex. When we back away from an emphasis on our message *sending* skills and seek to better understand the totality of what's going on, we develop a sensitivity to others that facilitates the process of making common our thoughts, feelings, impressions, goals, and policies. Being a better communicator means being a better understander. Constantly adjusting *your* message until it sounds better and better *to you* is not the ultimate communication improvement. The true communicator is concerned with "thou," not "I." Until we can sincerely develop a concern for understanding others, we cannot maximize our potential as communicators.

There are a number of popular misconceptions about managerial communication that can be attributed to a failure to see the broader context I've been describing. Managers who view problems in organizational communication in terms of faulty message sending techniques without clarifying the broader system of activities and variables at work cannot realistically expect to bring about long-range, enduring improvement in the ways they communicate.

Misconception 1:
Communication Is a Fringe Benefit

Too frequently managers consider effective communication as some sort of fringe benefit for employees. They see it as a way to keep workers happy or to boost their morale. In reality, communication is the essence of the manager's job. If we accept management as a process of accomplishing tasks through people under the most economical conditions with the most profitable results, we must accept the notion that the people we manage must be communicated with. This involves instructing, guiding, and motivating. Our effectiveness depends upon our sensitivity to the perceptions, the expectations, and the degree of involvement of those we manage. Such communication also involves creating conditions in which the development of mutual, two-way understanding can flourish.

The employee who, for whatever reasons, fails to be adequately involved in an organization's communication is not just missing out on a nice corporate perquisite. In a very real sense, that individual is not a part of the sustained patterns of coordinated action and the development of relationships which *constitute* the organization. Involvement in communication cannot be viewed as some special gift awarded to employees by beneficent leaders. It is instead the very process by which people become organized.

Misconception 2:
Communication Is Message Sending

Probably the most common view of communication is as an activity whereby an individual transmits information to another individual or group. This more accurately describes purposeful communication *events* or *activities* rather than the overall process. Here we are taking an "I" attitude (as opposed to a "you" orientation) and are primarily concerned with what happens when I purposefully construct a message and transmit it to others. A simple model describes the steps in this process:

Encoding ⟶ Transmitting ⟶ Receiving ⟶ Decoding
                via a medium

(Sender)   (Receiver)

As message senders, we put thoughts and feelings or perceptions into some form of language through the encoding process. We then send off that coded message via oral or written media to someone else. Our receiver, in turn, decodes or attempts to make sense out of the message he or she gets from us. Often our receiver goes through the same process and responds to us.

This is, of course, an oversimplified explanation of what happens. If we accept this at face value we might conclude that the only ways to improve our communication are to improve our message preparation skills and/or the integrity of the transmitting medium.

If we extract an isolated communication event from all that is going on in the organization, we can typically identify the activities described in the sender-to-receiver model. From a commonsense viewpoint, the approach seems satisfactory. If, however, we accept this as the definitive model of communication, we are likely to run into problems. Many communication processes going on in organizations cannot be realistically nor accurately diagnosed from this sender-oriented approach. Take for example, this short incident:

Paul Spearman, a district manager, had gone out on a limb for Dave Zaleski several times. He hired him despite the fact that Dave had no sales experience whatsoever. That decision paid off beautifully—within six months Dave was a top producer. Paul later pushed hard for Dave's promotion to sales manager when an opening arose. This took some effort to convince higher management. Although they were impressed with Zaleski's sales record, he had no management training, had been a sales representative only 18 months, and, frankly, had irritated more than a few people with his "cocksure" attitude. Nevertheless, Spearman prevailed and Dave was promoted. In the process, Paul and Dave developed a close rapport; they appreciated their mutually supportive relationship.

During his second month as sales manager, Dave boldly announced that his team would break the company's record for new customer orders. His self-determined quota was 48 units—200 percent of the normal quota. The previous district record had been 163 percent.

The month ended and Dave's team had indeed produced an outstanding record—194 percent of quota. Paul was delighted. He immediately sent off a congratulatory note, including a good-natured "needle" about just missing the 200 percent mark:

To: Dave Zaleski, Sales Manager

From: Paul Spearman, District Manager

Subject: Outstanding sales month!

200 percent it ain't; but not bad for a rookie.
Here's hoping you actually accomplish what you say
you're going to do someday. Way to go, champ.

Dave missed the humor completely. He was personally embarrassed about not making his goal, even though his accomplishment was outstanding. When Paul later visited Dave's office he was met with an icy reception. The message's intent was to congratulate and to stimulate continued excellence. Instead, it drove a wedge between the two men.

How does a sender-to-receiver model account for this communication problem? It doesn't. There are simply too many other variables, such as personal pride, values, and sentiments, which affect the communication but are left unexplained. Let's consider another example.

Wayne Johnson, a manufacturing plant foreman, was asked to teach two new employees how to work a machine. The first employee was a young man of a minority race who had been hired under a special program to train difficult to employ people. The foreman, whose views were not sympathetic to any of the affirmative action programs initiated by the company, begrudgingly took the young man to the machine and instructed him on how to run it: "Each time this metal part comes down this assembly line here, you pull it off, stick it under the press so that the edges line up here, and then push this foot pedal so the drill bit will come down and put the hole in the right place. Be careful to keep your hands away from the drill bit when you are doing it. Any moron should be able to do this. Ya got any questions?"

What could the employee say? If any moron could do this, surely asking questions would only make him look foolish to his new boss. "No, sir," he replied.

"Okay then, go to it. And good luck. If you have any problems let me know." In the foreman's mind there was little likelihood this employee would develop into a particularly effective worker. He had seen many of these minority employees hired under affirmative action who simply couldn't seem to cut it. And frankly he didn't understand exactly why it was like this. He treated them the same as anyone else. In fact he made it a point to use exactly the same language to explain this simple procedure. In a few days this employee fell seriously behind on both the quantity and quality of his work. Johnson was not surprised.

The second new employee, a young man that Johnson seemed to think looked pretty sharp, was given essentially the same verbal instructions. This new worker, perhaps sensing that the foreman seemed to like him, took the "any moron should be able to do this" comment in stride and asked for a few clarifying pointers, which he got. Soon he was on his way to meeting his production quota just like the old pros who had been there for some time.

Why the different results from essentially the same message? An analysis from a message-sent-to-receiver model sheds little light on what happened. Other variables played a part. Perhaps the most important one is that the foreman fully *expected* the first young man to fail. And because of this, the environment of the communication event was clearly different. Perhaps at the heart of the differences illustrated here is the sense of caring. As a wise manager once said, "When I love you, I teach you the art of the job. When I tolerate you, I teach you the technology."[1]

The point of both examples is that many factors affecting communication—such as expectations, receptiveness to questions, and a desire to express rapport and friendship through good-natured ribbing—are not accounted for when we view communication as mere message sending.

An Alternative to Misconception 2: Communication as Message Receiving

Another way to look at communication is the "nothing-happens-till-someone-gets-a-message" approach. Theoretically this view makes a lot of sense, but it requires adjustments in the way most of us describe communication. Let's contrast it with the more common but potentially misleading sender-oriented approach described earlier.

When people define communication as "someone *sending* messages to others" (or giving instructions, or directives, etc.) a couple of problems quickly arise. First, these explanations seem to imply that we are dealing with a distinct and clearly defined type of human activity which we can turn on or turn off as needed. It's not quite that simple. Communication doesn't start when we begin to talk or write and end when we stop. Human communication is a form of *behavior* and as long as we behave— that is to say, as long as we live—we are *constantly* communicating. Or at least potentially communicating. *We* don't determine when communication will take place, we simply provide the setting and some cues which, if we are successful, will be picked up by someone else and interpreted in a way we see as appropriate. In other words, we, like a radio or TV station, are constantly "transmitting" signals. But until these are picked up by someone, no communication has occurred.

A second problem with the notion of communication as "sending messages" is that it implies a lot more control over the process than we may actually have. In most cases we have too long focused on talking and writing skills and have not sufficiently emphasized anticipating audience reactions. We have too long accepted the responsibility for accurate communication when our control over the communication event is really quite limited. Our success as communicators is determined by our *receivers*.

Peter Drucker, the well-known management scholar, explains it this way:

> ... it is the recipient who communicates. The so-called communicator, the person who emits the communication, does not communicate. He utters. Unless there is someone who hears, there is no communication. There is only noise. The communicator speaks or writes or sings—but he does not communicate. Indeed, he cannot communicate. He can only make it possible, or impossible, for a recipient—or rather, "percipient"—to perceive.[2]

Anytime someone sees, hears, or otherwise experiences something new and relates that experience to something already known, we have the process of perception. This is the first step in the communication process. Again quoting Drucker:

> Perception ... is not logic. It is experience. This means, in the first place, that one always perceives a configuration. One cannot perceive single specifics. They are always part of a total picture. The "silent language," that is, the gestures, the tone of voice, the environment altogether, not to mention the cultural and social referents, cannot be disassociated from the spoken language. In fact, without them the spoken word has no meaning and cannot communicate.[3]

Once perception has occurred, we attach meanings to what has been experienced. W. Charles Redding sees these mental activities as the defining characteristics of communication. He says that communication refers to those behaviors of human beings, or artifacts created by human beings, which result in messages being received by someone. A "message," he goes on, is any kind of stimulus that arouses a response we call "meaning."[4]

More concisely, communication is occurring whenever someone attaches meaning to objects, processes, behaviors (including intentional message behaviors), and even to hard-to-define climates, or intangible events. A member of an organization has communicated, and is communicating, so long as someone is attaching meanings to what he or she does. And what one does includes words, actions, silences, and inactions. Any and all of these can and do communicate. This leads to misconception 3.

"Dear diary: Today the coffee cart failed to stop at my cubicle door. Was this an oversight? Or has some higher-up decreed this as punishment for some social slight I have unwittingly perpetrated while passing in the hall? Will this cause célèbre snowball, resulting in a demotion or termination of my employment, or is it but a temporary adjustment? Whatever the outcome, I have no coffee today to steady my nerves . . .

Misconception 3:
Managers Control Communication
in Their Organizations

Communication consultant Walter Wiesman has said,

> Whether management likes it or not, it must face the fact that all actions, by all people, on all levels, in all functions of the organization, constantly communicate; that all actions create impressions in employees, judged by each employee from his peculiar frame of reference. It makes little difference whether the employee's interpretation is correct—this is "his world" and he looks out of "his window." What he wants to see and hear is the impression he gains from the words and actions around him. The more diversified a workforce, the greater the challenge to reach all people with the maximum degree of effectiveness.[5]

Not only do we have relatively little control over what people pay attention to and draw meanings from, but we also cannot determine exactly *when* communication will occur. Again quoting Walt Wiesman,

> Communication takes place every time human beings use their natural facilities to listen, think, observe, be impressed (for better or worse), have doubts,

feel neglected, etc. This common trouble occurs when management takes the rather naive stand that "this is not the time to talk."[6]

Another complicating factor that precludes absolute control over communication is the ever-present "ripple effect." Even the simplest memo, announcement, or directive may have unforeseen impact on the organization. Here is an example:

One day a sales manager, Bob Tremont, distributed a memo with what appeared to be a simple message:

```
I am happy to announce that a member of our sales
team, Jim Hawk, has been promoted to Sales Train-
ing Instructor. Jim will start his new duties at
the Corporate Training Center on August 1. I'm
sure you all join me in congratulating Jim.
```

If we accept a sender-receiver viewpoint, we have a clear message and effective communication. There are a few simple points of information.

- Jim Hawk was promoted.

- His new title is Sales Training Instructor.

- He'll work at Corporate Training Center.

- He starts August 1.

But there was much more to this message than meets the eye. The manager who sent this memo was generally insensitive to ripple effects—his audience's potential reactions. If that manager had done a series of man-in-the-street interviews following this announcement, he would have been shocked. Here are some reactions:

Alan Travis, Sales Representative: "I can't believe what I just read! Hawk is the biggest donkey on the entire team. He's a loudmouth backslapper who'll stop at nothing to peddle equipment—whether the customer needs it or not! He takes the same approach for every prospect: sell them the most expensive machine whether or not they need it and can afford it. He never does customer surveys to see what they would really benefit from. Sure, he's had impressive sales results, but he has a gold-mine territory. Look, I don't want to sound like sour grapes, but this promotion is a joke. Jim Hawk represents everything we are taught not to do. There are a half dozen other people that should have been promoted first—or at least been given an opportunity to compete for the opening."

James Wilson, Sales Representative: "I'd heard that there might be an opening at Corporate Training and frankly, I thought I had a good shot at it. When Tremont just dropped that memo on us, I was really upset. Hawk has always been one of his boys, but you'd think he'd at least talk to a few of us who should have been considered. I'll put my sales abilities up against Hawk's any day. And I know I'm more effective at customer care. I don't believe in Hawk's sell-'em-and-forget-'em approach. To make him a trainer of new sales reps is ludicrous."

Barbara Anderson, Sales Manager: "It's really none of my business. Bob Tremont doesn't have to check with me when he promotes someone. But I have been a sales manager a lot longer than he has and I've seen situations like this before. The other folks on his team are fighting mad. It's not that they dislike Jim Hawk—it's just that he seems to represent the opposite of the professionalism the company is always stressing. When I face a decision like this one, I spend a lot of time talking to each of the people on my team. You can't just suddenly drop an announcement memo like that and expect that everyone will understand. The promotion situations are always tough but there's a lot you can do to smoothe ruffled feathers. I think Bob has a lot to learn about managing and communicating."

LeRoy Puckett, Sales Trainee: "I've got to be honest with you. I'm not positive I want to be a salesman in the first place. I've only been on board two months, but already I'm getting a little bit down. The company spends thousands of dollars sending me to the Corporate Training Center and stressing how important it is to be a professional representative. Then I come back here to my home office and the first guy who gets promoted is probably the least professional of them all. Frankly, I'm confused. I've seen this guy at work. He takes every shortcut (ethical or not), he spends half the time flirting with the secretaries and then feeds the customer the biggest line of baloney you've ever heard. I don't want to be like him, but I do want to get ahead. What do I do now?"

What initially appears to be a routine communication event has some very complex outcomes. For most members of the organization, Hawk's promotion was seen as a cruel joke. While the manager's memo was perfectly clear, the ripple effect was totally unpredicted. A more sensitive communicator could do much to take the sting out of such an announcement through use of different media, allowing for more adequate explanation of management's decision criteria, and through being more "in tune" with the message receivers' expectations and attitudes. Although a manager cannot anticipate and control the outcome of such messages, he or she can and must be sensitive to them.

An Alternative to Misconception 3:
Managers Influence the Creation of Understanding

If we don't give careful thought to the expectations and the wants and needs of those we are attempting to communicate with, we will surely fail to bring about understanding. The challenge for the manager lies in improving the *probability* that understanding will predominate in organizational relationships—by establishing and maintaining conditions under which effective communication can flourish.

As we seek to develop such conditions perhaps the three most important things we can keep in mind are that (1) we must expect to be misunderstood by at least some of our listeners and readers; (2) we must expect to misunderstand others; (3) we can strive to reduce the degree of such misunderstanding, but we can never totally eliminate it nor anticipate all possible outcomes. When we expect to be misunderstood we are likely to respond by considering ways to make the message sending circumstances more conducive to understanding. When we expect to misunderstand others we will be more conscientious about seeking out needed clarification. And when we recognize that we never absolutely eliminate misunderstanding or anticipate all outcomes, we are acknowledging reality.

While in the military service, I was trained to be an air traffic controller. It strikes me now as interesting that the precise language and procedures used by air traffic controllers are clearly aimed at overcoming such problems in communication. Controllers often restate important instructions given to pilots in an attempt to reduce misunderstanding; they also request that some messages received by pilots be repeated to check for accuracy. Nevertheless, even with meticulous language and procedures, occasional accidents due to communications breakdowns do occur. Communication will never be foolproof.

So how do we improve conditions for understanding? We can start by committing ourselves to ongoing self-analysis. We can increase our awareness of our own predispositions and expectations, and we can constantly reexamine them. We can continually evaluate the way our personality characteristics filter and distort the ways we see others. We must learn to anticipate what our recipients expect to see and hear from us. Only then can we know whether we should communicate so as to utilize their expectations or whether we need to shock them with an "awakening" that breaks through those expectations.

We are very quick to perk up our ears any time we hear something that confirms our beliefs. We also tend to literally tune out conflicting information that does not conform to what we expect. A friend of mine used to test this proposition at parties he would attend. Upon saying goodnight to the host and hostess he would shake their hands, smile and nod, telling them in a very serious tone that this was absolutely the worst party he had ever attended. They, in return, would smile, nod, and thank him for the compliment. While there are a number of factors that account for this confusion, the social expectations of the host and hostess play an important part in tuning out the actual language of that message.

When we come to recognize the interplay of our psychological characteristics with the managerial communication process we will look for factors which confound understanding. The key lies in a receiver-oriented approach coupled with the awareness that we really can't control communication. But we can, and must, seek to influence it. This is a frustrating state of affairs for the manager who wants to be a better director, persuader, or motivator. We all want to get our subordinates to produce more, our peers to accept our point of view, and our bosses to be impressed with us. But that's the old sender-oriented view. The broader and more realistic perspective tells us that communication is a lot more than just getting someone to say they agree. Real communication improvement means real sacrifices. It means developing more understanding. It means looking at the world through the eyes of others, walking the proverbial mile in another's moccasins. Most of us are hesitant to do this. Perhaps it is because, as business communication professor Richard Hatch has said, ". . . it's a little bit scary to think about other people's points of view too carefully; you may begin to think it makes sense!"[8] But it is exactly through this kind of empathizing that meaningful improvement of communication occurs.

All types of human communication are enhanced by more concern for "you" and less for "I." In many books on organizational communication, the distinction is made between "upward" (from subordinates to superiors) and "downward" (vice versa) communication. That distinction assumes again that the message source does the communicating, a notion of little value when we assume a receiver orientation.[9] What we have traditionally done is try to make the "manager as message sender" a better "communicator." But the only kinds of messages one can communicate downward are simple commands. We cannot "send" motivation or expectations—or understanding; these require interactive sharing between those who perceive our messages and us. When we reach out to better understand others we become the recipients, the real communicators.

Creation of a climate for understanding begins with self-analysis. It matures as we develop empathy for others. The ongoing process of creating a climate for understanding is no small task. It requires extensive effort, and it involves giving of ourselves to an extent that many are unwilling and perhaps unable to do.

The hard reality is that life is and will continue to be full of failures to communicate effectively. That is, people are assigning inappropriate meanings to what they perceive and managers are unrealistically assuming that accurate meanings are being created in the minds of the people they talk and write to. We tend to expect too much from communication attempts.

One final point: good communication beats the heck out of poor communication, but it is not a cure for every organizational problem. As one writer has expressed it, with tongue in cheek,

> An ailment called "lack of communication" has taken the place of original sin as an explanation for the ills of the world, while "better communication"

is trotted out on every occasion as a universal panacea. It is guaranteed to appear at least once, and usually several times, on any TV panel discussion. Usually it is offered with the mock modest air of one who is making a substantial contribution which is bound to be well received, while the correct response is solemn nods all around, strongly reminiscent of the amens in church. Indeed, ritualization of the whole sequence is far advanced.[10]

Good internal communication in itself will not guarantee that your organization will profit. Internal communication is a cost of doing business. Profitability is affected to the extent that efficient and effective communication saves the organization time, effort, and resources. Whatever efforts are expended to better comprehend the communication process are likely to be worthwhile if grounded in good theory and if tempered with realistic expectations.

Levels of Communication Activity

Internal and Interpersonal Levels

Communication can be studied from several different levels, each of which introduces additional complicating factors. We communicate *intrapersonally* when our minds process informational stimuli; when we talk to ourselves. Such internal communication is another way to describe thinking. *Interpersonally* (between two or more people), we transact or exchange thoughts to establish or maintain relationships with others. These interpersonal relationships help us gain a clearer understanding of our world by providing information from others. They also give us feedback concerning the appropriateness of our behavior or our self-image. When our interpersonal communication skills are poorly developed we tend to have emotional problems and social maladjustment. (Much of this book deals with the interpersonal level of communication.)

As managers we need also to be concerned with *group* and *organizational* levels of communication and the behavioral effects of organizing people toward task accomplishment. And *technological* considerations permeate the process at all levels. The model in Figure 1-1 illustrates these levels.

The manager's communication job involves all levels of communication activity, as indicated by the shaded area. Let me elaborate on the organizational and technological levels.

Groups and Organizations:
The Great Complicators

Earlier we said that 90 percent of those who work do so in organizations. This is simply a fact of our complex society.

People create organizations to do things they cannot or do not want to do alone. For years organizations have been studied to try to determine

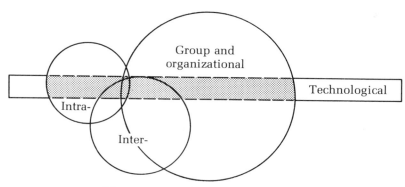

Figure 1-1 Levels of communication[11]

why they succeed or fail and how they can be improved. The more they studied, the more researchers came to realize that organizational success seems to be dependent upon countless variables, many of which are complex and unpredictable.

Several conclusions emerge from the development of organization theory. For one thing, we've learned that static models, like the ever-present organization chart, tell us very little about what really goes on. These

"For what it's worth, the new organization chart is out and you're not in your box."

charts with their boxes and lines actually create the misapprehension that there is a certain systematic rigidity to the organization—a rigidity that is less and less desirable as we recognize the frequent need to adapt to changing environmental pressures. Robert Townsend, in his famous book, *Up the Organization*, recommends that organization charts be drawn in pencil, if at all. He goes on to say, "Good organizations are living bodies that grow new muscles to meet challenges. A chart demoralizes people. Nobody thinks of himself as *below* other people. And in a good company he isn't."[12]

Another verdict of modern organization theories is that the process of drawing conclusions about overall organizational structure from isolated examples or events can be misleading. When foul-ups occur, it's often tough to decide if one person or group misfunctioned or if the organization structure is somehow faulty. Repeated ongoing evaluations of all aspects of organizational life—not just the financial bottom line— are crucial. In recent years we've seen the term *auditing* applied to far more than financial records alone. We now see enlightened companies conducting "social audits" to "assess and report realistically upon their performance in terms of benefits to society, rather than mere profit making."[13] Within companies the function of internal auditors has expanded to include ongoing appraisals of all organizational operations. Periodic studies of employee morale and communicative health are becoming standard procedure. The manager who attempts to run a modern organization by hunches or by casual, unsystematic observation is as out of date as the 1920s barnstorming pilot in the age of 747s.

Organization theorists have also found that organizations seldom work like well-oiled machines over the long run. No matter how carefully we assemble the parts (people, materials, information, and other resources) things still go wrong. Equipment breaks down. People throw temper tantrums or sulk. Competitors do something unexpected. Other outside influences intervene: government announces new regulations, customers quit buying, or suppliers quit supplying.

Managers, responding to organizational breakdowns, elaborate and complicate the organization structure by developing complex systems of roles, responsibilities, and positions. As people assume these positions, they are expected to behave—and to communicate—in ways appropriate to their place in the organization. This adds still another complicating dimension to the communication system. People must temper their own desires against the expectations and the tasks or goals of the organization. There arises a persistent tug-of-war between what we'd really like to say or do, and what we know we should say or do for the good of the group. Our personal understanding of and commitment to the group's goals often determines who wins the tug-of-war.

There are two classes of group or organizational objectives—those directed toward maintaining and solidifying group cohesiveness and those directed toward accomplishing group tasks. Both frequently require that members suppress what they'd really like to do and say for the collective good. The public relations director may find it useful to stifle his candid belief that a local civic leader is a jerk. The labor negotiator may resist introducing a new demand when agreement on a contract appears to be near. The newly appointed supervisor may feel he should no longer go out for a beer with former peers he now leads. Organizational integrity is maintained by appropriate role functioning. The maverick or "free spirit" who consistently says and does exactly what he or she wants to cannot long survive in an organizational world.

A formal organizational structure, although not necessarily of the traditional pyramid shape, emerges as groups become larger and more complex. This structure establishes clear differences in what people do (or are supposed to do); it distinguishes the amount of authority and responsibility and the number of rewards allocated to each.

Generally this emerging status hierarchy and job specialization is necessary for the organization to economically accomplish its objectives. But it complicates the communication process by imposing additional restrictions on individual communicators, restrictions required by virtue of organizational positions, roles, and expectations. Inevitably, formal organization structures also restrict the free flow of information. This is necessary to a point or the organization leadership would drown in a sea of unneeded data. But like leaks that develop from a flow-restricting crimp in a water hose, informal channels seep out which sometimes erode the intentions of the formal organization. Subgroups, with their own sets of objectives, roles, and procedures, emerge to further complicate things.

These subgroups are not always detrimental to the larger organization. In fact, Redding has said that "organizations frequently get their most important work done through various kinds of coalitions, factions, or alliances."[14] The point here is that we must be aware of such complicating factors. Organizational communication effectiveness may well depend upon recognition of these conditions and their effects.

Technological Level

Technological dimensions of communication concern more than simply hardware such as telephones, intercoms, copying machines, computers, and two-way radios. Lee Thayer broadly describes the technological level as "the focus upon the technology of communication including equipment, apparatus, and/or the formalized 'programs' for generating, storing, processing, translating, distributing, or displaying data—either for 'consumption' by other pieces of equipment or for ultimate translation into information and consumption by human beings."[15] Thayer goes on to remind us that the *languages* we use, whether verbal, graphic, or gestural, are just as much a part of the technology of communication as are other devices.

So the technological level of analysis can include everything from our language usage to the frequency with which we schedule meetings, to the apparatus we use to process data.

Just How Important Is Managerial Communication?

Communication scholar Gerald Goldhaber says, ". . . we are told by management and communication consultants that more than 10 percent of U.S. business enterprises fail every year primarily due to bad management and ineffective communication."[16] Raymond L. Hilgert, a professor of management and industrial relations with extensive consulting experience has said,

> . . . in every organization that I have come into contact with, communication is usually the number one problem, or it is at least associated with virtually every major problem which the organization faces. This ranges from basic problems of human misunderstanding, all the way to major financial, marketing, and production problems associated with the inability of people to properly communicate with one another.[17]

Henry Mintzberg's book, *The Nature of Managerial Work,*[18] reveals that managers are almost constantly communicating. Based on systematic observations of chief executives' work, Mintzberg calculated that verbal interaction accounted for 78 percent of managers' time and 67 percent of their activities. Mintzberg does not consider desk work as communication behavior, although it could be viewed as intrapersonal communication.

Communication is what managers do. It is the essence of managerial work. All levels of management must be involved in optimizing organizational communication. Staff expertise, either in-house or consultant, should be used when necessary, but ultimately success will lie with increased understanding, commitment, and effort on the part of working members of the organization.

All this is to say that getting your finger on the pulse of a living organization can be pretty tough.

Anything and everything that happens in the organization has a potential communicative effect on everybody. Some companies have attempted to deal with communication via a single staff element or designated managers who were given sole responsibility for a complete communication program. You cannot transfer communication into one office. What does

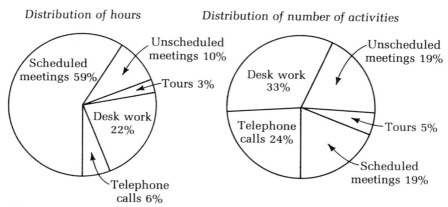

Figure 1-2 Distribution of time and activities by media (based on five weeks of observation of chief executives' work). Copyright © 1973 by Henry Mintzberg. By permission of Harper & Row, Publishers, Inc.

make sense is to "take inventory of all identifiable actions contributing to the total communication program, to phase these actions into the overall goal of the organization, to stimulate and assist segments and individuals responsible for such actions, and to have as a result a balanced, effective and timely program."[19]

Like any managerial program, communication improvement must be planned. Specific soft areas should be identified and targets established for improvement. Then we must follow up, follow up, follow up. An effective communication program is an ongoing effort. We can't apply a series of "quick fixes" and expect effective communication to run on perpetually.

Summary of Chapter 1 and Preview of Future Chapters

A theoretical base for this book is the notion that communication occurs any time someone attaches meaning to what's going on. Intentional communication efforts are successful to the degree that common meaning develops between the message receiver and the intent of the sender. Much communication, however, is unintentional and ripple effects of even seemingly simple messages are often unpredictable. Communication is not some distinct activity which we can turn on or off; we are constantly communicating so long as someone is around to attach meanings to cues they receive. The organizational context in which we operate greatly complicates the entire process. While we are interdependent as members—we need each other—we are too often unaware of the kinds of things that separate us from each other and reduce the probabilities of our attaching appropriate meanings to our interactions.

This book is about ways we can experience the communication going on around us while developing a clearer understanding of why it is as it is. Such experience can be, as someone once defined it, "the transition from cocksure ignorance to thoughtful uncertainty." In a subject as complex as human communication, thoughtful uncertainty is probably a healthy condition.

No one can say all there is to say about a subject as broad as managerial communication. My job has been to choose key areas that you and I can profitably investigate. Several questions served as criteria for determining what should be included:

1. Is this an aspect of communication that seems to be associated with frequent and serious communication difficulties in typical organizations?
2. Is this an aspect of communication that the practicing manager can influence? (At the risk of appearing overly pragmatic, I see little profit in dealing with areas on which we simply can't have a meaningful impact.)
3. Is this an area where I can concisely provide the reader with usable diagnostic information? Can the manager with little training in communication be taught to recognize difficulties in this area without too much difficulty?

I have also chosen to limit the scope of this book to internal communication behavior. While I recognize that organizations do interact with the public, their customers, stockholders, and myriad external audiences, this book focuses on the inner workings of the company. Instead of examining advertising, public relations, and the effects of external forces such as product acceptance, governmental regulations, etc., we are concerned with improving how people *within* organizations communicate.

In short, this book is a response to a need for pragmatic interpretation and application of organizational communication theory for the working or aspiring manager.

The chapters of this book deal with different contexts in which communication can flourish or flounder. In Chapter 2 we begin by viewing the broad picture of the *communication climate* within an organization. Chapter 3 looks at individual *processes*, such as the flow of messages, and the problems that arise when information flow is restricted or overloaded.

In Chapter 4 we deal with the various communication *media and tools* available to a manager, discussing the most cost-effective media for improving the probability that members of the organization receive accurate meanings.

Part Two of the book deals with oral communication activities. Chapter 5 focuses on one-with-one communication situations such as informal *conversation*, the more formalized *interviews*, and the use of the *telephone*. Chapter 6 deals with interactional communication situations or the use of *conferences* and *meetings*. Chapter 7 looks at communication effectiveness in the context of one-to-many or *presentational speaking*. Chapter 8 deals with *listening* skills.

In Part Three written communication activities become the focus. *Memos*, *letters* and more formalized (and usually more lengthy) *reports* are considered with an eye to increasing the likelihood that their readers will perceive their intended meanings.

Part Four narrows our focus a bit to deal with our personal communication *styles*, the way we use language.

I hope the materials in this book will be valuable to you. This book is written with the sincere belief that no single thing can be more important to improving productivity and overall effectiveness of an organization than maximizing understanding of experiences and ideas among the most valuable resources of that organization—its people.

As managers, we can profit most by establishing contexts in which understanding can germinate and blossom. Setting up such conditions requires recognizing the forces at work—and there are many in every organization—which stifle and inhibit, as well as those which enhance the development of common meanings. As one communication scholar has said, ". . . the best way to prepare a person for communicating—like painting—is to acquaint him with the repertoire of available techniques, train his judgement, and encourage him to become what he can."[20]

Questions for Further Thought

1. Consider other definitions of *communication* that you have heard (or make up your own). Are these definitions sender-oriented, receiver-oriented, or some combination of these or others? Based on what you read in this chapter, what drawbacks do these definitions pose?

2. Relate an experience in which you were given a task to perform and you felt that you were not expected to succeed. How was this expectation communicated to you?

3. How do your roles in an organization restrict the ways you communicate? (Consider the receiver orientation.)

4. When you have a particularly important idea you want to share with others, what do you do to cope with the maxim, "You must expect to be misunderstood"?

5. What steps can you take to move from the "I" approach to a receiver-oriented approach?

Notes

1. James L. Hayes, former president of the American Management Association, as quoted in a speech.
2. Peter F. Drucker, *Management: Tasks, Responsibilities, Practices* (New York: Harper & Row, 1974), p. 483.
3. *Ibid.*, p. 483.
4. W. Charles Redding, *Communication within the Organization* (New York: Industrial Communication Council, 1972), p. 25.
5. Walter Wiesman, *Wall-to-Wall Organizational Communication* (Huntsville, Ala.: Walter Wiesman, 1973), p. 4.
6. *Ibid.*, p. 3.
7. Drucker, *op. cit.*, p. 486.
8. Richard Hatch, *Communicating in Business* (Chicago: Science Research Associates, 1977), p. 19.
9. Drucker, *op. cit.*, p. 490.
10. Charlotte Olmsted Kursh, "Benefits of Poor Communication," *The Psychoanalytic Review*, Vol. 58, No. 2, 1971.
11. Based on a model by Lee Thayer, *Communication and Communication Systems* (Homewood, Ill.: Richard D. Irwin, 1968), p. 32.
12. Robert Townsend, *Up the Organization* (New York: Alfred A. Knopf, 1970), p. 134.
13. Carl Heyel, ed., *The Encyclopedia of Management*, 2nd ed. (New York: Van Nostrand Reinhold, 1973), p. 950.
14. Redding, *op. cit.*, p. 21.
15. Thayer, *op. cit.*, p. 31.
16. Gerald M. Goldhaber, *Organizational Communication* (Dubuque, Iowa: Wm. C. Brown, 1974), pp. 5–6.
17. Quoted from unpublished notes of Dr. Raymond L. Hilgert, Professor of Management and Industrial Relations, Washington University, St. Louis, Missouri.
18. Henry Mintzberg, *The Nature of Managerial Work* (New York: Harper & Row, 1973), pp. 38–39.
19. Wiesman, *op. cit.*, p. 4.
20. W. Barnett Pearce, *An Overview of Communication and Interpersonal Relationships* (Chicago: Science Research Associates, 1976), p. 33.

Recommended Readings

Pearce, W. Barnett, *An Overview of Communication and Interpersonal Relationships*. Chicago: Science Research Associates, 1976. In a very concise (35-page) booklet, Pearce develops the thesis that "Communication is the *activity* by which persons define and express their relationships, and relationships are the *context* in which communication occurs." It is stressed that sensitivity to our communication patterns and relationships can help us better identify possible problem areas. Although the book is concise, it is not light reading. Nevertheless, a few hours of study of this material could be very helpful in enlarging one's understanding of important communication theory.

Redding, W. Charles, *Communication within the Organization.* Industrial Communication Council, 1972. First, the good news: this 538-page book, subtitled *An Interpretive Review of Theory and Research,* is widely regarded as the most comprehensive book covering the field up to the early 1970s. Redding is recognized as an early scholar in organizational communication and developer of a fine academic program at Purdue University. The book is very readable and geared to both the academic and the practitioner. Now the bad news: it may be tough to get a copy. Privately printed by a professional communication association, the distribution was limited. Your best bet would probably be a major university library (perhaps via interlibrary loan).

Thayer, Lee, *Communication and Communication Systems.* Homewood, Ill.: Richard D. Irwin, 1968. Thayer's book is fascinating although heavily theoretical. You'll probably find yourself considering communication in an entirely new light.

Wiesman, Walter, *Wall-to-Wall Organizational Communication.* Huntsville, Ala.: Walter Wiesman, 1973. Witty recollections of the author's experiences as a communication consultant and Internal Communication Coordinator for the NASA Marshall Space Flight Center. This thoroughly enjoyable and thought-provoking book contains 58 pages of how-to information. It was privately printed by Wiesman, P.O. Box 466, Huntsville, Alabama 35804.

CHAPTER 2

ORGANIZATIONAL COMMUNICATION CLIMATE
Fair to Partly Confused

The climate of the organization is more crucial than are communication skills or techniques (taken by themselves) in creating an effective organization.[1] This is a conclusion drawn by Redding in his interpretive review of theory in organizational communication. Admittedly, *climate* is a tough concept to define. Most writers view climate as arising out of the way organizational leaders (1) define and express goals of the organization, (2) recognize and utilize talents and potentials of employees, (3) hold certain assumptions and attitudes about employees, and (4) regard the worth of individual members. In the ideal climate, people are valued and are used in ways that are satisfying and beneficial to both the organization and the individual.

Communication climate can be viewed as a psychological condition established by (1) the individual's relationship to his or her organization and (2) the individual's interpersonal relationships with other organization members. Much of this book deals with the interpersonal relationships and how they are affected by communication behaviors; this chapter focuses on the person-to-organization dimension of communication climate.

An organization's communication climate is defined by the answers its members get to eight key questions. I've labeled the climate dimension in parentheses following each question below.

1. What are we doing here? (Clarity of organizational goals)
2. What does the organization want from me? (Clarity of tasks and expectations)
3. Where do I fit into the organizational system? (Understanding of roles and functions of others)
4. What rewards will I get if I communicate in certain ways? (Motivation to communicate)
5. What punishments await me if I communicate in certain ways? (Motivation to not communicate)
6. To what degree should I take risks in communicating my ideas or feelings? (Supportiveness and risk encouragement)
7. How am I treated compared to others? (Fairness, trust, and credibility)
8. How am I doing? (Feedback and candor)

Organizational Goals; or Every Time You Aim Nowhere, You Get There

There are two things that an organization member needs to know about goals. (1) What are his or her personal goals, and (2) How do these coincide with the goals of the organization? Those two questions are often harder to answer than we might expect. Some background thoughts on goal setting may be helpful here.

Sometimes it's difficult for us to clearly put our goals into words, let alone communicate them to others. The question frequently asked in employment interviews, "Where do you want to be five years from now?" has thrown many a candidate for a loss. Thinking in detail enough to define a goal is troublesome for many people. When they do try to clarify their goals, the forces of change often intervene and seem to make meaningless the whole exercise of goal setting. The authors of *The Organizational World* illustrate some of the problems involved:

> "Tell me, young man," asks your prospective father-in-law, "what are your goals in life?" You stammer something about getting a good education and serving humanity and raising a happy family and perhaps getting rich. But you don't feel comfortable about the question, and even less comfortable about your answer.
> "Tell me," says the senior consultant to the young new company presi-

dent, "what are your company's long-range goals?" The president points to a framed document on the wall titled "The Long-Range Objectives of the Cymbeline Company." The document lists several goals: producing more and better widgets at the lowest possible price, providing the best possible service to consumers, acting like responsible citizens, making a reasonable profit in a way that is consonant with the glorious traditions of the American Free Enterprise System, and a lot of other stuff.

And if the president is a bright, sensitive person he will also feel a little uncomfortable about his answer. Both he and the prospective son-in-law feel, somehow, that their words have a hollow ring. Indeed, it's very difficult for any of us to have a clear and fixed idea of where we're going, of our long-run goals. We suspect that whatever we say today may not be what we feel tomorrow. We want to hold on to an option to change our minds.

On the other hand, if the prospective father-in-law or the consultant were to ask a couple of different, though closely related, questions, they could be answered much more confidently. Suppose the first question was simply the behavioral one: "What do you do?" Then the young man could answer firmly and proudly that he is a student majoring in social instability. And suppose the second was a short-term question: "What will you do next year?" He could answer that he will graduate, perhaps cum laude, at the end of next year; that he hasn't yet made up his mind whether he will go into the Peace Corps, join a commune, or work in his father's fish hatchery. And the company president could answer both questions quite clearly and confidently too: "We produce 900,000 plastic widgets a day in twenty-seven styles, thirty-nine colors. We have 19,000 people on our payroll in seven countries. Next year we will open sales offices in Peking and Murmansk." We can talk easily about what we now do—our tasks; we can talk a little less easily about our short-term objectives; and we usually have a great deal of trouble talking clearly about long-run goals.[2]

It's easier for individuals and for organizations to explain to people what they *do* (their tasks) than what they *want* (their goals). The process of setting effective goals is more complex than it may look. But the payoff is enormous.

Let's look first at personal goal setting and then elaborate to the organization. Few people question that specifying personal goals, preferably in writing, is a powerful tool for success. There are at least four reasons why written goals help us to achieve.

First, they force us to think about and focus our attention on important things. It's impossible to write out detailed objectives without focusing our thoughts and crystallizing our ideas. The last time I stopped in a supermarket for a gallon of milk and a loaf of whole wheat bread, I walked out with $23.64 worth of things I hadn't planned on. The problem: no "goals"—no list of what to get. A list would have (1) increased efficiency,

(2) reduced irrelevant purchases, and (3) saved me $21.36. Since we are constantly being bombarded by demands for our attention, our time, our money, and our efforts, we have to develop sophisticated selecting mechanisms. Our crystallized goals provide decision criteria which make for better and more efficient choices.

A second reason for personal goals has to do with the use of our unconscious mind. Maxwell Maltz's famous book *Psycho-cybernetics*[3] taught us that we do indeed have an "unconscious success mechanism" that silently works on our problems and objectives even when our conscious mind is doing something else. So long as we have clear objectives, this steering mechanism will move us toward their accomplishment. Many creative geniuses have testified of cases where solutions to problems which had long eluded them suddenly came to mind when they weren't consciously working on them. The selection of the appropriate material for filaments in electric light bulbs was said to have popped into Edison's mind while he rode in his carriage down a country road.

If the problem or challenge is clear enough, the unconscious mind will work on it by selecting bits of data from the world around us. This powerful selective perception solves problems and provides answers. Written goal planning forces us to clarify and focus on important issues.

A third advantage of written goal planning is that it provides a way for us to keep score. Few of us would be interested in watching a football game if we were never told the score. Yet many people don't record where they started in their personal plans, where they're going, or how fast they are getting there. Written goals with appropriate checkpoints provide a way to do these things.

And finally, as we succeed at achieving short-term or easy goals, we develop expectations of success—habits of success—which will apply to our long-range, lifetime objectives. Success breeds success. I know many habitual goal setters who could never be convinced that they are failures. They have years of written goals, each one crossed out with a red pen, to prove beyond any personal doubt that when they set a goal, they reach it. Period. The self-image of the effective goal setter cannot be shaken. He or she has documented "proof" of success and fully expects continued success.

When developing or improving goal planning programs for individuals or organizations, we should consider several factors likely to enhance the effort:

(1) *Goals should be established in several areas.* The individual or company who sets goals only for earnings or profits becomes awfully mercenary. As a goal planning consultant to individuals, I suggest establishing

goals in several different areas: career goals, family goals, educational goals, physical goals, spiritual goals, goals of service to others, and miscellaneous goals. The individual who attacks only career objectives and disregards all others is likely to be quite unhappy—and unhealthy. Similarly, the organization that sets only profit targets without considering service to its community, employee well-being, and social obligations objectives will suffer for it. Goal setting should not be directed only toward the financial bottom line, but should pervade every phase of the organization.

(2) *Establish short-term and long-term goals.* It's often useful for the novice goal setter (an individual or an organization) to begin with some short-range, readily attainable targets to build self-confidence in the goal-setting process. The best way to learn to putt a golf ball is to place it only a few inches from the cup and tap it in; then move it back a few inches at a time until you become proficient from greater distances. The same applies to goal setting. Begin with some easily reached targets and grow from there. Also consider long-run objectives in terms of more immediate steps of progression. As the saying goes, "There's only one way to eat an elephant—one bite at a time."

(3) *Whenever possible, make goals measurable in some way so you know when you've "got it."* Try to set goals you can count. Avoid phrasing goals such as "Every day I will. . ."; if you miss one day, you can't catch up. Instead say "Twenty times this month I will. . ." or "I will complete X employee appraisals this month." It usually doesn't matter whether you do it all in one day or it takes several weeks.

A word of caution is in order here. While quantification has obvious advantages, it cannot be applied to all worthwhile goals. Many creative measures of subjective concepts like "customer service" or "personal growth" can be developed. But good goals should not be thrown out simply because we cannot come up with a purely objective way to count our results. Indeed, frequent criticism of management by objective (MBO) programs is that they tend to measure only those things that are easy to measure. A subjective evaluation of target accomplishment is far better than having no objective at all.

(4) *Look at your goals frequently and mark them off as they are achieved.* I've known successful executives who spend several hours each week—uninterrupted hours—studying their goals. The more these goals are in the forefront of your mind, the more effectively they can do their job of crystallizing thoughts and focusing your energies. As you work on the goals, the goals work on you. Writing them down one time without reviewing them later is of little value.

In the organization it is crucial that objectives are clearly understood by its membership. Merely sending out a list of targets to those who will be involved in achieving them won't do the job. Clear understanding can be achieved only through participation in goal selection, clear communication of the agreed upon objectives, and frequent repetition and exposure to these goals.

(5) Finally, *build in a system of rewards—special rewards—when significant objectives are met.* For many goal-directed people, the satisfaction of crossing off an accomplishment on a list is enough. But a little extra reward, be it verbal recognition (an "attaboy") or some tangible prize can make goal setting and goal reaching a lot more fun.

Of course, writing down personal and organizational goals is no absolute guarantee of success. But when people become *committed* to goals they've set, these goals provide motives for action—motivation.

The optimum situation is to have members' individual goals pulling in the same direction as the organization's objectives. This can be done with effective communication, by creating understanding. When the objectives of both individual and organization are clarified and accurately perceived, it can be determined whether they can coincide. If they are diametrically opposed, there is little sense in going on. If they appear to be at least partially compatible, further clarification and commitment to each other can be the catalyst for success.

Although individual goal setting and organization goal setting are very similar, the process is more complicated and more political in organizations. Each member of the organization has a personal viewpoint and a personal domain that he or she seeks to protect. Like people everywhere, we tend to take "local" political issues (those affecting us personally) more seriously than distant ones (those that affect the larger organization). And as in politics there are factions, subgroups, and coalitions pushing for their pet priorities. Organizational goals grow out of negotiation, compromise, and some degree of personal sacrifice.

Ultimately, top management must be responsible for the process of organizational goal setting. Their decisions are influenced by this political give-and-take as well as their ability to digest relevant data and then to seek common understanding. The process is repeated by management at all organizational levels representing the subgroups within the larger organization. This is all further complicated by a chicken-or-the-egg dilemma. Middle managers complain, "Top management doesn't establish and communicate clear goals. If we knew what they wanted and what for, we could clarify our own goals and objectives." But an equally common complaint of top managers is: "Our middle managers aren't imaginative about proposing new goals and objectives. If they told us what they want to shoot for, we could say yes or no and clear the path for them."[4]

Sounds like a communication problem! It is only through effective communication that this dilemma can be resolved and the complex process of organizational and individual goal synthesis can come about.

After this fairly extensive discussion of goals, you may have forgotten that we are still talking about communication climate. The point is that without goals—without a clear sense of direction—organizations and people within them spin their wheels. A key dimension of organizational communication climate arises from the degree of mutual understanding about each others' goals that exists between the member and the organization. When individuals and/or the organization are sketchy about objectives, the ambiguity that exists can lead to communication difficulties and lower productivity. The effective manager will assist employees in personal goal planning while also conveying company objectives. A healthy climate is one in which each member has a pretty accurate response to the question "What are we doing here?"

Where Goals Go Astray . . .[5]

Common errors managers make in setting goals, based on a survey of 1,100 managers, are reported by Dr. George S. Odiorne:

- Doesn't clarify common objectives for the whole unit.
- Sets goals too low to challenge the individual subordinate.
- Doesn't use prior results as a basis for using intrinsic creativity to find new and unusual combinations.
- Doesn't clearly shape his unit's common objectives to fit those of the larger unit of which he is a part.
- Overloads individuals with patently inappropriate or impossible goals.
- Fails to cluster responsibilities in the most appropriate positions.
- Allows two or more individuals to believe themselves responsible for doing exactly the same things when he knows having one man responsible is better.
- Stresses methods of working rather than clarifying individual areas of responsibility.
- Emphasizes tacitly that it is pleasing him rather than achieving the job objective which counts.
- Makes no policies as guides to action, but waits for results and then issues ad hoc judgments in correction.
- Doesn't probe to discover what program his subordinate proposes to follow to achieve his goals but accepts every goal uncritically without a plan for its successful achievement.
- Is too reluctant to add his own (or higher management's) known needs to the programs of his subordinates.

- Ignores the very real obstacles that are likely to hinder the subordinate in achieving his goals, including the numerous emergency or routine duties which consume time.
- Ignores the new goals or ideas proposed by his subordinates and imposes only those which he deems suitable.
- Doesn't think through and act upon what he must do to help his subordinates succeed.
- Fails to set intermediate target dates by which to measure his subordinates' progress toward their goals.
- Doesn't introduce new ideas from outside the organization nor does he permit or encourage subordinates to do so, thereby freezing the status quo.
- Fails to permit his subordinates to seize targets of opportunity in lieu of stated objectives that are less important.
- Is rigid about not scrapping previously agreed-upon goals that have subsequently proved unfeasible, irrelevant or impossible.
- Doesn't reinforce successful behavior when goals are achieved, or correct unsuccessful behavior when they are missed.

Setting Goals to Measure the Unmeasurable...

(1) It is often necessary to devise measurements of present levels in order to be able to estimate or calculate change from this level.

(2) The most reliable measures are the real time or raw data in which the physical objects involved comprise the measures to be used (dollars of sales, tone of output, number of home runs hit).

(3) When raw data can't be used, an index or ratio is the next most accurate measure. This is a batting average, a percentage, a fraction, or a ratio.

(4) If neither of the above two can be used, a scale may be constructed. Such scales may rate "from one to ten," a nominal rating against a checklist of adjectives such as "excellent, fair, poor" or one which describes "better than or worse than" some arbitrary scale. These are useful but less precise than the above.

(5) Verbal scales are the least precise but can be extremely useful in identifying present levels and noting real change. Verbs such as "directs, checks, and reports" are indicative of actions to be taken.

(6) General descriptions are the least useful, but still have value in establishing benchmarks for change. "A clear, cloudless fall day" is obviously not the same as a "cloudy, foggy misty day" and the two descriptions could be used to state conditions as they exist and conditions as they should be.

(7) The statements of measurement should be directed more toward results than toward activity. (Much activity may prove impossible to state in specific terms, whereas results of that activity can be stated.)

(8) In stating results sought or defining present levels, effort should be

made to find indicative, tangible levels and convert verbal or general descriptions into such tangible scales, ratios or raw measures where possible.

(9) If you can't count it, measure it, or describe it, you probably don't
know what you want and often can forget about it as a goal.

What Does the Organization Want from Me?
Or What's a Girl Like You Doing in a Nice
Place Like This?

Depending on the nature of the organization, members may have similar
or widely differing tasks, roles, and activities. The organization itself may
exist to fulfill a clearly specified function (to manufacture automobiles) or
a very vague one (to study economic indicators). How the organization
goes about its work depends in part on the amount of "structure"
provided. A manufacturing operation typically has a fairly high degree of
structure. That is, the job to be done is clear: "You will assemble 314
three-wheeled, fiberglass skateboards today." Also, the way the job is to
be done is clear: "Insert wheel assembly into hole A." Training programs
evolve to instruct the worker on what to do. The worker is taught what to
do, how to do it, and what he or she will get in exchange for doing it.

A problem arises when employee behaviors not directly relevant to the
work are left unclear. An example may be the skateboard assembler who
produces at the desired level (task-relevant behavior) but who insists on
wearing unusually provocative and revealing clothing to work (non-task-
relevant behavior) to the eternal distraction of her coworkers. Organizational communication climate is affected to the extent that there is ambiguity about types of employee behavior deemed relevant by management.
Expectations of how we are to act in the organization are often communicated very subtly. But sometimes subtlety doesn't work at all. The results
for the worker can be confusion, frustration, and a very negative picture
of organizational leadership.

The employee may be receiving conflicting information as to what is
acceptable behavior. The department manager thinks her dress habits are
inappropriate while her immediate supervisor kind of likes things as they
are. Although the supervisor may be obligated to verbally express disapproval, it's entirely possible that his nonverbal message of approval over-
rides his perfunctory disapproval, and further confuses the worker.

Confusion about formal "rules of the game" and the informal customs
or standards of the organization can be frustrating for the employee. The
problem is further aggravated when different leaders apply different interpretations to what and how things are to be done.

One nationwide study found that nearly half of the workers inter-
viewed were working under conditions of noticeable conflict, where they

GRIN & BEAR IT

"Posting individual productivity reports has really created a competitive spirit among employees . . . they boast about who does the least."

were, from time to time, caught between two sets of people who wanted different things from them. About 15 percent of those studied reported this to be a frequent and serious problem.[6]

An important dimension of communicative climate arises from the degree to which a member feels comfortable with his or her understanding of what is expected on the job. These expectations apply to task behaviors as well as to social norms and standards of the work environment.

Understanding Roles and Functions of Others, or Where Do I Fit?

Once individuals understand and become committed to some degree to the organization's goals and expectations, they are likely to be interested in how their particular functions fit into the larger scheme of things. A recurring theme in the John Wayne type of war movies is the soldier who wants to "see some action" because he views his present role of, say, a mess sergeant, as unimportant. In reality, of course, the mess sergeant's job is crucial to a war effort, though less glamorous in the view of the job holder.

People in organizations want to know where they "fit." Helping members understand how the many organizational tasks mesh can be difficult because the position one holds often determines his or her perceptions of the organization. In other words, a mess sergeant could not perceive the army in the same way as a supply sergeant or an infantry officer or a general. Social psychologists Daniel Katz and Robert L. Kahn say "one's role in a social system dictates his perceptions of that system." They go on to explain that "organizational roles not only structure perceptions, but that changing one's role will result in concomitant changes in his perceptions."[7] Our view of the big picture is clearly affected by our vantage point. And when our vantage point changes due to a promotion, reorganization, or other change in job responsibilities, our understanding of the complex fabric of organizational functioning also changes. The movie starring Robert Redford called *The Candidate* a few years ago was a good illustration of this. An aggressive and dynamic young man seeks election to the U.S. Senate. He is very forthright in expressing exactly what should be done to solve governmental issues. The movie ends with the "hero" winning the election and coming to the stark realization that he is now faced with the enormous burden of *doing* the things he promised the voters. His role changes sharply from candidate to an elected official. In his closing scene, the bewildered senator-elect pathetically turns to his campaign manager and asks, "What do we do *now*?"

Every business person has encountered the employees or junior executives who have all the answers to the problems of the organization. But when it becomes their turn at bat, the problems suddenly become far more complex and solutions far more elusive.

A dramatic illustration of how organizational position colors perceptions is presented in a study by Dearborn and Simon.[8] These researchers were working with a group of executives from the same company in a training workshop. One of the exercises was to examine a fairly detailed (10,000 words) case study and write a brief statement of "what they considered to be the most important problem" facing the company described.

Although each trainee was instructed to respond from the vantage point of the "top executive in the company," the overwhelming number of trainees responded instead from their real frame of reference. Sales executives saw the fictitious companies' major problem as a sales problem 83 percent of the time. Eighty percent of the production executives saw the major problem of the case study as a production difficulty. Only 29 percent of the nonsales executives cited sales as the major problem and 20 percent of the nonproduction people saw the major problem as one of production.

Clearly, one's organizational roles affect one's perception of the big picture. Since perception is an integral part of communication, organizational position will affect communicative behavior. When we attempt to create understanding, this natural differing of views must be considered.

It is an oversimplification to expect that people could be brought to share precisely the same views about anything. In many cases we can get close enough to avoid serious problems. In fact, perceptual differences are okay as long as they fall within a "zone of indifference." Chester Barnard[9] coined this term more than forty years ago to mean a range of authoritative requests to which a subordinate is indifferent and therefore compliant without resistance. Requests falling outside this zone of indifference will receive critical consideration from the subordinate and consequently cannot be considered part of the authority relationship. Put another way, requests outside this zone will require either persuasion or power or both to gain compliance. People's role perceptions help determine their zone of indifference. When requests or orders overstep the zone, resistance and possible conflict are likely to arise.

An important issue is defining some tolerable limits to resistance and compliance. Conflicts arising from these different role perceptions become dysfunctional when they impair the organization's stability, adaptability, or productivity. At the first signs of destructiveness, steps to resolve conflict should be taken; however, conflicts of this type need not be destructive and, in fact, may well be productive, insofar as differing views often produce creative ideas. I'll talk more about this in Chapter 6.

So what can we do about the "Where do I fit" dimension of communication climate? First, recognize and help your people recognize that the positions each of us hold in the organization cause different viewpoints and different communication behaviors. Then provide opportunities to expand their understanding of the larger context. Orientation tours and employee training which include rubbing shoulders with people in other parts of the organization can go a long way toward developing empathy and more effective communication across functional lines.

Rewards and Punishments for Communicating:
Carrots, Whips, and Donkeys

In most organizations there are innumerable examples of reward systems that pay off for one behavior even though the rewarder dearly hopes for other, often the opposite kind of behavior. The fundamental idea of paying people by the hour encourages the taking up of time rather than productive use of efforts. The mechanic who fixes a machine so well that it never breaks down again finds himself out of a job. And the doctor who ostensibly is paid to make us well can make a lot more money if we stay sick and continue to visit him. This is not to say that hourly workers, mechanics, or doctors do these things, but the system rewards some behaviors that seem irrelevant or even counterproductive to the hoped for results. This principle can be easily applied to communication in organizations.[10]

How many times have we seen the ambitious junior executive suggesting a remedy to a problem and being instructed to "write up a report on it"? For a potentially useful suggestion the reward is to do more work. A clothing store owner constantly encourages his sales force to cooperate with each other—to share ideas with each other. Yet for his Christmas sales promotion he offers an award only to the top producer of sales. The results—salesmen tripping over each other to get to the customers, distrust, conflict. At a staff meeting, the member who suggests additional study of a particular problem is inevitably nominated to do the work.

In some companies, as part of an employee's performance appraisal, he or she is evaluated on communication effectiveness: how well she shares ideas with others; how well he keeps his superiors informed of activities they should know about. Yet seldom is there objective evaluation of this desirable behavior. Most appraisers don't know how to judge this kind of performance, so it becomes a "gut feel" evaluation—a guess. The employee who does nothing to open up communication channels has as good a chance of being favorably evaluated as any other.

Employee suggestion systems appear to motivate upward communication but are seldom as effective as they could be. The employee who makes the effort to pass an idea up is fairly often met with a rejection either because (1) he was unable to fully express the idea in writing (often on company forms) and/or (2) the evaluator of the suggestion didn't understand it or could care less if it was adopted.

As a staff employee at a large corporation I shared responsibility for evaluating employee suggestions. I had three options: accept the suggestion (in which case I would then need to see that it was implemented), reject the suggestion (I wouldn't have to do anything further), or refer the suggestion to higher organizational level where my counterpart would have the same options. The point is, there was little or no real incentive for me to approve suggestions even if they were pretty good. If I did accept a suggestion my work had just begun. I would then have to go to all our offices and teach the new procedure, create needed forms or equipment, arrange budget expenditures, etc. A rejection avoided all that work. Finally, my work evaluation was in no way affected by the number of employee suggestions I approved. In fact, these suggestions were simply extra work piled upon my "regular" duties.

So, where's the motivation to communicate?

This may be a fairly pervasive problem. Managers advocate employee openness until the first guy speaks up and is quickly labeled an "attitude problem." We tell our people to cooperate and avoid unnecessary inter-group conflict but do nothing to reward cooperative behavior and often unintentionally encourage friction or "friendly competition." We offer a $100 prize for a good suggestion while providing no good reason why those who will evaluate the suggestion should accept and implement it. The suggesting employee soon learns that his efforts at upward communication will be rejected. Finally, we see the stifling effect of putting members on the defensive so that their ideas must be substantiated (usually in written form) before they can be offered.

These kinds of things have profound effect on climate. The employee's response is too often likely to be "So why bother?"

Supportiveness and Risk Encouragement: I'm with You, Win or Tie

Closely related to the motivation to communicate are support and encouragement of creativity and risk taking.

The opposite of supportiveness is defensiveness. When people feel threatened—primarily threats to sense of self-esteem—a defensive climate develops. Behavioral characteristics of defensiveness and supportiveness in organizations have been studied by Jack Gibb,[11] who concludes that when climate is characterized by defensiveness we are likely to see frequent *evaluation* of people—a feeling among organizational members that they are being subjected to "good" or "bad" judgments. Also, a high degree of *control* over member behaviors is attempted in the defensive environment. People feel manipulated and burdened by lots of rules, regulations, and specified rigid procedures. In defensive organizations, leaders employ *strategy*—gimmicks or tricks—aimed at such things as getting the employee to think he is participating in important decisions when in fact the boss is making the decision. Gibb also describes the defensive climate as rather cold and impersonal with superiors tending to maintain their status by talking down to the "little people" in the organization and often being quite dogmatic and preachy.

The supportive environment is differentiated by the absence of the defensive characteristics. *Descriptive* language replaces evaluative comments and leaders take a *problem orientation*, that is, not simply calling up the rule or policy to stifle a difficulty, but getting to the root of the issue and seeking out underlying causes. The supportive climate is also marked by *spontaneity, empathy* for others, a sense of *equality* and fairness, as well as the replacement of dogmatism with *provisionalism*—a sense of

being not yet certain of the answer but rather engaged in a continuing search for solutions.

In the supportive climate, individual members have a sense of participation without threat to their ego or sense of self-worth. Risk taking and the freedom to make mistakes are accepted as normal states of affairs. Consequently, growth possibilities are broadened for the employee.

It is in the supportive environment that participative management may be utilized. Numerous studies have shown that participative decision making (PDM) frequently results in high quality solutions, reduced resistance to changes advocated, and a sense of cohesiveness and individual worth among participants.

A key dimension in communication climate is the degree of supportiveness present. Without this, communication becomes a contest of power plays rather than a search for common understandings. The waste of human resources in such an organization can be enormous.

Fairness and Equity:
Is This Any Way to Treat Your Partner?

The degree to which organizational leadership is willing to initiate communication has a profound effect on climate. This openness of downward communication has long been recognized as desirable. Few people would argue the wisdom of keeping members well informed. A more subtle aspect, however, is the *way* members are kept informed, the *equity* or fairness with which openness is applied to individual workers.

Some tentative and preliminary research has examined the effects of equitable distribution of communication rewards in organizations. By communicative rewards, I mean such valued outcomes as (1) receiving praise or verbal approval, (2) management's receptiveness to questions a worker may have, (3) management's willingness to directly answer such questions, (4) the degree to which additional questions or comments are encouraged, and (5) the timeliness of information given to members.

If managers have markedly different communication styles with different members of their work groups, the inequities are likely to be spotted by the employees. I recently tested this by setting up a series of experiments in which the supervisor responded differently to one half of the work group than to the other half. For some workers he (1) answered any questions they had and encouraged them to ask more questions as necessary, (2) gave each of them a number of compliments on the work they were doing, and (3) provided them with additional information, which clarified exactly what they were to do, early in the project. For other members of the same work group working in the same room, the supervisor (1) responded to their questions by telling them to "work it out the best you can" and did not encourage additional questions, (2) did not give any compliments, and (3) provided them with task-clarifying information only after they were almost finished with the project.

To test whether inequities are readily perceived, I manipulated *receptiveness, supportiveness,* and *timeliness.* Not surprisingly, these workers quickly saw that some people were being treated better than others. The communication climate was clearly marked by unfairness.

The experiments went on to examine how this perceived unfairness affected workers. Those who recognized the inequitable treatment tended to respond by downgrading their evaluations of the supervisor's effectiveness, by producing less, and by withdrawing (if not physically, at least psychologically) from participation in the task.[12]

Clearly the supervisor who used sharply different communication approaches with different members of his work group was seen as unfair. He was distrusted and rated lower in supervisory effectiveness.

In an ideal climate, there would be equitable distribution of communicative rewards. All members at the same organizational level would enjoy the same degree of receptiveness from his or her boss. Each would receive compliments for work well done and each would get new information at approximately the same time. This, of course, would be a pure ideal.

All this is complicated by the fact that perceptions of equity or fairness, like beauty or obscenity, are in the eye of the beholder. What appears completely fair to me may be a gross miscarriage of organizational justice to someone else. Since varying degrees of paranoia are widely distributed throughout most companies, achieving a pure state of communicative equity is highly unlikely. We do need, however, to avoid some of the more obvious favoritism.

If we keep in mind that the ways we interact with subordinates are in themselves potentially rewarding to them, we will recognize that communication meets important needs just as do tangible rewards allocated by organizations. We don't toss around money or "perks" indiscriminately, yet many managers go on passing out communicative rewards without any meaningful allocation strategy.

Feedback and Candor:
I Just Have to Tell You This

Employees have a basic need to know where they stand vis-à-vis organizational expectations. The degree to which management provides them with meaningful indicators affects climate. Formal feedback arrangements are usually established through management's policy for performance reviews. (These will be discussed at length in Chapter 5 of this book.) The degree of managerial *commitment* to such policy affects climate.

Often less formal feedback also creates impressions in the employee about organizational climate. For example, the physical conditions under which workers receive feedback can have diverse effects. As a rather extreme illustration, compare several contexts under which a manager could compliment a productive employee:

> *Situation 1:* The manager summons the employee to his plush, richly carpeted office. While seated behind the desk, the manager informs the standing employee that his good performance has been recognized and is appreciated.

> *Situation 2:* The manager happens to meet the employee in the restroom and informs the employee that his good performance has been recognized and is appreciated.

> *Situation 3:* The manager arranges a special visit to the employee's work location to inform him that his good performance has been recognized and is appreciated.

While we cannot absolutely predict which of these approaches would be most rewarding to the employee, the point is that reactions to the same message are likely to be quite different. Perhaps situation 1 would result in some resentment since status differences may be reinforced—possibly a painful reminder to the subordinate. Situation 2 might be viewed as too casual to be sincere; the compliment seems to be an off-the-cuff remark. At any rate, it is clear that little special effort was expended to compli-

Used by permission of King Features Syndicate, Inc. © 1977

ment the employee. Situation 3 would probably be viewed as the most sincere expression of the three since the manager made special arrangements to present the message in an appropriate context.

Candor of remarks to employees also affects climate. It's okay to be polite, but most employees want management to "tell it like it is." Give people the good news and the bad news. Share concerns and problems whenever appropriate.

Attempts by managers to suppress information they don't want the employees to have can be disastrous for communication climate. And it often doesn't work. As communication consultant Walt Wiesman has said, "There is never such a thing as a 'secret' in a working organization, at least not for more than 72 hours. If management creates a vacuum through silence, the employees will apply the boldest and weirdest imagination to fill it."[13]

Providing candid but supportive feedback to organization members is a key to developing a healthy communication climate.

All of the aspects of communication climate we have been discussing influence the ways people attach meaning and thus gain understanding about their organization. Answers to the eight questions on page 27 provide a composite view of organizational communication climate for that member. The degree to which that view coincides with some objective reality is less important than the fact that it does indeed exist in the mind of the employee and affects the ways he or she will interact in the organizational system.

Communication Climate:
Perceptions plus Policy

I've suggested that the practicing manager can understand one's person-to-organization communication climate by putting himself or herself into the position of an employee and seeking, to whatever degree possible, the answers to eight key questions. This of course is primarily a diagnostic exercise—and a highly subjective one at that. There is another managerial action that should be used in conjunction with diagnosis. That is the determination of organizational policy with regard to communication.

An organization's communication policy—whether formally stated or informally understood—expresses (1) a set of objectives the organization wishes to achieve through communication, (2) guidelines or directives to be applied to decision making about communication-related issues, or (3) a combination of both. The trend in large organizations is to formalize such policy by putting it in writing. As researcher David Burhans says, "In an organization where there is no formally written employee communication policy—as well as in one in which the formal policy is ignored or violated—a situation may exist in which each individual manager or supervisor has his own personal communication policy which may conflict with that of other managers and employees with whom he interacts."[14] Ideally, clear communication policies reduce ambiguity and inconsistencies and thus stabilize the communication climate.

Policy That Reflects Objectives

When communication policy is expressed as a series of objectives, it usually "paints with broad strokes." At times these objectives are so general they serve only to spell out underlying philosophy. Such proclamations standing alone, do not, in my opinion, constitute a bona fide communication policy. Below are brief excerpts from several corporate policy statements. These are taken out of context for illustrative purposes and are not intended necessarily to reflect good or bad examples. I have deleted any reference to the organizations' names.

The following example illustrates the expression of communication objectives by a large manufacturing company. It is an established policy of XXX Corporation:

A. To promote a better understanding that the personal objectives of XXX employees are closely related to the success of the company, by actively providing employees with timely, direct, pertinent and appropriate information on:

   1. Objectives, plans and operations of the Corporation

   2. Developments affecting our business and its employees, and

   3. Other matters of interest or concern to employees, including the basic economics of how private business enterprise operates in a free society.

B. To place on line management responsibility for maintaining at local level active and regular employee and management communication programs.

C. To insure that, whenever practicable, employees first learn of important matters which affect them and their jobs through internal channels—rather than through external sources.

D. To regard employee ideas, opinions and suggestions for the improvement of operations as an important corporate asset; to provide a uniform upward communication program—including specifically the establishment of a uniformly-administered, formal corporate suggestion plan which will provide awards to employees for usable suggestions.[15]

This organization's policy statement goes on to provide more details on implementation.

The philosophical ideal of many policy statements are tempered by recognizing limitations, illustrated as follows:

Some information, because of its nature, must be restricted to certain levels of management, or certain segments of the enterprise. In such instances, the confidence placed in the selected levels or segments must be maintained.

All members of Management are urged to develop a communicative attitude so they will consistently and consciously review each item they initiate, or that passes through their hands, and ask themselves "Who else needs to know about this—how is the best way to get it to them, orally or in writing?"[16]

Obviously there are limitations on what can be realistically achieved in employee communication. One ongoing area of managerial concern is just how far we can go with "openness." Archie McCardell, while president and chief operating officer of Xerox Corporation, addressed this issue in an article appearing in his corporate news magazine. His conclusion was that sometimes vital decisions in the works at Xerox couldn't be talked about. The article appeared at a time when business conditions were putting unusual stress on the company and its employees. And the people wanted to know what top management was doing about it. Here are the concluding paragraphs from McCardell's article entitled "Open Communication Is Our Policy, But Sometimes. . ."

So it comes down to this: Open communication is the policy at Xerox. I believe in it fully as a policy, even as a principle, though I realize that the more openly we communicate, the more opportunity we create for further questions. But sometimes, for good reasons, we can't answer certain questions— questions which are natural and legitimate in themselves. . . . Quite frankly, there has to be a point at which people accept a few things on faith.

I know that accepting things on faith is not always easy, and we can't always expect it—particularly when we are fortunate to have a group of bright and articulate people whose futures are tied to a major extent to the future of Xerox.

But I want you to have confidence that the management of Xerox Corporation *is* aware, *is* open to upward communication, *is* working on our problems in a priority manner—and wants you in on the process as early and fully as possible.[17]

In addition to the openness issue, some written policies also specify that objectives vary for communication *within* management and for communication *between* management *and* employees. The following excerpts from a corporation's policy statements illustrate this:

Communication Within Management

The objectives of communication within management will be to foster a complete understanding on the part of all management members of:

1. The aims, objectives, and plans of the business, both general and specific, long-range and immediate.
2. The organization of the Company and its elements, of who does what, and particularly the areas of responsibility and authority of management members.
3. The policies, regulations and procedures under which the Company operates, and the reasons for them.
4. The major problems faced by the business, and specifically what each member of management and what each employee can do to aid in the solution of these problems.
5. Up-to-date information on whatever lies ahead—business forecasts, contemplated changes in facilities, equipment, policies, practices, and organization.

Communication Between Management and Employees

The objectives of communication between management and employees will be to:

1. Facilitate the profitable operation of the business and to promote the understanding, approval and support by employees of its objectives in the free enterprise system. Cite (the Company's) tradition of leadership, thereby spurring the pride of accomplishment and good morale.
2. Create an environment of purposeful management in the eyes of employees, which is woven into the fabric of day-to-day operations at all levels, with supervisors held directly responsible for the effectiveness of communication.
3. Provide sufficient flexibility in communication methods so that they may be tailor-made to the problems of each organization, taking into account available information, the attitudes and interests of the group.
4. Provide a spirit of forthrightness so that the management will be willing to discuss openly and in detail the vital facts about the business which are of direct concern to employees and relate to their success and welfare as members of the corporation.
5. Provide the atmosphere, opportunity, and channels for communication so that employees may submit their ideas, project their attitudes, and set forth their grievances to management.

6. Recognize employee achievement and—again—to translate the meaning of these achievements for the overall benefit of (the Company).[18]

Finally, policies that express communication objectives sometimes (although perhaps not often enough) explain *why* internal communication is important. An examination of such statements can reveal a variety of assumptions held by the policy makers. For example, policies that say the employee has a *right* to know what's going on may view communication as a legalistic necessity, perhaps begrudgingly adhered to. Keeping employees informed because they *want* to know may be based in an assumption that information is a gift we bestow upon the underlings. I advocate that a view of internal communication as the vehicle for creating cooperative effort—effective participation—reflects healthier assumptions. When people are involved in information flow, there is the opportunity for synergy—the creation of a whole organization that is far greater than the sum of its individual members.

Policy as What, How, and When

Communication policy should go beyond the statement of principles to provide guidelines or directives about such things as what, how, and when to actively attempt the building of understanding. Peterson and Pace feel that an effective organizational communication policy should

1. Translate the plans and objectives of the organization into guidelines for managers and subordinates.

2. Be internally consistent—policies should develop logically and consistently with and from one another.

3. Be distinguished from rules and procedures—policies represent general statements that guide thinking and provide for discretionary action. Rules and procedures are designed to channel action and allow for little or no discretion.[19]

There is no one best communication policy for any and all organizations. My key point in discussing these is that policy affects communication climate which, in turn, affects the probability that understanding and organizational effectiveness is developing. Let's look at ways we as managers can analyze communication climate.

Diagnosing the Communication Climate in Your Organization

There are two general approaches to the analysis of communication climate in organizations: (1) evaluation of member satisfaction or dissatisfactions, and (2) measurement of discrepancies in perceptions of or assumptions about communicating.

Climate Satisfaction Measures

Communication satisfaction measures are often incorporated in other employee attitude or morale surveys. There are scores of questionnaires which measure aspects of job satisfaction and work attitudes. You can design questionnaires which focus on variables you are concerned about, such as trust and supportiveness, openness and candor, participation in organizational decisions, perceptions of organizational fairness, and receptiveness to suggestions.[20]

A common approach to designing measuring instruments uses Likert-type scales; that is, a statement is followed by a five- or seven-point scale on which respondents can indicate agreement or disagreement. Here are a few examples:

My supervisor expresses appreciation to me for work I do.
Strongly agree   5   4   3   2   1   Strongly disagree
I have ample opportunities to participate in decisions that affect me on the job.
Strongly agree   5   4   3   2   1   Strongly disagree

To avoid a response set whereby people answer all questions the same way, say "4," reverse the wording occasionally to reflect different meaning:

I never get a chance to participate in company decisions.
Strongly agree   1   2   3   4   5   Strongly disagree

With the above examples, a higher score reflects greater satisfaction with aspects of the communication climate.

A few words of caution are in order. Making up good questionnaires is seldom as easy as it looks. In most cases, they should be pretested and carefully evaluated before a great deal of confidence is placed in their findings. By all means, consult some books or resource people on how to do this before administering such questionnaires in your organization. I've listed several sources in the bibliography at the end of this chapter.

Discrepancy Measures

The second approach to diagnosing organizational communication climate focuses on certain discrepancies between what initiators of messages think they are communicating and what receivers really perceive. A pioneer of this approach, George Odiorne, devised a "communication audit" for the purpose of measuring the accuracy of management assumptions about its employees. The approach uses two identical questionnaires. Employees were asked to record their attitudes toward such things as the adequacy of the organization's communication channels, relationships with management, and satisfaction with aspects of their job. Managers were asked to complete the same survey *predicting how their subordinates would respond.* The responses were then compared.

David T. Burhans, Jr., who later elaborated upon Odiorne's technique, summarizes the findings of the original study: the management of the company was operating under a number of misassumptions about their employees. For example, management predicted that 87 percent of the engineers would answer affirmatively the question: "Do you feel that you are adequately informed on management aims and long range planning?" Actually, 83 percent of the engineers said no. Management assumed that engineers were interested only in the technical aspects of engineering work and would not want to be bothered with taking part in management planning. Consequently, management predicted that 90 percent of the engineers would answer negatively the question: "Would you like to participate more in company planning?" In fact, exactly 90 percent of the engineers indicated that they would indeed like to participate more in company planning. The point is that Odiorne's technique (the communication audit) revealed not simply misassumptions about the meaning of a few words—but fundamental misassumptions about the desires, expectations, and perceptions of their employees which until corrected caused pervasive and persistent misunderstanding between management and employees.[21]

On the following pages is the Burhans Communication Policy Preference Scale.[22] This carefully developed questionnaire employs the discrepancy technique used by Odiorne. Notice that two different instruction pages should be used—one for employees and one for supervisors. The procedure is simply to administer the questionnaires to appropriate organization members. Evaluation of results involves comparison of responses from employees with those of their supervisor. Serious discrepancies reflect areas where communication problems are likely to be present. A scoring form is provided on pages 55–56.

COMMUNICATION POLICY PREFERENCE SCALE

Employee's Instruction Page

On the following pages are 35 statements about the internal communication within this company, and, particularly, this office. You are to read each statement and then black out the number following the statement which best indicates your reaction to that statement.

Let the numbers stand for the following reactions:

(1)	(2)	(3)	(4)	(5)	(6)	(7)
Disagree very strongly	Disagree strongly	Disagree	No opinion	Agree	Agree strongly	Agree very strongly

Thus, if you disagreed strongly with the following statement, you would mark it as follows:

1. Quantity of communication between a supervisor and his subordinates is more important than quality of communication.
   _____(1)(●)(3)(4)(5)(6)(7)

There is no time limit. There are no right or wrong answers; the only right answer is your honest opinion. PLEASE BE SURE TO MARK A RESPONSE FOR EACH STATEMENT. If you wish to comment further on any of the statements, you may write your comments on the back of any of the statement sheets.

Supervisor's Instruction Page

Please read the Employee's Instruction Page. YOU ARE TO RESPOND TO THE FOLLOWING 35 STATEMENTS, HOWEVER, IN A DIFFERENT WAY: You are to read each statement and then black out the number following the statement which best indicates—*not your own reaction to it,* but—the reaction which you believe most employees under your authority will have to that statement.

For example, if you believe that most of your employees will agree strongly with the following statement, you would mark it as follows:

1. Communication is not one of the most important aspects of achieving teamwork. _____(1)(2)(3)(4)(5)(●)(7)

PLEASE BE SURE TO BLACK IN A RESPONSE FOR EACH STATEMENT. If you wish to comment further on any of the statements, you may write your comments on the back of any of the statement sheets.

1. Failure to inform employees regarding company policies, achievements, and future plans is an indication that management does not fully appreciate and value employees as individual persons. _____ (1)(2)(3)(4)(5)(6)(7)

(1)	(2)	(3)	(4)	(5)	(6)	(7)
Disagree very strongly	Disagree strongly	Disagree	No opinion	Agree	Agree strongly	Agree very strongly

2. This company should provide an orderly system by which employees will be given thorough and sympathetic consideration of any job or personal problem which they may have. _____ (1)(2)(3)(4)(5)(6)(7)

3. Employees should feel free to discuss with their supervisors any personal problems arising out of employment with the company. _____ (1)(2)(3)(4)(5)(6)(7)

4. The best way for management to communicate with employees is through the various informal means of communication. _____ (1)(2)(3)(4)(5)(6)(7)

5. Management should communicate to employees only those facts which are pertinent to the employees' work. _____ (1)(2)(3)(4)(5)(6)(7)

6. Whenever management decisions become firm, those decisions should be communicated to affected employees before any action is taken to carry out those decisions. _____ (1)(2)(3)(4)(5)(6)(7)

7. Consideration should be given to employees' views before reaching decisions that materially affect their jobs or interests. _____ (1)(2)(3)(4)(5)(6)(7)

8. The company should recognize the importance of maintaining a two-way flow of information between employees and management. _____ (1)(2)(3)(4)(5)(6)(7)

9. Management should give prompt and serious attention to each complaint or suggestion made by employees. _____ (1)(2)(3)(4)(5)(6)(7)

10. Employees should be informed of problems in their immediate work environment. _____ (1)(2)(3)(4)(5)(6)(7)

(1)	(2)	(3)	(4)	(5)	(6)	(7)
Disagree very strongly	Disagree strongly	Disagree	No opinion	Agree	Agree strongly	Agree very strongly

11. When management communicates pol-
    icy changes, it is important that they
    also communicate why those changes
    were made. _____ (1)(2)(3)(4)(5)(6)(7)

12. Well informed employees will be more
    cooperative and will work together bet-
    ter as a team. _____ (1)(2)(3)(4)(5)(6)(7)

13. Employees should be given information
    regarding company earnings, current
    profits, and the financial status of the
    company. _____ (1)(2)(3)(4)(5)(6)(7)

14. It is a supervisor's obligation to solicit
    and listen to the views of those whom
    he supervises. _____ (1)(2)(3)(4)(5)(6)(7)

15. Communication is an integral part of
    every job and is, therefore, every em-
    ployee's responsibility. _____ (1)(2)(3)(4)(5)(6)(7)

16. Members of an affected group should
    be informed on matters concerning
    their group before such information is
    given to the rest of the company. _____ (1)(2)(3)(4)(5)(6)(7)

17. Management should communicate to
    employees full information about the
    company's plans, both general and spe-
    cific, long-range and immediate. _____ (1)(2)(3)(4)(5)(6)(7)

18. An employee should feel free to consult
    any time he wishes with members of
    the personnel department. _____ (1)(2)(3)(4)(5)(6)(7)

19. Employees should be told not only
    when things are going well for the com-
    pany, but also when they are going
    badly. _____ (1)(2)(3)(4)(5)(6)(7)

(1)	(2)	(3)	(4)	(5)	(6)	(7)
Disagree	Disagree	Disagree	No	Agree	Agree	Agree
very strongly	strongly		opinion		strongly	very strongly

20. Employees should be informed in advance of any contemplated changes in facilities, equipment, policies, practices, and organization. _____ (1)(2)(3)(4)(5)(6)(7)

21. Performance in one's job is influenced by how well employees understand, accept, and support the action that management wants taken. _____ (1)(2)(3)(4)(5)(6)(7)

22. An employee should be given full information regarding his earnings and how they are calculated. _____ (1)(2)(3)(4)(5)(6)(7)

23. Effective internal communication can reduce costs, improve products or services, increase safety, improve working conditions, and improve or simplify methods of operation. _____ (1)(2)(3)(4)(5)(6)(7)

24. Management should communicate to employees all matters involving the company which affect the employee's job or welfare. _____ (1)(2)(3)(4)(5)(6)(7)

25. Employees should be kept informed about the company's progress and production. _____ (1)(2)(3)(4)(5)(6)(7)

26. Employees whose suggestions are rejected should be informed of the reasons for not following those suggestions. _____ (1)(2)(3)(4)(5)(6)(7)

27. Every employee has the right to express an opinion; the right to a definite answer; the right to appeal. _____ (1)(2)(3)(4)(5)(6)(7)

28. If matters arise which the employee would like to take up directly with the highest level of management in this office, the employee should feel free to do so. _____ (1)(2)(3)(4)(5)(6)(7)

(1)	(2)	(3)	(4)	(5)	(6)	(7)
Disagree very strongly	Disagree strongly	Disagree	No opinion	Agree	Agree strongly	Agree very strongly

29. Employees should feel free to discuss with their supervisors any matter troubling them whether it is directly job-related or not. _____ (1)(2)(3)(4)(5)(6)(7)

30. Most employees want to know more about the company of which they are a part. _____ (1)(2)(3)(4)(5)(6)(7)

31. This company has an obligation to establish workable channels of communication for its employees. _____ (1)(2)(3)(4)(5)(6)(7)

32. Employees should share a dedication to the company's objectives of earning a profitable return on its shareholders' investment. _____ (1)(2)(3)(4)(5)(6)(7)

33. The dissemination of vital company news to the employees is indispensable to the building of a feeling of participation on the part of the employees. _____ (1)(2)(3)(4)(5)(6)(7)

34. The active participation of all employees is essential to the success of this company's internal communication. _____ (1)(2)(3)(4)(5)(6)(7)

35. Employees should be well informed regarding the company's products and services. _____ (1)(2)(3)(4)(5)(6)(7)

(1)	(2)	(3)	(4)	(5)	(6)	(7)
Disagree very strongly	Disagree strongly	Disagree	No opinion	Agree	Agree strongly	Agree very strongly

COMMUNICATION POLICY PREFERENCE SCALE SCORING GUIDE

1. Add the scale scores (positions checked on the seven point scale from 1 = *disagree very strongly* through 7 = *agree very strongly*) of each employee for each item. Divide that total by the number of employees to get an average score for each item. Write these numbers in column 1 of the scoring sheet, pages 55–56.

2. Write in the scale score of the employees' supervisor for each item in column 2 of the scoring sheet.

3. Calculate the Supervisor Error Score in the following manner:

a. Subtract the supervisor's score (column 2) from the average of his or her subordinates' scores (column 1) and write the remainder in column 3. (Be sure to indicate + or −.)

b. Assign an error unit score to each item comparison (ignoring the + or − for now) in this manner:

Column 3 Score		Error Unit Score
.00	=	0
.01–1.99	=	1
2.0–2.99	=	2
3.0–3.99	=	3
4.0–4.99	=	4
5.0–6.00	=	5

c. For each item, compare columns 2 and 3 to determine severity of misassumption. For each comparison where the employee average score is 3 or less and supervisor score on the same item is 5 or more, or vice versa, add one to the error unit score in column 5.

d. Add column 4 and 5 to compute the Supervisor Error Score. Place this number in column 6.

Error Scores of 3 or more deserve immediate corrective action. The higher the score, the more potentially dangerous the misunderstanding.

Communication Policy Preference Scale Scoring Sheet

Scale Item	Employee Average Score	Super- visor's Score	Difference	Error Unit Score	Additional Error Unit	Supervisor Error Score
1						
2						
3						
4						
5						
6						
7						
8						
9						
10						
11						

Communication Policy Preference Scale Scoring Sheet (cont.)

Scale Item	Employee Average Score	Super-visor's Score	Difference	Error Unit Score	Additional Error Unit	Supervisor Error Score
12						
13						
14						
15						
16						
17						
18						
19						
20						
21						
22						
23						
24						
25						
26						
27						
28						
29						
30						
31						
32						
33						
34						
35						

Total Error_____

Developing Your Own Discrepancy Measures

Use of the discrepancy technique is relatively simple. Managers can adapt the questionnaires used to meet specific concerns of the organization. Listed below are a series of items which could be incorporated in questionnaires. Simply use the instructions for the Communication Policy Preference Scale and substitute these or other clearly worded statements. Be careful that each statement expresses only one thought. For example, do not say, "My boss listens to my ideas and he is honest." Such wording confuses the issue. Is the employee responding to "listening" or "honesty"?

Additional Climate Scale Items

1. Most people in the organization clearly understand the specific goals of the organization.
2. I have a very clear picture of what the organization wants from me.
3. Everyone in this organization is free to say what's on his or her mind without fear of negative consequences.
4. If I communicate good ideas upward to my boss, I will be rewarded in some way (at least complimented).
5. My boss frequently tells me when I have done a particularly good job.
6. I'm usually hesitant about suggesting new ideas because they will probably be ignored.
7. There is a strong sense of trust among employees and their bosses in the organization.
8. I clearly understand my job responsibilities and exactly where my job fits into the overall objectives of the organization.
9. Other people in the organization are usually given more prompt, meaningful answers to questions than I am.
10. My supervisor makes it easy to speak to him or her on almost any problem or topic.
11. I am constantly brought up to date on changes occurring in the organization.
12. My supervisor seems more prone to compliment other people in the work group and to ignore me.
13. I have no idea what the organization's long-range goals are.
14. Speaking out on organizational issues often leads to problems.
15. There is a general atmosphere of frankness, candor, and honesty among all members of the organization.
16. There are a number of avenues members of the organization can use to participate in goal setting and problem solving.
17. I am always one of the first to know of changes or new information in my work group.
18. Management encourages all employees to set personal goals as well as subscribe to organizational goals.
19. I could describe quite specifically the jobs and functions of most departments in the organization.
20. I know exactly how well I am doing at all times.
21. My boss seems to have a genuine open door policy. He is almost always available and willing to communicate to me.
22. When being evaluated on the job, I often feel that I've been put down when my work is criticized.

23. I really trust my boss and the organization's management in general.
24. I'm not sure what is expected of me on the job or in such areas as personal appearance and behavior on the job.
25. My boss seems to clearly understand my personal goals and what I want out of life.
26. My boss has never sat down and explained company policies to me on a personal basis.
27. My willingness to get involved in problem-solving discussions and to give work suggestions has an important impact on my performance appraisal.
28. My supervisor is open-minded to all kinds of ideas.
29. There is a widespread sense of trust and personal freedom in the organization.
30. I have all the information, including the "tricks of the trade" that I need to do my job in the best possible way.

(Note that items 6, 9, 12, 13, 14, 22, 24, and 26 are negatively worded. The discrepancy technique scoring procedure will not be affected by this. If, however, these questions are used as attitude survey questions, the scales should be reversed so that a higher number would not be mistaken for a positive response.)

Questions for Further Thought

1. How do your personal goals coincide or conflict with your perceptions of your organization's goals? Can differences be reconciled? Are they important?

2. How well do you understand the objectives or goals of your work group, club, organization, class, etc.? Talk with someone else about these and see how your perceptions may differ.

3. Develop a discrepancy measure of climate such as that suggested on pages 57–58. Gather some data and analyze your findings. What can or should be done (if anything) to improve?

4. What is your communication policy?
   a. Describe your goals or objectives with regard to communication in your organization.
   b. What specific rules or guidelines should be adhered to in order to attain and maintain desired communication effectiveness?

    c. Where do you or members of your organization tend to fall short? Where should managerial emphasis be placed to improve communication climate? Set three specific, attainable goals for improving the climate.

Notes

1. W. Charles Redding, *Communication within the Organization* (New York: Industrial Communication Council, 1972), p. 111.
2. From pp. 15–16, THE ORGANIZATIONAL WORLD by Harold J. Leavitt, William R. Dill and Henry B. Eyring © 1973 by Harcourt Brace Jovanovich, Inc. Reprinted by permission of the publishers.
3. Maxwell Maltz, *Psycho-cybernetics* (Englewood Cliffs, N.J.: Prentice-Hall, Inc., 1960).
4. Leavitt *et al., op. cit.*, p. 25.
5. Reprinted by permission of *Industry Week*, June 8, 1970.
6. Daniel Katz and Robert L. Kahn, *The Social Psychology of Organizations* (New York: John Wiley & Sons, 1966), p. 186.
7. *Ibid.*, pp. 193–195.
8. DeWitt C. Dearborn and Herbert A. Simon, "Selective Perception: The Departmental Identifications of Executives," *Sociometry*, 21 (1958), pp. 140–144.
9. Chester Barnard, *The Functions of the Executive* (Cambridge, Mass: Harvard University Press, 1938).
10. For elaboration on this line of thinking see Steven Kerr, "On the Folly of Rewarding A, While Hoping for B," *Academy of Management Journal*, December 1975, pp. 769–783.
11. Jack Gibb, "Defensive Communication," *Journal of Communication*, 1961, pp. 141–148.
12. Paul R. Timm, "Worker Responses to Supervisory Communication Inequity: An Exploratory Study," *Journal of Business Communication*, 16, 1 (Fall 1978), pp. 11–24.
13. Walter Wiesman, *Wall-to-Wall Organizational Communication* (Huntsville, Ala.: Walter Wiesman, 1973), p. 3.
14. David T. Burhans, Jr., "The Development and Field Testing of Two Internal Communication Measuring Instruments" (unpublished paper, California State College, Los Angeles, 1971), p. 5.
15. Geneva Seybold, *Employee Communication: Policy and Tools* (New York: National Industrial Conference Board, 1966), pp. 35–36. Reprinted by permission of The Conference Board.
16. *Ibid.*, p. 39.
17. Archie McCardell, "Open Communication Is Our Policy, But Sometimes. . . ," *Xerox World*, 21 (January 1976) p. 2.
18. Seybold, *op. cit.*, pp. 33–34.
19. Brent D. Peterson and R. Wayne Pace, "Communication Climate and Organizational Satisfaction" (unpublished paper, Brigham Young University, 1977).

20. One diagnostic instrument sold commercially which measures such things is the *Organizational Associates Communication Climate Inventory* (Organizational Associates, P.O. Box 7270, University Station, Provo, Utah 84602).
21. Burhans, *op. cit.*, pp. 3–4.
22. David T. Burhans, Jr., "The Development and Field Testing of Two Internal Communication Measuring Instruments." Unpublished paper, Department of Speech Communication and Drama, California State College, Los Angeles, December 1971. Used by permission of Dr. David T. Burhans, Jr.

Recommended Readings

Leavitt, Harold J., William R. Dill, and Henry B. Eyring, *The Organizational World.* New York: Harcourt Brace Jovanovich, 1973. This is the most delightful book on organization theory that I have read. It is both fascinating in its content and fun to read. As you can tell from the excerpt quoted on pages 27–28, the authors' tone is conversational and good-humored.

Katz, Daniel, and Robert L. Kahn, *The Social Psychology of Organizations* (2nd ed.), New York: John Wiley & Sons, 1978. If you have about a month with nothing to do you could profitably spend it reading Katz and Kahn. This book is clearly a classic. It is written in academic language and you have to chew your way through parts of it. But if you digest it, it'll give you an exceptionally deep understanding of what goes on among people in organizations.

Wiesman, Walter, *Wall-to-Wall Organizational Communication.* Huntsville, Ala.: Walter Wiesman, 1973. This is a spiral-bound collection of speeches and papers Walt has prepared over the years as head of the internal communication program at NASA Marshall Space Flight Center and as a private consultant. Witty and interesting reading is offered by this practicing communicator.

Sanford, Aubrey C., Gary T. Hunt, and Hyler J. Bracey. *Communication Behavior in Organizations.* Columbus, Ohio: Charles E. Merrill, 1976. Of the many recent textbooks in organizational communication, this one has a particularly interesting approach to communication climate.

For further information on my research in the area of communication equity, you might check Paul R. Timm and Paul L. Wilkens, "A Model of Perceived Communication Inequity and Job Dissatisfaction" printed in the *Proceedings* of the Academy of Management, 37th Annual Meeting, Orlando, Florida, August 1977. Also, Paul R. Timm, "Worker Responses to Supervisory Communication Inequity: An Exploratory Study," *Journal of Business Communication,* Fall 1978.

Kerr, Steven. "On the Folly of Rewarding A, While Hoping for B." *Academy of Management Journal,* December 1975, pp. 769–783. This article has become a classic. It describes the dangers of unforeseen outcomes associated with reward systems. The article is guaranteed to provoke thought, and is also more enjoyable reading than many journal articles.

One source of measuring instruments available in most university libraries is John P. Robinson, Robert Athanasion, and Kendra B. Head, *Measures of Occupational Attitudes and Occupational Characteristics*. Ann Arbor, Mich.: Survey Research Center, Institute for Social Research, The University of Michigan, 1969.

One clearly written book on research methods that I've found useful in designing and administering measurement instruments is Earl R. Babbie, *The Practice of Social Research*. 2nd ed. Belmont, Calif.: Wadsworth, 1979.

CHAPTER 3

ONGOING COMMUNICATION PROCESS AND FLOW
Gushers to Dribbles

A man once argued with his doctor over the high cost of medical care. "After all," the man contended, "a physician's job is really no different than that of an auto mechanic. Functionally, a human being is only a very complex machine that occasionally needs to be fixed." "The major distinction," came the doctor's retort, "is that I do my work with the engine running!"

The communication functions in an organization need to be examined and "tuned up" while the engine is running. To artificially stop the communication process and examine it in that static state tells us very little about the system's true health.

Human organizations are comprised of *components* such as people and other resources, working within certain *relationships* which arise from their *interactions* as they move toward some *goals* within their *environment*. Communication provides the glue that holds the system together.

We have already looked at communication environment or climate and how it emerges from members' orientation to goals, roles, and policies. In this chapter we will consider (1) how communication tends to "flow" in the organization, forming *networks of interactions*; and (2) who participates—that is, what *components* are involved in these networks of purposeful communication in the organization.

Communication Flow:
Fluid and Unpredictable

Information flowing through an organization provides the stimuli that members will respond to and create understandings from. Ongoing message processes are very fluid and often unpredictable. Communication networks serve to direct communication flow and improve the probability that understanding will develop. The effectiveness of a communication network is determined by the degree to which (1) messages maintain accuracy as they move through the system, (2) the people who need or want the messages get them at appropriate times, and (3) organization members avoid being overloaded with too many messages.

Network Accuracy

Managers are often called upon to initiate messages—to somehow manipulate words or symbols so that meaning will be created in the minds of others. These messages emerge from repetitive communication events among organizational members, that is, from habits of interaction. These habits arise from job needs, convenience, proximity, personality similarities, or any number of other factors.

Most organizations are quite careful about defining formal communication networks, especially when task-relevant messages are to be conveyed. For a downward flowing work directive, the plant manager gives it to section leaders who, in turn, give the message to supervisors, who give it to foremen. Similarly with "upward" communication, the worker conveys information to his or her immediate boss. It is usually considered inappropriate to go "over someone's head" to the next level. It is an unwritten assumption in most organizations that the higher level managers get work-related information and policy changes before the rank and file workers. Similarly, the immediate supervisor receives employee suggestions or complaints before higher level managers. When this protocol is violated, the message timing is thrown off and the network's effectiveness (at least from the viewpoint of those who organized the network) is impeded.

It is not coincidental that we tend to see communication networks as isomorphic with the organization chart. Job specialization and the principle of unity of command—the notion that each employee should have only one boss—are, in part, efforts to control the flow of information. If, however, we come to believe that communication flows in our organization only through designated channels, we are living in a dream world. In reality, the flow of information is seldom as predictable as we would like. More often than not our planned flow becomes an indiscriminate dribble.

Messages tend to ignore our carefully outlined network and instead take shortcuts, ending up with the wrong people—or the right people, but under the wrong circumstances. Or important information may simply be gobbled up by the system, ending nowhere. Perhaps the most dramatic examples of network failures leading to disaster come from history. The well-known debacle at Pearl Harbor is a classic case of a communication system that failed.[1]

The Serial Transmission Effect

Many of us have played the game where one person whispers a message in the ear of the person next to her who, in turn, passes it on to another player, etc. After 10 or 15 players, the message which is then announced aloud is very different from the original. Something happens to it as it moves from person to person. This is an example of the *serial transmission effect* on network accuracy. The distortion becomes even more pronounced when different organizational levels are involved. Opinion Research Corporation ran a series of studies to measure the integrity of information as it flowed from level to level in organizations. A survey in a metals producing company was initiated when top management, concerned over declining profits, sought to measure the degree of understanding of the severity of the problem at four levels in the organization. The results were startling:[2]

Of the top corporate officers	91% understood
Of upper middle management	48% understood
Of lower middle management	21% understood
Of first line supervisors only	5% understood!

The frightening point is that these results are probably not unusual. Why do messages get distorted or lost as they flow through different levels in the organization? There are a number of reasons, including personality characteristics of participants, power, status and roles, and the number of links in the network. The example below shows just how confused things can get.

Operation: Halley's Comet[3]

A *colonel* issued the following directive to his executive officer:

"Tomorrow evening at approximately 2000 hours Halley's Comet will be visible in this area, an event which occurs only once every 75 years. Have the men fall out in the battalion area in fatigues, and I will explain this rare phenomenon to them. In case of rain, we will not be able to see anything, so assemble the men in the theater and I will show them films of it."

Executive officer to company commander:

"By order of the colonel, tomorrow at 2000 hours, Halley's Comet will appear above the battalion area. If it rains, fall the men out in fatigues. Then march to the theater where the rare phenomenon will take place, something which occurs only once every 75 years."

Company commander to lieutenant:

"By order of the colonel in fatigues at 2000 hours tomorrow evening the phenomenal Halley's Comet will appear in the theater. In case of rain in the battalion area, the colonel will give another order, something which occurs once every 75 years."

Lieutenant to sergeant:

"Tomorrow at 2000 hours, the colonel will appear in the theater with Halley's Comet, something which happens every 75 years. If it rains, the colonel will order the comet into the battalion area."

Sergeant to squad:

"When it rains tomorrow at 2000 hours, the phenomenal 75-year-old General Halley, accompanied by the Colonel, will drive his Comet through the battalion area theater in fatigues."

Personality characteristics affect networks. The flow of communication through networks is quite different from the flow of water through pipes. For one thing, the "pipes" in the communication network are not clearly defined and there is a lot of spillover—for example, when someone listens in to or reads a message intended for another. Further, *people* are the conduit through which the messages flow and they are far less standardized in size, shape, or function than are their galvanized counterparts.

Indeed, an important determinant of network effectiveness is the people in it. Koehler, Anatol, and Applbaum[4] discuss the ways personality characteristics shape our perception of the world around us, including the way we hear or read messages passed to us. In the organization, we tend to pay close attention to messages which we see as somehow serving our needs or wants, while we are likely to ignore less relevant information.

Some people view their roles in the organization with *indifference.* They see their work as a necessary evil. They have little commitment to organizational values or goals and they often depreciate the company or the products it makes. Messages passed through them may lose a great deal of enthusiasm. *indifferent*

Other people have *authoritarian* personalities and tend to be very critical. Their thinking and language is likely to be marked by many *shoulds* and *oughts* and *musts*. In major research on the authoritarian personality some years ago, Adorno and others[5] concluded that several personality traits and "packages" of attitudes tended to occur together in the same people. The authoritarian dislikes and avoids any kind of ambiguity. He or she will reach firm conclusions, make judgments without qualifications, and stick to them. The world exists in black and white terms for this type person. Here are some characteristics considered typical in the authoritarian personality as summarized by Koehler et al.:[6]

1. Conventionalism—a rigid adherence to conventional middleclass values;
2. Authoritarian submission—a submission to authority figures and an uncritical attitude toward idealized moral authorities of the in-group;
3. Hostility toward those who violate social norms—a form of authoritarian aggression—a tendency to be overready to perceive, condemn, reject, and punish people who violate conventional norms;
4. Dislike of subjectivity—an aversion to the subjective, the imaginative, the aesthetic, the tender-minded;
5. Superstition and stereotyping—beliefs in mystical determinance of the individual's fate; the disposition to think in rigid categories;
6. Preoccupation with strength, power, and toughness—concern with the dominant-submissive, strong-weak, leader-follower dimension; identification with power figures; exaggerated assertion of strength and toughness;
7. Destructive cynicism toward human nature—rather generalized hostility—the vilification of the human;
8. Projectivity—a tendency to project unacceptable impulses—disposition to believe that wild and dangerous and wicked things go on in the world;
9. An exaggerated concern with sex and sexual goings-on.

Messages passed through the authoritarian personality are likely to come out sounding considerably more emphatic and dogmatic. Value judgments of right or wrong, good or bad, are likely to be added to the message.

A *Machiavellian** personality type is one we associate with a manipulative attitude toward others and a generally cynical view of other people's motives or character. The person with a strong Machiavellian personality (high Mach) tends to be self-centered and self-serving. As Koehler *et al.* explain, "his relative lack of emotional involvement in interpersonal relationships, his lack of concern for the conventional outlook, make it easy for him to manipulate and control others. The high Mach also distrusts his colleagues, and has little faith in human nature. He tends to rate fellow workers as less interesting, less assertive, less productive, less cooperative, and less intelligent. Since he disdains them, he experiences no qualms in taking advantage of them."[7]

This type of communicator will be less concerned with whether or not people understand his meanings and more concerned with how effective he has been at getting the message receivers to *do what he wants.*

There are, of course, many other personality types present in any complex organization. My point here is simply that personality affects the way we receive messages and the ways we attempt to create meaning in others. As messages flow through the organizational networks, these personality traits act as filters, each distilling the information and shaping the content.

Power, status, and roles affect networks. There are additional forces at work in communication networks which further determine effectiveness. Among these are power, status, and roles of member-participants. The way we perceive the power of someone affects the way we pass messages to her or him in the network. In a series of studies, French and Raven[8] determined that there are five types of power:

1. *Reward power* stems from the number of positive rewards, such as money, protection, and benefits, that people perceive that another can muster.
2. *Coercive power* arises from perceived expectations that punishment (being fired or reprimanded, for example) will follow if one doesn't comply with the bearer of such power.
3. *Legitimate power* develops from one's internalized values which dictate that the reference person has a legitimate right to influence and that one has an obligation to accept this influence (e.g., a policeman or organizational leader).

*Niccolo Machiavelli (1469–1527) was an Italian statesman and writer on government whose name has come to be associated with craftiness, deceitfulness, and manipulation of people of lesser status. The Machiavellian manager would not hesitate to communicate only messages which serve his or her ends.

4. *Referent power* is based on identification with the person and wanting to be associated with him or her or what he symbolizes (e.g., the son of a president or, the secretary to the chairman of the board).

5. *Expert power* results from the reference person's special expertise, knowledge, or ability in an area where influence is attempted (e.g., the lawyer or surgeon).

Other researchers have categorized these sources as *position* power—that attained by virtue of organizational position—and *personal* power—that derived from perceived personal attributes of the individual. Position power is bestowed upon a person from someone having organizational authority. Personal power comes from the perceiver's recognition of certain traits or capabilities and his decision to be influenced by these.

The way employees perceive power in others can greatly inhibit or facilitate the propensity to communicate. Whether or not messages are passed along, and, if so, in what condition, will be affected by perceived power. This will be especially true when the worker sees another's power as having direct influence upon him or her. No one wants to bear bad news to the powerful.

Status often relates closely with power. One may enjoy formal and/or informal status within groups. Formal status—often taking the form of organizational position, titles, and various symbols of rank—is conferred by those in authority. Informal status may be accorded one by peers, subordinates, or bosses but it reflects personal power dimensions, not formal position or rank within the group. It is important to keep in mind that people may have varying degrees of status in different realms. The entry level assembly line worker (low position power) may attain recognition for "pumping iron" in an athletic competition which affords him considerable status.

Organizational roles also affect network effectiveness. Role positions are typically arranged in a hierarchy which closely relates status and power. Roles entail certain rights, duties, and obligations which frequently call for different interaction patterns with others. Members tend to direct more messages to people they view as fulfilling important roles, such as those in organizational leadership positions.

In addition to our organizational roles, our sex roles also seem to influence the ways we communicate. Typically, men are more reluctant to exhibit their feelings, preferring instead to display a "toughness" that suppresses the sentimental or emotionally expressive. Evidence indicates that men do conceal more about themselves from others than do women. Women, who have traditionally been more expressive of sentiment, may now be modifying this kind of communicative behavior in light of new organizational roles. Nevertheless, our organizational and socially dictated sex roles do affect the ways we communicate.

We can see that there are many forces at work which can lead to confusion and distortion as messages flow through networks of people. But is there any way to predict how messages will change? Donald T. Campbell concluded that there are seven kinds of changes that occur as messages are serially transmitted:

1. The message gets abbreviated, simplified, and there is a loss of detail.
2. Participants in the flow tend to fill in the gaps—add information not specified in the original message.
3. Participants tend to accentuate, contrast, and highlight inconsistencies with other known information.
4. Participants draw comparisons to similar messages remembered from the past. They highlight the sameness of this message compared to other known information.
5. Distortion of the original message occurs to make it correspond to the participants' attitudes or personality traits.
6. The message is distorted to please the next person in the chain.
7. The message is distorted in the direction of oversimplification and "good-bad" evaluations.[9]

Managers interested in reducing such message distortions should look first at the possibility of reducing the number of links in the network. This can often be accomplished by selecting an appropriate transmission medium. (I'll discuss communication media and tools in the next chapter.) The major danger in reducing the links in the network is that it can lead to another problem, often as troublesome as serial transmission. When many messages flow indiscriminately to organization members rather than through a predetermined network, some people—especially the leaders—find themselves facing communication *overload*.

Communication Overload: Hold My Calls, Miss Findley

With the increase in organized activities and the growing sophistication of communications technology we are confronted with more information than we can possibly process. Managers are typically caught between the need to know and the ability to assimilate. People with strong "upwardly mobile" aspirations and those whose power and role positions put them in the middle of the informational mainstream are especially susceptible:

the upwardly mobile because they recognize the value of and hunger for information, and those in the mainstream because their job responsibilities demand that they be "in the know."

We have all experienced momentary overload. Driving down a city street is an exercise in handling countless messages which assault our senses. We listen to the car radio, talk to our passengers, read street signs and outdoor advertisements—all of which compete for our attention. Doing research in a large library, virtually surrounded by data, all of which could never be assimilated, can be psychologically and emotionally exhausting. As a recent advertisement by an office products company said, "Having all this information around can be an embarrassment of riches. But it can also be just an embarrassment unless . . . you organize it, edit it, transmit it, and store it so you can find it again."[10] When we are overloaded, our normal response mechanisms are forced to choose among countless informational stimuli. These choices leave many messages out. Psychologists tell us that we will attend to those items which best meet the conscious or unconscious needs or desires we are experiencing at that time. But since our needs are constantly changing, so are our selection mechanisms.

There have been a number of studies of what people do when faced with communication overload at work. When overloaded, we typically cope by some combination of seven options:[11]

1. *Omission.* We simply fail to attend to or handle some incoming messages. We ignore some information.
2. *Error.* If we are overloaded we overlook or fail to correct errors that have been made. We get sloppy in our information processing.
3. *Queuing.* We let incoming messages pile up and get to them as we can. This, of course, only works when we have hard copy—written information; spoken messages cannot as readily be lined up for later attention.
4. *Filtering.* We deal with incoming messages according to some predetermined system of priorities—for example, responses to customers get first attention and the employees come next.
5. *Approximation.* We may lower our standards of precision. Instead of clearly understanding details of a message, we may become satisfied with a summary or condensed version.
6. *Multiple Channels.* We may delegate or decentralize information processing procedures to reduce the load. For example, we hire administrative assistants to handle our mail.
7. *Escape.* We may simple refuse to handle any input at all or refuse to reach out for information available.

I've known managers who, upon taking over a new position, throw away all files kept by the previous manager, except those required by law or policy. This way their minds will not be cluttered with excess historical data. This reduces potential overload and has an added employee relations benefit: by starting off with a clean slate, rather than accepting someone else's perceptions of employee behaviors, we can *assume* the best from others. Who knows, they may even live up to our expectations!

The effective communication network should reduce the probability of communication overload. Periodic analysis of who is getting what messages for what purpose should be carried out in the organization. One way to accomplish such an analysis is presented later in this chapter.

Isolates:
Alone Again, Naturally

At the opposite end of the scale from the overload problem is the isolate. When any member of the organization is cut off from the communication network, we are wasting a precious human resource. Human resources management has taught us that every member must be considered an asset and should be utilized. We no longer hire a "hand." We hire the whole man or woman. People don't want only to be treated well, they want to be *used* well. Their potential for sharing thoughts, ideas, and perceptions comes as part of the package. To toss that aside doesn't make much sense.

Yet, in most organizations, some individuals become isolated. There are a number of reasons for this. One may be simply a matter of geography. An individual whose work location is away from other employees and/or who is not linked up by phone or intercom may become isolated. One study found employee satisfaction to be very low among bank tellers who worked in isolated drive-in facilities compared to that of inside tellers.[12]

There are also more subtle reasons for employee isolation. Often one's role or authority position in the organization, personality characteristics, ethnic background or race, or even personal hygiene habits can lead to ostracism from the larger work group. The problem is fairly widespread but it becomes tragic for the organization when high level leaders are the victims. One lesson learned from Watergate points out the dangers in becoming insulated from the buffetings of discrepant, yet necessary, information. Corporate leaders are no less susceptible to isolation than politicians.

Executive isolation, or the effect of losing contact with what is really happening in the organization, comes about when several factors are present:[13]

1. When there is a heavy reliance on downward communication alone.
2. When leaders fail to go into the organization and observe first hand what is going on.
3. When leaders develop a pattern of overreacting to bad news.
4. When delegating takes place without plans for follow-up.
5. When executives proclaim an "open door policy" but fail to recognize obstacles preventing people from coming in.
6. When leaders are fearful or they are embarrassed to ask about details of the work they don't fully understand.

When we recognize any of these characteristics in our own behavior, it is time to take a hard look at just how "in touch" we really are. There are several things a manager can do when executive isolation is recognized. These often call for fundamental changes in managerial behaviors. He or she should:

1. Cultivate a genuine desire to hear bad news as well as good.
2. Get out of the office and personally check to see how things are going.
3. Meet periodically with groups of subordinates to discuss operations and problems; meet them at their job location and demonstrate a genuine interest in what is happening. While the manager is with them, he can ask them to explain something about their job that he may not know. Develop the art of listening to the right people.

In short, the way to avoid isolation for the manager and for any other member of his or her workforce is to reach out and *ask questions*. Don't interrogate, but do seek out employee perceptions. Suggestions for being more effective in this are presented in Chapter 5, and the reading on pages 89–94, "How to Earn an MBWA Degree," also discusses the involved manager.

Participation in the Communication System: Any Number Can Play

Innumerable studies have shown that when members are included in decision making that affects them and their organization, they tend to be more satisfied. It is important, however, to recognize the limitations as well as the strengths of participative decision making (PDM).

Many managers tend to resist PDM for a number of reasons. It can be time-consuming and thus expensive. It can be viewed as a threat to one's ego in that it redistributes leadership functions, and thus power, to subordinates in the formal organization. It takes a degree of humility to accept their decisions.

In addition, it must be recognized that PDM is not practical in every decision situation. When emergencies arise requiring quick responses there simply isn't time for participation. Similarly, the cost of PDM must be worthwhile in relation to the benefits. Assembling a group of employees on company time quickly gets expensive; a one-hour meeting of eight or ten individuals can cost hundreds of dollars in salaries alone. The quality of the decision outcome and/or the reduction in resistance to change must be worth the additional cost.

PDM is likely to be most effective when:

1. The problems or issues dealt with are seen as relevant and important to the participants. The topics should have some recognizable effect on them; they should feel some "ownership" of the problem.
2. The employee has some expertise in the subject being discussed. Such expertise arises from education or experience.
3. Interaction between participants is free and open. Participants are in no way threatened by active exchanges of different ideas.
4. The group is allowed freedom to work within clearly defined limits. Off-limits areas—such as company policy, budgets, or legal responsibilities—which are not subject to change should be so stated before PDM gets under way.
5. Participants have sufficient interpersonal communication skills and a realistic understanding of the group process (see Chapter 6).
6. Organizational leadership acts from "Theory Y" assumptions. They recognize especially that "The capacity for creativity in solving organizational problems is widely distributed in the population."[14] (For a quick review of Theory Y assumptions see note 12, pages 104–105.)

While managerial leadership styles and assumptions about human nature go far toward determining whether participation will be effective, characteristics of the employees also play an important part. Hersey and Blanchard[15] have developed a situational leadership theory which provides a model for predicting whether participation will be effective in a given situation. The key to such predictions is the "task-relevant maturity" of the participants. Such maturity is defined by the group members' ability to set effective goals, willingness and ability to accept responsibility, education and/or experience, and self-confidence. (This approach is discussed in more detail in Chapter 6.) When these ingredients are taken together and considered in relation to the specific issue under discussion, a prediction about the potential effectiveness of participation is possible. The higher the level of task-relevant maturity of an individual or group, the higher the probability that participation will be an effective management approach. The lower the task-relevant maturity, the lower the probability that participation will be useful.

When maturity is very low, PDM would be simply pooling ignorance. When the maturity of certain individuals or small groups is extremely high, however, management may defer the decision to those having obvious expertise and capabilities rather than risk diluting a high quality decision with opinions of less qualified participants. Robert Townsend's advice on using professional advertising agencies provides an example: "Don't hire a master to paint you a masterpiece and then assign a roomful of schoolboy-artists to look over his shoulder and suggest improvements."[16]

A great deal more could be said about participation as a component of organizational communication processes. We will look at techniques for effective interactions in groups and committees in more detail in Chapter 6. For now it is important to recognize PDM as one way that ongoing communication processes can be affected by changing the participants in the information network.

The Grapevine:
Informally Speaking

Thus far we have been talking about formalized communication networks. Much of the information which flows through organizations, however, does not use formal networks or prescribed procedures. Instead it travels through the "grapevine."

For many years managers were very concerned about the grapevine. The general consensus was that people should use formal channels and we should defoliate this undesirable weed. But, as is the case with many things, when we take a close look at informal communication flow, we find it has some redeeming social value, some potentially constructive characteristics. Research by a number of people, most notably management theorist Keith Davis, has revealed some rather surprising findings.

First, despite the connotation that many of us associate with the grapevine (or "rumor mill" or "gossip chain"), information transmitted through this informal network is often very accurate. Several researchers meticulously counted details of messages received through the grapevine and determined that they ranged from 78 to 90 percent accurate. The accuracy was especially high when the messages did not deal with highly emotional or controversial data.[17]

A second finding is that the grapevine is very _fast._ People tend to receive and pass on information very quickly. The greater the communication opportunities, the faster it flows. As a manager for a telephone company, I was astounded at how organizational associates all over the country knew the "scuttlebutt" within hours of an event, often long before any official announcement. Easy access to long-distance phone service helped!

A third finding is that the grapevine is _active_ and carries large quantities of information in almost every organization. It is a fact of organizational life. Often it serves several constructive roles:

1. It provides a network for some types of information that would be inappropriate in the formal network. Often such scuttlebutt or personal information serves to strengthen relationships among organization members and helps develop a sense of comradeship.
2. It can also provide an outlet for voicing emotionally charged messages which, if not expressed, could fester into growing hostility among employees.
3. It can be useful in translating some of management's directives into language easily understood by employees.
4. It can prevent unfounded rumors or misinformation by providing clarifying details.
5. Finally, the grapevine provides feedback to management about employee sentiments.

The kind of information flowing through an organization's grapevine tends to depend on the supply of and demand for specific messages. Caplow explains that:

> The grapevine is most active when information is scarce and the demand for it is high; it is least active when the information is plentiful and the demand for it is low. If an organization's future plans are kept secret, there will be many rumors about future plans. If they are widely publicized, there will be few such rumors and perhaps none at all. Some sorts of information, like scandalous gossip, are always in demand and usually in short supply. When information in this category becomes available, the grapevine transmits it far and wide.[18]

Perhaps the most effective way to deal with a grapevine is to feed it lots of information. When employees feel they are being kept abreast of every detail in the organization's operation—maybe even more information than they want—the thirst for additional data is quenched.

The Two-Step Flow of Communication in Organizations

Studies of information diffusion reveal other facts about the grapevine that can be useful to the manager. Beginning with the sociological studies of voting behavior by Lazarsfeld and others[19] in the late 1940s, there emerged a "two-step flow hypothesis." Their findings indicated that the flow of mass communication messages (speeches, radio, newspaper articles, etc.) may have less direct effects on receivers than was commonly supposed. Instead, it appears, messages stemming from the mass media first reach "opinion leaders" who, in turn, "pass on what they read and hear to those of their everyday associates for whom they are influential."[20] Later studies examined the implications of this hypothesis. One line of research looked more closely at the nature of these opinion leaders, revealing several prominent characteristics. An opinion leader tends to

1. Personify certain values or attributes that his or her followers admire
2. Have competence, experience, or expertise in the area in which his or her influence is sought
3. Be in a strategic social location—a position that permits him or her to be "in the know" regarding an area of influence

We can all think of people whose opinions or ideas we especially value or whose behaviors, appearance, or demeanor we tend to imitate. Who would you turn to for investment advice? Who would you go to if you had marital problems? Who could recommend a good restaurant in Chicago? The people identified in answering these questions may be our opinion leaders.

It is important to note that there is very little overlap of opinion leadership: a leader in one area is not likely to be influential in another unrelated sphere as well. The individual we turn to for investment advice may not be the one whose opinions about clothing or hairstyles we'd value. Most of us have a number of individuals who help us make decisions about various topics.

One of the earliest studies of the effects of the two-step flow hypothesis in organizations was done by Jacobson and Seashore.[21] Their research examined the communication patterns of 200 employees in a governmental agency. These people were asked to name individuals in the organization with whom they had communication contacts, other than those they were linked to by the formal organizational structure. At all levels of the organization, the researchers discovered key persons (whom they termed "liaison" members) who served as opinion leaders within their subgroups. Jacobsen and Seashore's main purpose was to make managers aware of the opinion leaders in their organizations so more effective organizational communication could be attained.

Phillip Tompkins[22] is another researcher who applied the two-step flow hypothesis to organizational communication. His studies suggest that, as in the case of society at large, "individual local influentials" (opinion leaders) exist within the industrial or governmental organization. Just as the influentials in the earlier Lazarsfeld *et al.* research were found to interpret the mass-media-generated information and pass it on to the remainder of the public, the organizational opinion leader tunes in to organizational media and passes information on to other members of his or her organizational subgroup. They also pass along their interpretations of such information.

In his doctoral dissertation, Richetto[23] combined a study of the two-step flow in an organization with the *credibility* of a message source-person. Personal leadership was investigated within three separate spheres of influence: (1) task-related influence, (2) political (grapevine) influence, and (3) social-emotional (non-job-related) influence. Using interviews and rating scales, Richetto determined to whom workers turned for information in each area and how they perceived that source-person. He concluded that

1. Influentials were found to receive higher ratings on all measures of source credibility.
2. When subjects named immediate supervisors as influentials, the credibility of these supervisors did not differ significantly from the credibility of informal (nonsupervisory) influentials.
3. When credibility ratings between informal influentials and immediate supervisors were compared, the *informal sources rated significantly higher.*

This study indicated the importance of using informal leaders to disseminate organizational information. If employees rate opinion leaders higher on credibility than their own supervisors, then the need for managers to be aware of and understand opinion leaders is further substantiated.

Although research concerning organizational opinion leaders has been approached in a variety of ways with a number of conclusions, one thread seems to consistently hold the research together. This thread, both stated and inferred, is that for effective organizationwide communication to occur, managers should be aware of the role of opinion leaders and should attempt to identify and work through them. The diagnostic technique presented at the end of this chapter can help managers identify opinion leaders by indicating their locations in the informal communication network.

The wise manager knows the importance of being in tune to the grapevine. Informal networks need not exclude formal organizational leaders if those leaders are sensitive to potential problems of executive isolation which inhibit messages from coming to them. Getting an "ear to the ground" is a worthwhile expenditure of effort. Tap into the grapevine, instead of wasting time trying to chop it down.

Feedback Systems:
How's That Again?

I want to touch on feedback only briefly, for it is a topic that permeates this book. As mentioned in Chapter 2, there are characteristics of organizational communication climate which inhibit or prevent ongoing feedback. Managers need to be sensitive to two aspects of the way they encourage or discourage employee feedback: *receptiveness* and *responsiveness*.

Receptiveness involves a general willingness to accept and encourage feedback *as perceived by your subordinates.* Saying you are open doesn't make it so. It's the impression your people have of you that determines your receptiveness. Feedback *responsiveness* involves the degree to which you are willing and able to *do* something about the information you receive from subordinates. Again, this is in the eye of the beholder.

While most managers tell their employees that their "door is always open," often that's true only in a physical sense at best. Psychological barriers remain. The new mayor in a city where I once lived dramatized his openness policy by physically removing the door to his office. While this may have had symbolic effect, in reality it was no easier to get an appointment to see His Honor than it was to see his predecessor who was roundly criticized for being "aloof." Visitors still had to get by one of the most deviously protective secretaries I've ever seen. After a few weeks and several encounters with unsavory characters who conned their way in, the mayor developed the habit of working in a "hideaway" office in another part of city hall so that his secretary could dutifully report that he was not in.

An open door policy must be more than a symbolic gesture. To be open we must be aware that we're likely to be spending a certain amount of time talking about things that seem trivial or talking to people we'd rather avoid. We'll get a lot of chaff with the wheat. But under all that chaff we're likely to find valuable nuggets of information. The object of the game is to maximize the income of useful data while accepting a tolerable amount of useless verbiage. We can't simply open the door and expect only useful information to come tumbling in. What we can do is develop patterns of behavior that convey to our subordinates our active interest in what they have to say, especially when their ideas are relevant to the organization.

Since feedback receptiveness and responsiveness are perceptions of us held by others, we may be unaware of how we're doing. In "Encouraging Feedback" (see p. 94), William G. Dyer shows some constructive things the individual manager can do to get useful reactions to his or her managerial efforts.

It is possible to go overboard in reaching out for information from others. Gelb and Gelb make some excellent points about "forced, fuzzy or filtered" feedback in "Strategies to Overcome Phony Feedback," p. 99. Clearly, how we solicit feedback is an important determinant of the quality of information we receive.

A Case in Point

At the Bank of America, the need to open up a feedback system to respond to changing business conditions was handled as described in the following case study, "Coping with Change."

Bank of America: Coping with Change[24]

Change is an inevitable facet of modern business. Reorganization, expansion of services, increased worldwide activities, and more complex technology are changes that affect many industries—including the banking industry. How to cope with such change is a major dilemma. Bank of America has some 45,000 employees located in over 1,000 offices throughout California. At B of A World Headquarters, San Francisco, a face-to-face employee communications program was designed in 1974 to help managers at all levels to increase their awareness of the effects of change, and to provide them with an efficient tool for identifying and solving problems.

Called the Open Meeting Program, this service is offered by B of A's 40-person (Employee) Communications Department, headed by a vice president and administered by an assistant vice president. The program is consistent with B of A management's objective to encourage open communication at all levels, and meets the recommendation of a task force on intra-bank communication for better horizontal communication within the bank.

The Problem

It is generally recognized that many employees hesitate to bring their concerns to the attention of their supervisors or department heads for fear that their comments will not, to put it mildly, be appreciated. Thus, many problems go unidentified and unsolved. The Open Meeting Program recognizes this problem by giving employees a confidential means of communicating their opinions and feelings.

The Strategy

The credibility, and thus the success, of the Open Meeting Program hinges on each manager's agreement to:

1. report to his or her total staff the information learned in the meetings, and

2. develop, communicate and implement an action plan to deal with the issues raised.

Also important is the Communications Department's ability to build trust in interactive meetings conducted according to the principles of behavioral science.

Implementation

Bank of America completed a pilot Open Meeting Program in 1974 in the Systems and Equipment Research Department (650 people). Working together, Communications people and the Systems Department head developed a program format to meet the department's needs. There were many options: the specific "how, who, when, where, and how often" were choices made by the department head. Prior to the actual meetings with employees, presentations were made to the department's top management, about 30 people in all, in order to acquaint them with the program. They, in turn, held meetings with their staffs to describe the program and to distribute a letter from the department head inviting each staff to participate.

There were 18 open meetings held in the pilot program. Both technical and non-technical staff members at all job levels participated. Approximately one out of four employees at each job level in the department was impartially selected from a computer payroll list, and attendance was voluntary. The groups ranged from five to 13 people of equal status. Employees, from vice presidents to clerks, were invited to meet with their peers in a private, comfortable place for an hour or so to talk about their views of their jobs, the work environment, and other aspects of working at B of A—concentrating on the things that got in the way of their job satisfaction and effectiveness.

Candor and informality were encouraged at these meetings. Participants pulled a few chairs into a semi-circle, drank coffee, walked around, or left the room at will. Some groups became quickly involved in earnest discussions, while others were slower to begin; often this factor depended on the previous contact between group members.

Over all, people were serious and positive in their comments. Some strong feelings surfaced. There was also laughter and relief when a consensus about certain problems was encountered. The understanding that the participants' concerns would be heard and acted upon, gave an optimistic air to all the meetings.

A staff meeting "facilitator" was present at each meeting to guide the discussion impartially, act as a catalyst, and establish an atmosphere of trust. Most importantly, the facilitator meticulously recorded the shared opinions, attitudes, and ideas—exactly as they were spoken—on flip charts in full view of each group. In addition to the spoken material, the facilitator measured and made note of group consensus and intensity of feeling. The Open Meeting sessions often ran well over the hour-and-a-half anticipated. Many groups left only at the insistence of the facilitator—with one or two people still staying on for a last comment or word of thanks.

After each group meeting, the material gathered was carefully categorized according to major areas of concern, then ranked in the order of importance conveyed in the meeting. It was found that employees who held decision-making positions tended to raise issues about authority and responsibility; employees at every level noted problems in departmental communication. Other frequently-raised points included training and orientation needs, working conditions, the reward system, career development, administrative procedures, and a wide range of staff support matters such as clerical and administrative personnel, and photocopy, keypunch, and library services.

At the end of the pilot program, a detailed, 140-page report, including a concise statement of all major issues uncovered and verbatim quotations to support them, was prepared in confidence for the Systems Department head alone. No employee identities were revealed in this report. It was left to the department head to choose whether or not to share the data upward or with other departments. The format of the report issued to the total staff could be written, oral, or both, and contain as full or as general a statement as desired.

The Results

Top Systems and Equipment Research Department personnel were given the complete report of all comments recorded (anonymously) in the meetings. These people collaborated with the department head in devising an elaborate system to disseminate the full report via peer groups throughout the department. Subsequently, task forces were assembled at levels throughout the department to seek solutions for the issues raised in the Open Meetings.

After the final meetings had been held, it became apparent that some staff members were unaware of the progress being made to *solve* problems revealed through Open Meetings. To remedy this, the Communications Department helped to prepare a newsletter, "Open Meetings Update." Issued every week, this letter deals with one or two specific problems identified at Open Meetings and reports on work underway to solve them.

The first update reported on major organizational changes within the department, and stated that "Open Meeting comments were used in reporting to senior management these department moves."

According to the program's administrator,

> Too many professional communicators, trained in journalism, tend to see the print media as the answer to all communication problems. We don't think so. Employees today want to be heard and involved in a way that print doesn't allow. We have a first-rate publications program and are committed to TV and various upward media—including a "speak up" program we call "Open Line." Open Meetings, in a sense, are a small-group Open Line. We surface opinions and attitudes quickly and confidentially, and can get action in a very efficient way.

As a result of the successful pilot program, Open Meetings are now becoming an integral part of B of A's efforts to maintain candid communication with employees at all levels throughout the bank.

Summary

Analyzing and correcting organizational communication flow problems is like rebuilding an engine while it's still running. It's tricky. In this chapter I have suggested five areas of concern which affect the accuracy and reliability of communication process and flow: (1) the serial transmission effect, (2) communication overload, (3) isolates, (4) participation in the communication system, and (5) the stimulation of useful feedback.

order does not agree with page 63 order

Diagnosing Your Communication Process and Flow

Perhaps the most widely used technique for diagnosing communication flow in organizations is ECCO analysis. Initially developed by Keith Davis of Arizona State University, ECCO (episodic communication channels in organizations) analysis provides a simple method of tracing the movement of messages through the organization. It provides an after-the-fact picture of how certain messages moved through the communication networks. From this picture we might logically predict how future messages will flow. Upon careful data analysis, this technique can clearly identify problems of distortion, overload, and communication isolation, as well as identifying potential opinion leaders.

This diagnostic approach can be relatively simple or highly sophisticated, depending upon how many variables are checked, the size of the sample, and the number of messages traced. The technique presents brief sample messages to organization members, followed by a questionnaire which solicits details about how much of the message was actually received. If, in fact, the employee had received all or any part of the message, a questionnaire asks where, when, and from whom the respondent received the information. The "from whom" question asks for a code number rather than the name of an individual. These code numbers, assigned to each employee or organizational member, indicate demographic characteristics of the source-person. Additional numbers may be used to identify message sources outside the organization. Even if the employee received the message from an impersonal source such as a newsletter or mass meeting announcement, he or she should be encouraged to identify the *person* who originated the message.

Assigning Code Numbers

Begin the process by listing in alphabetical order the members of the organization or work group to be studied. Following each name, put an appropriate code number which will be used by respondents. Each digit of the number provides a bit of data: the number of digits used will depend on how many variables you are interested in. If, for example, you suspect that messages aren't flowing across departmental boundaries, you would use one digit to designate the individual's department. Other possibilities include organizational level, age, sex, race, work location and seniority level. The number of demographic characteristics included is limited only by the researcher's imagination and willingness to process complex data. Generally, digits should be included for variables deemed likely to have significant effect on the flow of messages.

For example, you may want to assign seven digits as shown in the sample list of Figure 3–1.

Sample Messages

Once your coding has been established, you are ready to select sample messages and administer the questionnaires. Figure 3–2 shows an ECCO analysis data-gathering instrument. Sample messages should be sufficiently detailed to include several facts. One or two sentences are usually enough. They need not be all task-relevant messages. Here are examples of the types of messages you might use:

The order processing department has now completed the replacement of all keypunch machines with new visual display computer terminals. The order error rate has dropped to 4 percent, the lowest it has ever been.

Effective in January, an optional retirement annuity program will be available to mid-level managers which will provide a way of tax sheltering up to 10 percent of annual income. Personnel will be holding meetings during November to explain who is eligible and how it works.

John Franklyn, the former office manager who left the company to return to college, has been rehired as a commercial supervisor in the company's Jacksonville office. He will be responsible for job enrichment programs throughout the North Florida District.

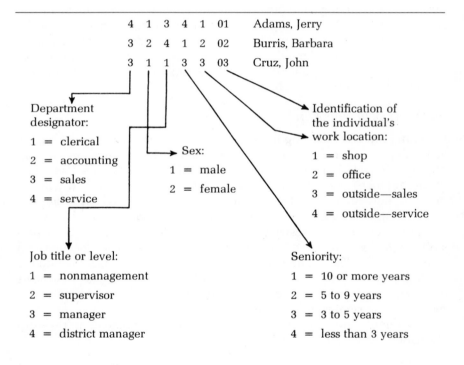

To account for the possibility that a respondent may have received information from persons not on the list, additional codes may be used:

9 0 0 0 0 00   an individual outside the organization

8 0 0 0 0 00   a competitor

Figure 3-1 Assigning code numbers for ECCO analysis

Analyzing the Results

Analysis of the responses can be both objective and creatively subjective. A large tally sheet should be drawn up to keep track of responses to all the structured response questions. Items asking employees to explain (such as how the facts they received differed from the sample message) will need to be evaluated more subjectively. Trends toward persistent misunderstanding or distortion can often be identified via these responses.

Note: Your individual reply to this questionnaire is very important to the overall project. Your answers and identity are known only to the surveyor. The results of this study will be presented in a statistical form which will iden-tify no one.

(enter date and time)

Question 1: By no later than _____did you know the information in the box below or *ANY PART OF IT?*

```
┌─────────────────────────────────────────────────────────┐
│                                                          │
│                  (INSERT SAMPLE MESSAGE)                 │
│                                                          │
└─────────────────────────────────────────────────────────┘
```

Check One: _____ Yes, I knew all of it.
_____ Yes, I knew part of it. Please circle the part you knew . . .
(LIKE THIS.)
_____ No, I did not know any of it.

IF YOUR INFORMATION GAVE FACTS DIFFERENT FROM WHAT I HAVE GIVEN YOU ABOVE, WRITE THE DIFFERENT FACTS HERE.

_____

_____

_____

IF YOUR ANSWER TO QUESTION ONE ABOVE WAS "YES" PLEASE ANSWER THE NEXT SIX SHORT QUESTIONS.
IF YOUR ANSWER WAS "NO," PLEASE STOP HERE AND RETURN THE QUESTIONNAIRE.

Question 2: From *whom* did you FIRST receive the information in the box? Place the source's code number on this line _____

Question 3: By what method did you *first* receive the information in the box? Check one:

Figure 3-2 ECCO analysis data-gathering form

WRITTEN AND VISUAL
METHODS
____ Personal letter from the
     company.
____ Bulletin board.
____ Company booklet of any type.
____ A company record
____ Public newspaper or magazine.
____ I did it, or I originated the
     information.
____ I saw it happen.
____ Other (please explain).
     _____

TALKING AND SOUND
METHODS
____ Talking with one other person in
     his presence.
____ Talking over the telephone.
____ Talking (and listening) in a small
     group of two or more persons.
____ Attending an organized group
     meeting or conference.
____ Overhearing what someone else
     said.
____ Listening to radio or television.
____ Other (please explain).
     _____

Question 4: Aproximately how long ago did you first receive the information in
the box?
Circle the appropriate answer: Today   Yesterday
This Week: Mon.   Tue.   Wed.   Thur.   Fri.
Last Week: Mon.   Tue.   Wed.   Thur.   Fri.   2 weeks ago
3 weeks ago   More than 3 weeks ago

Question 5: How many people did you pass this information on to in the
company?
Circle: None   1   2   3   4   5   more than 5

Please check to see that you have answered all the questions correctly before
returning this questionnaire.

THANK YOU FOR YOUR COOPERATION.

The space below is for your comments regarding this piece of information or this
questionnaire.

Figure 3-2 (cont.)

The flow of the message from point to point can be reconstructed by
looking at the code numbers of those identified as the respondent's message source. By checking the first digit of the code numbers assigned to
both the respondent and the person identified as the information source,
we can identify, for example, the degree to which cross-departmental
communication is occurring. Diagrams like Figure 3–3 can graphically de-
pict what is going on. Let us say there are four departments in the
organization.

Respondents with code numbers beginning with 1 (all clerical personnel) are placed in a stack. Their responses to question 2 indicate the code
number, including department designation, of their message source. For
fairly small samples, we could simply draw in a line for each respondent

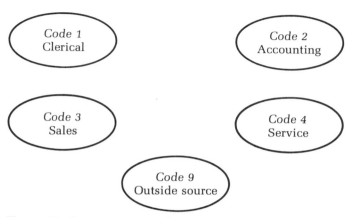

Figure 3-3 Departments or information sources for
organization being analyzed

to develop a graphic display. A computerized sorting would be used with
a larger number of respondents.

Looking at the sales department in Figure 3–4, we see that six salespeo-
ple got the message from someone in the clerical department while two
got it from someone in service. One person received the sample information from accounting department personnel, and one employee reported
someone outside the organization as her source. The number who received it from within their own department is indicated in the box.

A quick glance at such a chart indicates a far greater proportion of
information exchange between sales and clerical with other departments

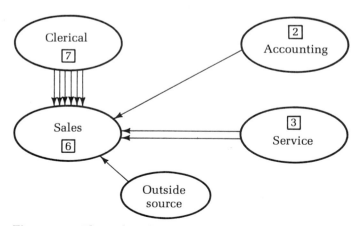

Figure 3-4 The sales department's sources of
information

being somewhat isolated from the flow of *this particular sample message.* Similar charts would be worked out for message receivers in the other three departments until a total picture is described.

Evaluating flow between organizational levels can prove interesting in determining to what degree data flows through the formal organizational hierarchy.

A chart like the one in Figure 3–5 would indicate that the sample message examined flowed, by and large, down the organizational hierarchy. Most respondents got the word from someone at the next higher organizational level.

Another important type of information to be gained from this analysis is the kinds of communication *media or tools* that are being used most effectively. As we'll discuss in Chapter 4, the appropriate use of media can be very important to the organization's profitability.

Finally, ECCO analysis tells us something about the *speed* with which messages are disseminated through the organization, and which people seem to act as liaisons—passing information on to others. Opinion leaders are likely to arise from those frequently mentioned as sources as well as those who have passed on the information to others.

As you can see from this brief description, ECCO analysis offers numerous possibilities for evaluating message flows in the organization. Repeated administration of the ECCO instrument will provide additional insights. The larger the sample (both in number of respondents and number of messages) the more valuable the data are likely to be.

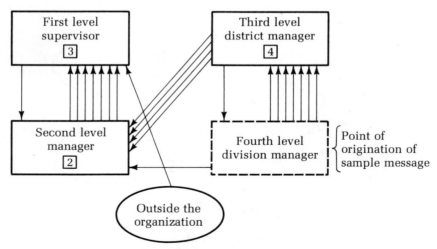

Figure 3-5 Communication flow down the organizational hierarchy

An important advantage of this diagnostic technique is that it can gather information quickly and efficiently without disrupting the organizational routine. Once the coding system is established, frequent checks of communication health can be made by simply presenting employees with a new sample message and questionnaire.

Some Other Thoughts About Ongoing Communication Process and Flow:
READINGS FOR CHAPTER 3

How to Earn an MBWA Degree[25]

James H. Lavenson

The last time I was in Chicago, I was making a speech before the Executives Club. I don't know if you're familiar with that organization, but it's impressive for a couple reasons. First, they have over 3000 paid up members. Second, they get anywhere from five hundred to a thousand of the members to come to a luncheon speech every Friday. The week before my speech, they'd had Senator Charles Percy. The week after me, they had Nelson Rockefeller. I felt good about the company I was in until I was introduced with the polite explanation to the audience by the club's president that a "change of pace" was desirable.

Anyway, the point of my telling you about this organization is that before each luncheon, they ask the speaker to meet with a half dozen high school kids whom they've invited as guests. When I met with them, they took one look at me, looked at each other, and almost in one voice wanted to know what kind of education you needed to be in management. Was there a major course of study, a *degree* in management which they could pursue in college?

Naturally, I refused to answer a stupid question like that.

But if you know kids, you know they don't let go, especially if they smell a phoney. They'd been told I had been president of the Plaza Hotel and had had no previous hotel experience, no hotel schooling and they seemed skeptical about what the B.S. degree I'd gotten in college really stood for.

"Mr. Lavenson," one particularly obnoxious little smart alec asked me, "If you had no experience running a hotel and you started at the top, how did you know what to do? Just what did you do?"

"I ran the place, that's what! Next question?" I snapped back and figured I'd won. I hadn't.

"Come now, Mr. Lavenson, these students won't accept that answer." It was their teacher who interrupted this time, a guy with a beard and a pipe and a very high forehead and I hated him on sight. "What about an MBA degree? Wouldn't you say that a master's degree in business from a school like Harvard or The Wharton School would qualify a man or woman for management?"

I didn't have an MBA degree and it was painfully obvious this teacher did. If I let him win that point, I knew I was lost, so I resorted to a trick I'd learned through years of experience: I lied.

"Not an MBA degree," I said very calmly. "It takes an MBWA degree to qualify as a manager." With that one, I'd stopped the beard and pipe dead in his tracks. But he recovered and just before someone came in and announced lunch was starting, he growled a last question. "Just exactly what *is* an MBWA degree?"

I gave him my most generous smile, and gave him a pearl of wisdom in one sentence that I'm going to stretch out into a full speech today. You see, I'd never really thought about it before and my glib answer to that poor teacher and his group of kids was the lucky, accidental, off-the-cuff, wise-guy response of a cornered rat. On my way home from Chicago, I thought a lot more about the questions those kids were asking and my answer. The longer I thought about it, the more I realized that MBWA *is* the qualification for management, and it's one I'd unwittingly been using in every job I'd been in. And when I'd started each of the management jobs I've had over the past twenty years—in advertising, in toy products, in luggage, in publishing, in food processing, in sun glasses, T-shirts, dresses and, yes, if you'll excuse the expression, in women's pants. There's one thing you can say about me without fear of contradiction from anyone with whom I ever worked. I didn't know from beans about any of those businesses. I don't really mean I didn't know *any*thing. Naturally, since I was over thirty, I did know a thing or two about ladies pants. But what I didn't know about any of the businesses when I started in them was how to *run* them. And I certainly didn't have any of the technical experience necessary to mold a doll, sew leather into a suitcase which would come out the other end of the production line as Hartman luggage, or how to dig clams out of the Atlantic Ocean, clean them, vacuum pack them into cans labeled Doxsee. And what I knew about ladies sportswear was confined to whistling—mostly at my wife's bills from Saks Fifth Avenue and Bergdorf Goodman.

A long time ago, and this is hindsight, I remember a man I admired a great deal during World War II being quoted and what he said must have made a subconscious impression on me. Today I repeat it to myself every morning.

The man was General Sommerville, and he'd spent his entire life in the army. Then came the end of the war, he was retired as a multi-starred general and suddenly it was announced he wasn't really retiring at all. He was made the chairman of the Koppers Company, a gigantic corporation which had nothing to do with the army, war, tanks, guns, airplanes or VD training films. Some wise guy reporter asked General Sommerville at the press conference announcing his election to the chairmanship of Koppers—he must have been related to that young teacher in Chicago—just why the general thought he was qualified to be the chief executive officer of a large corporation in the business world, when all his experience had been in the army. Not business, just the army. The general's reply was a classic and if I had my way would replace all those think signs you see in offices all over this country wherever an IBM man has been able to get his foot in the door.

What the general replied to the reporter's questioning his qualifications for a job in business was this: "You don't have to be a chicken to smell a rotten egg." Here it comes again: "You don't have to be a chicken to smell a rotten egg."

Isn't that nifty? Aside from the fact that it gives every idiot like me an open season license to take on a management job in any field, it happens, also, to be true. Think about it a little longer than we're going to be together here today. Think about it tonight, and tomorrow. Think about it for a week. I believe you'll come up with your own examples and experiences, either yours or a manager you admire, and you'll agree that what General Sommerville was saying is that he had an MBWA degree.

Maybe the president of International Harvester, that gigantic farm equipment company, was saying the same thing when he was asked what he looked for in men he hired to help him run the company. "More than an agricultural degree or courses in business management, I look for men who know what manure smells like at five o'clock on a frosty morning." I submit that he, too, like General Sommerville, was talking about an MBWA degree.

Oh my, that's right! I still haven't told you what MBWA stands for, have I? MBWA stands for *Management by Walking Around*. Just walking around with your eyes and ears open, asking questions like crazy and trying to understand what the guys working for you are doing. A good place to start is to see if *they* understand what they're doing.

But, of course, to start you have to get up off that big over-stuffed leather throne in your paneled office, and actually *walk* around by yourself. Granted it's hard exercise, particularly because most of us bosses are used to being carried and guided by well-meaning subordinates. Don't take your secretary with you and have her scribbling notes of your observations, don't take a portable dictation machine and mumble into it in front of the guy you're talking to, either. Have you ever had that happen to you? A guy comes up, asks you a question, then pulls a little machine out of his pocket and starts talking, or rather whispering, into it like he was right out of 1984? Make you nervous? It scares the hell out of me! I figure he's calling in a hit man.

A couple years ago, I was asked to consult with the management of the Tour Hassan Hotel in Rabat, Morocco. They had service problems and profit problems and they wanted me to help fix them. This was really funny because, at that time, I'd not yet been in the hotel business. In addition, in Morocco they only speak French and Arabic. I spoke little of one and none of the other. Unwittingly in Morocco, I got a degree in MBWA, and it was in a language I didn't even understand. I flew to Morocco not having the remotest idea how to start and just checked into the hotel like any other guest. The first morning I wanted my breakfast in the room and walked around trying to figure out how to order it. There were two buttons over the bed with a single sign over both saying "Service" in English. I pushed one button, waited five minutes and then pushed the other one. Nothing happened, so I got dressed and went downstairs for breakfast. The hotel's manager was there and again, like any guest, I was quick to tell him his buttons didn't work. He wasn't the least bit upset. "They've never worked since I've been here and that's five years. You have to call for room service on the phone" he said casually.

"Can't you get them fixed?" I asked.

"Cost too much," was his answer, which I've learned to expect from management in almost any business.

"How much?" I wanted to know.

"A lot" was his enlightening answer.

Not satisfied, I went to the Controller and asked if he'd seen a bid on repairing the buzzer system from the rooms. He hadn't, but he knew it would cost too much. I went to the chief engineer and asked him if he knew how much it would cost. Do you know what he said? He told me it wouldn't cost anything because there was nothing wrong with the system. It was just turned off. All that was required to make it work was to throw a switch. So why was it turned off? Because, since the two buttons were never identified as to which was which—food or maid—guests batting an even 500 would push the wrong button every other time. The maids got exasperated, the room service waiters were sick of people crying "Wolf, Wolf," or rather, "food, food," when what they really wanted was a clean towel. So the housekeeper persuaded the chief engineer to throw the switch. Nobody had told the manager, and he never asked to find out. Believe it or not, I got a citation from the king of Morocco for a stroke of sheer genius . . . putting labels over each of the two buttons, marking one "food" and one "maid" and asking the engineer to throw the switch.

One day about ten years ago, I suddenly found myself chairman of the

Hartman Luggage Company. Like you, I'd know the name for years and before I'd seen the figures, I would have guessed Hartman was at least a ten or twenty million dollar company. I was shocked to learn its sales volume was under two million, so I started by walking around the territory with a couple salesmen to see why they weren't selling more. They all told me the same thing—Hartman was a prestige name without a truly prestige product—a real top of the line, expensive piece of luggage which by its very price, had the snob appeal to get it into stores like Saks Fifth Avenue and Neiman Marcus. I brought that story back to the president who pooh-poohed the idea, but reached into a secret compartment in his office safe and produced the loveliest, richest looking attache case made of belting leather and brass trim that I'd ever dreamed of. "Why isn't that in the line?" I wanted to know.

"Too expensive. It would never sell. We'd have to retail this thing for close to two hundred bucks."

I walked around again, taking the sample attache case with me and asking the salesmen if this was the kind of thing they had in mind. "Yeah, man!" was their reaction.

"How much should it sell for?" I wanted to know from the guys who had to sell it. The consensus was three hundred bucks. That MBWA attache case went into the Hartman line along with overnighters and two-suiters all made of belting leather with price tags that would shock the Shah of Iran. Today Hartman is stocked by Saks and Neiman Marcus and doing one helluva lot more than two million dollars in sales.

Probably the most important principle of MBWA is really a philosophy—a philosophy which says that the boss' job is to make sure of three things: first, that his staff understands what they are doing: second, that his staff has the tools *they* think they need to do the job: and last, that the boss lets the staff know he has an *appreciation* of what the employee is doing.

You hear a lot of management types talk sanctimoniously about their "open door" policy. Their door is "always open to the staff," they tell you. In my book, the best reason for a boss' open door is so he can go *out* the door and walk around.

On the wall of the office of Eddie Carlson, chairman of United Airlines, is a sign with the word Netma printed on it. He told me that represents the most serious deterrent to success in managing an organization. Netma stands for "nobody ever tells me anything." Just because you told the vice president doesn't mean he told his subordinates. Get up, walk out of your office and ask if they know what they are doing? And why? And does it make sense to them? The question is the single most powerful tool of management. You'd be amazed, even in a business you know nothing about, how you can smell the answer. You don't have to be a chicken to smell a rotten egg. You can kill the Netma in any business with an MBWA degree.

I'm going to burden you with one of the oldest management stories of all time, but it's the best one I ever heard. It goes back to early Egyptian times when the Pharoah came across a beehive of activity out in the middle of the desert. Slaves all over the place, busy as all get out, he went up to one who was cutting stones up into blocks and asked him what he was doing.

"I'm cutting stones into blocks" was the workman's reply. Then the Pharoah went to a man weaving long strands of rope and asked him what he was doing.

"I'm weaving long strands of rope."

Then he saw a third man mixing mortar in a wooden trough and asked him what he was doing.

"I'm building a pyramid for you, Pharoah," the man said.

So, in closing, let me suggest to all you Pharoahs that you go back to your plants and your offices and find out how many people you've got who are cutting stones into blocks and how many are building a pyramid.

Thank you for listening.

Encouraging Feedback[26]

William G. Dyer

In much of our current organization life, people have learned to mask, hide and cover up their feelings, particularly those towards people in positions of power and influence. Because of this, it is often difficult for a manager to know what his true impact on others has been. He may see only the polite smile, the ready agreement, the apparent consensus and may assume, falsely, that the external feedback cues really represent the total impact.

The person with good interpersonal skills has ways of checking out the data to determine his actual impact and to ascertain whether the problem, if any, is his own inability to correctly communicate his conscious intentions or if it is in the filter systems of others.

In the process of improving one's performance, probably no skill is more important than being able to gather accurate and honest feedback about one's impact on others. Yet this is also an area of sensitive skill for most people feel fearful and inept when it comes to sharing their feelings about someone's performance directly with that person.

It is not easy for a person in a lower status position in an organization to go to a more powerful, higher status person and give feedback that is un-solicited and presumably unwanted. The risks involved, from the lower sta-tus person's perspective, are so great that unless the situation becomes intolerable or he is ready to quit, the safest course appears to be remaining silent and hope the passing of time will improve conditions.

This silent strategy seems to be widely used for coping with people who have negative impacts on us. It is also a minimal change strategy that masks the real conditions and keeps frustration and negativism underground. And until it surfaces, the negative consequences of a poor relationship are difficult to deal with.

If a manager initiates a process where he is asked for feedback and sets a climate where a person feels safe or even rewarded for sharing information, more people seem willing to share sensitive feedback. So how do you go about doing this?

Individual Direct Request

Probably the simplest method is to invite another person to a private, one-to-one session. This could be preceded by a written memo or verbal request stating the purpose of the meeting, thus giving the person time to prepare. (Example: Dear Ed: I would like very much to get your reactions about my management performance. Do you see anything I do that creates problems for others? Do you have any suggestions as to how I might improve my effectiveness? I'd like to get together with you next week and talk about this. I'll have my secretary call and set up a time when I can come to your office to discuss this. Thanks. Don.)

In discussing this method with managers, they nearly all agreed that they would appreciate their boss coming to their office for such a discussion. Others felt it would not be inappropriate to discuss this in the boss's office at a regular report or discussion meeting.

Written Feedback

A second method is to request (either verbally or by memo) the person to share his feeling in writing. (Example: "Ed, I'm trying to improve my own management effectiveness. Would you be willing to take some time out and write down any suggestions you have for my improvement. Try to be as honest as possible. I want the feedback and feel it's important that I find out what my impact on others is, both positive and negative.")

In the direct request for either verbal or written feedback the person to whom the request is directed may feel on the spot. If his boss is making the request, he may feel obligated to say something but feel uneasy because of the risk involved. Direct request data are not anonymous and the person may wonder how direct he can be without creating problems. To stimulate the feedback, the following technique can be used.

Priming the Pump

This is a method of stimulating the flow of data by sharing some data already known. This process was observed in a training program where one participant was generating negative feelings in others. Every time a serious, deep or sensitive discussion was underway, this man would sit with what was later described as a sneer on his face. It was apparent that the other participants resented this and rumblings were evident.

The second day this man addressed the group. "Whenever I get emotional or nervous, I know that my face twitches up. It's something I can't seem to control. Some people have said it looks like a sneer. Have you been aware of this?"

This was a great releasing factor and people talked freely about their reaction to him. It became easy for them to discuss his behavior since he had opened the subject and had some awareness of it. A manager could help release feedback in similar fashion. (Example: "Ed, I have been told that I cut people off in staff meetings and appear to reject their contributions. Have you been aware of this? Have you seen anything else I do that disturbs people? Do you have any suggestions how I might improve?")

Sub-group Feedback

To assure more anonymity, managers can divide the staff into sub-groups of three or four people at a staff meeting. The sub-groups meet for 30 to 45 minutes following a request like this: "I am very concerned about my effectiveness as a manager. I would appreciate it if you all could help me. At the next staff meeting I would like to have each of you get into a sub-group and identify those behaviors that seem to reduce the effectiveness of our operation. Would you also list those things that you like and would want me to continue?

"It would be helpful if you could give me any concrete suggestions for improvement. I won't be present while you meet and you can just turn in a written summary to my secretary. No names need be attached. I'm more interested in getting the information than knowing who said it. If any sub-group would like to talk with me directly, I would also welcome that opportunity."

Total Group

It is possible for a manager to use his total staff at a staff meeting to discuss his managerial style and to give him suggestions for improvement. This is usually an identified agenda item and people are aware this issue is going to be discussed. The dialogue is more open than in the sub-group format and there can be more direct exchange between the manager and his subordinates. Such a meeting requires a general climate of openness, a spirit of dealing directly with human issues in an atmosphere of concern and mutual help.

The meeting's format can vary. The manager can summarize his impressions of his own style and ask for reactions. He can ask each person to express his reactions and share his feedback and suggestions. The group can form sub-groups for a few minutes and then come back for a total staff discussion.

Instrumented Feedback

The use of instruments provides another avenue for anonymous feedback. Here the manager or the personnel department circulates an instrument or questionnaire that gathers data about his managerial performance as experienced by peers or subordinates. Such instruments are the Blake-Mouton Grid, Likert's Four Systems, Hall's Telometrics Instruments and the Dyer-Daniels-Moffitt Management Profile.

The data collected are tabulated and presented to the manager. Such information gives a general picture of impact but may not include any specific suggestions for improvement, nor will it provide specific information on how to improve performance with any one individual.

The advantage of the instrumented process is that it can be given to a large number of people, it focuses on common areas, can be repeated at a later date and protects the anonymity of the respondents.

Shared Assessment

Similiar to pump priming, here the manager writes an assessment of his own performance and asks others to confirm or deny it, to share additional reactions and to make any suggestions for improvement.

Example: Memo. I have written up the following assessment of my own performance as a manager. Would you indicate whether you agree or disagree with the various points, what your own reactions are and any suggestions you have for improvement?

As I see myself, I feel I do the following things well: 1. I think I am punctual and never miss appointments or keep people waiting. 2. I feel I am dependable in taking care of assignments or requests given to me. 3. I see myself as a hard-working person who has great dedication and loyalty to the company and its goals.

I also see the following critical things about my performance: 1. I feel that I am a rather closed person and that I don't communicate very much or very easily. I would like to improve this, but I'm not sure exactly how to do it. 2. I think I tend to cut people off in staff meetings and am somewhat rejecting of new ideas. I'm not exactly sure how people see or react to this. 3. I also think people are a little afraid of me and feel a bit uncomfortable talking with me. I don't know what gives people that impression or what I can do to reduce it.

Opposite each of these comments should be space for the reviewer's comments and suggestions.

Outside Consultant

The assistance of an outside person is another common method for gathering feedback data. This person can be from outside the organization or a person in the company's training or personnel department but not from the manager's department.

The consultant can use a variety of methods to gather feedback. He can observe the manager in action at meetings, problem solving sessions or in the work setting. He can interview peers and subordinates and get their direct expressions. He can administer instruments and tabulate a summary profile.

The advantage of the outsider is that he can often see things to which insiders have become oblivious and can probe in areas not available to the manager. A disadvantage is that the manager and subordinates may become dependent on the consultant and never learn to give and receive helpful feedback as a regular part of their on-going relationship.

After Feedback

For most people, sharing data with a superior is an especially high risk activity. When it is first attempted, the person usually watches his superior closely to gauge his reaction. And this reaction usually determines whether such feedback will be given again.

Listen, don't explain or justify. There is a tendency to explain or justify actions when we receive feedback we feel is unwarranted or stems from a misunderstood action. When you ask for feedback the burden is on you to listen and try to understand. This does not mean you are obligated to believe or accept the information but your responsibility is to try to understand why the other person feels and reacts the way he does. Defensive behavior usually stifles the flow of feedback communications for it tells the other person you are more interested in justifying yourself than in understanding him.

Ask for more. Especially in the open, verbal feedback process, there is an opportunity to get additional information. If the person eliciting the data can honestly keep saying, "That's extremely helpful. Tell me more. Is there anything else I should know about that?", this will support and encourage the continual flow of feedback.

Express an honest reaction. The person giving the feedback often wants to know what your reaction is to the data he has presented. The best guideline is to express your honest reaction.

Express appreciation and plan for the future. Acknowledge the risk that was involved for the person giving feedback and share your appreciation for his efforts. It is also a good time to plan ahead for future feedback sessions, which should be less disturbing and more productive than the initial encounter.

Sometimes the negative impact a person has is a result of an inability to translate his intentions into appropriate behavior. At other times the other person's misperceptions lead to undesired consequences. In either case the manager needs to discern the impact and engage in a process of exploring intentions, behavior, filter and impact with the goal of reducing negative affects in mind.

Gathering feedback is the skill that starts the improvement of impact in motion. Several methods may be appropriate in stimulating a greater sharing of feedback from peers and subordinates. Such methods as personnel discussion, sub-groups, written communication, instruments and outside consultation assistance are available to the manager who is willing to take the risk to begin this sensitive, difficult but much-needed process.

Strategies to Overcome Phony Feedback[27]

Betsy D. Gelb
Gabriel M. Gelb

You are sitting in a restaurant muttering about the slow service when finally the food comes—cold. You eat reluctantly, get up to pay the check, and hear the cashier ask, "Was everything all right?"

Somewhere up the organizational pyramid from that cashier is a manager who thinks he is going to find out something useful from your answer to the cashier's question. He supposes that forcing customers to offer answers because they are in a social situation provides *feedback*, as he calls it.

Likewise, somewhere high up on a number of organizational charts sit managers who once believed that suppliers would warn them about impending shortages. Or they thought their own purchasing people would sound the alarm. And everywhere are managers reviewing computer printouts and narrative summaries hoping to discover what threatens their organizations or where their opportunities lie.

Unfortunately, all these managers may find themselves the victims of feedback that is forced, fuzzy, or filtered—in sum, *phony* feedback. They—and all of us—need to look carefully to distinguish the useful from the deceptive; only then can we understand how to obtain dependable news about the results of our organization's efforts.

The whole feedback concept entered organizational thinking from the world of thermostats; therefore, it is hardly surprising that its usefulness in a world of human beings was overestimated. Seeing an organization as a system, various writers on organizational theory seized on the analogy to a heating system, in which the temperature in the room provides the feedback to direct the furnace to begin. Charmed by the efficiency of such a system, they envisioned a world where, for example, rising profit margins of a firm's Product A as contrasted to its Product B would automatically shift advertising dollars to A, until such time as A's margin dropped due to high advertising expenses, at which time B's margin would be higher and the advertising dollars would shift over to B.

Even in this kind of application, problems arose. A business differs dramatically from a situation where the cause of a cold room may be of interest in the long run, but in the short run the occupant wants heat. In a business, by contrast, more advertising may not always be desirable for a hot product; the Federal Trade Commission may be ready to swoop in if market share reaches 50 percent. Furthermore, the spurt in umbrella sales in Kansas City that diverts advertising funds to umbrellas can hardly prove a useful guide for allocation of advertising expenditures during a Midwestern drought.

Therefore, more sophisticated writers shifted to defining organizations as *open systems*, affected by the outside world as well as by the results of their own output.[1] They began to take into account the human element that influences the reporting of results, understanding that this human element distorts reality as part of the process of supplying a manager with feedback. The cashier's question to the restaurant patron, for example, is a device conspicuously different from the thermostat: for the restaurant manager, the measurement of results involves people. And the presence of people offers the hazard of forced, filtered, or fuzzy feedback.

Forcing an Answer

Forced feedback results from social pressure: it is rude to ignore a face-to-face question. So a restaurant patron mumbles that "everything was fine" to the cashier, knowing perfectly well that he's lying. Then, of course, he dislikes the restaurant on two counts: it served him a cold meal and forced him to lie. Similar results await the salesman who asks a buyer of his company's valves, textiles, or real estate what the buyer thinks about the company's products or service. Fudging the truth seems preferable to giving an honest answer that will provoke an argument or at least provoke more questions.

The Fuzzy Answer

Fuzzy feedback provides another substitute for either of the two honest answers of "I don't know" or "It wouldn't be smart strategy for me to give the facts." It arises, for example, when a purchasing agent, in times of scarcity, asks a supplier how prospects look. If things look grim, the supplier reports them as "so-so" rather than admit how scarce the product is, which will send a buyer shopping elsewhere. Hedging represents a common kind of fuzzy feedback—and it's just as fuzzy when dignified by a formal report format. Not much can be gleaned from the organizational equivalent of a weather report that reads: *Fair today, unless it rains.*

Organizational Filters

Filtered feedback results when a manager asks a subordinate what's happening in the organization. Inevitably, as noted by Robert Heilbroner, "Armies and corporations alike have ways of sweetening the news as it ascends the hierarchy of command."[2] As one example, a clerk reports "No more orders from Widget, Inc.—they're mad at us." The supervisor's interpretation reads, "Widget, Inc. will not be placing further orders." The manager notes, "We do not expect further orders from Widget, Inc. at this time." The vice president reports "Widget, Inc. is not ordering this month," and the executive vice president passes along, "It will be next month before we receive an order from Widget, Inc."

What Can Managers Do?

If forced feedback, fuzzy feedback, and filtered feedback are dangerous to an organization's health, what does a manager do to find out what's happening? "Phony" data is obviously no use in decision making, but how do you avoid it?

Four suggestions may help: cultivating feedback rather than forcing it; rewarding and acting on useful feedback; avoiding unnecessary dependence on feedback; and reporting on feedback results. Specifically:

- You don't force feedback—you cultivate it. In the restaurant, the cashier might simply smile and offer the conventional "We hope you enjoyed your meal." Then a week later, a sample of customers get a phone call or post card from a consultant asking for comments (he got the names from credit card slips). He doesn't hit 100 percent response, but because he is independent of the firm and promises anonymity, the people who do answer have no reason to lie.

- You reward useful feedback and you act on it. In a tight supply situation, a supplier who tells you forthrightly that deliveries will be a month behind is still supplying something timely: information. But that is a commodity that brings him no commission or profit—unless you provide the payoff, like a promise to give his firm priority if all delivery times turn out to be equal. Accurate reports from employees merit rewards, too—from the conventional "suggestion box" bonus to the obvious reward for a middle-manager: an offer to put him in charge of correcting the problem he's found, or an offer not to put him in charge of that particular can of worms if he prefers to avoid it. That last reward is important: many subordinates hesitate to bring in news of something wrong for fear they'll automatically be told to make it right.

- You circumvent the need for feedback—you go and take a first-hand look. Peter Drucker offers a rationale for top managers to become the "sensing organ" for the organization; he notes that

  > if they remove themselves from market and customer and come to rely on reports and inside information, they will soon lose their ability to sense and anticipate changes in the market and to perceive, let alone to appreciate, the unexpected.[3]

- Specifically, a department store executive can shop at his own store and the stores of competitors. Any company president can, as Robert Townsend suggests, personally use every new form proposed for adoption in his company.[4] What discourages first-hand investigation is usually fear of being caught: "How would my people feel if they thought I were spying?" But of course the way they would feel depends largely on how many compliments, not just complaints, flow from your office as a result of direct observations.

- You report on feedback results—in other words, feed back the feedback. Employees and customers are naturally delighted when you tell them how their ideas have led to improvements in products or services. This can be done in employee publications, mass mailings to customers, mentions in the annual report, or even in media advertising. Almost nothing affects people in a more positive sense than to let them know that "We hear you," in Bell Telephone's excellent phrase.

One final roadmap to a disaster area: some managerial actions result in feedback that is forced, fuzzy, *and* filtered. Suppose, for instance, that a manager sets a pet project in motion, then asks a subordinate how the project is doing. Forced to answer, the unlucky underling fuzzes and filters wildly: a favorite example is the "assistant to" who scanned the red ink on a project he had secretly opposed, then announced to his beaming boss: "Sir, that idea of yours has met my every expectation."

1. Among many examples of authors advocating the systems approach are Daniel Katz and Robert L. Kahn, *The Social Psychology of Organizations* (New York: John Wiley & Sons, 1966) and John A. Seiler, *Systems Analysis in Organizational Behavior* (Homewood, Ill.: Richard D. Irwin, 1967).
2. Robert Heilbroner and others, *In the Name of Profit* (Garden City, N.Y.: Doubleday & Company, 1972), p. 226.
3. Peter F. Drucker, *Management: Tasks, Responsibilities, Practices* (New York: Harper & Row, 1973), p. 662.
4. Robert Townsend, *Up the Organization* (New York: Alfred A. Knopf, 1970), p. 84.

Questions for Further Thought

1. Make a brief list of your opinion leaders. For example, who would you ask to recommend a good course for next semester, a new stereo, a good restaurant, a good doctor? Why do you look to them?

2. Think of an organizational leader who claims to have an "open door policy." What kinds of things make that policy successful or unsuccessful? Identify some nonverbal cues which may make a person hesitant to accept that openness policy at face value.

3. Develop your own variation of an ECCO analysis questionnaire. What variables do you think should be examined? Administer the questionnaire to a relatively small group of people (not more than 25) and analyze the results. What do they show? What problems did you encounter with the technique?

Notes

1. For a moment-by-moment description of the communication failures at the Pearl Harbor invasion, see Hugh Russell Fraser's "56 Minutes before Pearl Harbor," *American Mercury*, August 1957, pp. 80–85.

2. Opinion Research Corporation, *Avoiding Failures in Management Communications*, Research Report of the Public Opinion Index for Industry (Princeton, N.J.: Opinion Research Corporation, January 1963).

3. Reprinted from "Permutation Personified" in *Boles Letter*. Copyright 1962 by Edmund D. Boles & Associates.

4. Jerry W. Koehler, Karl W. E. Anatol, and Ronald L. Applbaum, *Organizational Communication: Behavioral Perspectives* (New York: Holt, Rinehart & Winston, 1976), Chapters 6 and 7.

5. T. Adorno, E. Frenkel-Brunswik, D. Levinson, and R. Sanford, *The Authoritarian Personality* (New York: Harper & Row, 1950).

6. Koehler *et al.*, op. cit., p. 92.

7. Koehler *et al.*, op. cit., p. 93.

8. John R. P. French and Bertram Raven, "The Bases of Social Power," in *Group Dynamics*, 2nd ed., eds., Dorwin Cartwright and A. F. Zander (Evanston, Ill.: Row, Peterson, 1960) pp. 607–623.

9. This list is based on research by Donald T. Campbell, "Systematic Error on the Part of Human Links in Communication Systems," *Information and Control*, 1958, 1, pp. 334–369.

10. From an advertisement by Xerox Corporation appearing in *U.S. News and World Report* (July 24, 1978), p. 32.

11. Summarized by W. Charles Redding, *Communication within the Organization* (New York: Industrial Communication Council, 1972). Based on earlier work of J. G. Miller, "Information input, overload, and psychopathology," *American Journal of Psychiatry*, 1960, 116, pp. 695–704.

12. T. R. Cheatham and M. L. McLaughlin, "Effects of Communication Isolation on Job Satisfaction of Bank Tellers." Paper presented at International Communication Association annual conference, Portland, Oregon, 1976.

13. Adapted from Christopher J. Quartly, "Executive Isolation: Can It Be Prevented," *Personnel Journal* (December, 1974), pp. 902–905.

14. Douglas McGregor contended that our assumptions about people affect the ways we deal with them. He categorized managerial assumptions into his famous "Theory X–Theory Y." Below is a list of McGregor's assumptions as presented in Paul Hersey and Kenneth H. Blanchard, *Management of Organizational Behavior*, 3rd ed. (Englewood Cliffs, N.J.: Prentice-Hall, 1977), p. 55.

Theory X	Theory Y
1. Work is inherently distasteful to most people.	1. Work is as natural as play, if the conditions are favorable.
2. Most people are not ambitious, have little desire for responsibility, and prefer to be directed.	2. Self-control is often indispensable in achieving organizational goals.

3. Most people have little capacity for creativity in solving organizational problems.

3. The capacity for creativity in solving organizational problems is widely distributed in the population.

4. Motivation occurs only at the physiological and safety levels.

4. Motivation occurs at the social, esteem, and self-actualization levels, as well as physiological and security levels.

5. Most people must be closely controlled and often coerced to achieve organizational objectives.

5. People can be self-directed and creative at work if properly motivated.

15. Hersey and Blanchard, op. cit., especially Chapter 7.
16. Robert Townsend, *Up the Organization* (New York: Alfred A. Knopf, 1970), p. 20.
17. These studies include work by Keith Davis, *Human Behavior at Work* (New York: McGraw-Hill, 1972); Evan Rudolph, *A Study of Informal Communication Patterns within a Multi-Shift Public Utility Organizational Unit.* Unpublished Ph.D. Dissertation, University of Denver, 1971; Eugene Walton, "How Efficient Is the Grapevine?" *Personnel* 78 (1961), pp. 45–49.
18. Theodore Caplow, *How to Run Any Organization* (Hinsdale, Ill.: Dryden Press, 1976), p. 77.
19. Paul F. Lazersfeld, Bernard Berelson, and Hazel Gandet, *The People's Choice* (New York: Columbia University Press, 1948).
20. Elihu Katz, "The Two-Step Flow of Communication: An Up-to-Date Report on an Hypothesis," *Public Opinion Quarterly*, 21, (1957), p. 61.
21. Eugene Jacobsen and Stanley E. Seashore, "Communication Practices in Complex Organizations," *Journal of Social Issues*, 7 (1951), pp. 28–40.
22. Phillip K. Tompkins, "Organizational Communication: A State-of-the-Art Review," *Conference on Organizational Communication.* Monograph, National Aeronautics and Space Administration, MSFC Form 454, 1968.
23. Gary M. Richetto, "*Source Credibility and Personal Influence in Three Contexts: A Study of Dyadic Communication in a Complex Aerospace Organization.*" Unpublished Ph.D. dissertation, Purdue University, 1969.
24. *Case Studies in Organizational Communication* (New York: Industrial Communication Council, 1975), pp. 9–13. Reprinted by permission of ICC and Bank of America.
25. Delivered before the Kings Dominion Management Group, Pinehurst, North Carolina, March 12, 1976. Reprinted by permission of *Vital Speeches of the Day*, City News Publishing Company. © 1976.
26. Reprinted from *The Personnel Administrator* (June 1974) by permission of American Society for Personnel Administration. © 1974.

27. Betsy D. Gelb and Gabriel M. Gelb, "Strategies to Overcome Phony Feedback," pp. 5–7, *MSU Business Topics*, Autumn 1974. Reprinted by permission of the publisher, Division of Research, Graduate School of Business Administration, Michigan State University.

Recommended Readings

Goldhaber, Gerald M., *Organizational Communication*. Dubuque, Iowa: Wm. C. Brown, 2 ed., 1979. The first edition of this book was one of the earliest of a series of organizational communication texts since the mid-1970s. The second edition is a good update. It is thorough and well organized. Although written as a college text, it provides considerable information which would be directly applicable for the working manager. Each chapter is followed by an extensive bibliography of additional materials.

Koehler, Jerry W., Karl W. E. Anatol, and Ronald L. Applbaum, *Organizational Communication: Behavioral Perspectives*. New York: Holt, Rinehart & Winston, 1976. These authors tie in management theory with communication perspectives focusing on behavioral aspects. The ideas covered in the present book on personality and power factors affecting network accuracy were drawn in part from Koehler *et al*.

Case Studies in Organizational Communication. A joint project of Industrial Communication Council and Towers, Perrin, Forster & Crosby, 1975. This paperback book details 20 separate real-world cases, each written up like the Bank of America case I've included in the chapter. The problem is described, a strategy explained, implementation and results reported. The cases are brief but provide excellent ideas for working managers. A copy of this book could be purchased by contacting T, P, F & C (they're a consulting firm) at 90 Park Avenue, New York, New York 10016, or the Industrial Communication Council (a professional association of corporate communication specialists), P.O. Box 3970, Grand Central Post Office, New York, New York 10017.

Davis, Keith, "The Care and Cultivation of the Corporate Grapevine," *Dun's Review* (July 1973), pp. 44–47. In one of his many articles on informal networks, Davis recommends that managers not attempt to kill company gossip but instead listen to it.

For an example of how a computer can be used in the application of ECCO analysis to a large, complex organization, see Jay Terry Knippen, *An Episodic Study of Informal Communications in a Retail Chain Store*. Unpublished DBA dissertation, Florida State University, 1970.

CHAPTER 4

COMMUNICATION MEDIA
The Manager's Tool Kit

Gaining the attention of potential message receivers is a critical first step in producing intentional messages. The method we use to communicate is a signal to our receivers, providing cues about our estimation of the audience's importance, the significance and urgency of the message being conveyed, and so forth. A routinely distributed photocopied memo conveys a very different immediate impression than a neatly typed and personally signed letter—even though the actual message may be identical. In some organizations the memo is regarded as a way we as managers "cover our tracks" so that we can later produce proof that a message was distributed. Receivers come to view the memo's message as insignificant. Form letters and one-way lecture sessions also tell the message recipient that he or she is not important enough for a face-to-face, individual dialogue with the message source.

At the heart of media selection problems in organizations is a failure to recognize the distinction between communication *efficiency* and *effectiveness*. Efficiency is simply a ratio between the resources (including time, materials, and effort) expended in generating intentional messages and the number of people to whom the message is sent. To improve efficiency we simply increase the number of people reached or reduce the message preparation costs. The widely distributed memo or mass meeting is an efficient communication method.

$$\text{Communication efficiency} = \frac{\text{resources (including time) expended}}{\text{number of recipients reached}}$$

Communication *effectiveness* is quite another matter. In Chapter 1 we suggest that communication is the creation of understanding. In organizations, effective communication creates understandings which orchestrate effort in much the same way as the nervous system arranges an organism's thoughts and behaviors. Management theorist, Saul Gellerman, concludes that organizational communication "may be said to be 'effective' when a message is:

received by its intended audience,

interpreted in essentially the same way by the recipients as by the senders,

remembered over reasonably extended periods of time, and

used when appropriate occasions arise.[1]

The dilemma for the manager is that in most cases the communication methods that are most efficient are least effective and vice versa. In almost every case, face-to-face dialogue with individual organization members is the least efficient, least convenient, and most costly method of communication. It is also the most effective.

Gellerman concludes that an unwillingness to pay the price for effec-

tiveness in communication may well be false economy. "A very large part of the blame for ineffective communication ... falls on management's persistent efforts to communicate with the most people at the least cost. Alas, communication is one function where it does not pay to be efficient."[2]

In some cases, of course, a message is simply not important enough to transmit via individual, face-to-face interaction. In many cases, the organizational structure and complexity forbids it. The manager must then strike a balance between efficiency and effectiveness. Unfortunately, many managers choose a communication method out of habit, without considering the merits or drawbacks of possible alternatives. In this chapter, we'll explore some considerations which should enter media decisions, and discuss a number of communication tools found to be useful in internal communication programs.

The Medium:
Ground Rules for Exchange

Often the term *media* is associated with mass communications—radio, TV, newspapers and so forth. A more generic description of the term involves the choice of a *channel or mechanism for* transmitting messages from point to point. Typically we think in terms of hardware such as telephone, videotape, letters, or telegrams. But these might better be viewed as communication *tools*. Another way to conceptualize media may be more useful to the organizational communicator: *A medium is a generally accepted set of ground rules for structuring and exchanging messages.*

The ground rules are usually assumed by participants rather than prescribed in advance. Here is an example from communication professor Richard Hatch. A medium called "conversation among friends" usually works under the following ground rules:

- Whoever is talking may continue to talk until he or she appears to be finished.

- No speaker should talk for "very long" at a time, which may vary from a few seconds to two or three minutes, depending upon the circumstances.

- Nobody may interrupt the speaker unless he or she agrees to be interrupted.

- When a silence occurs, each participant has an equal opportunity to begin talking, that is, nobody is intentionally excluded.

Some Possible Ground Rules	Spoken Media				Written/Graphic Media		
	Conversation	Interview	Committee	Presentation	Letter/Memo	Report	Poster/Display
Receivers may interrupt and/or seek clarification	yes	yes	yes	no	no	no	no
Participants may change the subject	yes	sometimes	yes	no	no	no	no
Source may talk for extended periods of time	no	no	no	yes	no	yes	no
Participants have equal opportunity to initiate ideas	yes	sometimes	yes	no	no	no	no
Messages are presented in a standard arrangement or format	no	sometimes	no	yes	usually	yes	no
Supporting data of considerable detail are presented with conclusion	sometimes	no	no	yes	sometimes	yes	no
Artistic or aesthetic qualities are conveyed	no	no	no	somewhat	no	no	yes

Figure 4-1 Examples of ground rules for media

- Anybody who is talking may change the subject without getting permission from other participants.[3]

When such ground rules are violated, participants in the communication situation are thrown off. Visualize a friendly conversation in which any of the rules listed above are violated—say, interruptions abound—and you're likely to picture an ineffectual and decidedly unfriendly conversation.

Obviously we don't consciously consider these rules every time we communicate, but they are there. They've just become so familiar that we no longer notice them. These rules do, however, provide a rational basis for making decisions about what medium to use for specific messages. If, for example, we need to convey some highly technical, intricate, and complex information, we would be likely to avoid the friendly conversation medium. Such messages may involve talking for "very long" periods of time and listeners would be expected to refrain from changing the topic. Recognizing the ground rules in operation may alert us to potential communication failures.

When we describe media in this broad sense, we discover that there are quite specific advantages or disadvantages to the use of different communication approaches in different circumstances. For the manager, a wise selection is based on consideration of the (1) media characteristics inherent in each and (2) relative costs of written versus spoken communication.

Media Characteristics

Although there are many nonverbal cues present in any organization which communicates to its members, most conscious communication efforts involve either the spoken or written word, or some combination of both. Graphic or pictorial information often accompanies written messages or may, on occasion, stand alone (such as on a poster or sign). Spoken language is occasionally accompanied by music or other aural stimuli.

Let's look at some of the characteristics of business communication media that make one medium preferable to others in given situations.

Speed

How fast or slow a medium is may depend on what you are measuring. A letter is generally slower getting from sender to receiver but an oral presentation of the same information may take considerably more preparation time. The time-consuming work of producing a videotape may be offset when repeated showings can efficiently present the same information to many employees or customers. Normally the spoken word is faster than a print medium, except when we are comparing a formal oral presentation with a handwritten note. Informal conversation and telephone generally provide quickest information transfer.

Feedback

The amount and promptness of feedback are other media characteristics. Written media elicit no feedback from your audience while you are writing the message. Unfortunately, the usefulness of responses that come later is limited; it is too late to adjust and clarify the original message for your receivers.

Telephone conversations provide immediate feedback in the form of questions, comments, or tone of voice, pauses, and hesitation. Face-to-face communication situations provide all this plus other nonverbal feedback in facial expression, body movement, and posture.

Record

Whether or not a permanent record of the message is *normally* retained is another media characteristic. Ordinarily interviews, informal conversation, and telephone messages leave no record. (Of course these can be

Reprinted with permission from The Saturday Evening Post Company © 1976

"Didn't you get my memo?"

recorded, but that is not routine practice in most organizations.) Written communications such as letters, reports, and most memos are usually maintained on file. An informal note, however, may be discarded and is therefore usually a nonrecord medium. A nonrecord medium can have distinct advantages where candid expression "off the record" is called for. Putting it in writing seems to make the message more formal or "official," a situation which may also call for less openness in expression.

Message Intensity and Complexity

The impact a message is likely to have on its receiver and the inherent complexity of the message affect its format and medium. A high intensity message may be one which has a strong effect on the receiver's emotions. Bad news or persuasive messages which require careful explanation of underlying reasoning are often best communicated by a medium which can carry complex data in a relatively structured format. Typically a formal letter, a carefully planned oral presentation, or a written report would be best. Friendly conversation or a brief memo would be less appropriate.

Formality

Some media are more appropriate for formal occasions while others fit well in informal settings. A letter of congratulations to you announcing your promotion seems more formal and has a rather different impact than, say, a phone call conveying the same information. The letter makes it official. A handwritten note, on the other hand, sent to members of the board of directors by a worker would probably be considered disrespectful. When the message is intended for internal consumption only (within the "family") its format may be more informal than if it were to be publicly disseminated outside the organization. This accounts in part for the differences between memos, which are internal documents, and letters, which go outside the organization.

Cost

There are many different costs to be considered in media comparisons. Usually the highest expenditures are people costs: the wages and benefits paid to employees. There are also *technical* costs, such as paper, postage, copiers, typewriters, telephone, and videotape players. A simple face-to-face conversation between two executives may involve no technical cost but considerable people cost.

Since communication activities are a cost of doing business, they do consume profits. Cost effectiveness in the selection of best media for messages can have considerable impact on an organization's profitability.

Media	Fast/Slow	Feedback (High/Low)	Record/Nonrecord	Formal/Informal	Inside/Outside	Complex/Simple	Cost (High/Low)
Informal conversation	Fast	High	Nonrecord	Informal	Either	Simple	Low
Telephone conversation	Fast	Medium	Nonrecord	Informal	Either	Simple	Low-Medium
Formal oral presentation	Medium	High	Nonrecord	Formal	Either	Medium	Medium
Informal note	Medium	Low	Nonrecord	Informal	Either	Simple	Low
Memo	Medium	Low	Record	Informal	Inside	Medium	Low-Medium
Directive	Slow	Low	Record	Formal	Inside	Medium	Medium
Letter	Slow	Low	Record	Formal	Outside	Complex	Medium
Formal report	Very slow	Low	Record	Very formal	Inside	Complex	High

Note: Italicized items are the specific biases which would ordinarily cause a communicator to choose that medium for his message.

Figure 4-2 Some biases of business media. From *Communicating in Business* by Richard Hatch, p. 113. © 1977, Science Research Associates, Inc. Reproduced by permission of the publisher.

Often we overlook some of the more subtle cost dimensions. For example, written media processing also includes costs of operating the mail room, filing cabinets, in/out baskets, and the square footage of valuable floor space occupied by these ingredients of the communication system. Even disposing of waste paper can cost money and should be figured into the total cost picture. When all such factors are considered and added to people costs, written communication can amount to between a penny and ten cents a word.[4]

The cost of a simple dictated business letter can be surprisingly high. Figure 4-3 illustrates this.

A look at some U.S. Postal Service statistics provides an idea of just how enormous these costs are to business. In round numbers, the postal service handles approximately 90 billion pieces of mail each year. About 74 percent of this volume—66.6 billion pieces—is business mail. Even if only one-third of these business messages were dictated and typewritten, that would be about 22.2 billion letters per year. The average cost of such a letter has been estimated by a number of research studies in recent years. The current figure as provided by the business information service

	Dictator $12,000/Year Secretary $8,000/Year	Dictator $25,000/Year Secretary $10,000/Year	Dictator $75,000/Year Secretary $15,000/Year
Dictator Costs: Reading time, research, and dictation = 10 min.	$1.00	$2.08	$6.18
Secretarial Costs: Taking dictation and transcribing = 10 min.	.67	.83	1.25
Stationery/Postage	.25	.25	.25
Total Costs	$1.92	$3.16	$7.68

Note: Dictator and secretarial costs are based on a 250-day year at eight hours a day. Thus the $12,000-a-year dictator would earn $48 a day or $6 an hour. The time of ten minutes for reading, research, and dictating is equal to 1/6 of an hour or $1.00. Overhead costs for rent, utilities, and depreciation have not been included.

Figure 4-3 Letter-writing costs for 200-word letter[5]

of my public library is $4.77. Such estimates include technical and people costs but do not reflect unusual expenses such as mistakes that require redoing the letter and misuse of expensive office machinery, all of which can run the cost of a letter up to $15 or $20, as calculated on the basis of consultant observations. And the most expensive cost of all—the cost of *ineffective* letters that make a customer into a former customer, or a collaborator into a competitor—are not calculated into any of these estimates. These *real* costs can only be guessed at.

Using even a conservative estimate of $4.00 per letter multiplied by 22.2 billion amounts to a staggering $88.8 billion a year. I don't think any of us can really visualize how much money that is. To try to put this into perspective, we might consider that if we were to spend $1000 per day, every day, it would take us about 2739 *years* to spend $1 billion. At that same rate of $1000 per day, it would take almost *61,000 years* to spend as much as American business spends on letters sent through the mail in one year. And this does not include written messages distributed internally or via other delivery services.

Combining Media

Managers are, of course, not limited to the use of a single medium, although many seem tied to the conventional ways "it's always been done." Often a combination of several media does the job very nicely. Some message repetition can be an important learning device; disadvantages of one medium can be compensated for by another. For example, the low feedback characteristic of written media can be offset by accompanying the message with an oral medium. Several ways to combine media are suggested in Figure 4-4.

Empirical studies of the effects of combining media have produced rather confused results primarily because it is difficult to keep nonverbal variables constant. We cannot absolutely control what our receivers will pay attention to. Nevertheless some tentative findings have emerged.

In one type of experiment, specific factual information was transmitted and the following media and combinations of media were compared: (1) oral only, (2) written only, (3) use of a bulletin board, (4) the grapevine (no formal message sent), (5) oral and written. The general procedure was to have a message distributed by different media for different groups in the organization. After several days, the recipients of the message were tested to see how much content they could accurately remember. The results were usually the same: the written-plus-oral message combination resulted in the greatest retention. The oral exchange alone was second in effectiveness, followed by a written message, the bulletin board, and the control group who received the information only by the grapevine.[6]

Medium	Major Limitations	Supplemental Media
Informal conversation	no record; deals with simple messages	informal note to acknowledge; additional written information to clarify complex topics
Telephone conversation	little nonverbal feedback; no record	informal conversation; memo or note to confirm; tape conversation
Formal oral presentation	preparation time; no record	written report of briefing (outline format) to follow up
Informal note	low feedback; deals with simple messages	telephone or conversation follow-up
Memo	low feedback	telephone or conversation follow-up
Directive	preparation time; low feedback	meeting or presentation to amplify and get feedback
Letter	preparation time and cost; low feedback	telephone follow-up to test for understanding

Figure 4-4 Combining media for effectiveness

In another study, supervisors were asked to rate the effectiveness of (1) written, (2) oral, (3) written and then oral, or (4) oral and then written communication for different types of situations. In general, the oral-followed-by-written technique came out best. Supervisors saw it as most effective for situations which (1) required immediate action, (2) passed along a company directive or order, (3) communicated an important policy change, (4) reviewed work progress, (5) called for praising a noteworthy employee, and (6) promoted a safety campaign. The written-only technique was judged best for passing along information that (1) required action in the future or (2) was of a general nature. An oral-only message was suggested for reprimands or to settle a dispute among employees.[7]

A general but tentative conclusion we might draw from all this is that a combination of the oral and written message seems to improve communication effectiveness in most settings.

Media Expectations

One final point about media is that people come to expect certain types of messages to be communicated via certain media. While these expectations differ in various organizations, habits of communicating do develop and become the norm.

To give extra impact to a message, a manager may want to use a different medium or different combination of media. If, for example, a change in work schedule is normally posted on a bulletin board, a supervisor may get better audience attention by calling a meeting or talking with each worker individually about an unusual change. Similarly, a letter sent to a worker's home will have a very different impact than will a general public address system announcement. Creativity, a consideration of media characteristics, and some educated guesses about likely effects of messages provide the manager with some real opportunities to develop an interesting and effective media mix.

Tools of the Manager-Communicator

Developing creativity and communication innovation starts with a look at what's being done now. In the following pages, a number of communication tools used to promote organizational functioning and health are described. After reviewing well over a hundred internal communication tools, I have developed a classification system based on what seems to be the *primary intent* of messages generally conveyed with particular tools. These categories are:

1. Tools used to convey work directives, specific policy and other *job-related information*. These are used primarily for downward communication.
2. Tools used to keep members informed of general organizational matters and provide them with *information* which may be *of interest* but which is not specifically necessary to their jobs.
3. Tools which develop *organizational identification*. These are used to create employee pride and a sense of loyalty to the organization.
4. Tools which provide *upward feedback* to higher management.
5. Tools which tend to build stronger *interpersonal relationships* on the individual level.

Here are some examples of tools in each of these categories. Keep in mind, of course, that there are other options and other combinations which may be more effective. This listing represents popular usage, not necessarily the optimum use of communication tools. Many of these are discussed in depth in other chapters of this book.

Job-related information, such as work directives and policy, is frequently conveyed downward via tools such as these:

- *Introduction or orientation programs for new employees*
- *Published job descriptions*
- *Procedure or policy manuals*
- *Bulletins* (Brief announcements of something that has just happened or is about to happen, transmitted orally or via a written handout, are especially useful in "clearing the air" and stopping counterproductive rumors.)
- *Instructional interviews or briefings*
- *Performance reviews*
- *Conferences and meetings*
- *Training activities* (including on-the-job training)
- *Bulletin boards*
- *Maps or floor plans* (to direct people around the organization's plant)
- *Company reference library*
- *Reports,* written
- *Benefits statements* (individual accountings of the value of an employee's benefit package)
- *Reprints of technical articles*
- *Subscriptions* (to magazines or journals which provide job-related information)
- *Tuition aid programs* (to provide additional job-related training)
- *Visits* (to other locations or other organizations to gather information on procedures)

For your-information tools convey messages which are likely to be of some interest but are not crucial to the job functions of employees. These serve to keep organization members "in tune."

- *Announcement folders* (used to explain personnel changes, promotions, appointments, etc.)
- *Information/reading racks* (stocked with pamphlets, how-to-booklets, and magazines or journals of varying topics)
- *Bulletin board*

Reprinted by permission of the Chicago Tribune–New York News Syndicate

- *Booklets* (containing subjects such as health and safety; inspirational and self-improvement topics; how-to-do-it materials)
- *Company library*
- *Grapevine* (informal channels)
- *Classes or instruction* (may be on non-job-related topics such as handicrafts and self-development)
- *Company advertising awareness* (programs inform employees of upcoming promotions)
- *Posters, bulletins*
- *Letters and memos* (letters may be sent to the home rather than work location for greater impact)
- *Distribution of union contracts*
- *Visits, trips to other plants or organizations*
- *Videotape presentations* (Some companies tape a question and answer session between rank and file employees and top executives for showing in all plant locations. Employee questioners are free to ask about any topic.)
- *Answerline column* (in organization publications to address employee questions or concerns)
- *Newsletters or organizational magazines*
- *Progress reports* (covering topics such as new product acceptance, plant mechanization, and civic involvement programs)

Organizational identification and loyalty can be built by the creative use of communication tools such as these:

- *Anniversary book* (Such a book emphasizes the history and growth of the organization to convey a sense of tradition and pride. Often pictures of employees are included.)

- *Auto windshield decals, bumper stickers, or license plates*

- *Directory of employees or members* (with brief biographical sketches)

- *Open house or "family night"* (programs including tours of the plant, exhibits, demonstrations, samples, and refreshments)

- *Alumni or retiree activities* (systematic visits, banquets, picnics, and explanations of any changes in their retirement benefits; maintaining retirees' mailing lists for company publications and annual directory of names and addresses so they can keep in touch. Many companies are also developing preretirement orientation and planning programs. Such an attitude of caring is not lost on present employees who someday will join the ranks of the retired.)

- *Newsletters, in-house magazines*

- *Contests* (competition in art, photography, games or puzzles, writing—including slogans, captions for cartoons, essays, letters, model making, and, of course, sales)

- *Letters and memos* (especially congratulatory)

- *Recreational and social* activities (such as athletic leagues, picnics, and outings)

- *Tours of plant*

- *Uniforms, coveralls, hardhats marked with company logo*

- *Workplace design and appearance*

- *Samples or discounts on company products*

- *Tuition aid programs*

- *Training programs*

- *Displays and exhibits* (photos, artwork, videotape or slide presentations accompanied by dramatic lighting and sound effects on subjects such as company history, company products, or statistical data regarding employees, management, and stockholders. Occasionally a display can be used to highlight a special problem. One company exhibited "actual examples of broken TV sets and crushed cartons to provide dramatic evidence of results of mis-handled shipping. . . . To carry out a theme of traffic safety, wrecked cars and mock graveyards have been used in exhibits.")[8]

Upward feedback tools provide for communication from subordinates to management.

- *Advisory councils on human relations* or similarly named groups provide feedback on employee concerns to management. (Employees, usually elected, serve as representatives of their departments for the purpose of better communication between all organizational levels.)

- *Observation* (preferably systematic observation by trained communication observers, primarily of nonverbal indicators)

- *Attitude surveys*

- *Grievance interviews* (informal or via formal procedures)

- *Grapevine*

- *Conferences or meetings*

- *Exit interview*

- *Junior board of directors program* (where promising subordinates are given an opportunity to identify, research, and recommend solution strategies for organizational problems)

- Readership surveys (for company publications)

- Reports and analyses of employee concerns

- Rumor control programs

- Suggestion systems

- Communication audit

Interpersonal relationships on the individual level can be strengthened via communication tools such as these:

- Counseling interviews

- Announcements of personnel changes, accomplishments

- Cards sent to others on birthdays, holidays, or to mark special events for the employee or members of his family (e.g., births, graduations, Junior's first little league home run, marriages)

- Sympathy cards/flowers
- Nameplates at work locations
- Identification badges or nametags
- Get-well cards
- Recognition (oral and written)
- Informal conversation
- Social get-togethers such as picnics and Christmas parties
- Sports or other activities

This represents only a sample of tools often used in organizational communication. Many of the communication tools just described are, of course, prepared by specialized departments within an organization such as advertising, employee relations or employee communications.

It remains an important communication responsibility of the individual manager to determine which of these or others will best meet the needs of his or her organization. These decisions should be based not on habits of use but on sound consideration of media characteristics and cost.

Diagnosing Your Use of Communication Media and Tools

A communication log, as illustrated in Figure 4-5, can increase your awareness of the frequency with which you use certain communication media and tools while functioning in an organization.

Select a specific time period of at least six or seven hours and keep a careful accounting of your communication activities. If you are a practicing manager or full-time employee you will want to do this on the job. If you are a student you may evaluate your educational organization. Or if you are interested in analyzing your communication effectiveness in your church group or civic organizations, you may need to take two- or three-hour samples over several days or weeks. Select times that closely reflect your normal activities. For example, you'd want to avoid monitoring your activities during exam week or inventory time.

During your sample time period, take a moment at the end of each hour to estimate the time you spent using each of the media listed. If you use others simply note them and the time spent at the bottom of the form. When your form is complete, total the times for each column. These data should provide ideas for more effective utilization of available communication media and tools.

ORGANIZATION: _____

COMMUNICATION MEDIA USED

Time Period	Informal Conversation (Unplanned)	Telephone	Oral Presentations or Briefings (Planned)	Informal Notes (handwritten)	Memos or Directives (Typed)
8–9 AM	____ min.	____ min.	____ min.	____ min.	____ min.
9–10	____ min.	____ min.	____ min.	____ min.	____ min.
11–12	____ min.	____ min.	____ min.	____ min.	____ min.
12–1 PM	____ min.	____ min.	____ min.	____ min.	____ min.
1–2	____ min.	____ min.	____ min.	____ min.	____ min.
2–3	____ min.	____ min.	____ min.	____ min.	____ min.
3–4	____ min.	____ min.	____ min.	____ min.	____ min.
4–5	____ min.	____ min.	____ min.	____ min.	____ min.

Total
Time
per
Medium

Other communication media used: _____

Time Period	Letters	Formal Written Reports	Meetings or Committees	Interviewing (Planned Conversation)	Listening
8–9 AM	____ min.	____ min.	____ min.	____ min.	____ min.
9–10	____ min.	____ min.	____ min.	____ min.	____ min.
11–12	____ min.	____ min.	____ min.	____ min.	____ min.
12–1 PM	____ min.	____ min.	____ min.	____ min.	____ min.
1–2	____ min.	____ min.	____ min.	____ min.	____ min.
2–3	____ min.	____ min.	____ min.	____ min.	____ min.
3–4	____ min.	____ min.	____ min.	____ min.	____ min.
4–5	____ min.	____ min.	____ min.	____ min.	____ min.

Total
Time
per
Medium

Other communication media used: _____

Figure 4-5 A communication log

Questions for Further Thought

1. Describe in your own words the dilemma of communication efficiency versus communication effectiveness. Why don't we always use individual, personal media?

2. What kinds of messages can or should be transmitted by the most efficient means? Give specific examples.

3. What kinds of messages require a high degree of effectiveness regardless of efficiency? Give specific examples.

4. Think back to experiences you have had where an inappropriate medium or tool was used to convey an important message to you. Describe what happened in the form of a short case or critical incident description.

Notes

1. Saul W. Gellerman, *The Management of Human Resources* (Hinsdale, Ill.: Dryden Press, 1976), p. 61.
2. *Ibid.*, p. 62.
3. Richard Hatch, *Communicating in Business* (Chicago: Science Research Associates, 1977), p. 96.
4. From *Business Communications, Principles and Methods*, Fifth Edition, by William C. Himstreet and Wayne Murlin Baty. © 1977 by Wadsworth Publishing Company, Inc., Belmont, California 94002. Reprinted by permission of the publisher.
5. *Ibid.*
6. T. L. Dahle, "An Objective and Comparative Study of Five Methods of Transmitting Information to Business and Industrial Employees," *Speech Monographs*, 21 (1954), pp. 21–28.
7. D. A. Level, "Communication Effectiveness: Method and Situation," *Journal of Business Communication*, Fall 1972, pp. 19–25.
8. Geneva Seybold, *Employee Communication: Policy and Tools* (New York: National Industrial Conference Board, 1966), p. 53.

Recommended Reading

Seybold, Geneva. *Employee Communication: Policy and Tools*. New York: National Industrial Conference Board, 1966. This book provides the most detailed discussion of communication tools I have seen anywhere. The material includes a forty-page description of tools arranged in alphabetical order from Advertisements to Visits. Any manager would gain a number of useful ideas from a review of this material.

PART

ORAL COMMUNICATION ACTIVITIES

CHAPTER **5**

ONE-WITH-ONE COMMUNICATION SITUATIONS

Conversation:
An Exchange of Perceptions and Strokes

People talk to each other to establish and maintain relationships which, in turn, serve certain needs. Specifically these needs are (1) to gain a better understanding of "reality," (2) to develop and clarify our self-image, (3) to satisfy a normal hunger for affiliation with others, and (4) to gain support for our personal growth.

Reality and Self-Image Clarification

We get a better picture of how things are by bouncing our perceptions off others. We develop satisfying relationships with others by sharing our view of the world and getting confirmation or correction of that view from them. In organizations, other members fill us in on the details of the way things work as we learn "the ropes"—the way things really are.

But there is another type of reality that is clarified by our relationships with others. It is our self-concept. We develop a healthy self-image (or an unhealthy one) through our communicative relationships with others. From our earliest recollections, others—most often our parents—provided feedback to us about our personal worth. We were told that we were a "good boy" when we finished our cereal. Our teachers commented that we were "bright" or "better at gym class than academics." Our peers noted that we "danced pretty good for a fat kid." Each evaluative comment could magnify or discount our self-image.

By the time we reach adulthood we have a fairly stabilized self-image; nevertheless, we continue to seek out information from others that reinforces the way we see ourselves. Among the tragic outcomes of the negative self-image is that it can be reinforced most effectively by negative "strokes"*—by put-downs, humiliation, and failures. The tendency is to establish relationships with those who provide the kind of self-worth confirmation we really want—negative or positive.

In addition to seeking our favorite strokes from others, there is another communicated phrase that is music to our ears—our name. Dale Carnegie's famous book on "winning friends and influencing people" made a point of this more than forty years ago and it hasn't changed a bit since. Few things can affect a person's sense of self-worth more than having others remember and use one's name.

Our Need to Talk with Others

People's needs for affiliation with others are met through their conversational relationships. All of us have some degree of need for social belonging. We want to identify and be identified with other individuals, groups, and organizations. Being deprived of human associations is most distressing. During the Vietnam war, servicemen who were prisoners of war suffered long periods of isolation from all others. They later spoke of the ecstatic relief they felt upon hearing even tapping on the dungeon walls by another prisoner. Periods of almost total deprivation from human interaction were broken by even the primitive communication that said, "I know you are there."

Fortunately, few of us need to endure the agony of total isolation. Nevertheless, each person faces new and unusual experiences that may bring momentary deprivation of familiar forms of interaction with others. Travel to a foreign country where we do not speak the language or beginning an unfamiliar job in a strange city are examples. In such situations we are likely to gravitate toward others who seem to understand us best. Affiliation salves the discomfort of uncertainty. Meaningful relationships established by conversations satisfy this social need.

---

*A *stroke* can be any communicated expression of recognition. Arising from transactional analysis (TA), the term is sometimes misapplied to refer only to expressions of verbal approval. See Recommended Readings for sources that explain TA concepts.

Effects on Personal Growth

Clarifying reality, strengthening self-image, and satisfying affiliation *good to in* needs all contribute to our development as persons. The expectations of our associates can inhibit or facilitate our personal growth. Communicative interaction forms the stuff that holds relationships together.

Interaction with employees is a key management tool. Touring work areas or circulating among organization members should be a regular function of the manager as recommended in Jim Lavenson's "How to Earn an MBWA Degree" on pages 89–94. Look for opportunities to provide recognition and support. Then do it. And mean it. The payoff goes beyond more pleasant interpersonal relations; it can show up in the maximization of human resources.

A manager can have a profound effect on his or her employees by simply thanking or complimenting them. It sounds simplistic but the fact remains that, as Robert Townsend said in *Up the Organization,* "Thanks [is] a really neglected form of compensation."[1]

Management consultants have implemented systematic approaches to expressing verbal approval based on behavioral principles that have demonstrated remarkable results. In one division of a major American corporation, such a program led to one-year cost savings conservatively estimated at $3.5 million "and that is not including employee morale, which is difficult to quantify." With such results, it's not surprising that successful managers are increasingly attempting to systematically use verbal rewards to alter employee behavior.

This approach is known by several names: *behavior modification* (a term that conjures up Orwellian manipulation in some people), *operant conditioning* (you may picture salivating dogs ringing a bell), or the more euphemistic—and more acceptable—*performance improvement* or *contingency management. Business Week* reports how one consulting service implements such a program. First, a series of meetings are held in which managers and employees discuss mutual needs and problems as well as potential solutions. These diagnostic sessions provide a base for determining job performance standards and how they will be met. The meetings also identify reinforcers that managers may use to "modify" the employees' behavior. One company, for example, held a three day session which revealed that

> What workers, such as clerk typists, want most is a sense of belonging, a sense of accomplishment, and a sense of teamwork. . . . In return, managers ask for quicker filing of reports and fewer errors.
>
> The second step is to arrange for worker performance to be observed with a reliable follow-up; the third is to give feedback often, immediately letting employees know how their current level of performance compares with the

level desired. At an airline company for instance, five telephone reservation offices employing about 1,800 people keep track of the percentage of calls in which callers make flight reservations. Then they feed back the results daily to each employee. At the same time, supervisors are instructed to praise employees for asking callers for their reservations. Since the program started, the ratio of sales to calls has soared from one in four to one in two.[2]

Whatever the name of the program, the objective is to provide communicative rewards in such a way that they motivate performance and reduce dissatisfaction. The timing of this feedback system should meet the criteria of high speed. Face-to-face conversation would normally be the best choice, with a phone call ranking second as media choices.

At the heart of any such performance improvement efforts is the premise that future behavior is influenced by the outcomes of past behavior. If the outcome immediately following an act was in some way rewarding, we are likely to repeat the behavior. If the response was punishing, we're likely to not do it again, unless we prefer punishment to other outcomes such as simply being ignored.

Managers can provide three types of responses to employee behaviors: positive reinforcement, negative reinforcement, or no observable response at all. The effects of each on the behavior it follows are shown in Figure 5–1.

There are some questions about just how far we can go with verbal approval as a motivator. Theoretically, it should work indefinitely so long as appropriate *schedules of reinforcement* are used. The two main reinforcement schedules are *continuous* and *intermittent*. Continuous reinforcement means the individual receives reinforcement (a compliment or

Types of Responses to Employee Behavior	*Effect on the Recurrence of the Behavior*
Positive reinforcement	tends to increase or strengthen the recurrence of such behavior
Negative reinforcement	tends to decrease or weaken the recurrence of such behavior *unless* the employee is seeking negative reinforcement to coincide with his or her self-image
Reinforcement withheld	tends to decrease or weaken the recurrence of such behavior; can lead to extinction of the behavior

Figure 5–1 Behavior responses to different reinforcement

supportive statement) every time he or she engages in the desired behavior. This approach is useful when the person is being taught a new behavior and needs to be shored up to develop confidence in this new ability. People learn very quickly, at least initially, under continuous reinforcement. You can readily observe this when teaching a child how to do something like catching a ball. Each time the ball is caught, you praise the child and the child will develop this skill very quickly. The principle generally holds for employees working on unfamiliar tasks.

There are three main problems with continuous reinforcement. First, it takes too much time—and therefore costs a great deal—in supervisory effort. It is just not feasible to always be there complimenting each job done; you might as well do it yourself! Secondly, there is a problem of "inflation." Just as dollars lose value when too many are in circulation, verbal approval is cheapened by overuse. The third problem is that once continuous reinforcement is expected, it is tough to wean people away from it without certain risks. If we suddenly drop continuous reinforcement—that is, we no longer express verbal approval for each good behavior—the message to our worker may be that the behavior is no longer appropriate and should be stopped. In short, we may extinguish the desired behavior.

The drawbacks to continuous reinforcement are largely overcome by using intermittent reinforcement. Here, instead of expressing approval of every act we use another system to allocate compliments. We may decide to express approval at intervals, such as each time a unit of work, say a day's or week's quota, is completed. Most organizations use intermittent reinforcement in the payment of wages. Workers do not get paid $.15 each time they assemble an item. Instead they are paid at the end of the week or twice a month. The same principle can apply to communicative rewards.

Another intermittent reinforcement approach is to provide reward at completely random times. Much of the lure of slot machine gambling comes from the anticipated random windfall. It is the anticipation or hope of a sudden big reward that keeps the players engaged in the "desired behavior"—putting money in the slot.

Under random intermittent reinforcement the worker doesn't know exactly when he or she will be rewarded. So long as there remains any hope of eventually receiving a reward such as verbal approval, extinction of the desired behavior is delayed. If the rewards are too far apart, of course, the worker will not continue to produce unless he or she is particularly good at working hard today for some far-off, but certain-to-be-worthwhile reward. Relatively few workers today are content to "get their reward in heaven."

The best approach is to use continuous reinforcement when new behaviors are being developed and then gradually move to an intermittent schedule so the desired performance won't be inadvertently extinguished. In other words, shift the employees' expectations so that longer intervals between reinforcement are seen as normal.

Finally, we need to be aware that the use of praise coupled with appropriate criticism doesn't always produce desired results. When you're dealing with human communication and motivation, nothing is a sure thing.

Praise and Criticism

Sometimes praise is downright embarrassing and so-called constructive criticism just plain makes you mad. Morrison and O'Hearne, in their book, *Practical Transactional Analysis in Management*, have developed an explanation of why praise and criticism seem to have such an on-again, off-again value.[3] These authors suggest that both praise and criticism can be broken down into two types. Type 1 praise consists of those statements that have little effect on the performance of the receiver. They are accepted like water off a duck's back. Type 2 praise consists of those statements that *might* have a positive effect on performance under certain circumstances. There are no guarantees, but these kinds of "attaboys" might motivate or at least build stronger authentic relationships between the giver and the receiver. Some examples of Type 1 and Type 2 praise are offered in Figure 5–2.

A similar classification of criticism is illustrated in Figure 5–3. Type 1 criticism results in defensiveness and deterioration of performance while Type 2 criticism is at least potentially constructive in that it *might* result in improved future performance.

Interviews:
I'm Glad We Had This Little Chat

Effective interviewing is conversation which is *planned* and which has specific *purposes*. Although we often associate interviewing with the job-getting process, it has equally important functions in the organization's internal communication program. Interviews can be an organization's most effective information-sharing activities. In many situations there is no substitute for them. Too often, though, managers sit down to an interview with an employee without doing his or her homework first. The key question for the interviewer must always be: "What am I attempting to accomplish in this interview?"

The three key ingredients of the successful interview are a *clear* purpose for having the discussion, a *planned approach* to maximize the value

Type 1 praise—has little effect on performance of the receiver.	Type 2 praise—may have a positive effect on performance and build an authentic relationship.
1. Generalized praise—such as, "You're doing a good job, Charlie." This is meaningless and it generally rolls off the back of the individual without effect. It is often seen as a "crooked" stroke.	1. Specific praise—such as, "Charlie, you did a great job handling that unpleasant customer with a complaint this afternoon." This communicates to the receiver that the boss has actually observed or heard about the praised action ...
2. Praise with no further meaning. There is no analysis of why a praised behavior is being commended. This "discounts" the persons being praised by assuming they will respond with higher productivity and better morale merely as a response.	2. Continuing with, "The reason I think it was such a good job is because you acted interested, asked questions, wrote down the facts, asked the customer what she thought we should do to make it right." Analysis of this kind permits the employee to internalize the learning experience ...
3. Praise for expected performance, when it may be questioned. Mabel, who always gets in on time and is met one morning with, "Mabel, you're sure on time today, you're doing great," from her boss, may wonder what's really going on.	3. Praise for better than expected results ... for coming in over quota ... exceeding the target ... putting out extra effort.
4. The "sandwich" system—praise is given first to make the person be receptive to criticism (the real reason for the transaction), which is then followed by another piece of praise, hoping, thereby to encourage the person to "try harder" next time, feel better about the criticism.	4. Praise, when deserved, given by itself is believable; when mixed with critique it is suspect. Authentic relations develop better when people talk "straight." When positive conditional recognition is in order, do so; when critique is deserved, do so. Don't mix the two.
5. Praise perceived by the receiver as given in the nature of a "carrot," mainly to encourage the receiver to work even harder in the future.	5. Praise that is primarily to commend and recognize, and does not seek to put a mortgage on the future.
6. Praise handed out lavishly only when the "brass" or higher-ups are present. Employees soon recognize the boss is trying to impress superiors with what a good human being he or she really is in dealing with subordinates.	6. Praise given when it is deserved, not just on special occasions, when it seems to build the image of the praiser to some third party.

Figure 5–2 Ineffective versus effective praise*

*Morrison/O'Hearne, PRACTICAL TRANSACTIONAL ANALYSIS IN MANAGEMENT, © 1977, Addison-Wesley, Reading, Massachusetts. Pp. 118–119. Reprinted with permission.

Type 1 criticism—tends to produce a defensive reaction in the receiver and worsen performance.	Type 2 criticism—a type of constructive criticism that may improve performance.
1. Criticism that involves use of the personal "you," e.g., "You're having too many accidents on the lift truck, Bill. What's the matter with you anyway?" It is almost always seen as a "discount" or put down by the receiver . . .	1. Criticism using a situational description, e.g., "Bill, we're experiencing an increase in lift-truck accidents. What's going on?" This indicates the manager is open to looking at all the facts leading to the unfavorable result.
2. Criticism that is unanalyzed. The subordinate then tends to rationalize the criticism as a personal opinion of the manager. . . . Or, the manager is viewed as unable to analyze the problems effectively.	2. Discussion of cause and effect with the unfavorable condition perceived by both as the result of one or more causal factors, one of which might even be the manager!
3. If the situation has been properly assessed, some managers are at a loss to provide coaching necessary for the subordinate to improve. This may be the result of ignorance or lack of competency in deciding on the corrective steps.	3. If steps 1 and 2 above have been properly accomplished, it is important for solutions to be outlined and agreed on. If the subordinate can't do this, the manager must provide, or arrange, for a resource that can develop corrective measures.
4. Critique of an individual in public is not only regarded as humiliating by the subordinate involved, but sometimes even more so by other members of the organization.	4. Individual criticism given in private is usually more acceptable. "Saving face" is almost as important in Western cultures as it is in the Orient.
5. Criticism given *only* in the interests of the boss (to get the boss recognition, promotion, or raise) or the organization (more profit or status in the marketplace). These may all be legitimate interests, but *authentic* relationships are not likely to develop.	5. Criticism given *also*, or even chiefly, in the interests of the employee (to provide greater competencies, future achievements, or a more secure future with the organization).
6. The manager does all the critiquing which sets the stage for a Parent-Child [relationship].	6. The subordinate participates in the critiques, even to the point of taking the lead role in defining the unsatisfactory condition, analyzing causes, and suggesting corrective steps.
7. Criticism used as a [calculated] game to justify withholding raises or promotions.	7. Game-free criticism leading toward candor and [authentic interactions].

Figure 5–3 Destructive versus constructive criticism*

*Morrison/O'Hearne, PRACTICAL TRANSACTIONAL ANALYSIS IN MANAGEMENT, © 1977, Addison-Wesley, Reading, Massachusetts. Pp. 120–121. Reprinted with permission.

of the time spent together, and ample opportunities for *interaction* between participants.

Interview purposes may be generally categorized as (1) giving and getting information, (2) seeking attitude or behavior changes, and (3) solving problems. There are, of course, many situations which call for a combination of purposes.

The *planning* phase of the interview process involves careful consideration of (1) exactly how you hope to accomplish your purpose; (2) the characteristics, needs, and *motivations* of the other person; (3) the *climate* or setting in which the interview will take place; and (4) specific *questions* and general *structure of questions* to be used.

The effectiveness of interaction between participants will depend in large part on purpose and planning. The overall climate of the interview situation will affect the degree and quality of both verbal and nonverbal communication. Interaction means that both parties have ample *opportunity* to participate. If the interviewer finds herself talking uninterruptedly for as long as two or three minutes she is very likely failing to maximize this communication medium. There should be a good deal of give-and-take, even when the manager's key purpose is to give instructions.

Giving Instructions

In some organizations the most frequent communication contact a manager has with his or her employees is the giving of orders, directions, or instructions. Although we tend to think of this as one-way, boss-to-subordinate communication, the interview format is usually far more appropriate. The key ingredient to effective instruction is *planning* to achieve a specific *purpose* with allowance for *interaction.*

It seems self-evident that a manager needs to know exactly what action he or she wants to result from instructions given. Yet this step is occasionally overlooked. When we give a subordinate instruction to "clean up this area" we may not have a clear picture of what the finished product will look like. And we might be disappointed. Instead we need to mentally clarify our purpose—our reason for giving the order—and then *plan* the best way of creating understanding with the employee. As we plan, we should *expect to be misunderstood.*

Providing sufficient details and *repetition* are good ways to minimize misunderstandings. The journalist's "who, what, where, when, why, and how" provide a good framework for giving instructions. Be sure you know the answers to each of these before directing someone else. And be sure to encourage questions from the message receiver. A simple "Do you have any questions?" probably isn't the best technique. The question calls for a yes or no response and many people opt for "no" to avoid showing ignorance. Changing the wording to "What questions do you have?" presup-

poses some ambiguity and encourages task-clarifying requests. Be sure to pause long enough to let your listeners know you are serious about getting questions from them.

When explaining instructions use simple, specific terms. Start with something the employee already knows and move to the new or more complex. Show how the two are related. Give reasons for what's to be done so that the task won't be seen as busywork. Demonstrate or dramatize where this could enhance understanding. And follow up to evaluate the completed job. Give the employee a sense of success and give yourself an opportunity to reinforce positive behavior.

Five Specialized Interview Formats

I've suggested that instructions, orders, or directives can best be given in an interview context. The same characteristics that make the instructional interview useful also apply to the more traditional interview situations. There are five types* of interviews that are especially important in managerial communication: (1) *performance review,* (2) *counseling,* (3) *reprimand,* (4) *grievance,* and (5) *exit* interviews.

---

*I do not deal with employment interviewing because the focus of this book is on *internal* organizational communication, not interaction with nonmembers. The principles presented here are, of course, relevant to employment interviewing. There are many books available that specifically address recruiting interviews.

The Performance Review:
How Am I Doing and What Do I Do Next?

A poorly prepared or improperly conducted performance review can undo in an hour all the good manager-employee relationships that have developed over a period of months or even years. On the positive side, the effective appraisal session can clarify expectations and objectives for both parties and can provide a base for a supportive, mutually beneficial relationship.

Management theorists agree that periodic performance reviews have proved vital to the management of people. Ideally this type of interview combines information giving and information getting. It is not talking *to* subordinates, it's talking *with* them. The manager's role is and must be that of an evaluator but it should not be judgmental in matters going beyond the work context. "Order accuracy in your work group needs to be improved" would normally be appropriate in an appraisal interview. "You need to get a haircut and stop living with your girlfriend" would probably be out of line.

Purposes of the performance review. Norman Maier cites several purposes for the performance review interview: (1) to let employees *know where they stand,* (2) to *recognize* good work, (3) to communicate to subordinates *directions* in which they should improve, (4) to *develop* employees in their present jobs, (5) to develop and *train* employees for higher jobs, (6) to let subordinates know the direction in which they may make *progress in the organization,* (7) to serve as a *record* for assessment of the department or unit as a whole and show where each person fits into the larger picture, and (8) to *warn* certain employees that they must improve.[4]

Ideal climate. The interviewer should strive for a climate of objectivity—evaluating the subordinate's work while avoiding irrelevant judgments about personal characteristics. Tact and skill are required but touchy job-related issues should be addressed head-on. Don't expect the dialog to always be warm or pleasant. Many things discussed in the performance review are hard for most people to talk about. Occasionally confrontations will arise. These should be expected.

Obstacles. Certain attitudes on the part of the manager can set the stage for failure. Among these are:

(1) Failure to accept the subordinate as a person, unconditionally. A fundamental respect for the worth of people is required for effective performance appraisals to take place. This does not mean that the manager accepts the subordinate's behavior or value system. It means, instead, that

the subordinate's potential and intrinsic worth to the organization is implicitly assumed.

(2) Being overly concerned with why the subordinate behaves as he or she does rather than with what can be done to improve is another unproductive managerial attitude. Overemphasis on specific causes tends to lead to the making of excuses and to rationalization by the subordinate. When this approach is carried too far, we find the manager playing amateur psychologist. Diagnosing a psychological condition and giving it a label such as "poor self-image," "lack of aggressiveness," or "too hot-tempered" can lead to self-fulfilling prophecies. Once we have identified a problem in such a way we are likely to see more and more evidence that supports our diagnosis as correct. We will selectively pay attention to examples of "hot temper" or apparent lack of self-assurance so we can say, "Aha—just as I thought!"

(3) A third attitudinal problem is an underlying belief that appraisal sessions should be used to punish the employee. If you find yourself thinking, "Wait till his performance review—I'll get that SOB then," you are missing the point. Review sessions based in confrontation are seldom productive.

Performance reviews categorize people's behaviors and make judgments about behaviors in light of organizational needs. Some people, of course, feel uncomfortable being so evaluated. Perhaps this accounts for satirical guides to appraisal categories like the one on the next page found circulating in one company:

The article, "Nonevaluative Approaches to Performance Appraisals," by Les Wallace (p. 163), discusses practical communication techniques that can make your employee performance reviews more effective. It addresses one of the most common weaknesses in the appraisal system: the creation of employee defensiveness rather than performance improvement. In one extensive study cited by Redding,

> researchers found that the typical employee reacted defensively about 54 percent of the time when criticized. Moreover, constructive responses to criticism were *rarely* observed ... Finally, and most significant of all, the actual on-the-job performance suffered ... on those very items to which the bosses had paid special attention."[5]

The intelligent manager would do well to pay special attention to the creation of a supportive climate conducive to information sharing as well as evaluation.

Counseling Interviews

When an employee is experiencing specific, personal difficulties—rather than a general pattern of performance which would be dealt with in an appraisal interview—a counseling interview may be in order. Counseling

Guide to Employee Performance Appraisal

Performance Factors	Far Exceeds Job Requirements	Exceeds Job Requirements	Meets Job Requirements	Needs Some Improvement	Does not meet Minimum Requirements
Quality	Leaps tall buildings with a single bound	Must take running start to leap over tall buildings	Can leap over short buildings only	Crashes into buildings when attempting to jump over them	Cannot recognize buildings at all
Timeliness	Is faster than a speeding bullet	Is as fast as a speeding bullet	Not quite as fast as a speeding bullet	Would you believe a slow bullet?	Wounds self with bullet when attempting to shoot
Initiative	Is stronger than a locomotive	Is stronger than a bull elephant	Is stronger than a bull	Shoots the bull	Smells like a bull
Adaptability	Walks on water consistently	Walks on water in emergencies	Washes with water	Drinks water	Passes water in emergencies
Communication	Talks with God	Talks with the angels	Talks to himself	Argues with himself	Loses those arguments

sessions can address matters such as marriage difficulties, drugs or alcohol dependence, or inability to cope with stress. Although personal problems may not have directly measurable impact on work performance, they can lead to serious organizational problems if unattended. You as a manager are certainly not expected to have the solutions to these problems, but it sometimes becomes necessary to confront the more obvious situations, lend a sympathetic ear, and know the procedures for referrals to professional help where appropriate.

Purpose of the counseling interview. The counseling interview addresses and seeks resolution to employee problems, often of a personal nature, which may have eventual impact on the organization if left untreated.

Ideal climate. Trust would be the key word in describing a productive climate for counseling. The manager must assure the employee that strict confidentiality will be observed and that this counseling will have no detrimental effects on the subordinate's opportunities on the job. The climate should also be *permissive*—the employee should feel free to introduce any subject for discussion without fear of offending, alienating, or embarrassing the interviewer. The words and nonverbal cues of the interviewer should be *nonjudgmental* and approach should be *nondirective*—that is, the employee determines what subjects will be considered. It is important that the manager feels a sense of empathy—"is able to sense the feelings and personal meaning of the interviewee as though he or she personally were experiencing them."[6] The atmosphere should be unhurried if possible.

Obstacles. Most managers are not professional counselors. Most tend to get impatient with the often time-consuming and frequently discouraging process of counseling people with problems. It costs a lot of time and therefore money. Often professional counselors are preferable. These may be in-house psychologists in larger organizations or, in many cases, the manager can do the most good by recommending—strongly—that the troubled employee seek professional advice outside the organization. If a productive worker can be salvaged, the time and effort is, of course, justified.

Reprimand Interviews:
The Gentle Art of Chewing Out an Employee

The survival and growth of any organization requires order. Organizational discipline which brings about unity and order is not a natural condition of human groups. Rather it grows out of the behavior of its leaders. Responses to members who violate norms of order determine what further behaviors will be deemed acceptable. When individuals act in ways that are blatantly destructive to organizational functioning, simply ignoring their behavior in hopes that it will go away may not work. The reprimand interview can and should be regarded as an opportunity to turn around unacceptable behaviors. It must be followed by positive recognition when improvement materializes.

As with the performance review, some managers hold underlying assumptions which are *counterproductive* to the reprimand situation. Among these are certain failures to recognize the limitations within which the manager must work. They go wrong when there is

(1) A failure to recognize that discipline implies rules, not personal desires. The belief that a manager has legitimate authority to reprimand those who violate his or her personal sense of what should be, without regard to whether or not organizational rules have been violated, is a misconception. Management has no "divine rights" to act above or around organizational law.

(2) A failure to remember that discipline implies *correction* of error and a belief that it is unnecessary to be specific in citing violations. Some managers mistakenly feel that all they really owe employees is to tell them they're "wrong-headed."

(3) An overemphasis on "who's to blame" rather than "what's wrong." This tends to arise from an implicit and oversimplified belief that there is a single cause for any given malady.

(4) A failure to recognize the need for equitable treatment for all subordinates. Some managers feel that they can make an example of one violator while ignoring similar behaviors of others.

(5) A belief that one's supervisory rights extend to robbing a person of his dignity. Some managers assume a legitimate right to humiliate employees.

There is probably no quicker way for a manager to open mouth, insert foot than to commit one or more of what George Odiorne lists as the "Seven Deadly Sins of Reprimanding":[7] *

1. *Failure to get facts.* Be sure you have all the facts before leaping. Don't accept hearsay evidence, or go on general impressions.

2. *Acting while angry.* Don't act while you've lost your temper. Be calm in your own mind, and as objective as possible in making a decision to reprimand. Ask yourself, "Is it possibly my fault that the error or violation occurred?"

*From the book, *How Managers Make Things Happen* by George Odiorne. © 1961 by Parker Publishing Company, Inc., West Nyack, New York, 10994.

3. *Let person be unclear of offense.* Let the person know the general charge, and the specific details of the offense. Don't allude to general complaints, or refuse to give details.

4. *Not to get the other person's side of the story.* Always let the persons have their full say about what happened and their reason why they did what they did. There may be mitigating circumstances, conflicting orders, or even orders you gave unclearly which were at fault.

5. *Backing down when you are right.* Compromise and understanding are virtues, but once you've decided and announced your decision it is a mistake to relent. It merely indicates you were wrong in your first decision, and you'll lose the effect of your reprimand.

6. *Failing to keep records.* Disciplinary reprimands should always be recorded in the personnel folder of the person. This becomes part of the work history of the person and provides evidence in the event of further disciplinary requirements. In many cases people who were known to be unsatisfactory employees over the years have been reinstated after discharge because the company could produce no evidence that the person had ever been told of his shortcomings.

7. *Harboring a grudge.* Once the reprimand has been administered and any sanctions or punishments administered, don't carry a hostile attitude forever after. The person required discipline and received it. Assume now that they are starting with a clean slate and let them know that you consider it a thing of the past.

The effective manager who puts aside counterproductive attitudes and avoids Odiorne's deadly sins has successfully clarified the real reason for the reprimand interview.

Purpose of the reprimand interview. The reprimand interview attempts to correct inappropriate behavior.

Ideal climate. Reprimands should always be handled in private. There need be no special efforts to reduce anxiety or equalize nonverbal power positions, but conversation should be measured and unemotional. A concerted effort to avoid highly judgmental or emotion-loaded terms should be made. Keep the transactions on the adult level. Never reprimand while upset, angry, or after a three-martini lunch.

Obstacles. Most managers hate chewing out people. This is normal. We'd prefer to maintain amiable relationships, and reprimands make that difficult. The subordinate's defensiveness—his need to justify what he's been doing—may make it hard to change behavior. Personal dislike can color the reprimand and make it unfairly harsh. There is always the danger of counteraccusations and even coming to physical blows if a participant is

unduly offended. Long-term interpersonal relationships can be inaltera-
bly damaged.

A final comment about the reprimand. Although it is sometimes necessary to rebuke others' behaviors, we should afterward show an increase
in our concern for that individual so that he or she does not see us as an
"enemy." Be quick to reinforce performance improvements which follow
the reprimand. Both you and your subordinate will then look back upon
the experience as a useful one.

Grievance Interviews: A Reprimand in Reverse

Although a subordinate cannot generally chew out his boss, he can make
known his views of organizational neglect or errors. In many organizations, the grievance procedure is formalized through labor unions or other
internal employee representatives. The interview type discussed here is
less formal and may logically precede the filing of a formal grievance. In
this sense, if well handled, it can provide an early warning of potentially
more serious industrial relations problems. The grievance interview
should be regarded by management as an information-gathering opportunity. Don't take it as a personal affront.

Purpose of the grievance interview. The grievance interview provides a
subordinate with a format for airing a complaint to higher management.

Ideal climate. It should be recognized that status and power difference
between the employee and the boss may make it difficult for the subordinate to express his or her views. This is not likely to be comfortable for
the grievant. Since the information he or she will provide can be potentially valuable to the organization, attempts to create a relaxed atmosphere are usually worthwhile. A friendly greeting or light remark may
help break the ice and make the exchange more pleasant and productive.
As with the reprimand, there should be an opportunity for both sides of
the story to be aired. Participants should avoid "blowing off steam" and
leveling personal attacks and should keep their exchanges on the adult
level, maintaining a problem orientation.

Obstacles. As with the reprimand, there exists the possibility of emotional
blowups that can only be counterproductive. When either participant is
bent on vindication or on destruction of a relationship, serious long-range
problems can arise.

Exit Interviews: More Than Parting Shots

One of the most frequently overlooked interview situations is the exit interview. I have left a number of jobs in my career and can never
remember having an effective exit interview. On a few occasions I could

have provided some useful information which, if acted upon, could have reduced later turnover problems. Often it is the exit interview which provides us with the opportunity to "get it with both barrels"—get our most candid (although perhaps not most pleasant) feedback. The mature manager will welcome this unique opportunity for data gathering.

Obstacles. James Lahiff suggests several obstacles to successful exit interviewing:

> In the exit interview the interviewer is confronted with a number of unique obstacles to frank disclosure of reasons for leaving the job. A feeling of suspicion on the part of the interviewee is one of them. It is natural for him to wonder why, all of a sudden, has the company gotten interested in his thoughts and feelings. Another obstacle is presented by the interviewee's desire, often unspoken, to get a favorable recommendation from his employer. Another possible explanation for the interviewee's hesitancy to give reasons is his wish to keep a "foot in the door" by departing on a pleasant note and hence making it possible to return to this employer should his plans for the new job go awry.[8]

Special features. To maximize the value of the exit interview it is important to talk in specifics. The skillful interviewer will probe general comments to get past abstractions and down to concrete examples. If the employee cites "supervisory methods" as a reason for leaving, be sure to find out *which* methods and *which* supervisors. Encourage him to name names and cite specific cases. You don't have to agree with what's being said but you should bring it out into the open.

Timing of the exit interview is very important. It should be near the employee's last day but not on the termination date when he is going through other separation procedures and paperwork.

Don't expect this interview to be particularly pleasant. It may be uncomfortable to hear negative things about your organization and maybe even yourself. But the information gathered can be of considerable value. Leave the interviewee on a pleasant note and thank him or her for the candid comments. In a very real sense, these people are doing the organization a favor.

One side benefit of the exit interview is that it can provide important information about labor market conditions which may help the organization remain competitive in terms of salaries, benefits, organizational opportunities for advancement, and the like. Departing employees are happy to tell you about their new position if you'll simply ask.

Figure 5-4 summarizes the interview types discussed and salient characteristics of each.

Type of Interview	Manager's Purpose(s)	Key Dimensions of "Ideal" Climate	Key Obstacles to Authentic Communication	Payoff if Successful
Performance review	Evaluation of work Feedback to employee Development of employee Recognition Warning	Objectivity Fairness Avoid personal attack	Judgmental nature Defensiveness Barriers created by personality differences	Motivated worker Properly directed efforts Work improvement Positive outlook toward organization Optimism re: opportunities Clear understanding of "Where I stand"
Counseling	Address personal problems Solution or referral to professional help	Trust/ confidentiality No fear of reprisals Low defensiveness Permissiveness Nonevaluation Nondirective questioning	Managers not trained Impatience Reluctance to take time High cost with indirect payoff to the organization	Problem solution or referral for professional help Avoidance of organizational problems "Rehabilitated" worker Appreciative and loyal organization member
Reprimand	Correct inappropriate behavior	Privacy Objectivity Adult level Address facts not personality	Emotionalism Defensiveness Reluctance to face offender Fear of reprisals	Corrected behavior Clarification of expectations and laws
Grievance	Receive complaints which may be correctable without formal union or legal intervention	Same as for reprimand Attempt to develop air of mutual problem solving rather than confrontation	Same as for reprimand	Grievance solved Confrontation or legal action avoided
Exit	Determine reasons for employee's decision to quit Gain constructive criticism about employees' work conditions Learn about relative benefits in the labor marketplace	Nondefensive No persuasion to reconsider Reduce power/ status differences Seek objective information	Employee's desire to avoid "burning his bridge" by being highly critical Manager's reluctance to hear unflattering facts about himself/herself or others in the organization	Valuable feedback from the employee's viewpoint Good feelings between ex-employee and organization Data about labor market conditions

Figure 5-4 Summary of interview types

Specific Questioning Techniques

The quality of an interview is largely determined by the kinds of questions asked. There are several types of questions, each useful under certain conditions. (The term *question* is used here to refer to any comments made to elicit responses from the other party. Sometimes these take the form of statements or even commands.)

The Closed-Ended Question

This type of question allows the respondent little or no freedom in choosing his or her response. Typically there are only one or two possible answers. Examples: "Were you on duty last Tuesday at 11 A.M.?" "Have you completed the Tompkins report yet?" "Do you prefer the standard retirement program or the optional annuity?" "How long have you been on your present job assignment?"

Use of closed-ended questions permits the interviewer to exercise close control over the exchange. It is, of course, the technique most frequently used by trial lawyers or police interrogators to elicit specific information. Its drawback is that it rigidly structures the interview and, while often efficient, it may completely miss opportunities for exchanging other relevant information.

One of the major features of closed-ended questions is that they can be manipulative. Respondents often feel frustrated when they must choose between one or two possible answers without opportunity to clarify. Sometimes, however, these kinds of responses are the most useful to the questioner. Yet in most business interviews, the nondirective, open-ended question makes more sense.

The Open-Ended Question

This kind of question allows the respondent maximum freedom in responding by imposing no limitations on how it may be answered. Examples: "How do you feel about our new benefits package?" "What would be a better way to handle that job?" Often open-ended questions are in the form of statements such as, "Tell me about your experiences with the new machine," or "Explain that procedure to me."

This questioning approach can produce considerable information which may not come out in closed-ended questioning. Its success depends in large part on the respondent's ability to express his or her thoughts clearly. Often it is necessary for the interviewer to seek additional clarification by using "probes" when the respondent is talking in generalities or using unfamiliar language.

The Probing Question

Frequently used with open-ended questions, the probe asks the interviewee to clarify a response for better understanding. Examples: "Could you give me an example of something he did that upset you?" "What do you mean when you say she's 'ruthless'?" "Why do you say that?" "Exactly what happened?"

Probes serve to move the language level down the "ladder of abstraction" toward more concrete, specific, and descriptive terms. Another function of the probe is to determine intensity of feelings. Let us say that an employee has just commented that his supervisor is "tough to get along with." How tough is he, you wonder. Try a sympathetic or mildly supportive probe like this: "I've heard several comments like that recently." Drop your comment and wait. This often encourages the interviewee to elaborate. "I think he must be having trouble at home. He comes to work first thing in the morning grouchy as a bear." Now some useful information may be coming to the surface.

The Leading Question

While a probe leads the respondent to elaborate his or her own feelings, the leading question typically suggests the response desired. Occasionally this is helpful, but more often it is a block to the emergence of authentic information. Examples: "I'm interested in your work experiences over in R & D. Did you learn a lot while you were there?" (Obviously the interviewer wants the respondent to say "yes.") "Don't you think it's important for our people to be informed on policy decisions?" (Of course. What else could be said?) When the question is prefaced by a remark that suggests the kind of answer the interviewer would like to hear, the range of responses is reduced. "I've always loved the exciting atmosphere of the newsroom. How do you feel about your job there?" (I love it, just like you do!)

The Loaded Question

Loaded questions also suggest the desired response to the interviewee primarily through the use of highly emotional terms. Sometimes it is used to determine a respondent's reactions under stress, and when a questioner seeks to "crack" the reluctant respondent. The interviewee who is wearing a mask or acting a role may be angry enough to let his true feelings or honest answers emerge. This questioning strategy is illustrated by a "Doonesbury" cartoon that appeared several years ago when Nelson Rockefeller was being confirmed as Vice President:

Interviewer: "Mr. Rockefeller, could you tell us your net worth?"
Rockefeller: "This is not the proper forum for such discussion."
Interviewer: "How about just a rough figure?"
Rockefeller: "No, not at this time."
Interviewer: "Sir, the reason we ask is that what with the Agnew incident, the American people want to be reassured that the new Vice President isn't in it just for the money."
Rockefeller: "Are you KIDDING? I'm worth over *four billion dollars!*"
Interviewer: "Thank you, sir."[9]

Other examples of loaded questions rely heavily on the use of dysphemisms—terms that conjure up negative associations. Examples: "How can you work effectively in this *filth*?" "Some of your coworkers claim you're a *racist*." "I've heard reports that you are satisfied with *slipshod* quality. How would you respond to that?" He'll probably respond by attacking. The loaded question, like a loaded gun, occasionally goes off in the wrong direction. Avoid them under all but the most desperate circumstances.

The Hypothetical Question

This questioning technique can be used to see how a respondent might handle a particular situation. It is helpful in identifying creativity, prejudices, ability to conceptualize the "big picture," and other respondent characteristics. Examples: "If you were promoted to sales manager, what programs would you implement?" "Put yourself in the shoes of the production manager and suggest some approaches he might take." "Let's assume that you discovered one of your employees intoxicated on the job. What would you do?"

The hypothetical question can be very useful but be careful of underlying meanings which may arise in your receiver's mind. If you ask an employee to picture himself as a manager often enough there is bound to be some implication that he is being considered for promotion. If the promotion doesn't, in fact, materialize, he may be pretty disappointed.

The Mirror Response

This technique is useful in getting at underlying meanings which might not be clearly verbalized. It also helps to maintain the communicated exchanges on a we're-both-adults level rather than a parent-child relationship. Example: An employee says to her supervisor, "Some days I'd like to take that damn typewriter and throw it." The first reaction might be, "You throw that and you'll pay for it" or some other such critical response. The underlying meaning of the employee's statement would remain suppressed and antagonism toward the supervisor may emerge. The supervisor using a mirror response might say something like, "That typewriter makes you angry?" Now the opportunity is presented to explain the source of her anger. "The stupid thing continually vibrates. It's driving me nuts." Supervisor: "You find the vibrations annoying?" Employee: "Yes, can it be fixed?" Supervisor: "Sure, I'll call a repairman."

Often the mirror response sounds like a rather dull statement of the obvious. But it lays the groundwork for more specific expressions of information from the interviewee. Psychologists find the mirror response especially useful in getting perplexities phrased in specific terms. The manager in the counseling session may find this technique especially effective since it is nonevaluative and nonthreatening.

In a well-executed interview, each question is asked for a particular reason. The interviewer needs to lead, to keep a step ahead of the respondent. Don't worry about pauses in the interview. It is not necessary to fill every moment with the sound of someone's voice. It makes more sense to think through each question and response rather than to babble on with ill-defined and meaningless exchanges which do little to create understanding.

When the interview is over, the manager should summarize briefly and be sure the respondent understands what to do next. There should be a clear agreement about the outcome of the discussion. Often, testing for such understanding is appropriate. We might ask, "Okay, Tom, now what did we agree must be done next?" Each participant may explain the interview's outcome as he or she sees it. Then close on an upbeat and express gratitude for the employee's participation in the interview.

Telephone Usage:
Like We Say Down at the Phone Company, "Hello"

The telephone has the media advantages of speed, efficiency, and relatively low cost. It permits one-with-one communication when participants are geographically separated. It provides, as the telephone company ads say, "the next best thing to being there." In fact the only significant drawback to the phone is that it does not permit most nonverbal communication cues.

There are approximately 39,498,000 business telephones in the United States today. The total number of telephone calls made (both business and personal) exceeds 640 million per day. That's an average of three calls for every man, woman, and child in America. The increasing volume of calls from people outside the organization as well as from other employees makes telephone equipment and use a major item of expense.

This expense must be measured both in terms of payments to the telephone company and, more importantly, in the expenditure of people time. It is imperative that we use the phone and our time efficiently. To do so, think about some of the unique characteristics of this medium.

Each telephone call creates interactions where people are operating blind—without the visual feedback which helps us assign meaning to language and events. To compensate for this lack of visual stimuli, we draw many conclusions from what we hear alone. And what we hear includes some very subtle cues such as tone of voice, word choice, pauses, and the occasional mumble. Two of the most irritating telephone use errors are the failure to respond to statements made by the other party, and cutting off the conversation. Here is a recent personal example.

As I was driving to work, I noticed a sports car in an automobile dealership's lot. Sensing that such a car would do a lot for my image, I decided to inquire about it. I dialed the telephone number of the dealership, and here is how the conversation went:

A receptionist with a pleasant voice identified the name of the dealership and I asked to "speak with someone in used cars, please."

"One moment please," she replied.

After a pause, a male voice said, "Hello?"

"I'd like a little information about the Triumph TR-6 you have on your lot," I said.

"Ya mean the red one?"

"Yes, could you give me some information on that car?"

The male voice hesitated for a moment and said, "I think that's the owner's daughter's car. She's been driving it around. Let me check and see what the deal is on it."

There was a long pause, and while I waited on hold, another male voice came on the line, "Hello? Hello?" to which I replied, "I'm already being helped." There was a *click* as he hung up without acknowledging my explanation.

After a few more minutes, the original salesman came back and said, "Yeah, I think that's the car the boss's daughter's been driving around. If they sell it, they'll want an arm and a leg for it. I think it's a '75 model."

"Well would you check and let me know if it is for sale?" I asked again, getting a bit exasperated.

"Just a minute, I'll ask the owner" he said as he put me on hold again. After a few moments the salesman again picked up the phone and abruptly said, "The owner says it's not for sale."

As I began to say "Thanks for the information" I was cut off in midsentence by the click of the phone as he hung up.

I doubt that this salesman was being intentionally rude, but he sure came across that way to me. Failing to acknowledge the comments of someone else with a "thank you," or "okay," or "you're welcome" can make your conversation sound very abrupt and discourteous. Frankly, in this case, I was irritated to the point where I would definitely *not* do business with this dealership.

Placing and Receiving Your Own Calls

Some business people think it's a sign of status to have their secretary place telephone calls for them. It probably does convey some of that and most of us wouldn't expect it to be any other way for major corporate or governmental leaders. But when a supervisor or mid-level manager has his secretary place a call to someone at the same or higher organizational level, it can be poorly received. One businessman reports his experience of calling a company president this way.

> I'll never forget the first time I called Jack on the telephone. I asked my secretary to get him, and when she said, "Mr. Sordoni's on the line," I picked up and said, "Hello."
> "Are you calling me?" asked Jack.
> "Sure," I said.
> "Then how come your secretary called me?"
> "I just asked her to get you on the phone," I said, beginning to squirm.
> "So I could wait on the phone while you get ready to let me have the honor of hearing your voice? You're calling *me*, remember?" And he hung up.
> I dialed his number again myself, and sure enough he answered. No switchboard, no secretary, just Jack Sordoni, president of the Commonwealth Telephone Co., saying, "This is Sordoni."[10]

When you place your own calls you are telling your listeners that you value their time. If you are willing to personally make the effort to contact another person they are likely to feel more obligated to expend some effort and converse with you.

Each individual should be encouraged to answer his or her own phone unless they are engaged in face-to-face conversation which should not be interrupted. Routine screening of calls by a secretary or receptionist often creates resentment in the caller. The indiscriminate use of "May I say who's calling?" is often recognized as a dodge—an opportunity for the manager to decide if he wants to talk to the caller or not. Even if the call legitimately cannot be accepted the phrase may well be considered a snub. Your secretary or receptionist should serve to expedite communication, not impede it.

The appropriate way to answer a business call is by simply stating your name. Use of a Mrs., Miss, Ms., Mr., or Dr. may sound a bit stand-offish.

A male employee might simply use his last name, unless this would be confusing to the caller. In my own case, my short last name used alone seems to throw off the caller so I say "Paul Timm" when I pick up the phone. (A friend of mine used to have all kinds of problems when he'd answer with only his last name. His name was Paul Waite. His greeting was often followed by a very long pause.)

Use of "May I help you?" following your name is a pleasant way to start off a conversation. This approach tells your caller (1) whom they are speaking with and (2) that you are ready to converse with them. So let's be sure we are ready.

It's Your Dime, Start Talking

This wisecrack, occasionally used by TV hoodlums and teenagers, reminds us of a need for efficiency in telephone use. Although small talk is sometimes useful to create a personable relationship between callers, I've found that the more important the organization member, the more efficient he or she is with phone use. The real pro can make a call very concise without being curt.

When placing a business call, plan ahead, preferably in writing. What is the *purpose* of your call? What information do you want to get or give? Is this likely to be a good time to call? Jot down the key questions or items you need before you begin to dial. And be sure to identify yourself immediately—business people don't like playing "guess who?"

Since your voice is the only source of informational clues available to your listener, be especially careful to speak clearly into the mouthpiece. Make sure you provide verbal feedback to your caller so that he or she knows you're still there. Long pauses can be disconcerting. One good way

to convey appropriate voice is to visualize the other person and then visualize yourself talking directly to that person, perhaps using a few gestures as you talk to feel more comfortable and natural.

Diagnosing Your One-with-One Communication

Evaluating our effectiveness in one-with-one communication requires (in order of importance) an open mind and some systematic way of observing our own behavior. An excellent approach is to tape record or, better yet, videotape record ourselves in actual interactions with others. Then play back the recorded conversation and systematically analyze it. It is very helpful to have several other "observers" also analyze the tape to pick up points you may have missed and to confirm correct evaluations. (If it is awkward or impossible to tape real interview situations, the use of role-playing in training sessions can be the next best thing.)

Professor G. Hugh Allred has developed a technique for systematically observing interactions between two people which he calls Allred's interaction analysis (AIA). Although this is only one of many such techniques, it is a good one for our purposes. It is simple to learn and provides meaningful data.

Allred describes two categories of responses we can make to others: vertical interaction and horizontal or level interaction. *Vertical* interactions are those which move us *away from* authentic, open, and constructive relationships. Such movement makes one or both parties unhappy, angry, defensive, and so forth. The relationship is not strengthened. Vertical interaction is marked by competitiveness, distrust, and a reduction in the probability of mutual understanding. The vertically oriented communicator seeks to create win-lose situations and is prone to playing psychological games, often from a manipulative position, which prevent him or her from having authentic, honest relationships.

Horizontal interactions do just the opposite. Such communicative exchanges *foster positive relationships* and the development of understanding. Horizontal interactions can convey unpleasant information, but when they do so, it is in a constructive manner. Interactions are straightforward, candid, and yet sensitive to the needs of others. The horizontal communicator tends to operate from Theory Y assumptions, having a high regard for the self-worth of others.

In the chart in Figure 5-5 Allred identifies ten categories of communication behavior—five of which indicate level or horizontal interaction, four of which are vertical, and one which is a miscellaneous category. Take a few moments to study this table and identify types of behaviors likely to occur between individuals. It is important that you can identify

Categories	Typical Behaviors
Level	
1. Voices observations:	Reveals ideas concerning self, other(s), the relationship, events, or places; expresses observations; gives facts or opinions; asks rhetorical questions; answers other person's questions; gives feedback
2. Seeks meanings:	Asks questions, seeks to understand or clarify; asks for a response to accuracy of higher perception; hypothesizes or guesses about meanings (may misunderstand, but works respectfully to understand)
3. Discusses alternatives/ commits:	Discusses/questions alternatives, explores/ questions their advantages and/or disadvantages; negotiates; agrees; consents; commits self to a decision (influences, using democratic methods)
4. Gives support:	Says such things as "please go on"; praises; makes encouraging statements; identifies, recalls and/or predicts others' feelings; accepts others' feelings; makes empathic statements; paraphrases others' feelings or thoughts
5. Discloses emotions:	Reveals own feelings concerning self, other(s), the relationship, things, events, or places; discloses negative feelings in a courteous manner

Allred, G. Hugh. *How to Strengthen Your Marriage and Family.* Provo, Utah: Brigham Young University Press, 1976.

Figure 5-5 Allred's interaction analysis of communication style

these kinds of behaviors and categorize them from memory before going into an observing situation.

Following are some sample expressions illustrating the five horizontal categories. The individual who uses such expressions in a sincere way will promote mutual understanding. Become familiar with these expressions and add others of your own. Strive to become sensitive to such relationship-building comments.

Category 1. Voices Observations:

- The way I see it ...

Categories	Typical Behaviors
Vertical	
6. Solicits attention:	Monopolizes the conversation; interrupts; overtalks; talks with little or no request for feedback; competes for focus; draws attention to self at expense of others; brags; parades self; seeks service from others; seeks to obtain approval or to please
7. Bosses/punishes:	Bosses; lectures, preaches, orders, makes intrusive statements; talks down to others; fights to/for control; justifies oneself; talks angrily; whines; cries; complains of being ill; uses autocratic methods to control the other person(s); punishes; belittles; demeans, blames; uses faultfinding, sarcasm, ridicule
8. Creates/maintains distance:	Talks in an aloof, uninterested manner; wanders; talks continuously or incongruently; uses humor that creates distance; ignores feelings; intellectualizes; talks like a robot; agrees automatically with little or no assertion of self; talks evasively; avoids closeness
9. Surrenders	Gives in; abandons own wants, wishes, and desires (often as a result of another person's vertical behavior, classified in category 7); gives up
Miscellaneous	
10. Silence/confusion:	Silence; more than one person talking at a time

Figure 5-5 (cont.)

- It seems (or appears) to me that ...
- As I recall, it was ...
- My thinking may change but I now believe ...
- I could be wrong but ...
- My perception is ...
- As best I can figure it out ...

    (Add yours) _____

    _____

    _____

Category 2. Seeks Meanings:

- I'm not sure I understand ...
- Help me to clarify this in my mind ...
- What do you mean when you ...?
- How do you feel when I ...?
- Let me see if I understand what you mean ...

(Add yours) ――――――――――――――――――
――――――――――――――――――
――――――――――――――――――

Category 3. Discusses Alternatives/Commits:

- What do you think we could do ...?
- How do you think we could solve the problems of ...?
- What options do you see as open to us ...?
- As I perceive it the advantages are ... while the disadvantages are ...
- Let me see if I understand. The alternatives available seem to be ...
- Which alternatives do you prefer ...?
- I prefer alternative ...
- I am willing to ... if you are willing to ...
- As I understand it, you agree to ...
- I agree to ...

(Add yours) ――――――――――――――――――
――――――――――――――――――
――――――――――――――――――

Category 4. Gives Support:

- That's interesting. Continue with that line of thinking ...
- Please go on ...
- You work hard ...

- That was respectful of you . . .
- Your efforts at . . . really helped out . . .
- I appreciate your suggestions . . .
- That's a good idea . . .
- I like the way you handled that . . .

    (Add yours) _____

    _____

    _____

Category 5. Discloses Emotions:

- I feel that we have a good relationship . . .
- It's a good feeling to . . .
- It's a real sense of satisfaction to . . .
- I am confused/sad/angry/hurt when . . .
- I feel confident when . . .
- I feel uncomfortable expressing myself when . . .
- I enjoy working with you when . . .
- It's really awkward to say this . . .

    (Add yours) _____

    _____

    _____

These examples illustrate the five level or horizontal categories of interactions. The next four categories reflect types of vertical interactions—those which tend to be counterproductive to successful communication. Many vertical interactions are characterized by nonverbal cues such as failure to maintain eye contact, the appearance of boredom, and indications of disinterest or disapproval. Nonverbal cues also play a part in conveying horizontal communication behaviors, but their impact seems to be greater in vertical interactions. The category descriptions in Allred's chart provide a number of examples of vertical communication behaviors. Jot down other examples of such relationship-disrupting behaviors you've experienced.

Once you have memorized the categories you are ready to systematically observe your communication behavior. Using a simple tally sheet, record the number of each category of remarks you hear in the tape of your one-with-one interaction. You may want to tally the behaviors of both participants or only your own behavior. Figure 5–6 is a tally sheet for scoring interactions.

A number of types of information can be gleaned from interaction analysis. As we can see, percentage of tallies in each category can readily be calculated, indicating horizontal and vertical interaction habits. We

Date _____
Topic _____
Observer _____

Categories	Subject A	Subject B
Level		
1. Voices observations	1 Sum ____%____	Sum ____%____
2. Seeks meanings	2 Sum ____%____	Sum ____%____
3. Discusses alternatives/ commits	3 Sum ____%____	Sum ____%____
4. Gives support	4 Sum ____%____	Sum ____%____
5. Discloses emotions	5 Sum ____%____	Sum ____%____
	Total L ___%L___	Total L ___%L___
Vertical		
6. Solicits attention	6 Sum ____%____	Sum ____%____
7. Bosses/ punishes	7 Sum ____%____	Sum ____%____
8. Creates/ maintains distance	8 Sum ____%____	Sum ____%____
9. Surrenders	9 Sum ____%____	Sum ____%____
	Total V___%V___	Total V___%V___
Miscellaneous		
10. Silence/ confusion	10 Sum ____%____	Sum ____%____
	Total of sums ___	Total of sums ___

Figure 5–6 Interaction analysis scoring guide

might also compute a talk ratio score between the interviewer and the interviewee. This may reveal an unrealized domination of the conversation. In Figure 5-7 we see some additional ways of calculating scores from the AIA.

Over a period of time it might be very useful to portray progress through the use of a graph. After repeated observations of interview situations, the percentage of different types of responses can be plotted on a graph such as the one shown in Figure 5-8. This particular figure shows encouraging progress in the reduction of vertical interactions. A similar chart could show increase in level or horizontal actions indicating a healthier communication between this employee and those she or he deals with. Such calculations might also be useful in determining the effectiveness of certain communication training programs by applying analysis of interactions between people before and after training has taken place.

The reliability of interaction analysis is improved when several people observe or listen to the same conversations. The scores then tallied by

---

1. Percent in Each Category

   Calculate the sum of tallies and the percentage of time spent in each category for each partner.

   $$\% = sc/T$$

   where sc = sum of tallies in a given category and T = the total from all categories for a given participant.

2. Manager/Employee Talk Ratio Score

   To calculate the manager/employee talk ratio score, divide the total of sums for the manager by the total of sums for the employee. A score of 2.5 means that the manager talked 2½ times more than the employee. A score of .50 means that the manager talked half as much as the employee.

3. Manager's or Employee's Level/Vertical Ratio Score

   To calculate the level vertical ratio score, divide the sum of manager/employee tallies in categories 1 through 5 by the sum of manager/employee tallies in categories 6 through 9.

   Level   =   total of sums for categories 1 through 5
   Vertical =   total of sums for categories 6 through 9

   Level/vertical score of 5.0 means that the person observed made 5 level responses for every vertical response.

Figure 5-7 Calculations for scoring the AIA

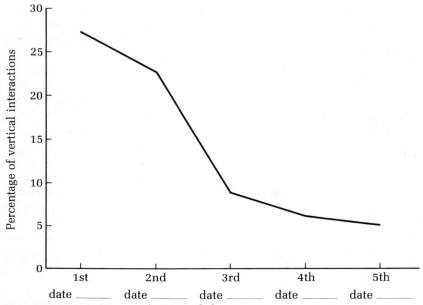

Figure 5-8 Interaction analysis trend sheet

each observer can be compared using a simple formula to determine their intercoder reliability.

$$\text{Reliability} = \frac{A}{A + D}$$

where A = tallies in agreement among observers and D = tallies in disagreement among observers.

Interaction Category	Observer 1	Observer 2	Agree	Disagree
1	12	15	12	3
2	5	4	4	1
3	20	18	18	2
4	6	8	6	2
5	4	3	3	1
6	10	8	8	2
7	5	5	5	0
8	2	0	0	2
9	0	0	0	0
10	5	4	4	1
		Totals:	60	14

Figure 5-9 Calculations of intercoder reliability

Applying the formula to the data in Figure 5-9, we can calculate the reliability as follows:

$$R = \frac{60}{60 + 14} = .81$$

The higher the reliability figure, the better. A typical cutoff point for research is at .70. Anything below that reflects observer inconsistencies which should cause the researcher to question the validity of his or her approach. If you get low intercoder reliability, check first to see how well your observers understood the categories of interactions. It takes time and practice to get used to this analysis approach but it can be very fruitful once learned.

Although preparation for observing and the time used in the actual observations is rather costly, real improvements in communication effectiveness can be plotted in a meaningful way using this diagnostic procedure.

Some Other Thoughts About One-with-One Communication: READINGS FOR CHAPTER 5

Nonevaluative Approaches to Performance Appraisals[11]

By Les Wallace

For the supervisor who deals predominantly with high-quality performers, the performance appraisal process is not a frightening one. But though every supervisor would prefer to work in this type of situation, most find themselves working with employees whose performance ranges from unacceptable to exceptional and therefore having to adjust their discussion appraisals to fit each employee. For the supervisor untrained in counseling on different kinds of performance problems, adjusting his or her approach to fit the needs of high-quality and lower-quality performers can be difficult—and in some cases, disturbing.

For example, during a conversation I had recently with one production supervisor, he bragged that he thoroughly enjoyed writing and discussing the performance evaluations of his 26 subordinates. But two weeks later this same supervisor was back on the phone, frantically asking for advice on how to handle a poor performer and complaining that this difficult appraisal was taking all the fun out of the process.

So this is the most common appraisal situation for supervisors: They have employees at all levels of performance—good, poor, and mediocre—and they have personnel forms and management strategies by the dozens to follow in carrying out the appraisals. But the biggest problem for supervisors is that employees react to the appraisal on a personal level, *not* on a professional one. And unfortunately many supervisors lack the communication skills to get the essential message of an appraisal across to the employee without causing bigger problems in the process. As Douglas McGregor pointed out some 20 years ago, problems with adequate performance appraisals revolve around "a normal dislike of criticizing a subordinate and perhaps having to argue about it and a lack of skill needed to handle the interview."

Questions for the Supervisor

Now that we have some idea of the problems supervisors face when they enter the appraisal arena, let us ask: What communicative approaches could a supervisor use to more clearly communicate to an employee what he or she must do to improve performance? At the same time, what approaches would help reduce employee hostility and defensiveness and also generate cooperation in working to improve performance?

Most suggestions that have been made for improving the appraisal process *deal more with the theory of performance appraisal and the goals of a supportive exchange rather than with concrete skills and examples on how to achieve these goals.* Whether one looks at the problem-solving interview, the participative approach to performance improvement, or the supportive-defensive climate contrasts, these are all theories suggesting a particular approach but omitting the specifics on how to put the approach into practice. As one personnel manager remarked to me recently, "Who could disagree with such ideas? I just want my supervisors to learn how to make these theories useful."

Consequently, I want to make some specific suggestions for the supervisors who have to face their subordinates eyeball-to-eyeball during performance appraisals. By utilizing such suggestions, a supervisor should be able to get much more mileage out of the performance interview and be able to approach counseling sessions with high, medium, or low performers with the same self-assured attitude.

Evaluative vs. Descriptive

First, what are the conditions in an interview that lead to employee defensiveness rather than to the more desired cooperation? Of course, we know that when a supervisor exhibits *evaluative*—that is, blame-putting—behavior, this will almost always elicit defensive behavior from an employee. But beyond this, the more personal, negative, and accusatory the evaluation by a supervisor is, the more hostile and defensive the employee will become.

The way to avoid evoking such defensive behavior is by using *descriptive* rather than evaluative approaches to the problem. By simply stating, in a nonpersonal way, that a problem exists and then describing that problem, the supervisor makes it possible for him and the employee to arrive at a joint decision—or even an employee-initiated decision—on how to resolve the problem. Some examples of both evaluative and descriptive comments that the supervisor might make in performance appraisals are as follows:

Evaluative	*Descriptive*
"You simply can't keep making these stupid mistakes."	"We're still having a problem reducing the number of scrap parts produced."
"Bob, you're tactless and undiplomatic."	"Some people interpret your candor as hostility."
"You're too belligerent when dealing with co-workers."	"Many employees perceive your attitude to be belligerent."
"The accident was your fault. You ignored the safety regulations on that project."	"This accident appears to involve some differences in interpreting the safety regulations."

Using descriptive, nonevaluative comments in the appraisal interview, the supervisor is signaling to the employee that he wants to analyze and discuss a problem, not look for an "easy out" or demean the employee. In such a way, the interview can then move on to the more constructive elements of the appraisal process.

The Threat of Control

Sometimes in a performance appraisal the supervisor will make the mistake of assuming a *control* communicative stance. This stance emphasizes the superior's power over the subordinate, and it reflects an error in the supervisor's thinking because, like most of us, employees don't like to feel dominated by another person and react defensively when they do.

Opposed to the control stance is *problem orientation,* which is a communicative approach designed to allay an employee's fear and increase his sense of personal control over whatever problems exist. Problem orientation conveys a respect for the employee's ability to work on a problem and to formulate meaningful answers to the problem. Examples of these approaches that could be found in many performance appraisals are:

Control	*Problem Orientation*
"John, I'd like to see you doing X, Y, and Z over the next week."	"John, what sort of things might we do here?"
"I think the only answer is to move you over by Margaret on the line."	"One possibility is to have you move over by Margaret on the line. Is that likely to help?"
"I think my suggestions are clear, so why don't you get back to work?"	"Let's think about these possibilities and get back together next week, after you've thought about them."
"Arthur, you'd better tone down your criticism of co-workers."	"Arthur, this sensitivity among co-workers requires us all to try for a bit more diplomacy."
"You've got a problem here."	"We've got a problem here."
"I've decided what you must do to reduce mistakes."	"Have you thought about what we might do to reduce mistakes?"

Problem-oriented communication will generate more options for solving the problem by encouraging the employee to make suggestions and inducing a mutual concern for controlling the problem, *not* the person. Furthermore, problem orientation can also improve the appraisal discussion by aiding both parties in truly listening to what the other is saying, by encouraging both parties to offer suggestions, and by fostering a more open climate in which disagreement is not only tolerated but invited.

Neutrality and Empathy

Just as inimical to the appraisal process as control is a supervisor's *neutrality*, which is usually interpreted by the subordinate to be disinterest about the outcome's impact on the employee. Like the rest of us, employees tend to be more guarded and less communicative when their superior lacks real concern over their welfare. Ironically, supervisors who display such unconcern often are very interested in their employees, but they don't realize that some of their actions are interpreted by subordinates to be indicative of a neutral attitude.

Showing *empathy*, on the other hand, signals a clear concern for the employee and his situation. But to get this message across unequivocally, the supervisor must make an overt communication attempt—one that the employee cannot help but notice. Some examples of neutral and empathetic approaches are:

Neutrality	**Empathy**
"I really don't know what we can do about it."	"At this point I can't think of anything, but I know where we might look for help."
"Well, that's one way to look at it."	"I get the feeling you don't feel confident with our original plan."
"I didn't know that."	"I wasn't aware of that. Let me make sure I understand."
"Too bad, but we all go through that."	"I think I know how you're feeling. I can remember one experience I had that was similar . . ."
"You could have something there, but let's get back to the real problem."	"I'm not certain I understand how that relates to this problem. Why don't you fill me in before we go on?"

Supervisors communicate empathy best when they listen well, when they follow up on suggestions, and when they inquire how employees feel about questions and solutions raised in the appraisal. Displaying a concerned sympathy about difficult problems will also signal an understanding attitude by the supervisor and encourage the employee's cooperation.

A Need for Equality

In any discussion between a superior and a subordinate—whether the distinction has been brought about by legal, financial, or emotional factors—if the superior uses communicative techniques that emphasize his *superiority,* this will correspondingly induce feelings of unworthiness in the subordinate. For example, the supervisor who keeps the subordinate at arm's length by stifling feedback and overtly rejecting his help only increases the employee's need to defend himself and prove his self-worth.

However, the supervisor who tries to reduce the distance between himself and his employees encourages the employees to feel they share a certain *equality* with the supervisor. This feeling can be aided by a supervisor showing concern for sharing information with the subordinates and gaining their input in solving problems. Some characteristic differences between superiority- and equality-evoking comments can be seen in these examples:

Superiority	*Equality*
"Bob, I've worked with this problem for ten years and ought to know what will work."	"This idea has worked before. Do you think it might work in this case?"
"Well, I don't think I need to give you all the background. Why don't we just do it this way for now?"	"Arthur, you might find some of the background information helpful, so let me fill you in a bit."
"The supervisory staff thought this policy through pretty thoroughly."	"We've only discussed this policy at the supervisor's meetings and I'm interested in your reactions and thoughts."
"Oh, the rationale should be of no interest to you people on the line."	"Let me go over the rationale with you. Some of you might find it helpful."
"Look, I'm being paid to make these decisions, not you."	"I'll have to make the final decision, Mary, but why don't you get your suggestions in to me right away?"

Of course, workers generally do not expect complete equality from their bosses, nor are they interested in sharing the supervisor's responsibility for decisions that are implemented. Instead, they appreciate a supervisor who shares information with them, seeks their feedback, and listens to their concerns. Such communicative approaches can easily be made part of the performance appraisal process, and the supervisor should see a more enthusiastic and less defensive attitude among employees as a result.

Who Has the Last Word?

Supervisors who emphasize *certainty* tend to phrase everything they say as if the last word had been said and a decision could never be changed. Such a dogmatic stance makes the employee feel that there is no need to offer new ideas or different solutions to the approach already outlined by the supervisor. This in turn leads to loss of morale and a feeling of powerlessness among employees.

But a supervisor who shows *provisionalism* demonstrates that he is willing to have his own ideas be challenged in order to arrive at the best possible solution to a problem. Communication that encourages analysis and investigation can restore enthusiasm and provide a challenge for employees that might otherwise not be there. Examples of certainty and provisionalism are:

Certainty	*Provisionalism*
"I know what the problem is, Tom. I don't think I need another opinion."	"I have a view of the problem, Tom, but I'd be interested in your perception."
"This is the way we're going to do things. Period."	"Let's try this for a couple of weeks, then we can reconsider, based on that experience."
"I've thought these suggestions through thoroughly, Mary, so let's not waste time arguing."	"I've tried to think these suggestions through pretty thoroughly, Mary. Can you see anything I may have left out?"

Let us add that a provisional approach does not deny the fact that decisions have to be made and policies adhered to. Instead, it suggests that decision making is an alterable process and that employee suggestions and creativity are important to and appreciated by management.

From Appraisal to Analysis

These examples of communicative approaches are all designed to help the supervisor reduce the defensiveness of employees, and as such they all share a common base: They emphasize a process of *analysis,* rather than *appraisal,* of employee problems. Of course, inherent in any analysis is some evaluation of past performance, but hopefully the employee will be led to approach this evaluation from a more participative and less defensive position. Instead of being told simply that he or she failed, the employee's help is enlisted to pinpoint problems and come up with answers to problems. An analytical process should emphasize the employee's personal worth and demonstrate the confidence that management has in the employee's ability to learn from and improve on past behavior.

Unfortunately, not all employees will be able to recognize and resolve their performance problems, no matter what supervisors do. But the supervisor who validates an employee's worth through supportive, nonevaluative communicative techniques will at least find that his suggestions to the employee on improving performance are received with less defensiveness and anger. Similarly, supervisors I have talked with report several other benefits that result from using nonevaluative communicative techniques, including:

- Improved creativity in solving problems, due to greater employee input.

- Less supervisory reluctance to discuss employee performance problems.

- A clearer understanding by the employee of why and how he or she needs to change work behavior.

- The growth of a climate of cooperation, which increases individual and group motivation to achieve performance goals.

- Greater employee self-reliance, which improves the individual's ability to diagnose problems and react quickly with less supervisory assistance.

The supervisor who implements constructive, nonevaluative appraisal techniques becomes more of a leader and teacher to his or her employees and less of a disciplinarian. This also means that employees come to see the supervisor as more of a friend and helper who assists them when their own ideas and abilities run short and less a management representative looking for a scapegoat on whom to blame poor performances. Of course, implementing such techniques does not essentially change the performance appraisal; a supervisor's suggestions and high performance goals remain part of the process. But constructive communicative techniques, when correctly used, should make the process a little less painful and intimidating for all concerned.

There Is an Alternative to "Shape Up or Ship Out!"[12]

By Anliko Galambos

Is there any one right way of communicating with subordinates? Probably not. There are as many different techniques of successful communication as there are managers and employees. However, one especially helpful way—it seems to me—to create effective communication is outlined in the theories and ideas put forth by noted psychologist Carl Rogers. This method of communication he characterized as being "helping relationships," and it can be applied quite easily and productively to a work environment.

A helping relationship—whether between two persons or among a group of persons—is that kind of relationship in which at least one of the parties has the intent of promoting the development, maturity, and adequate functioning of the other. To do this successfully, the helping person must always be aware of—and avoid the use of—those behaviors that tend to create barriers of communication rather than help the subordinate. Such behaviors would include evaluation and judgment, emotionalism, autocratic rejection, and remoteness and distance. On the other hand, the helper should strive to show such positive attitudes as understanding, empathy, respect and unconditional acceptance, genuine interest, and sensitivity and openness.

When effectively transmitted to the subordinate, these positive attitudes will result in the creation of an environment in which the individual feels free, trustful, friendly, understood and appreciated, and independent. This in turn reduces the need for fear and defensiveness, false fronts can be dropped, and an expression of true feelings will become possible.

The point of all this effort on the manager's part is to create a less emotion-charged atmosphere in his department. Then when an employee problem crops up, he doesn't have to fall back on such pejorative techniques as telling the subordinate, "Shape up or ship out." An example of how this improved atmosphere can help the manager accomplish his tasks is shown in the following example. The situation is that manager *Brook* must correct a "people problem" his department is having with new employee *Larry*. Brook wants to keep Larry and retain his good will, but he also realizes that a change in Larry's attitude is essential.

> *Mr. Brook:* Hi, Larry. Come in and have a seat. You're right on time. I didn't think being punctual meant anything to anyone nowadays. I appreciate it.
>
> *Larry:* Well, I know from my own experience—especially with women—what it feels like to be kept waiting, and it's not exactly pleasant.
>
> *Mr. Brook:* Ha! Brings back the good old days, doesn't it? Before you were married? Yes, that goes for me too. But I guess, looking back on it, at the time the waiting was really worth the anticipation. Like in the ketchup commercial.
>
> *Larry:* (smiling) For some of them it was really worth it, but for some others, well . . .
>
> *Mr. Brook:* Sounds like we dated the same girls. By the way, how's your family?
>
> *Larry:* No problems, sir. They're just fine.
>
> *Mr. Brook:* You know, that reminds me. I meant to ask you this before. Eveyone calls me Bob. Is there any particular reason why you don't? Something wrong with my first name?
>
> *Larry:* (laughing) I guess I feel there's too much familiarity in calling people by their first names. They say familiarity breeds contempt, and I believe it. Respect is very important for me, especially having respect for the person I work for.
>
> *Mr. Brook:* In that case, do you mind if I call you Larry?
>
> *Larry:* Not at all. It fits the situation perfectly.
>
> *Mr. Brook:* Okay, then, Larry, let's get down to business. You're probably wondering what this meeting is about. The truth is, you've been with the department now about four months, and I simply wanted to find out if you're satisfied, dissatisfied, or what. Are things turning out the way you thought they would?
>
> *Larry:* I guess so. More or less.
>
> *Mr. Brook:* Any particular problems? Boy, I sound like a doctor!
>
> *Larry:* None that I can think of.
>
> *Mr. Brook:* Really? I know I certainly don't agree with everything that happens around here. I've got my own boss, and he likes to run things different from the way I would. What about you? Do you have any particular qualms about me?
>
> *Larry:* (hesitantly) No.
>
> *Mr. Brook:* Then let's say if you were in my shoes, is there anything you would change?

Larry: If you put it that way, sure, I'd change a few things. Some things appear to me to be old-fashioned, outdated. But then, it's easy for me to criticize. I see everything with a fresh eye.

Mr. Brook: I wouldn't call it criticism, Larry. Or maybe I'd call it constructive criticism. As the poet said, no man is an island. Everyone needs feedback. And you're exactly what we need around here—someone with a fresh, new approach. So let's make a deal. You write up a list of the things you feel should be changed, and I'll be happy to discuss them with you, one by one. How's that?

Larry: (surprised) What can I say?! It's more than a fair deal.

Mr. Brook: Okay. Now that I'm out of the way, what about the others? Listen, I remember how difficult it was for me when I first came here. Everyone considers you an outsider for a long time. All the clerks, secretaries, bosses, colleagues— you name it—they all have the same attitude toward you at first. I don't know if you've had the same experience, but it's a rough stage to go through. Cigarette?

Larry: Yes, thanks. (pause) I know what you mean. Everybody can be pretty tough. I keep asking myself, why are they doing this to me?

Mr. Brook: Who do you mean? Who's doing what to you?

Larry: Everyone! All those people you mentioned—but especially the first and second levels—they're just not cooperative. They resent me and I can never understand why. If you say they did the same thing to you, that makes me feel better. But the truth is, I really don't know what to do about it; I don't know how to change them.

Mr. Brook: Okay, let's take this step by step. How exactly are the others uncooperative? In what sense?

Larry: They don't help me! They don't give me the data I need. I have to look through the files a hundred times before I can find anything because no one is willing to tell me where to look. I'm not familiar with things, and they take advantage of that. I don't know who has what information, everyone gives me the runaround, and I end up wasting half my time. Do you really want specifics?

Mr. Brook: No, but you've confirmed some things that I've been feeling for some time. Tell me, Larry, are you cooperative with these people?

Larry: I haven't had the chance to be. I'm new around here, so how can I help them?

Mr. Brook: For one thing, you've got a very good reputation for knowing all there is to know in some fields; that reputation followed you from your former department. Don't these people ever approach you with questions that you could help them with?

Larry: Well . . .

Mr. Brook: Let's say, for instance, the DCF method—you're an expert in that. Or capital budgeting—that's your field too.

Larry: Yes, I suppose they have approached me in those areas. The truth is, I'm not very willing to help out. I do to them what they do to me.

Mr. Brook: Don't you think there's a vicious cycle taking place here?

Larry: Sure, I realize that. But, you see, when I asked for a transfer into this department, I had a good reason. Once I was here, I told myself there was no way I was going to let the same thing that happened to me in economics happen to me here.

Mr. Brook: What exactly was that?

Larry: To make a long story short, I did almost nothing while I was there except teach, give lessons, and tell them how to do projects. Everyone was always coming to me for help. And what happened? Two idiots got promoted over my head, all on *my* brains. It just wasn't fair. And that's when I asked for the transfer.

Mr. Brook: Then you think there's a risk involved in helping people?

Larry: Yes, sir, that's exactly what I think.

Mr. Brook: Tell me, Larry. Now you're 23, one year out of college. How old are the others who got promoted?

Larry: I guess Tremblay is 50 and Jackson is about 35—maybe 40. Okay, they're a lot older and they've been with the company longer. But does that mean they can take advantage of me?

Mr. Brook: What makes you think they took advantage of you? Why do you think you were hired in the first place?

Larry: I know what you're getting at, Mr. Brook. But if I was hired because I'm smart, don't you think I should get some reward for it?

Mr. Brook: Yes, I do, and I think you did. We knew about your reputation, and that's why we were so eager to have you in the department. You were able to get out of an unpleasant situation and had no problems in finding another job. How many people could have done what you did?

Larry: I suppose you're right, in that sense.

Mr. Brook: And what about those two men? Do you think that after being with the company for so long, they suddenly became smart—so to speak—without their boss realizing what was going on?

Larry: No, I guess not. Maybe they got promoted for other reasons. But it was an emotional situation, and I guess I couldn't really handle it.

Mr. Brook: You were talking about respect before. Who do you think merits respect?

Larry: People who are intelligent, people who have something to offer.

Mr. Brook: Do only intelligent people have something to offer?

Larry: (pause) No, there are others. I guess people who know every single damn detail about this company. And God knows there's a lot of detail. Those are the people with seniority. That's the answer you were looking for, isn't it?

Mr. Brook: I'm not looking for any answer.

Larry: Okay, then you want to show me that people who have dedicated so much of their lives to one company should be eligible for some sort of reward.

Mr. Brook: How long do you think you'll be with the company?

Larry: I have no idea. (pause) Maybe you're right. I don't seem very dedicated right now, do I? Perhaps seniority has value in its own right. No, I take that back. Ignore the perhaps.

Mr. Brook: Now if you really tried, Larry, to see things in another way, do you think you could explain—not rationalize—what really happened?

Larry: Looking back on it all, I don't know exactly. Maybe I was hired at a time when there was some form of reorganization; that seems to be a recurring disease in this company. Or maybe the promotions of those two men were long overdue. Who knows? In any case, I guess it's egotistical of me to think that they got promoted because of me. But that's my problem. I guess you realize that by now. Maybe I'm in too much of a hurry and too competitive as well.

Mr. Brook: There's nothing wrong with either of those attitudes.

Larry: I think there is, if they become self-defeating. You know that vicious cycle you were talking about? That's what I mean. And I was talking about trying to find some way to change *them*. It sounds stupid now.

Mr. Brook: What do you mean, Larry?

Larry: I mean maybe *they* are the ones reciprocating *my* uncooperativeness. But the truth is, in the other department, it was my first job and I had a rotten experience with the people over there.

Mr. Brook: Or maybe you simply misinterpreted what happened?

Larry: It's beginning to look that way, isn't it? Look, Mr. Brook, I've been sitting here and thinking about all this.

Mr. Brook: And?

Larry: I just figured out that if I could drop this hassle with the people in the department and somehow make a complete turnaround, it might be to my advantage too.

Mr. Brook: Sounds interesting. How does it work?

Larry: Well, first, I wouldn't be wasting so much time on useless things, and, second, I'd probably like the atmosphere a lot better. Basically, I like people. I just haven't worked long enough to really know how to behave. Well, I guess I have some time yet to do constructive work and also prove I'm capable of doing things other people can't handle.

Mr. Brook: If that's the case, I'm sure you'll see the rewards of having a different attitude. (pause)

Larry: Well, Mr. Brook, your phone messages must be piling up. I'd better go. Is there anything else?

Mr. Brook: Not unless you can think of something.

Larry: By the way, I promise you won't get anymore complaints about me.

Mr. Brook: I never said I did.

Larry: No, you didn't. But you didn't have to. Have a good day. And I'll have that list to you by tomorrow.

Questions for Further Thought

1. Think of a one-with-one communication you participated in recently. It may have been an interview such as those discussed in this chapter or a discussion with someone in your family, a friend, or a sales representative. What specific behaviors or exchanges can you recall which led to developing understanding? What things tended to "turn you off" to that person? Be as specific as possible.

2. Recall recent praise or criticism you received on your job or in school. How did you feel and respond? Was it Type 1 or Type 2? Give some examples.

3. What could you do to create an appropriate climate for a performance review interview? A counseling interview? A reprimand interview? An exit interview? A grievance interview?

4. Listen to yourself in conversation with others. To what extent do you tend to use closed-ended questions? How could open-ended questions be more useful? Give some examples.

5. Use the diagnostic technique suggested in this chapter to evaluate a tape-recorded interview. Get someone else to observe and tally the same tape. Calculate intercoder reliability. How did you do? How could the participants improve communication?

6. Carefully reread the article by Galambos, "There Is an Alternative to 'Shape Up or Ship Out' " and analyze the kinds of one-with-one communication going on there. What questioning techniques are used? What are the results of these? Apply interaction analysis to it.

7. Review the telephone conversation the author had with the car salesman (p. 152). What went wrong? How could the salesman have responded to improve the quality of the interaction? What are your pet peeves about telephone manners? How can we avoid coming across poorly to others on the phone?

Notes

1. Robert Townsend, *Up the Organization* (New York: Alfred A. Knopf, 1970), p. 184.
2. "Productivity Gains from a Pat on the Back," *Business Week*, January 23, 1978, pp. 57–58.
3. James H. Morrison and John J. O'Hearne, *Practical Transactional Analysis in Management* (Reading, Mass.: Addison-Wesley, 1977), pp. 118–121.
4. Norman R. F. Maier, *The Appraisal Interview: Objectives, Methods and Skills* (New York: John Wiley and Sons, 1958), p. 3.
5. W. Charles Redding, *Communication within the Organization* (New York: Industrial Communication Council, 1972), pp. 54–55. Redding is describing research by Herbert H. Meyer, Emanuel Kay, and J. R. P. French, Jr., "Split Roles in Performance Appraisal. *Harvard Business Review* 1965 (January–February), 43, 1, pp. 123–129.
6. James M. Lahiff, "Interviewing for Results," in *Readings In Interpersonal and Organizational Communication* (Boston: Holbrook Press, 1973), pp. 341–342.
7. George S. Odiorne, *How Managers Make Things Happen* (West Nyack, N.Y.: Parker Publishing Company, Inc., 1961) pp. 138–139.
8. Lahiff, *op. cit.*, p. 345.
9. Quoted in S. Bernard Rosenblatt, T. Richard Cheatham, and James T. Watt, *Communication in Business* (Englewood Cliffs, N.J.: Prentice-Hall, 1977), p. 213.
10. Jim Lavenson, *Selling Made Simple* (New York: Sales Management, 1973), pp. 59–60.
11. Reprinted, by permission of the publisher, from SUPERVISORY MANAGEMENT, (March 1978) © 1978 by AMACOM, a division of American Management Associations. All rights reserved.
12. Reprinted, by permission of the publisher, from SUPERVISORY MANAGEMENT, (November 1977) © 1977 by AMACOM, a division of American Management Associations. All rights reserved.

Recommended Readings

Many books and articles are available to help us improve our one-with-one communication. Several that I have found useful are listed below.

Rosenblatt, S. Bernard, T. Richard Cheatham and James T. Watt, *Communication In Business*. Englewood Cliffs, N.J.: Prentice-Hall, 1977. Chapter 10, "Communication with One: Interviewing." This 25-page chapter covers types of interview situations, structuring the interview, and a condensed listing of suggestions for participants that is very well done.

Morrison, James H. and John J. O'Hearne, *Practical Transactional Analysis in Management*. Reading, Mass: Addison-Wesley, 1977. This is an exceptionally straightforward and clearly written book for the practicing manager. Written by two business professionals, it strips away the academic jargon and provides the clearest explanation of TA applications to management I have seen. Very enjoyable reading.

Fear, Richard A., *The Evaluation Interview* (2nd ed.). New York: McGraw-Hill, 1973. The author is especially strong on the psychological aspects of interviewing strategies and questioning techniques. The orientation tends toward the interviewing of perspective employees but can readily be adapted to other situations.

Lahiff, James M. "Interviewing for Results," in *Readings in Interpersonal and Organizational Communication* (3rd ed.), pp. 395–414, eds. Richard C. Huseman, Cal M. Logue, and Dwight L. Freshley. Boston: Holbrook Press, 1977. This is more recent than the Lahiff article cited in the chapter, note 6. Well written and concise, it covers important strategies for planning and carrying out effective interviews in several contexts.

Scott, Dru, "Motivation from the TA Viewpoint," *Personnel*, 51 (January–February 1974). A concise and very readable application of transactional analysis to management by a well-known consultant.

CHAPTER 6

INTERACTIONAL COMMUNICATION
Meetings and Conferences

The fifty salesmen from all over the country arrived the night before; but it's nine-thirty a.m. when the nine o'clock sales meeting begins. The welcome message from the president was naturally delayed until he arrived. But waiting for the president is not only polite, it's smart, and what's a half hour? Actually, for fifty salesmen it's only 25 hours or three full days of selling time.

"Gentlemen," says the president, "good morning and welcome to home base. I don't want to take any of your valuable time, but I asked Artie if I could say a few words before you get down to work. I know it will be a fruitful and busy day for you men who are, in my opinion, the most important asset this company has. Welcome! I'm sorry I can't spend time with each of you, but I've got to catch a plane." And the president leaves, smiling to the applause of the salesmen who give him a standing ovation, principally because the chairs haven't arrived yet.

"Men," says Artie the sales manager, "you've heard from our president; now let's get down to business. But to use the time until the tables and chairs arrive, I have a few housekeeping announcements. The coffee break will be at 10:30 instead of 10:00, so make a note of that on your agenda."

"I didn't get an agenda," one of the salesmen says.

"Those of you who got an agenda can share it," says Artie and continues.

"Although our president has already set the tone of this meeting, I want to add a few words before we get down to the nitty-gritty. You men represent the finest sales organization in our industry. Why? Because your company demands, and *gets*, selling skills and performance above and beyond the call of duty. That's why at this year's meeting there are so many new faces."

"Artie, a question please?" comes a plea from one of the salesmen.

"Sure, Joe, fire away. But before you do, for the benefit of the new men, let me tell them who you are. Men, Joe is our man in the Midwest who is doing one helluva job. Really knows the market, his customers, and the product. How long have you been knocking 'em dead for the company, Joe? Four years? Five?"

"Eight months," says Joe.

"Oh, yeah, right. Now, what's the question?"

"Are we going to talk about the competition today?"

"What the competition is doing right now, you worried about?"

"What they're doing now," says Joe.

"You tell me. What is the competition doing now?" Artie is smirking.

"What the competition is doing right now," says Joe, "is calling on our customers while we're in this sales meeting."*

You're Probably Wondering Why
I Called You Here Today

Try asking someone in your organization "Been to any good meetings lately?" and you're likely to hear "You've got to be kidding!"

Many of us spend too much time in meetings. A lot of organizations have too many meetings and/or ineffective meetings. The frustration or cynicism of those who have too long suffered through overuse or misuse of the "group method" is reflected in statements like: "A meeting brings together a group of the unfit, appointed by the unwilling, to do the unnecessary." Or, "When all was said and done, a lot was said but nothing was done." Meeting is something we do instead of making decisions.

Why is it that for many managers, meetings lead to feelings of restlessness, disgruntlement, and raw boredom? Do meetings have to be a burden for the manager? What can be done to make the group process live up to its potential to produce high quality outcomes? To get at these questions, let's first look at qualities of small group communication as used in organizations. Meetings have some very significant potential advantages as well as some serious limitations.

Advantages of Meetings

One characteristic of organizations as social systems is called the principle of equifinality. In the language of systems theory this means that "a system can reach the same final state from differing initial conditions and by a variety of paths."[1] In the language of clichés it means there is more than one way to skin a cat. The problems or issues facing the organization could have come about by a number of different sequences of events and they can be solved by an equally diverse number of remedies.

*Jim Lavenson, "Meeting the Issue" from *Selling Made Simple*. Reprinted by permission from Sales & Marketing Management magazine. Copyright 1973.

Since our range of experiences as individuals is limited, it follows that several individuals working on the same problem, issue, or decision can bring more relevant information to light. Each participant represents a unique frame of reference—an individual way of looking at the world—that may provide the key to a better solution. The usefulness of these multiple inputs is, of course, limited by the extent to which the group can assimilate the different viewpoints. To be successful the group must develop procedures for (1) sharing ideas and perspectives so that members may build upon one another's insights, and (2) resolving differences among group members which, if left unattended, would prevent eventual consensus. In short, groups must work under conditions which foster the creation of understanding. When successful, the group process creates a synergistic effect with the end product being greater than the sum of its parts; a better decision will be reached than if the same people worked individually on the problem.

The nature of the group's task seems to affect the degree to which a group's decision or solution is likely to be superior to an individual's. Research by behavioral scientists suggests that there are certain kinds of problems groups handle best. For example, studies show that groups are better at solving problems that require the making of relative rather than absolute judgments. That is, groups can better solve problems for which there is no single correct solution and for which solutions are difficult to verify objectively. This finding suggests that groups are not much better than individuals at handling certain kinds of clerical tasks (such as adding up columns of figures) or at solving logical "brain teasers" which require purely rational answers.[2]

In addition, groups tend to be more successful than individuals working alone when the task problem is complex, having many parts and requiring a number of steps to solve. Groups also seem better at dealing with controversial or emotionally charged problems.

When the problem is relatively simple or noncontroversial, or involves routine logical tasks, group discussion does not seem to offer significant advantages. Many organizational problems, however, are clearly candidates for the group process.

There is a second significant advantage to the discussion method which, in many cases, may be even more important than the quality-of-the-solution advantage discussed above. There is likely to be a higher degree of commitment to a group decision and a concomitant reduction of hostility or resistance to it (at least among those who participated). Similarly, if those who participated are commissioned to execute the decision, they will do so more faithfully because they understand why and how the decision was reached. In one well-known study conducted more than thirty years ago, Coch and French[3] compared workers' resistance to technological changes in their jobs. It was found that when workers participated in discussions regarding the implementation of the changes there was significantly less resistance than among workers who were excluded from such participation. Since this important study in 1948, other research has shown similar results among American workers in industrial settings.

The significant advantages of meetings and conferences, then, are (1) potentially better quality decisions and (2) less resistance to implementation. There are, however, situations under which these advantages can be completely negated by inept or unqualified participants and leaders as well as by some other factors we'll discuss later.

Disadvantages of Meetings

Important disadvantages to the use of meetings can be categorized into three general types. First, meetings in many organizations have become substitutes for action.

Some managers use meetings as an alternative to making the tough decision. They confuse the appearance of such activity with the hard reality that nothing substantive is happening. Consciously or unconsciously they hope that by "talking it out" they can avoid the unpleasant necessity of acting. For some, it's hard to face up to the fact that filibusters are seldom a useful management technique.

Either the participants or the leader who initiates a meeting or committee can create a problem by not really wanting to take action. By definition, an operating meeting calls for participation, involvement, and commitment of each member. To gain commitment from members of a group, management has to inspire some motivation to participate. It makes little sense to assign a person to a committee without regard to his or her values or interests. Don't assume that because we recognize a problem which should be handled by a committee others recognize and feel the same need for resolution. Too often, I've seen people drafted for committees that cope with issues the participants couldn't care less about. They have nothing personally vested in the issue. The likelihood of such people being productive participants is low. They may go through the motions but their only motivation for reaching a conclusion will be to simply get it over with.

A second general disadvantage of meetings is that they cost a lot of money. A group decision inevitably takes more time than an executive action. And the costs of such time can really add up. Example:

Meeting Cost:
Estimated salary of meeting participants
    (@ $20,000 year) hourly $10
Number of participants 12
Hourly meeting cost $120

A four-hour meeting can easily cost $480 in labor costs alone. And this figure doesn't include the added "burden" costs for each employee—

fringe benefits, social security, medical coverage, etc. This is only the *direct* labor cost. There is also a ripple of psychological costs to the individual and the organization which can be staggering. Work done by subordinates is often tied up while the boss is in conference. Talented employees engage in monotonous busywork while waiting for direction from the absent leader. Customers are annoyed that they cannot talk with the conferring manager. The manager's work piles up, so that she is faced with a stack of phone messages to respond to, a pile of papers in her in-basket, and a half dozen people who just have to talk about some pressing matter when the conference ends. Each of these kinds of things saps psychic energy from people who are paid to use their minds. And each of these things adds to the aggravation of the manager's job. For some, it is likely to end in turnover, depression, or worse. The question is one of opportunity cost: what could the meeting-goer do with that time if he or she weren't tied up in the meeting? The manager must ask, "Is this meeting worth it?"

In addition to these disadvantages of meetings—their use as substitutes for action and their potentially enormous cost—the group process can result in _low quality decisions._ I said earlier that one advantage of conferences *may be* higher quality decisions, but there are some situations where the group process may backfire and negate that potential advantage. There are two general situations where this can' occur: (1) when the group members lack sufficient expertise to deal with the problems, and (2) when pressures censor the free flow of information. In the former case, the solution will reflect pooled ignorance. In the latter situation, the quality of the group's decision is distorted by either *groupthink* or *individual dominance* of the process.

The term *groupthink* was coined by Irving Janis to describe a condition of likemindedness which tends to arise in groups that are particularly cohesive. While cohesiveness is normally a desirable condition in groups, it can be carried so far that it becomes counterproductive. This is especially likely when the group has a high esprit de corps and where members' desire for consensus or harmony becomes stronger than their desire for accuracy. Under such conditions critical thinking and the independent and objective analysis of ideas are foregone in deference to a smooth running group. The likelihood of groupthink increases if the group becomes insulated from outside influences and the fresh flow of information. Based on Janis's concept, VonBergen and Kirk describe eight symptoms of groupthink:[4]

1. Illusion of unanimity regarding the viewpoint held by the majority in the group and an emphasis on team play.
2. A view of the "opposition" as generally inept, incompetent, and incapable of countering effectively any action by the group, no matter how

risky the decision or how high the odds are against the plan of action succeeding.

3. Self-censorship of group members in which overt disagreements are avoided, facts that might reduce support for the emerging majority view are suppressed, faulty assumptions are not questioned, and personal doubts are suppressed in the form of group harmony.

4. Collective rationalization to comfort one another in order to discount warnings that the agreed-upon plan is either unworkable or highly unlikely to succeed.

5. Self-appointed mindguards within the group that function to prevent anyone from undermining its apparent unanimity and to protect its members from unwelcome ideas and adverse information that may threaten consensus.

6. Reinforcement of consensus and direct pressure on any dissenting group member who expresses strong reservations or challenges, or argues against the apparent unanimity of the group.

7. An expression of self-righteousness that leads members to believe their actions are moral and ethical, thus inclining them to disregard any ethical or moral objections to their behavior.

8. A shared feeling of unassailability marked by a high degree of esprit de corps, by implicit faith in the wisdom of the group, and by an inordinate optimism that disposes members to take excessive risks.

It is apparent that each of these symptoms of groupthink damages realistic thinking and effective decisions. A combination of several or all of these can be devastating to group effectiveness.

A second type of pressure which censors the free flow of information is _individual dominance._ In many groups, certain individuals become excessively dominant by virtue of their personality, organizational position, or personal status. Other participants become reluctant to interact freely, perhaps feeling that their contributions are of lesser value.

While individual dominance can speed up the decision process, it does so at the cost of a potential reduction in decision quality.

Managers need to be sensitive to how differences in status and expertise as well as communication styles can put a damper on free discussion. And one of the committee leader's chief concerns must be with drawing out the participant who may feel suppressed by other dominating members. I'll talk more about leader responsibilities later.

The point is that hindrances to group decision quality can be caused by lack of group expertise, by groupthink, and by individual dominance.

Still another problem which has been identified by social scientists can affect the quality of group decisions. Cartwright and Zander,[5] two researchers well-known for their studies in group dynamics, pointed out what they called the _risky shift phenomenon._ A series of widely replicated experiments showed that groups tend to make more daring or more risky decisions than individuals working alone. Again, social pressures from within the group result in potentially counterproductive behavior. Risk taking is viewed as a positive personality characteristic which we demonstrate to others as we work in groups.

The potential danger in this is that some groups adopt a "safety in numbers" position and recommend extreme solutions that they wouldn't dream of taking responsibility for as individuals. You end up with a lynch mob mentality.

One final disadvantage of group decision making is simply that it is sometimes inappropriate because of time constraints imposed by the problem. A battle group in combat cannot use participative decision making while the enemy awaits their solution. Similarly, in business, some decisions must be made quickly. To delay a decision may squander a potential competitive advantage or organizational opportunity.

Although advantages and disadvantages must be carefully considered in decisions about conferences or meetings, many such decisions are still likely to come down on the side of continued and even expanded use. *Of what?* Most of the disadvantages can be overcome; they are not inevitable. As Richard Dunsing said:

> "When you accept poor meetings as a fact of life, you are in collusion with many others doing the same thing. In effect, you are aiding and abetting them on clogging the system and in eroding the quality of working life. Managing means changing things that aren't what they need to be. Surprisingly often, it is merely the management of the obvious."[6]

While griping about the overuse or misuse of "those miserable meetings" has certain cathartic value, the real issue is how to maximize the value of needed committees. *purging* ?

Let's first look at the types of committees typically used in an organization and then focus on variables that determine effectiveness of this potentially powerful communication activity.

Types of Committees

There are three general types of committees frequently used in organizations: the *standing* committee, the *special* committee, and the *ad hoc* committee.

Standing committees serve to relieve the manager of administrative burdens and substitute collective judgment for his individual judgment in certain recurrent, noncritical situations.[7] Since standing committees act as a form of work delegation, it would be self-defeating for the manager to act as chairman. The committee membership should be representative of the organization and should be chaired by a ranking member who can comfortably allocate work to others. The work of standing committees is ongoing so long as there is organizational need.

Special committees may be assembled to deal with a single specific issue which cannot be realistically handled via ordinary organizational procedures. Often these situations are too controversial, too complex, or deal with issues of symbolic or highly emotional significance which are simply too important to be handled in a routine manner. When the work of a special committee is done, it should disband. Problems arise when special committees don't disband but become self-appointed standing committees. The manager should ensure that this does not happen unless there is a clear need to "upgrade" to standing status.

Ideally, the organizational leader should assemble the special committee, give it its "charge" in clear unequivocal detail, and step back to let it work. Its membership should include representatives from all factions who stand to be affected by the decision or outcome. This often means a larger than usual number of participants which, in turn, calls for a chairperson who is skilled in parliamentary procedures, is reasonably high in seniority or rank, and, as one writer says, has gray hair. The key to the special committee's effectiveness lies in the degree of clarification provided by the manager who calls it together. His or her instructions should describe the task in detail, indicate clearly what the end product (usually a written report) should be like, and explain what resources are available from the organization. Deadlines and instructions about conditions of secrecy or publicity under which the group should work should also be spelled out. Equally important, once this information is presented to the group, the manager should remove himself from the process except for occasional briefings or further clarification.

Ad hoc committees, like special committees, deal with nonrecurrent, special tasks. They differ, however, in that ad hoc committees typically handle relatively noncontroversial tasks, are smaller in number of participants and do not necessarily represent the views of all organization members. Members should be selected on the basis of interest in and/or competence with regard to the committee's assignment. The group may consist of as few as two members and seldom more than five. Like the special committee, their work should be temporary and they should not develop into standing committees unless the needs of the organization clearly demand this. Typically their work is somewhat less complex than the special committee. Examples of ad hoc committee assignments may be inspecting an item for sale, developing a one-time analysis of office equipment needs, or arranging facilities for a convention or training session. The manager who assembles the ad hoc committee should have no regular involvement in its deliberations.

Figure 6-1 summarizes key points about consulted committees.

	General Purpose of Committee	Examples of Such Committees	Ideal Type of Membership
Standing	relieves manager of administrative burden substitutes collective judgment for individual judgment on recurrent noncritical situations	Safety committee Professional school admissions committee Loan committee of a bank Computerization committee Personnel committee	Widely representative of all departments that may be affected by decisions reached Wide range of organizational rank, personal characteristics
Special	Considers particularly knotty problems too complex, too controversial, or too important to be handled in a regular way Appointed to defer or avoid an otherwise pressing decision To deflect the onus of an unpopular decision or to allay suspicions that have arisen in connection with a particular issue To cope with problems that are intrinsically unimportant but have acquired symbolic significance.	Committees to iron out conflicts between organizational factions Disciplinary action committees Decision appeals or policy review committees	Representative of all relevant shades of opinion and every important faction of the organization which is likely to be affected by the decision
Ad Hoc	Deals with some nonrecurrent, noncontroversial task	Drafting a statement Inspecting an item for sale Arranging convention facilities Surveying organization needs	Compatible with each other Competent with respect to the committee assignment Do *not* need to be representative of organization members.

Figure 6-1 Rules of thumb for consulted committees*

(continued)

*Adapted from Theodore Caplow, *How to Run Any Organization* (Hinsdale, Ill.: Dryden Press, 1976), pp. 59–61.

	Number of Members	Qualifications of Chairperson	Manager's Participation
Standing	5 to 9	Senior to most other members (so can comfortably allocate work to others) Not holding extreme position with respect to committee's task Not someone new to organization who does not understand its informal norms	As ex officio member
Special	10 to 30 (limited only by size of organization's largest conference table)	Manager of considerable seniority Good command of parliamentary procedures Organizational maturity	Should start the committee off with unequivocal charge; describe the group's task in detail; indicate clearly what type of report should be produced; state time interval, resources available, and conditions of publicity or secrecy under which group should work Is kept posted of progress via informants
Ad Hoc	2 to 5	Interested in the assignment	None after group's assignment is given

Figure 6-1 (cont.)

Five Major Elements of the Effective Meeting

The effective manager needs to build some flexibility into his or her approaches to meetings and conferences, for there is no one best way to run all types of meetings. There are, however, five major elements upon which effective meetings are built:

- The goals of the meeting
- The climate of the meeting
- Leadership and the internal workings of the meeting
- The decision strategy
- Post-meeting evaluation and follow-up

Group Goals:
Everyone Knows Why We're Here, Right?

More often than not, wrong! Although the person who called the meeting probably has a pretty good idea of why it's been called, others are seldom so clear. If you don't believe this, try asking everyone in the group to write down specifically why the meeting is being held and compare answers. As we try to work down the ladder of abstraction from general expression of the topic (solving our morale problem) to more concrete objectives (reducing high absenteeism rate among keypunch operators), we introduce a clearer focus to the meeting. It's not necessary to predetermine exactly what all possible goals are before meeting, but it should be the priority activity in the early part of the discussions. Otherwise, how will you know when the job is done? That may be the key question to be answered before setting out to discover solutions.

Although we may come to agree on the discussion topic, committee meetings seldom have just one goal. There are other, subsidiary objectives even when the task seems clear. Sometimes these "hidden agenda" items, real though they may be, are implied but never stated. For individual participants they may include such things as

- getting some "exposure" (i.e., to favorably impress others)
- providing a status arena in which we can assert our power or abilities
- filling some perceived quota for having meetings
- providing a chance to socialize with others
- providing a chance to assert dominance of one group or department over others (or a chance to break that dominance)
- working on leader and participant communication skills
- diffusing decision responsibility so one person won't have to take all the heat if a decision fails
- getting away from unpleasant work duties

By fulfilling such personal objectives as these, the conference can be a genuinely satisfying experience which may motivate additional participation. A good group work experience will go a long way toward reducing employee reluctance to work on future committees.

The three key questions that must be answered early in a discussion are:

- What exactly are we here for?

- What exactly will we have when we've completed our job?

- How will we go about accomplishing our task?

Agreeing on the answers to these three questions is crucial to the effective meeting. If the primary task objective and procedures are never clearly established, participants will never know when they are finished. Then the likelihood of time-wasting, extended meetings increases sharply.

The Meeting Climate

Clarity of goals is a legitimate part of the climate of an organization or group, as discussed in Chapter 2. But several other equally important climate characteristics affect the communication of participants. These are *physical* factors and *interactional* characteristics.

Physical dimensions of climate include such things as room temperature and lighting, presence or absence of distracting noises, odors or interruptions, the arrangement of furniture, and the availability of tools such as chalkboard, paper and pencils, flip charts, and the like. Seating arrangement allowing participants to comfortably talk to each other and to have unobstructed view of others and of visual aids is a must. Often the impressive, large wooden table of the board room is not the best for working meetings. People should feel free to get up, move around, and not be chained to their chairs. Avoid meeting in rooms with auditorium style seating where all participants see is the back of others' heads. Do not seat some people at "power positions" while others are placed in clearly subordinate places. Planning for good physical climate is a preconference responsibility of the leader.

Leadership and the Internal Workings
of the Meeting

For many years social scientists attempted to define specific personal traits or characteristics inherent in individuals that seemed to make them effective leaders. This research approach predominated in the studies of leadership for the first half of this century. The underlying assumption was that leaders are somehow different from other people in the population. If we could but identify what makes them different we would be able to "scientifically" select the best leaders. One of the earliest studies, for example, indicated a positive correlation between a person's height and his or her organizational position. Other studies looked at such attributes as "general intelligence," "self-confidence," "persuasiveness," or "intuition" as these relate to leadership.

Several problems arose from this avenue of study. For one thing, some of the labels for the traits being studied were pretty ambiguous. A more important criticism is that the findings were largely inconclusive when applied to different task situations. An effective sales manager may not be successful as a railroad crew foreman, for example.

Social scientists who came to recognize the importance of the situational variable began to regard the search for universal leadership traits as virtually worthless. But before we write off more than fifty years of research, it may be well to consider a massive review of such leadership literature prepared by Ralph Stogdill. His analysis of almost 300 studies did conclude that leaders, when compared to nonleaders, tended to be more goal-directed, venturesome, self-confident, responsible, tolerant of interpersonal stress and frustration, and capable of influencing behaviors of others. He also concludes, however, that these "characteristics, considered singly, hold little diagnostic or predictive significance. In combination, it would appear that they interact to generate personality dynamics advantageous to the person seeking the responsibilities of leadership."[8]

Perhaps one reason some totally discredit the traits approach to leadership studies is that it seems to imply that either a leader has the desired characteristics or he/she doesn't—an implication that questions the value of leadership training. If you've got it, you don't need the training; if you don't, the training probably won't help.

Clearly there have been methodological and theoretical problems with trait studies. But, as Hampton, Summer, and Webber say, "the complete denial of any (leadership) traits could be an overcorrection."[9]

Before we conclude this discussion, let's consider an interesting variation of the traits approach that is potentially useful to our understanding of leadership dynamics. John Geier[10] applied what was later referred to as a "method of residues" to conclude that certain personality characteristics consistently *eliminate* an individual from leadership consideration in almost all situations. The individual who is seen as (1) uninformed about issues important to the group, (2) a very low participator, or (3) very rigid in thinking will be passed over when groups select leaders.

In view of the serious limitations of many of the traits studies, how can we predict leadership success? What should we consider when diagnosing and responding to leadership opportunities? Researchers today would contend that there is a complex network of factors at work in any leadership situation. From the situational perspective, three classes of variables predominate in accounting for leader effectiveness:

1. the nature of the task to be accomplished by the leader's group
2. the leader's personality compared to the predominant personality characteristics of the group's members
3. the leader's power

The first two variables arise from the way people interact in groups. To understand such interactions we must recall the two classes of activities at work in every meeting: *task activities* and *maintenance activities*. Task has to do with *what* the group is doing; *maintenance* is concerned with *how* they do it. The process of goal clarification is primarily a task activity while the establishment of climate is mostly a maintenance activity. Most leaders understand their task roles—they see a job to be done and know they're responsible to see that it is accomplished—some, however, underestimate the importance of maintenance. Although one can go too far with either activity, the degree of emphasis is an important management judgment. While it is the task activities that get the job done, neglect of maintenance can lead to serious dissatisfaction which could undermine the entire process. The manager who rams through his solution may find himself facing group resentment that eventually will more than offset his "victory." And there are cases where the maintenance activities are, legitimately, the most important outcome of the meeting, making participants just plain feel good about the opportunities for affiliation and participation in group work. The manager's sensitivity to an appropriate balance between task accomplishment and interpersonal need satisfaction will be reflected in her or his personality. The degree to which group members view such personality characteristics as appropriate will affect their willingness to go along with leadership efforts.

The third variable which affects the leadership situation is power. People bring two types of power to the group: *personal* power and *position* power. Personal power is that which is given to an individual based on how others perceive him or her. It usually arises when one is seen as possessing expertise, skills, ability, and other characteristics the viewer deems important. There is a natural attraction toward people with high personal power. Position power, on the other hand, is conferred upon an individual by someone in a higher level of authority. It is made known by rank, position, status, and the capability of providing others with rewards and/or punishment. Most leaders exhibit some combination of both types of power.

The newly announced political candidate may run initially on his or her personal power (personality, appearance, experiences, etc.) until position power in the form of endorsements and party nomination is granted. After being elected, the office holder has position power (having been legitimately selected by the voters), which adds significantly to his or her potential for leadership effectiveness.

Fred E. Fiedler has developed a leadership contingency model which focuses on the three variables I have mentioned. He refers to these as *leader-member relations, task structure,* and *position power.* His research has suggested that emphasis on *task* or *maintenance* leadership efforts should be determined by the *"favorableness of a situation"* which he defines as "the degree to which the situation enables the leader to exert his influence over his group."[11] The most favorable situation would be one where the leader is well liked by the participants, is directing a

Too complicated
Not practical info

clearly defined task, and has recognized status or position power. An unfavorable situation would be the negatives of these. Some mixture of posi-
tives and negatives would put the leader in an intermediate situation.

Fiedler's research concludes that when the situation is either very favorable or very unfavorable to the leader, he or she would do well to
stress task activities and not be overly concerned with maintenance activities. When the favorableness of the situation is intermediate, the
leader needs to be more concerned with maintenance activities and
should emphasize the building of good relationships. Figure 6-2 illustrates
shifts in leadership emphases.

A skillful leader should be aware of these two channels of activity and
be capable of switching emphasis as needed. As changes appear in, say,
task clarity and relationships with group participants, a marked increase
in situational favorableness may call for a shift in emphasis from maintenance (building rapport, etc.) to getting down to tasks.

Management theorists Paul Hersey and Kenneth H. Blanchard have
synthesized the ideas of Fiedler and a number of others to develop their
"situational leadership theory." According to their approach, a leader can
determine an appropriate mixture of relationship building and task directing behavior to increase the probability of effectiveness. "To determine what leadership style is appropriate in a given situation, a leader
must first determine the maturity level of the individual or group in rela-

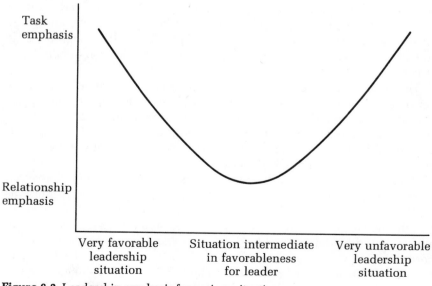

Task
emphasis

Relationship
emphasis

Very favorable   Situation intermediate   Very unfavorable
  leadership   in favorableness   leadership
  situation   for leader   situation

Figure 6-2 Leadership emphasis for various situations

tion to a specific task that the leader is attempting to accomplish through their efforts."[12]

What is this "maturity level"? According to Hersey and Blanchard, the *task-relevant maturity* of a person or group can be diagnosed by considering four characteristics of the group *in relation to the specific job the group is called upon to accomplish*. These characteristics are:

1. the capacity to set high but attainable goals
2. the willingness and ability to take responsibility
3. education and/or experience (or a combination of both) relevant to the task
4. personal maturity on the job in combination with a psychological maturity or self-confidence and self-respect

Let's look at an example. You have been asked to lead a committee to recommend a marketing strategy for a new product line. In gathering information about those who will work on the committee you determine that

1. The participants have a good record for setting ambitious yet realistic targets for themselves.
2. The participants have shown an eagerness to work on the committee and to take responsibility for marketing this new product line in a vigorous manner. If it goes over well, they expect to get credit; if it flops, they expect to shoulder the blame.
3. Each participant has been in on the new product development from the ground floor. They know how it's made, why it's built the way it is, and, based on past experience, they have a good idea of potential markets.
4. The participants are seasoned professionals in their field. They are success-oriented people with a proven track record.

Obviously in such a scenario, we have a committee with very high task-relevant maturity. But what if our team consists of quite another group?

1. They tend to take excessive risks (they have a record of "biting off more than they can chew").
2. They want credit if their plan works but won't accept blame if it fails.
3. They have never worked on a committee like this one before.
4. They are "rookies" in this business.

Under these circumstances, the leader's job is likely to be quite different. Hersey and Blanchard would classify the first group as high in task-relevant maturity and the second example as very low. Most groups, of course, are likely to fall somewhere in between. Figure 6-3 indicates how the effective leadership style would be determined.

As shown in Figure 6-3, once the maturity level of the participants is identified (or realistically guessed at), "the appropriate leadership style can be determined by constructing a right (90°) angle from the point on the continuum that represents the maturity level of the follower(s) to a point where it intersects the [curve] in the style-of-leader portion of the model. The quadrant in which that intersection takes place suggests the appropriate style to be used by the leader in that situation with follower(s) of that maturity level."[13]

Or we could say that the leader's predominant communication behavior changes in relation to the group's maturity:

Group Task-Relevant Maturity Level		Leader's Predominant Communication Behavior
Low	- - - - -	Telling
Moderately low	- - - - -	Selling
Moderately high	- - - - -	Participating
High	- - - - -	Delegating

Telling, selling, participating, and delegating all call for a different mix of communication skills to establish understanding. In moving from behaviors appropriate for the immature worker toward those for the more highly mature, communication skills become more important to effective leadership because of the increased complexity of communication interaction between the leader and follower(s). For example, the high task, low relationship quadrant of the model is characterized by one-way communication where the leader simply gives directives—tells the follower(s) what to do and when to do it. The leadership attempt is successful to the extent that the follower does the desired thing. As workers become more mature, communication is more interactive; there is more emphasis on sharing information for mutual benefit rather than simply getting compliance.

The leadership style appropriate for highly mature employees calls for a substantial reduction in communication interaction, since the follower(s) start to run their own operation. The leader steps into the background, and the leader's function moves away from what we've viewed as tradi-

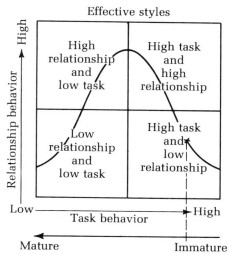

Figure 6-3 Determining an appropriate leadership style*

tional leadership toward less involvement and more "group-centered" leadership.

Current thinking on leadership seems to be that the mature group can function effectively with very little intervention from the designated leader. The leadership *process* of guiding and directing the group's activity is likely to move from person to person within the mature group rather than be centered in one individual. Leland Bradford[14] contrasts individual-centered, traditional conceptions of leadership with such group-centered leadership.†

Traditional Leadership	Group-Centered Leadership
1. The leader directs, controls, polices the members, and leads them to the proper decision. Basically it is his group, and the leader's authority and responsibility are acknowledged by members.	1. The group, or meeting, is *owned* by the members, including the leader. All members, with the leader's assistance, contribute to its effectiveness.

*Paul Hersey, Kenneth H. Blanchard, *Management of Organizational Behavior: Utilizing Human Resources,* 3rd edition, © 1977, p. 165. Reprinted by permission of Prentice-Hall, Inc.
†Reprinted from Bradford, Leland P. *Making Meetings Work: A Guide for Leaders and Group Members.* La Jolla, CA: University Associates, 1976. Used with permission.

2. The leader focuses his attention on the task to be accomplished. He brings the group back from any diverse wandering. He performs all the functions needed to arrive at the proper decision.

2. The group is responsible, with occasional and appropriate help from the leader, for reaching a decision that includes the participation of all and is the product of all. The leader is a servant and helper to the group.

3. The leader sets limits and uses rules of order to keep the discussion within strict limits set by the agenda. He controls the time spent on each item lest the group wander fruitlessly.

3. Members of the group should be encouraged and helped to take responsibility for its task productivity, its methods of working, its assignment of tasks, its plans for the use of the time available.

4. The leader believes that emotions are disruptive to objective, logical thinking, and should be discouraged or suppressed. He assumes it is his task to make clear to all members the disruptive effect of emotions.

4. Feelings, emotions, conflict are recognized by the members and the leader as legitimate facts and situations demanding as serious attention as the task agenda.

5. The leader believes that he should handle a member's disruptive behavior by talking to him away from the group; it is his task to do so.

5. The leader believes that any problem in the group must be faced and solved within the group and by the group. As trust develops among members, it is much easier for an individual to discover ways in which his behavior is bothering the group.

6. Because the need to arrive at a task decision is all important in the eyes of the leader, needs of individual members are considered less important.

6. With help and encouragement from the leader, the members come to realize that the needs, feelings, and purposes of all members should be met so that an awareness of being a group forms. Then the group can continue to grow.

As the group evolves toward higher levels of task-relevant maturity over time, the leader must be ready to adjust his or her behaviors accordingly. As communication scholar Franklin Haiman said almost thirty years ago, "The man officially called *leader* performs only those tasks which the group itself is not yet mature enough, intellectually or emotionally, to handle for itself. The leader's goal is to work himself out of a job."[15]

The Decision Strategy

Problem solving is the most frequent use of the group discussion process. Most educated people readily understand the process of problem solving; i.e., they easily learn and can talk or write about the steps involved. Yet many people seem incapable of or unwilling to apply them in actual discussion. Understanding the decision process does little good until this knowledge affects our behavior.

There are two phases in the development of a decision strategy: problem description and problem solution. The description phase seeks to crystallize the nature of a disquieting situation which has come to the attention of group members. Such a situation may be attributed to an inability to achieve desired objectives, a dissatisfaction with the speed at which goals are reached, an uncertain sense of morality or ethical standards, or just a general condition of wondering whether or not the very best is being achieved. Removal of such feelings of dissatisfaction presupposes a clear problem description. There are three phases of problem description:

(1) *Problem Definition.* What exactly is exerting pressure on us? Participants, in the initial stage of discussion, should attempt to identify, in specific terms, the elements of the problem. This process of defining contributing factors usually involves defining critical terms. The group called together to "do something about employee morale" should define what they mean by *morale.* How do they know when morale is good or bad? Often, an *operational definition*—one that defines in terms of something clearly measurable—works well. In this case we might say that bad morale is what we have when absenteeism, number of grievances filed, and employee turnover reaches some specified level.

It is crucial to get on the same wavelength by clarifying all relevant terms. And be sure group members use the terms only in the agreed upon way.

(2) *Problem Analysis.* Once the problem is defined, there should be a general discussion of objectives, where we stand now vis-à-vis the objectives, and what obstacles we face. The objectives or ideal solution should be described in terms of criteria. That is, we might say, an ideal solution to our perceived morale problem would

- reduce absenteeism to less than 2 percent per day
- reduce grievances filed to one per month
- reduce turnover to .5 percent per month

This operationally defines the objective. We should also develop additional qualifying criteria. An *ideal* solution would

- not undermine the authority of the supervisor in any way
- not cost additional money for wage or benefit incentives
- be easily implemented
- serve as a prototype for future employee motivation programs
- be based in sound management theory

These criteria should be listed on a chalkboard or chart so that everyone can refer to them as possible solutions are evaluated. You may not get full agreement on each criterion but strive for a general consensus that the criterion does reflect a highly desirable condition.

Once criteria are established, solution ideas generated in the discussion can be weighed against them. Evaluating any potential solution is extremely difficult if the requirements of the solution are hazy.

(3) *Problem Reformulation.* At times discussion of the "obvious" problem breaks down and people get frustrated by a seeming inability to come up with workable ideas. If the problem definition and analysis processes have been carried out, and still we have no luck, the problem may be due to underlying assumptions we may be holding. The effective problem solver recognizes that even the best groups sometimes "bark up the wrong tree." Here's an example:

> . . . an automobile manufacturing company . . . was concerned because they were running out of drying sheds in which to store their cars while the paint dried. At first the problem seemed to be simply the need to build more sheds. Land was expensive; buildings were expensive; and construction was time-consuming. But one person had an idea: If the paint dried faster, more cars could be accommodated in the existing sheds. This problem reformulation led to the discovery of faster drying paint [which solved the problem].[16]

In my earlier example of an employee morale problem resulting in absenteeism, grievances, and turnover, a problem reformulation might be useful. The group's predominant and perhaps unspoken assumption may be that supervisor-subordinate relations are at fault. In reality, some physical environmental condition such as the presence of a harmful chemical may become suspect as the root cause of much absenteeism. Evidence pointing to previously unsuspected problem variables can require new ways of viewing the problem. Reformulation means taking a new tack, and often it can lead to more productive results in the group.

Once problem description has been satisfactorily achieved, the solution stage begins. This may involve four more steps.

(4) *Solution Proposal.* There is a general tendency among participants to jump to this step before the problem description phase is complete. What may emerge could be an excellent solution—but to a different problem! Depending on the nature of the problem, it may be desirable to collect as many potential solutions as possible, especially where the task calls for creativity.

One popular way of generating lots of solutions is by using the *brainstorming* technique. This approach requires a communication climate in which free expression of all kinds of ideas is valued and encouraged—no matter how offbeat or bizarre they may seem. Brainstorming was developed by Alex Osborn, an advertising executive, to stimulate creative and imaginative problem solving. There are four basic rules:

    a. don't criticize any ideas
    b. no idea is too wild
    c. quantity of ideas generated is important
    d. seize opportunities to improve or add to ideas suggested by others[17]

The rules of brainstorming are easier to state than to obey—especially rule (b). Unless great care is taken, nonverbal cues can be interpreted as evaluations of ideas which can discourage additional "wild ideas." When using brainstorming, the participants should prominently post the rules as a constant reminder.

(5) *Solution Testing.* Once ideas have been generated, they may be tested against the criteria established back in the problem description phase. Which ideas, alone or in combination with others, would be most likely to solve the problem? It is possible that no proposal will meet all criteria fully. You must then predict which is most likely to rectify most of the problems, most of the time.

(6) *Action Testing.* Now comes the acid test. When the chosen solution is implemented, we have the final step in the decision process. Since solu-

tions are seldom perfect, or everlasting, rechecking over time is important. Problems have ways of recurring in a cyclical pattern or reemerging in different variations. Seldom can a solution settle the matter once and for all. Action testing checks on implementation and should be read-ministered periodically.

Post-Meeting Evaluation and Follow-Up

Evaluation and adjustment should be ongoing processes for leadership during any meeting. In addition, taking a retrospective look at the meeting can be very useful in overcoming problematic areas in future meetings. Let's discuss for a moment some of the elements that should be observed.

Think about a recent meeting you attended. How would you answer these questions about task activities? Did the meeting participants

- State exactly what the meeting was to accomplish? Set goals and objectives, list priorities, identify clearly the problem areas to be dealt with?

- Apply a systematic, logical decision-making strategy?

- Combine useful ideas while sorting through possible solutions? Was background information gathered when needed? Were more details called for when appropriate?

- Examine potential solutions in terms of their impact on others, their costs and benefits, and the need for support from others in order to be effective?

- Seek creative and innovative approaches? See new relationships by linking other issues into the problems that were being evaluated?

- Delegate assignments and agree on such things as time limits and resources to be used? Determine times for follow-up sessions when necessary?

- Process the final decision into a usable form, usually a written report?

Now recall the group maintenance activities. These included the ways participants thought, acted, and felt while they were immersed in the task. Did the meeting participants

- Clearly understand the reasons for the meeting? Did they share a common view of its urgency?

- Interact in constructive ways through supportive word choice, body language, "strokes," and a sense of caring?

- Avoid patterns of excessive dominance and passivity?

- Share in commitment to cooperate? Avoid factionalism or the "hard sell" of personal viewpoints?

- Freely express feelings as well as information?

- Manage disagreement and conflicting ideas in constructive ways?

- Mix seriousness with playfulness?

- Seem to enjoy the work and feel good about being together?

The degree to which these kinds of things are happening determines the likelihood of meeting effectiveness. Before we leave this topic, there is one other area which should be addressed—the role of conflict in meetings.

Coping with Conflict

I said earlier that interactional characteristics which affect meeting climate include the effective use of conflict. This deserves clarification.

Traditionally, it has been assumed that conflict should be avoided in meetings. The term conjures up images of fistfights or people screaming at each other. In reality, conflict is simply a state of incompatibility, and incompatibility itself is neither good nor bad. What makes that incompatibility either desirable or undesirable is the participants' reaction to it. Communication professor Elliott Pood[18] suggests several responses to conflict:

(1) We can attempt to avoid conflict by not expressing opposing views and by withholding even nonverbal feedback which indicates disagreement. Here we keep from rocking the boat and minimize the possibility of being subjected to rejection or reprisals from others. By so doing, however, we also preclude a full sharing of ideas and feelings within the group. And without a free sharing of information, the group cannot maximize its potential for producing superior solutions.

(2) A second response to conflict reflects the opposite view. We can engage in unregulated confrontation, which is traditionally characterized by a win-lose orientation, leading to a no-holds-barred, open warfare among participants. The goal here is to win over others at any cost. Unregulated conflict becomes very personal rather than group task-oriented

and results in the elimination of some group members, usually by their psychological withdrawal from participation. The result again is the reduction of information sharing and lower quality group decisions.

(3) A third and most beneficial response to group confrontation is what Pood calls *conflict management*. The effective management of conflict seeks to regulate but not eliminate confrontation. Recognizing that the abrasive actions of opposing views polish the final product, the skillful leader seeks free exchange of information but without the win-lose destructiveness of unregulated conflict. Accomplishing this calls for effective communication skills which encourage the generation of information without inhibiting or turning off participants. These skills are essentially those which I've discussed throughout this book: establishing and maintaining a supportive, constructive climate, avoiding defensiveness, and freely exchanging feelings as well as data to create mutual understanding.

So, What's a Good Meeting Like?

If your committee meetings could be described as polite, orderly, and carefully led, with each participant taking his or her turn to address the group or the leader, your meetings are probably a flop. Good, effective meetings, where people wrestle with tough problems, are likely to bear little resemblance to parliamentary discussions in hushed conference rooms among polite and scrupulously "reasonable" people. Some good meetings are more likely to resemble cattle auctions.

Good meetings are often noisy, with hard-thinking, challenging people talking straight and bouncing ideas off each other. Under effective leadership, which often rotates from person to person as the need arises, participants debate, discuss, and even argue about the problems before them. The meeting often looks disorderly and, in fact, the phrase "wrestling with problems" conjures up a rather accurate picture of an effective meeting. Before we get too carried away with this rough-and-tumble metaphor, be reminded that there remains method to the madness of a good meeting.

The key to success is that participants never lose track of what they are doing. The objective of the meeting remains clear and commitment to accomplishing the goal is unwavering. Sure, there will be momentary sidetracks to explore possibilities that ultimately may not prove productive, but the focus remains on the issues. When the job is done, the meeting ends, period. Even if it is way before scheduled quitting time.

These are the kinds of goings-on you'll find at a good, productive conference. Many managers have never been to such a thing. Perhaps this is because we've come to expect something different. Let's look at some expectations of how meetings "should be" that are actually counterproductive to effectiveness.

I'VE CALLED THIS MEETING TO GET
YOUR IDEAS ON HOW WE CAN QUIT
HAVING SO MANY MEETINGS.

*Misconception 1: Meetings Should Be Orderly, with
the Leader Managing the Flow of Information*

If your meetings are characterized by the raise-your-hand-and-be-recognized syndrome, participation is being stifled and you're not getting the maximum benefit from the process. *Robert's Rules of Order* are fine for large groups and formal proceedings but not for most business conferences. If you need such tight structuring to avoid total chaos, your group probably has too many members.

The designated leader need not function like a traffic cop. Tight leader control on the group's activities, according to Dunsing, results in

> . . . a lot of "reporting." Each member is choreographed to give his or her view of things in one blurt: "Here's how we see it down in the laboratory." No one is permitted to interrupt. Dialogue is cut off. There is no free flow. Participants need not pay close attention because they can't respond naturally to ideas as they are presented—so they cast off into dreamland or start rehearsing their big moment.
>
> . . . a bizarre kind of human interaction results: People don't talk to each other directly—they talk to each other through the leader.[19]

Such tight control destroys the vibrant, free-flowing *interaction* that makes meetings work.

Misconception 2: Conflict Should Be Avoided in Committee Meetings; We Should Seek Cooperation at All Cost

If there is a free exchange of ideas, there is bound to be some conflict. One reason for the group process is to subject ideas to the abrasive action of other ideas. That's the way we smooth out the rough edges. Conflict should be managed, not discouraged. Managed confrontations remain issue-oriented, not people-oriented. The use of appropriate communication skills allows all the benefits of assertive information exchange without the destructiveness of unregulated, win-lose warfare.

The real apprehension people associate with verbal conflict arises from a fear of hurt feelings—our own or others—from such interaction. If, however, the conflict remains on the adult level, where issues, positions, evidence, and reasoning are attacked without the advocate's *self-worth* being questioned, conflict can be useful. This, of course, is easier said than done. We have skin of varying thickness that at some point is penetrated when our pet idea is put down or unfairly (we think) criticized.

If we go into the committee meeting knowing that such useful confrontations will take place as a normal course of events, we puncture this misconception and improve the quality of the meetings. Maybe we should all shake hands before we come out swinging.

Misconception 3: The Leader Is Totally Responsible for the Success of the Meeting

Effective communication can never be assured by one participant in the interaction. As I said in Chapter 1, communication means the creation of common meanings—understanding—among two or more parties. If a conference or meeting is to work, it will require efforts from several participants. A designated leader does have some special responsibilities, however. He or she can (1) set the tone and establish patterns of interaction, (2) clarify the task to be accomplished and guide participants back on track when they stray too far, (3) mediate conflicts to be sure they remain productive, (4) arrange pre-session agenda and post-session follow-up, and (5) make assignments as appropriate. While these responsibilities are considerable, they do not constitute *control* over the outcome of the committee's deliberations.

The effective leader will share responsibility with participants in an adult-to-adult relationship. Participants need to accept responsibility for the group's success and not permit a child-parent relationship with the leader to permeate the committee.

An effective committee meeting is one in which these popular misconceptions are not assumed. Overemphasis on orderliness, "correct" procedures, and elimination of conflict can only detract from the usefulness of the group process. When the leader and the led share a mutual sense of responsibility for getting the job done, your group will succeed.

Diagnosing Your Meetings and Conferences

There are many ways we can diagnose the quality of conferences held in our organization. Some very simple procedures will produce feedback from participants immediately after the completion of a conference assignment. To assess the effectiveness of the designated leader, we might simply ask participants to complete a ballot such as the one in Figure 6-4.

In addition to such a simple balloting procedure, it is also easy to ask participants to complete a group performance index such as the one shown in Figure 6-5 on the next page. This easy-to-complete question-

---

"If you were called to participate on a committee dealing with the topic that you have just completed, who would you designate to be the official conference leader?"

Why did you feel the leader was effective or ineffective?

Figure 6-4 Post-meeting response ballot

Listed below are seven statements relating to group competence. Please circle the number on the scales which best describe the performance of the group you have just participated in as you see it.

1. There was a high degree of involvement among participants.

| agree strongly | 5 | 4 | 3 | 2 | 1 | disagree strongly |

2. Commitment to group decisions by most members was:

| high | 5 | 4 | 3 | 2 | 1 | low |

3. Leadership (i.e., responsibility for moving the group along toward task accomplishment) moved from person to person as the meeting went on.

| agree strongly | 5 | 4 | 3 | 2 | 1 | disagree strongly |

4. Feelings were openly dealt with.

| agree strongly | 5 | 4 | 3 | 2 | 1 | disagree strongly |

5. A systematic approach was used to clarify the problem (issues), establish criteria before solutions were considered.

| agree strongly | 5 | 4 | 3 | 2 | 1 | disagree strongly |

6. Confrontation and conflicting ideas were managed to improve quality of the group's decision.

| agree strongly | 5 | 4 | 3 | 2 | 1 | disagree strongly |

7. The overall success of the group's performance should be evaluated as

| high | 5 | 4 | 3 | 2 | 1 | low |

Total Score_____
(sum of scales)

Figure 6-5 Group performance rating form

naire provides useful feedback to the manager. These should be completed anonymously and tallied by a disinterested third party. A total score may be useful to easily compare different meetings.

Like other diagnostic instruments, these will provide some indicators which can help you as a manager to make decisions about leadership assignments and the general effectiveness of the group process in your organization. Although I would caution against using this raw data at face value, it can be used very effectively in developing trends. For example, the data obtained from each meeting of a particular committee could indi-

Name of committee or meeting: _____

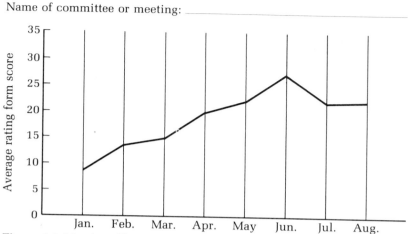

Figure 6-6 Meeting effectiveness trend sheet

cate deterioration or growth in the potential of that particular committee. Similarly, data obtained for the same leader in different situations may provide interesting information as to where that individual can be most effective. A simple trend form could be constructed by plotting rating form scales over time as illustrated in Figure 6-6.

Some Other Thoughts About Meetings and Conferences: READING FOR CHAPTER 6

How to Sabotage a Meeting[20]

Alfred Fleishman

Lots of people talk about "communication" as if they know what they're talking about. They don't.

These people usually know more about how to sabotage communication than they do about how to promote it.

Of course, we're all would-be saboteurs. Most of the time, we do this unconsciously; and since sabotage is a risky business, sometimes we do succeed in communicating in spite of ourselves, having inadvertently stumbled upon some principle of general semantics—like the notion that the words we use may have a different meaning to the person we're talking to than they do to us, even though we both read the dictionary—diligently.

But there are some people around who have really studied the art of sabotage. They like to attend large gatherings ostensibly devoted to the practice of serious discourse—any meeting will do. Meetings offer them the perfect opportunity to be disruptive. The serious student is advised to study their methods.

If you adhere to the following seven rules, and apply them judiciously, you, too, can be an expert at semantic sabotage.

meaning in language

Interruption

The secret of breaking up any meeting by using the interruption method lies in your timing.

Let the speaker talk just long enough for you to get a general idea of what he's trying to say. Before he has a chance to conclude, interrupt. Arrange it so that you supply the clincher to *his* argument before he can get a word in edgewise. Even if you don't agree with his point of view, it isn't difficult to twist his words to support whatever different point of view you may be advocating at the moment. Of course, the speaker may insist on plodding on. Let him. This not only gives you a chance to interrupt him again, but, by demonstrating how patient and tolerant you are, wins *you* the support of the audience.

Diversion

The diversion technique begins where the interruption technique leaves off. Changing the subject is the best method of diversion, and the easiest for the beginner to follow. The only thing to remember is CHANGE THE SUBJECT COMPLETELY. You can talk about anything—the latest space shot, civil rights, the "good old days"—just so you change the subject completely.

There are, however, more sophisticated ways of creating a diversion. For instance: if several persons are engaged in a seminar, start talking in semi-hushed tones to the person sitting next to you. Put your hand in front of your mouth to make it even more obvious that you are carrying on a separate conversation. This may earn you some dirty looks, but the main thing is that people's attention is being diverted away from the speaker.

There are a few special techniques to cultivate if you use this device. It is important to be able to pitch your voice at a low enough level so as not to drown out the speaker completely. Yet you must create a "buzz." This takes some practice, but it's worth trying. People will attempt to listen to both you and the speaker. They won't be able to. Their heads will begin to turn and their minds to wander away from what the speaker is trying to say. You've won!

Name Calling

Name calling is a more advanced technique. Here, you don't interrupt, you wouldn't dream of creating a diversion. You are completely and totally cooperative. BUT, when the speaker has completed his address or succeeded in making his point, call him a name. It's as simple as that. The name should, of course, cast doubt on his character, or on his ability as a thinker. Suggest that he must be "off his rocker" or "out of his mind." Imply that nobody with a grain of sense could say such things or hold such views.

It isn't necessary to use foul language in your implementation of this technique. In fact, it's better if you keep your remarks "clean," because the effectiveness of this device hinges upon loudness and self-confidence. You want to make sure everybody hears what you are saying, and you want to sound extremely sure of yourself. Only as a last resort should you make a statement such as "I don't want to discuss that woman we both know." The distraught speaker will insist on knowing "what woman." All you have to do now is keep repeating that you don't want to embarrass anybody by going into details. This ploy is practically infallible. People being what they are, many of them will be very interested indeed in knowing all about "that woman." But *you* haven't said anything. Can you help it if other people have "dirty" minds?

Challenging the Speaker's Integrity

To make this particular method of sabotage work, you must permit the speaker to finish what he has to say—however much it hurts. Your aim is to disarm him. Never raise your voice; for you must appear to be in complete agreement with him. Then pounce:

"Who's *really* making the money out of this?"

"What are you trying to hide?"

"What's in this for you?"

"Why aren't all the facts being brought out in the open?" (You can allow yourself a great deal of moral indignation here.)

This will put the speaker on the defensive all right!

Contradiction

You shouldn't have any difficulty with this technique. All you have to do is sit back, wait until the speaker is finished, and then contradict him. Don't attempt to engage him in debate. Just say authoritatively: "You're wrong."

The speaker will probably try to defend his position. Don't pay any attention to him. Simply shrug your shoulders and repeat your original remark. (He's dead wrong, and you know it.) Never make the fatal mistake of actually arguing with him. And whatever you do, don't let him trap you with specifics.

Laughing It Off

As demonstrated in the interruption technique, one good way to deflate a speaker is by showing his audience how tolerant you are—by laughing him and his subject off.

Remember, it's within your power to turn any discussion into a farce. Of *course*, you'll stay and listen to what the speaker has to say—patiently and with good-natured amusement. But really, you imply, the whole thing is so ridiculous that if you weren't such a "good Joe," you'd get up and walk out right now.

The Brush-Off

The brush-off is often used ineffectively. The student should be thoroughly versed in the other techniques before he tries this one. Only the real expert can successfully maneuver a speaker away from the podium by opening his briefcase and starting to rearrange its contents.

The beginner often makes the mistake of thinking that he can employ the same tactics to disrupt a meeting as he uses to get rid of an unwanted guest or client. In a public situation, he can't pick up the phone, dial the golf pro at the Country Club, and ask if he can have a quick lesson. That would not only be impractical, but openly rude. The saboteur has to play by the rules, even if he is playing a different game.

No, if you're a beginner, your best bet is to carry the interruption technique to the point of absurdity. Your first attempts will certainly result in chaos—not necessarily semantic chaos, but chaos nonetheless—and you will have achieved your goal. Cut off communication quick!

Questions for Further Thought

1. What are the potential advantages of traditional leadership (as described by Bradford on pages 195–196)? Name some specific situations where such an approach is likely to be effective.

2. What are the potential advantages of group-centered leadership (as described by Bradford)? Name some specific situations where such an approach is likely to be effective.

3. Think about a problem or issue faced by your organization. Go through the seven steps suggested as decision strategy and write out your ideas for each. Compare them with the ideas of someone else in the same organization.

4. Try applying brainstorming to a problem your organization faces which calls for creativity. Remember the four basic rules.

5. How do you tend to respond to incompatibility (potential conflicts) on the job? Is your style of response productive?

6. What do your meetings tend to be like? Describe them in detail. Based on what you've read in this chapter, are you satisfied with this description? What would you like to see changed?

Notes

1. Daniel Katz and Robert L. Kahn, *The Social Psychology of Organizations*, 2nd ed. (New York: John Wiley & Sons, 1978), p. 30.
2. Corwin P. King, "Decisions by Discussion: The Uses and Abuses of Team Problem Solving," *S.A.M. Advanced Management Journal*, Autumn 1976, p. 33.
3. Lester Coch and John R. P. French, Jr., "Overcoming Resistance to Change," *Human Relations*, 1 (1948), pp. 512–532.
4. Reprinted from Von Bergen, Clarence W. and Kirk, Raymond J. "Groupthink: When Too Many Heads Spoil the Decision," *Management Review*, March 1978 (New York: AMACOM, a division of American Management Associations) p. 46.
5. Dorwin Cartwright and Alvin Zander, eds., *Group Dynamics: Theory and Research*, 3rd ed. (New York: Harper & Row, 1968).
6. Richard J. Dunsing, "You and I Have Simple Got to Stop Meeting This Way" (Part 1), *Supervisory Management*, September 1976, p. 9.
7. Theodore Caplow, *How to Run Any Organization* (Hinsdale, Ill.: Dryden Press, 1976), p. 59.
8. Ralph M. Stogdill, *Handbook of Leadership* (New York: Free Press, 1974), pp. 81–82.
9. David R. Hampton, Charles E. Summer, and Ross A. Webber, *Organizational Behavior and the Practice of Management*, 3rd ed. (Glenview, Ill.: Scott, Foresman 1978), p. 597.
10. John Geier, "A Trait Approach to the Study of Leadership," *Journal of Communication*, 17 (1967), pp. 316–323.
11. Fred E. Fiedler, *A Theory of Leadership Effectiveness* (New York: McGraw-Hill, 1967), p. 13.
12. Paul Hersey and Kenneth H. Blanchard, *Management of Organizational Behavior*, 3rd ed. (Englewood Cliffs, N.J.: Prentice-Hall, 1977), p. 165.
13. *Ibid.*
14. Leland Bradford, *Making Meetings Work* (La Jolla, Calif.: University Associates, 1976), pp. 11–12.
15. Franklin S. Haiman, *Group Leadership and Democratic Action* (Boston: Houghton Mifflin, 1951), pp. 38–39.

16. R. Victor Harnack and Thorrel B. Fest, *Group Discussion: Theory and Technique* (New York: Appleton-Century-Crofts, 1964), pp. 66–67.
17. Alex F. Osborn, *Applied Imagination: Principles and Procedures of Creative Thinking* (New York: Scribner's, 1953), pp. 300–301.
18. Elliott A. Pood, Assistant Professor of Communication at the University of North Carolina at Greensboro. Interview, March, 1979.
19. Dunsing, "You and I Have Simply Got to Stop Meeting This Way" (Part 2), *Supervisory Management*, October 1976, p. 12.
20. Reprinted from ETC. Vol. 24, No. 3 by permission of the International Society for General Semantics.

Recommended Readings

Although there is a wealth of printed material available dealing with small group communication, the items listed below are those I have found to be particularly useful to the practicing manager. Each of them has a very practical orientation. Each can provide some tips on making meetings more effective.

Bradford, Leland P., *Making Meetings Work*. La Jolla, Calif.: University Associates, 1976. Bradford combines his extensive experience in educational psychology and training to produce a very useful, readable guide for leaders and group members. The book elaborates on many of the points covered in this chapter; in addition, it shows the reader how to be effective in larger meetings. His chapters on giving a large assembly the qualities of small group meetings, and planning the work group conference give additional insights that may be useful to the manager. Several appendices at the end of this book provide alternatives to the diagnostic techniques I have suggested.

Dunsing, Richard J., "You and I Have Simply Got to Stop Meeting This Way," *Supervisory Management*, September 1976–February 1977. This six-part series by Professor Dunsing is especially enjoyable to read and full of good information on meetings. The first three sections discuss problems that typically arise with the meeting format. In Part 4 he details analyses and diagnoses of your meetings. In Parts 5 and 6, he identifies changes that leaders can make in organizations as well as changes that individual participants can make. These are some of the most interesting and well-written articles I've seen on the topic of effective meetings. I highly recommend your looking at this material.

Caplow, Theodore, *How to Run Any Organization: Manual of Practical Sociology*. Hinsdale, Ill.: Dryden Press, 1976. As Caplow's title implies, this is a very practical orientation to being effective in leading organizations. One chapter of this book deals specifically with communication.

Jay, Anthony, "How to Run a Meeting," *Harvard Business Review*, 54, (March–April 1976), pp. 43–57. This excellent article illustrates the kinds of things that can go wrong in meetings and how to put them right.

CHAPTER 7

SPEAKING BEFORE GROUPS
Briefings and Oral Presentations

The thought of giving a talk in front of others has a way of unraveling even the most self-confident individual. Surveys have indicated that of all things people fear, giving a public speech is at the top of the list. Comedian George Jessel once said, "The human brain is a wonderful organ. It starts to work as soon as you are born and doesn't stop until you get up to deliver a speech."

Despite the anxiety that often accompanies the thought of "giving a speech," oral presentations are a normal and very useful way of communicating in organizations. In this chapter we will discuss the preparation and presentation of *briefings*, a term I'll use interchangeably with *oral presentations*. The principles presented here apply to speaking before public groups, as well as to the kind of presentation typically made within the organization.

There are four types of briefings commonly used in organizations: persuasive, explanatory, instructional, and progress reports. An element of persuasion—getting agreement or action from the audience—is present in any briefing, but the first type focuses on this extensively. An attempt to sell upper management on the need for a bigger budget, more employees, or different methods is one common type of persuasive briefing. Others may try to sell changes in operations, need for additional coordination, adoption of a new procedure, and so forth. The key feature of the persuasive briefing is that it attempts to get others to "buy" your idea, plan, or recommendation. And buying generally involves more than simply agreeing with what you say. It means getting some desired *action* from your listeners. The success of your briefing will be readily observable by how much of the desired action actually occurs.

In *explanatory* or *instructional* briefings we are not trying to sell anything but are providing opportunities for the listener to gain knowledge, understanding, or skills. *Explanatory* briefings generally present a "big picture" overview such as orienting new employees to the company, acquainting staff members with what is involved in opening a new branch or division in the company, or showing how each function of the organization fits in with others. *Instructional* briefings get more specific. They teach others how to do or use something such as a new machine, procedure, or paperwork system. This usually involves more audience involvement than the explanatory briefing. Testing for knowledge gained fits naturally into the instructional briefing.

The *progress report* brings the audience up to date on some project they are already familiar with. Examples of this may be reports on research and development of new products, briefings on money and manpower expenditures compared against budgets, and checking the organization's success against objectives or goals.

The remainder of this chapter will deal with the ways we can get maximum results from briefings, beginning with an overview of the whole process of developing an effective briefing.

Here's the Password: TIMM'S CAT

Here's a mnemonic device—a memory aid—to help put together a presentation: TIMM'S CAT.* Briefly, these key letters refer to the ingredients of an effective presentation.

T	*Topic*	Determine specifically what your presentation is about; give it a label to help identify the message.
I	*Intent*	Determine specifically what you want your audience to learn, think, do, or feel. Why is the presentation to be given?
M	*Materials*	What references, notes, props, visual aids, handouts, films, charts, equipment, etc. will be needed or helpful to achieve your intended results?
M	*Message*	Determine specifically what you are going to say to your audience. This will include at least three main parts: (1) *introduction/attention getter*; (2) *body*—the "pitch" consisting of a theme and supporting information aimed at getting some desired reaction from your listeners; and (3) *a conclusion/action step.*
S	*Summary*	Restate the main points to tie them together in some easy-to-remember format. Often more than one summary is appropriate.
C	*Checkup*	Test or otherwise check for understanding and retention of the message. Did the audience get the message? Was the intent fulfilled?
A	*Assignment*	Give the audience something specific to do or think about in the days to come.
T	*Take-home*	Use handouts, samples, reading lists—something for the audience to take with them that can go on reinforcing your message.

Let's take another look at TIMM'S CAT and elaborate on each part.

*TIMM'S CAT and its description copyright 1979 by Paul R. Timm. Reprinted by permission of the author. All rights reserved.

Topic

In most situations the topic, in general form, arises from some felt need or a particular assignment given to us. Our topic should be specific, yet it need not sound like a newspaper headline; indeed, a longer and more descriptive title is often better. Instead of talking about "plant safety" we might deal with "improving plant safety in the welding shop." "Billing order accuracy" might become "reducing errors created by keypunch operators." Start from a general problem or topic area and narrow it to a specific statement or title for your talk. (I'll discuss some techniques for doing this later in this chapter.) Also, put into your title something to indicate the importance of the topic to your audience. Usually a verb such as "improving" and "reducing" (in the examples above) will suggest the benefits of the talk to the listeners.

Intent

What specifically do you want from your audience? Why are you giving this presentation? Often your intent will be for the listener to *learn* or *do* something. Sometimes you may simply want to bring them up to date or even entertain them. The clearer your understanding of exactly what you are attempting, the greater your likelihood of success. In education, the modern approach is to set clearly measurable *learning objectives*. The same might apply for most presentations in organizations. The speaker should be able to recognize when the intent is met. If your intent is unclear, unrealistic, or unproductive, don't waste your audience's time. Communicate for a specific desired response.

Materials

What kinds of things will be needed to reinforce what you are saying? First, the speaker has a responsibility to establish an environment conducive to good communication. The layout of the room, furniture, lighting, temperature control, sound system, etc. should be checked. Second, the speaker should develop materials that amplify or reinforce the ideas presented orally. Charts, tables, graphs, handouts, sample equipment, films, slides, overhead transparencies, and the like should be gathered and used as appropriate. A third type of materials is the speaker's notes and references. In every speaking situation, some research is needed. Methods of gathering information, condensing and organizing it, and presenting it in such a way as to enhance credibility will be developed later in this chapter.

Message

What exactly are you going to say to your audience? Your actual message should be organized with a clear plan in mind. Assertions made should be appropriately documented. The briefing should be aimed toward your specific audience and should consist of (1) an attention-gaining introduction, (2) a logically organized body, and (3) an action-oriented conclusion which seeks to have the audience try out or practice the intended behavior or way of thinking.

One very important point to keep in mind: in most briefing situations, the speaker need *not* be tied to an I-talk-you-listen format. Audience participation can be a key ingredient to making your presentation successful. Audience involvement following the body of your talk is one effective approach keyed at getting the listeners to apply the ideas you've presented. Sometimes, however, it is useful to get the audience involved earlier—perhaps by having them complete a questionnaire or respond to some ideas before you present the main part of your message. Hopefully this gets them thinking along appropriate lines. Everyone likes to participate, and the speaker who can get the audience into the act is always that much more interesting to them.

Occasionally we are hesitant to use audience involvement in presentations. I can think of a personal example. While still fairly new at consulting, I was asked to do a training session for an organization of businessmen. I felt that I should "*teach,*" that is "*tell* them" a lot of information. After all, I was being paid good money for teaching. Despite a carefully prepared module of instruction and the use of some of my best one-liners, the presentation seemed to fall flat. Afterward a colleague who also worked with this group gave me some very good advice. He reminded me that these business people are already very successful in their own fields and are often more interested in demonstrating their abilities to each other than in "being taught" in the traditional sense. The trainer should *manage* the learning process, not force-feed information. I later revised the same program to include lots of discussion, cases, and "experiential learning activities" (academic jargon for games). The change in audience response was dramatic. The moral of the story: just because you're the "speaker" doesn't mean you should do all the talking.

One further thought on audience involvement is offered by Frederick C. Dyer: "When in doubt, schedule *twice* as much participation as seems adequate. Most speakers err on the side of too little participation rather than too much. The audiences love it; they enjoy it; they will never protest against too much talking or action on their part, but they will regret too little. One often sees speaker evaluation sheets with the comment, 'not enough group participation; too much monologue.' One never sees the comment, 'too much group participation.' "[1]

Summary

Another key ingredient of the oral presentation is the use of summaries. Summaries tie together main points and help the listener organize and assimilate the ideas presented. Few people have the ability to grasp exactly what is being said the first time through. Repetition and restatement of key points is crucial to effective communication. Within the body of the talk we should use internal summaries to tie together clusters of three or four points at a time. The use of memory aids (like TIMM'S CAT) can be very helpful for your audience. And don't forget to summarize what has been demonstrated or learned from audience participation activities. It is difficult to summarize too much. Many speakers do not use this important tool as frequently as they should.

Checkup

The checkup ingredient fulfills two purposes: (1) it helps you as presenter find out what the audience has learned, and (2) it provides valuable feedback about errors or weaknesses in your presentation so that you can improve it.

You might feel that testing for audience understanding is inappropriate or even impossible in a business presentation. "After all, this isn't school where a teacher administers a pop quiz." I'd disagree. If your topic is important enough to the organization and its members to present in the first place, it's certainly important enough to test for understanding.

Often, this testing phase requires creativity and perhaps a heightened sensitivity to your audience's responses. Here are a few techniques for checking up:

1. Ask some questions orally or in writing to test for understanding of key points. Focus the questions on issues that are important to your talk and avoid exceptionally detailed information which is presented only as support for main points.
2. Observe nonverbal reactions to what you are saying; look for indications of uncertainty and ask if you can clarify. Be sure to do this in a nonthreatening manner and be sincere about your desire to have your listeners understand.
3. Use recognition methods—for example, hold up a picture, object, a large card with a formula, or diagram, and ask audience members to identify the parts and purposes.
4. Get the audience to demonstrate different segments of your presentation.
5. Have the audience provide examples they have experienced that relate to your main points.

The key to effective checkups is to keep looking for ways to get feedback from your audience which indicates understanding or acceptance of what you are selling or explaining. Then use the feedback to improve this presentation or future ones.

Assignment

The same arguments for resisting the use of checkups could be used against the giving of assignments. After all, we can't assign *homework* to our listeners! Or can we?

Assignments can be effectively used to reinforce and strengthen thoughts presented. If the talk itself is planned with the audience's interests in mind—that is, they are shown how *they* will profit from this information—an assignment to help them further *profit* is perfectly natural and will be readily accepted. Usually the assignment shows the listeners how they can, on their own, maximize the ideas presented in your talk. Few people can be sold, converted, or even taught on the basis of a one-shot speech. Follow-up is necessary to make knowledge, attitude, or behavior changes. A good assignment tells the listener specifically what can be done to reinforce or perfect the newly learned information or behavior. Some typical assignments might be:

1. Recommendations for *further study* citing specific books, articles, movies, TV programs, etc.
2. Recommendations for *practice* by setting a self-training schedule, applying principles to different situations, explaining points to others, etc.
3. *Observations* of situations in which the topic of your presentation works. Once a person starts looking for specific things he or she can learn much.
4. Exposure to other *teaching situations* or learning opportunities such as recommending membership in a professional group or attendance at some workshop or conference.
5. A *challenge* to apply taught behaviors for a specific period of time to get the listener to try on new ways of doing or thinking.
6. Invitation to *follow-up sessions* to check progress and compare notes or implementation of new ideas.

Again, creativity is needed to develop effective assignments for your listeners. Follow-up activities which are genuinely beneficial to your listener work as a natural extension of what you have said in your presentation and will be eagerly accepted.

Take-Home

The logic of providing some sort of handout to your audience is similar to that applied to the assignment step. They can keep on teaching after you're gone. Take-home items can take many forms, including samples, outlines, charts, letters, brochures, and badges. They may incorporate a mail-back card or sheet which further tests the audience's grasp of the presentation. Take-home items serve as reminders and as sources of clarifying or amplifying information. These provide message reinforcement for those who use them and may be "advertising" for others who did not hear your talk.

Be sure take-home items are pertinent to your topic and intent. I've seen speakers pass out very attractive copies of case studies or articles which have little bearing on what was presented in their briefing. Also, be sure the quality of the handouts is appropriate both in appearance and content. Take-home items should be selected very carefully for the particular audience. It may be useful to maintain a "family resemblance" in things you give out; a familiar motif or logo may be repeated on each printed item to show that these go together and are not simply a hodgepodge of miscellaneous materials you had lying around.

Call attention to your take-home items during your presentation and take time to explain their use to your audience. Do *not*, however, pass out reading materials while you are speaking or you'll lose your audience. Often it may be appropriate to tie in the take-home with the *checkup* and *assignment* phases of your presentation.

Prepare Your Mind

You have been given the assignment (or you see a need) to prepare a briefing. Once you have considered the ingredients and have firmed up your topic and your intent, it may be useful to consider your own expectations. What will it be like addressing this audience? For some people, even experienced managers, speaking before groups is a very uncomfortable ordeal. Here are some suggestions of ways to reduce anxiety and actually *enjoy* presentational speaking.

Your Audience Wants You to Succeed

In almost every situation your audience wants you to succeed in your presentation. People come to a briefing hoping it will be a good one. They are rooting for you. If you are suspicious of that statement think back on a situation where you were in the audience of a briefing or speech that went poorly. Perhaps the speaker was unusually nervous or poorly prepared. Recall how uncomfortable *you* felt *for* that speaker. Your audience will empathize with you and will seldom consciously do anything to heighten your anxiety. Your business audience is far more likely to be considerate and friendly—but also expectant. They come to the briefing expecting to receive useful information presented in digestible form. So long as you're prepared to provide that, you will have their complete support.

Controlling Anxiety: Flying in Formation

The only people who experience no nervousness before an audience are drunks or fools. If we have any self-regard we'll be concerned about how others see us and respond to us. This concern quite naturally leads to some nervousness. The skillful speaker seeks to *control* this nervous energy, not to eliminate it. As the Toastmaster's* handbook says, effectiveness training in speech "won't completely eliminate those butterflies in the stomach, but it will keep them flying in formation."

There are a number of things we can do to cope with stage fright. Communication professors Harold Zelko and Frank Dance talk about developing your "coping quotient" by reducing the number of things you must give conscious attention to. In other words, as different aspects of presentational speaking become natural and spontaneous, we can channel our concentration toward the specific purpose of our briefing. It's like typing or playing a musical instrument. So long as we must consciously think about how each finger should be positioned to print a letter or produce a note, we will never be effective in putting together the entire composition.

Here are several ways to reduce the number of specific things that call for your attention in order to bring the presentation comfortably within your coping quotient:[2]

(1) *Prepare!* There is absolutely no substitute for adequate preparation. If you are well prepared, your capacity to cope with problems rises significantly. Nothing reduces anxiety like being well prepared to the point of being overprepared—totally confident of your grasp of the subject matter. Preparation should go beyond the content and delivery of the presentation to include practice in handling anticipated questions. This is where the high cost of the presentation medium comes in. A rule of thumb is that you should spend up to one hour of preparation for each minute of speaking.

---

*Toastmasters International is an organization aimed at improving members' communication and leadership skills. For more information about their programs, consult your local phone directory or write them at P.O. Box 10400, Santa Ana, Calif. 92711.

(2) *Be idea-conscious, not self-conscious.* Having your specific purpose in mind helps reduce overconcern for irrelevant details. The principle of the "unconscious success mechanism" enters here. We are most effective when we don't think of each step or each procedure needed to complete a task but instead focus on the desired result and let our subconscious mind help us get there. The baseball outfielder going after a high fly ball doesn't consciously think, "I'll take six steps to my left, two steps forward, raise my glove with my left hand and shield my eyes from the sun with my right hand. . . ." Instead he fixes his eye on the ball and visualizes the desired result of catching it. His unconscious success mechanisms go through the mechanics of bringing that to pass and free him from concerns about tripping over his shoelace, taking the wrong size of steps, or raising his glove too late.

The same principle applies in presentational speaking. Overconcern with mechanics at the point of doing the briefing can only be distracting and anxiety producing. Zelko and Dance give this example:

> Self-consciousness tends to be self-destructive. If you are overly worried about the way you look, you often overcompensate and this draws to yourself attention which would not ordinarily be centered on you. It's when you are trying to walk nonchalantly that you walk stiffly or affectedly. It is when you are trying to smile naturally ("Say 'cheese' ") that your smile tends to look artificial. If you are caught up in a conversation or in telling a story and the conversation or the story causes you to smile, you are usually unaware of the smile itself, and it is at that point that the smile is, and appears, most natural. Similarly with speaking in public. When you are caught up in the message of your speech, when you are interested in communicating the ideas of the speech to the listeners, you are not usually uncomfortable or noticeably concerned with how you look or how you sound—it's the idea that is at center stage, not the self. Simple remedies: Be audience-centered; be message-centered; not self-centered.[3]

(3) *Relax.* If you are well prepared and idea-conscious, not self-conscious, you are raising your coping quotient to a level where anxiety should not be a problem. If you still feel that flush of nervousness just as you're being introduced, don't worry about it. It's perfectly natural and it is seldom visible to your audience. When you get up to speak, take a moment to arrange your notes, look at your audience and smile, and take a few slow, deep breaths. Even professional entertainers use these kinds of movements to prepare themselves and their audience. I recently saw a TV special about Elvis Presley's last concert tour and was interested to see the king of rock and roll, visibly nervous, pause for several minutes to take relaxing deep breaths just before going on stage.

Use Your Background and Experience

Every speaker talks from a wide background of thought and experience. We each bring unique experiences, attitudes, and ideas to any presentation we do, yet for some reason, speakers tend to depreciate the value of such experience and ideas and instead turn to other, more "authoritative" sources. There are, of course, situations where it's important to cite recognized authorities on a topic, but don't hesitate to add your own ideas too. We are usually more comfortable as we bring more of ourselves into the talk. We can better explain and answer questions about *personal* experiences. Your preparation for this briefing makes you a bona fide authority in your own right.

Audience Analysis: Discovering Attitudes

We constantly look at others and make guesses about how they will act or what they will do. As we walk down a busy city sidewalk we anticipate the actions of others based on what we see them do and on our past experiences in similar situations. We suspect that the lady in front of us may suddenly stop to look in a store window. We feel pretty confident that if we stay to the right of the sidewalk we'll be in the flow of traffic. We expect that the young panhandler will approach us next. These guesses, suspicions, and anticipations cause us to adjust our behavior.

Analysis of our audience is every bit as natural and can be done with considerably more accuracy. Our guesses become more educated as we learn more about individual listeners. Such analysis is an *ongoing process* that we conduct during the preparation and throughout the actual presentation. The primary purpose is to discover audience needs, attitudes, values, and predispositions so that your talk will be seen as relevant to these. You'll also learn not to unintentionally insult or offend your listeners.

Another function of audience analysis is to determine how much your audience already knows about your subject and how much they need to or would like to know. Going over detailed information that is already known can be taken as talking down to your listener and can insult their intelligence. On the other hand, presenting complex information to people who don't understand the basics can result in frustration for you and your listeners.

The organizational communicator often has an advantage over the public speaker in audience analysis. He or she can—and should—go directly to the people who will be briefed to get information about their attitudes and foreknowledge. The more thorough this analysis, the more potential objections or misunderstandings will surface in time for preparation of additional arguments or clarification. All of which means you'll

2.

have your "ducks in a row" when the actual presentation comes about. Visit or phone individual members of your audience before you prepare your briefing. This will be time well spent. One caution: be sure you are *gathering* information, not jumping the gun on your pitch. You need to do lots of listening and very little talking at this point. Your turn to talk comes later.

Figure 7-1, an Audience Analysis Audit,[4] suggests some of the questions that you should ask yourself as you develop your presentation.

Developing a Preliminary Plan

Once your purpose is clear and you have analyzed your audience, there is one more step to prepare your mind before you begin to prepare the subject matter of your talk. Developing a blueprint—a preliminary plan—can help you decide how much and what kind of material to put in your briefing. This is not a speaking outline but rather a conceptual approach to what will most logically lead to accomplishing your objectives.

Main Ideas

A key objective of the preliminary plan is to spell out the main ideas or concepts that the audience must get if you are to be successful. Your main ideas should be stated in the form of conclusions you want your listeners to reach. For example, your main ideas for a persuasive briefing urging the hiring of a plant safety inspector may be:

1. It is essential that the company get the expertise needed to cope with its increasing accident rate and more frequent government inspections.
2. The costs of hiring a safety expert would be offset by reduced lost-time injuries and avoidance of government penalties.
3. This company cares about its employees' well-being and is committed to creating a safe and pleasant place to work.
4. A search committee must be appointed to find a qualified safety inspector.

For some presentations there is only one main idea which will be approached from several directions. A progress report may simply stress that "We are on target" or "We will meet our objectives in spite of certain temporary setbacks."

When developing these main ideas or concepts—those the audience *must* understand if you are to be successful—be sure to

1. State the main ideas as conclusions, preferably in complete sentences.

1. Identify the objectives in presenting your briefing to THIS audience. What do you want to happen as a result of it?

(Keep these objectives in mind as you consider the items below.)

2. Specific Analysis of members of this audience—

   a. Their knowledge of the subject:

   High level   General   Limited   None   Unknown

   b. Their opinions about the subject and/or the speaker or organization represented:

   Very favorable   Favorable   Neutral

   Slightly hostile   Very hostile   .

   c. Their reasons for attending this briefing:

   d. Advantages and disadvantages of briefing results to them as individuals:
      Advantages _____
      Disadvantages _____

3. General Analysis of members of this audience—

   a. Their occupational relationships to speaker or his organization:

   Customer   Top management   Immediate management

   Co-workers   Subordinates   Other management

   Other workers   Public

   b. Length of relationship with company as customer or employee:

   New   Less than two years   More than two years

   Unknown

   c. Their vocabulary understanding level:

   Technical   Nontechnical   Generally high

   Generally low   Unknown

   d. Open-mindedness (willingness to accept ideas to be presented)

   Eager   Open   Neutral

   Slightly resistant   Strongly resistant

4. Information and techniques most likely to gain the attention of this audience:

   High technical information   Statistical comparisons

   Cost figures   Anecdotes   Demonstrations   Other

5. Information or techniques likely to get negative reactions from this audience:

Figure 7-1 Audience analysis audit*

*From Morrisey, *Effective Business and Technical Presentations*, 2nd. Ed., © 1975, Addison-Wesley, Reading, Massachusetts. Pp. 23–24. Reprinted with permission.

2. Be sure each idea leads to a specific objective such as securing agreement, convincing, or gaining a desired action. (In the example above, the first three ideas aim at getting agreement or inducing belief. The fourth seeks action.)
3. Express ideas in thought-provoking ways.
4. Use only a few main ideas, probably not more than five.

Support for main ideas. Once key ideas are stated, determine what factual information is necessary to help your audience understand them. Write down simple descriptions of such supporting information. Do not elaborate or go into excessive detail. The main ideas of the "safety inspector" briefing might be identified like this:

1. Company records showing increased accident rate and increased number of government inspections.
2. Estimate of cost of employing a safety inspector.
3. Amount of fines levied by government inspectors in similar industries.
4. Description of company policy and programs that indicate high concern for employees' well-being.

Using a preliminary plan as a guide will help focus your energy toward the goal of your presentation. It also helps reduce wasted time and results in a more cohesive briefing.

Morrisey provides a guideline for developing the preliminary plan in Figure 7-2. The manager who makes frequent presentations may want to make a copy of this and tape it to his or her desk for easy reference.[5]

Figure 7-3 presents samples of preliminary plans for explanatory, persuasive, and progress report briefings.[6]

Prepare Your Matter

Once your preplanning is complete it is time to assemble the contents of your briefing. The three major parts of the presentation are the introduction, body, and conclusion. Transitions tie each of these together.

If your introduction fails to gain sufficient attention and interest, your message will not be received. Typically, audiences are alert as a speaker begins to talk. Their attention span curves downward as the presentation goes on and then perks up as the speaker gives his concluding remarks. If your conclusion is not effective, audience retention of what has been said suffers. For these reasons, special emphasis should be placed on preparing strong introductions and conclusions.

1. Identify specific objectives for the briefing, keeping in mind the following criteria:

   a. They should answer the question, "Why am I giving this briefing?"

   b. They should state the results desired from the briefing, in effect, completing the sentence, "I want the following things to happen as a result of this briefing: . . ."

   c. They should be designed to accomplish whatever hidden objectives you have for the briefing.

Note: If the body of knowledge to be presented must be identified in the objectives, use a sentence such as "I want to tell about . . . so that . . . will take place."

2. Identify the specific audience for whom you are designing this briefing and state in a one- or two-sentence summary pertinent information about their knowledge, attitudes, and so forth.

3. State the MAIN IDEAS OR CONCEPTS that the audience MUST get if the objectives of the briefing are to be met. These should:

   a. Be in conclusion form and preferably in complete sentences.

   b. Definitely lead to the accomplishment of the specific objectives.

   c. Be interesting in themselves or capable of being made so.

   d. Be few in number, usually no more than five.

4. Identify under each main idea the types of factual information necessary so that this audience can understand these ideas. Avoid excessive detail.

This Plan Should Be Used as a Guide:

1. For the briefer in selecting materials, keeping ideas channeled, and determining emphasis points.

2. For support personnel who may provide the backup data, prepare charts and other aids, and assist in the briefing itself.

Figure 7-2 Guidelines for preparing a preliminary plan*

Introduction: Grabs You, Aligns You, Locks You In

The advertisement for a television set that "takes the color, grabs it, aligns it, and locks it in" pretty well describes what a good introduction should do. The introduction that just gets attention does only part of the job. You can get attention by pounding on the desk, tapping a waterglass with a spoon, shouting obscenities, or telling an elephant joke, but that doesn't

*From Morrisey, *Effective Business and Technical Presentations*, 2nd. Ed., © 1975, Addison-Wesley, Reading, Massachusetts. Pp. 27-28. Reprinted with permission.

Topic: Orientation of New Employees

Objectives:

1. To provide an overview of the company's history, organization, and products so that new employees can more readily understand and identify with the company's philosophy and objectives and feel a sense of responsibility for the part they will play in the organization.

2. To identify, in broad terms, company policies and benefits so that the employees will be able to apply or take advantage of them with a minimum of wasted time and effort.

Audience:

New employees at all levels. Most will have at best a limited knowledge of the subject matter, will be somewhat nervous and unsure of themselves, will be unable to retain the majority of the detail presented, but will be positively motivated to learn.

Main ideas the audience MUST get:

1. This is a strong company with a good product line and a firm future for competent, conscientious employees.

2. Company management personnel are interested in the growth and well-being of their employees.

3. Capable assistance is available to all employees in the application of policies and procedures and in the interpretation and use of company benefits.

4. Employees are expected to meet their company responsibilities and, in return, will be treated fairly and equitably.

Factual supporting information related to all the main ideas:

1. Company historical highlights and major product lines.

2. Company organization and key management personnel.

3. Highlights of relevant company policies and procedures.

4. Company benefit programs and sources of information.

Figure 7-3 Preliminary plan sample,* explanatory briefing   *(continued)*

serve as an introduction *unless* it also leads the audience into the body of the talk.

Several standard devices you can use for an effective introduction are illustrated here. Your audience analysis, preliminary plan, and your own personality will help you select the best approach.

*From Morrisey, *Effective Business and Technical Presentations*, 2nd. Ed., © 1975, Addison-Wesley, Reading, Massachusetts. Pp. 39–42. Reprinted with permission.

Topic: Need for Increased Training in the Company

Objectives:

1. To create an awareness of the need for increased training.

2. To gain management approval and support for increased training so they will act to:

   a. Authorize necessary funds,

   b. Authorize time for training, and

   c. Give verbal and written support to training efforts.

Audience:

Members of top management plus other management personnel at Director level or higher. Most will have a general knowledge of the subject, a few will be favorably inclined, but most will be neutral, skeptical, or slightly hostile.

Main ideas the audience MUST get:

1. Increased training is essential if we are to survive in the industry.

2. Money invested in training now (charged to Overhead or taken from Profit) will be returned manyfold in the future.

3. Time spent in training now (taken from urgent current work) will result in a much more profitable use of time in the future.

Factual supporting information:

Idea 1

   a. New technology requirements.

   b. Training experience in other similar companies.

   c. Potential application of new management concepts.

Idea 2

   a. Recent training progress in the company.

   b. Comparative cost of operation figures (before and after).

   c. Personnel training versus replacement costs.

Idea 3

   a. Comparative (before and after) time-investment ratios.

   b. Intangible time benefits, for example, increased confidence and effectivity of personnel resulting in more productive use of time.

(continued)

Figure 7-3 (cont.) Preliminary plan sample, persuasive briefing

Topic: Progress Report on XYZ Project

Objective:

To keep upper management informed in a regular monthly briefing on the current status of the XYZ Project and to draw their attention to any potential trouble spots so that corrective action can be initiated.

Audience:

Department Manager, Section Director, Chief Engineer, related staff personnel. They are familiar with the project and will be interested primarily in adherence to schedule.

Main ideas the audience MUST get:

1. Project is currently one week behind but can be brought back on schedule with the following adjustments:

    a. Authorization of 100 overtime hours in next month.

    b. Elimination of second reinforcement tests which will serve merely to validate the results of the first test.

2. Costs will remain within budget if both these adjustments are made.

3. All performance standards are being met.

Factual supporting information related to all the main ideas:

1. Factors affecting schedule.

2. Comparative cost figures.

3. Test results.

4. Key performance measurements.

Figure 7-3 (cont.) Preliminary plan sample, progress report

Startling statement. "The river behind our assembly plant has been declared a fire hazard." or "By the year 1989—less than ten years from now—we will run out of the primary materials we use to manufacture our products." These kinds of straightforward statements can get your listeners' attention if they are interestingly worded and not too complicated. The natural reaction is to perk up and mentally ask for more information.

Statistics. Statistics can often be worded in ways that grab our attention. "Today more than 64 percent of our female employees utilize day care facilities for their children at a cost of more than $90,000 per year." "Today, on May 10, you begin working for yourself and your family. Since the first of the year you've been working to pay your taxes." There are many ways that statistics can be expressed to make them sound smaller ("only 93¢ per day") or larger ("over its contract life the service will cost $75,000"). How you word this depends on your intent.

Rhetorical question. This is the use of thought-provoking questions for which you don't expect an answer. "Just how much more government interference can our company take?" or "How would you feel if you were turned down for a promotion because your skin was not the right color?" Sometimes a whole series of these is effective:

> What will you do when there is no gasoline to drive your car?
> —when there is no fuel to heat your home?
> —when our electrical generators go silent?
> —when the oil supply runs out?
> What will you do?

Be careful not to overwork this approach. And remember that there is always the danger that some wise guy will *answer* your question and completely deflate your introduction. "How many more people do we have to lose to the competition before we wake up?" If someone in the audience deadpans, "Eleven," your intro may fizzle.

Quotation, definition or short narrative. Often a short story, quote, or light remark can effectively lead into the body of your talk. A briefing advocating expenditures for additional training might build upon a quote from Benjamin Franklin: "If a man empties his purse into his head no man can take it away from him." If a man invests in learning he has made the greatest investment.

Here's an example I recently heard. A newspaper editor was critical of President Jimmy Carter's call for personal sacrifice to solve the inflation problem. He began this way:

> Chutzpah is a Yiddish word for nerve or gall. It's best defined by the story of the boy who murders his parents and then begs for the mercy of the court on the grounds that he's an orphan.
> You've got chutzpah, Mr. President.
> Our government wrecks our pocketbook and ruins our dollar. Then our president goes on TV and appeals to us to put the house in order.
> Some nerve, some gall.

Everybody loves to hear a story. So it's no surprise that the narrative or short anecdote, especially if a personal example, often works beautifully. Simply relate your interesting experiences as though you were telling a friend. Strive for a conversational tone. Don't drag out the story; use it only as a lead-in to the meat of your talk.

You need not be a professional entertainer to come up with useful attention-getting materials. Your local library will have dozens of books of humor and interesting anecdotes which are likely to fit into your theme. Here's one I used while addressing a training workshop of retail department store executives. The theme of the conference was maximizing sales through customer service. I changed the wording of the story slightly to make it sound like a personal experience.

A man went into a clothing store to buy a suit. The salesman asked him his name, age, religion, occupation, college, high school, hobbies, political party, and his wife's maiden name.

"Why all the questions?" the customer asked. "All I want is a suit."

"Sir, this is not just an ordinary tailor shop," the salesman said. "We don't merely sell you a suit. We find a suit that is exactly right for you.

"We make a study of your personality and your background and your surroundings. We send to the part of Australia that has the kind of sheep your character and mood require.

"We ship that particular blend of wool to London to be combed and sponged according to a special formula. Then the wool is woven in a section of Scotland where the climate is most favorable to your temperament. Then we fit and measure you carefully.

"Finally, after much careful thought and study, the suit is made. There are more fittings and more changes. And then . . ."

"Wait a minute," the customer said. "I need this suit tomorrow night for my nephew's wedding."

"Don't worry," the salesman said. "You'll have it."[5]

"Now *that's* customer service!" I concluded. The audience enjoyed it and I had their attention.

A word of caution: always *practice* a joke or story *out loud* several times to be sure it *sounds* as good as it reads.

Statement of topic or reference to occasion. If your audience is already interested in what you'll be saying, a simple statement of your topic may be sufficient. "I am going to outline the new sales representative compensation program." Reference to the occasion may sound like this: "As you know, Tom has asked me to take a few minutes at each staff meeting to update you on the computerization program."

There are, of course, other introductory approaches and combinations that will work. There are also a few sure-fire ways to flop, some of which are discussed here.

Sure fire ways to flop

The apologetic beginning. The unaccustomed-as-I-am-to-public-speaking type of remark has no place in a briefing. Neither do opening statements like, "I'm here to bore you with a few more statistics" or "I'm pretty nervous, so I hope you'll bear with me." If you haven't prepared well enough to be effective it will become obvious to your audience soon enough. You accomplish nothing by announcing it.

The potentially offensive beginning. An off-color joke, a ridiculing statement, or use of the same, standard opening remark regardless of the audience or occasion will eventually get you in trouble.

> The story is told of a rather timid governor who spoke to the inmates of a men's penitentiary. He began conventionally with "Ladies and . . . ," but there was laughter before he could get out the word "gentlemen." After he recovered, he began a second time with "Fellow inmates," and again there was a burst of laughter. A moment later he blundered on with "Glad to see so many of you here." Undoubtedly, more planning should have gone into the governor's opening remarks to make them appropriate to his audience.[6]

Other openings may be inappropriate because they are trite or excessively flattering, or just plain phony: "I am filled with a deep sense of personal inadequacy when I presume to speak authoritatively in the presence of so many knowledgeable men."

The gimmicky beginning. Resist the temptation to blow a whistle, sing a song, role-play a violent scene from a play, or write the word SEX on the blackboard saying, "Now that I have your attention . . ." These just don't work. They tend to put your audience on the spot—they don't know how they should respond. It's embarrassing and distracting.

In summary, your introduction should be brief and direct. It should get the audience's attention and prepare them for what is to follow. Just ask yourself, would this introduction get my attention? If not, rework it. The introduction is probably the single most important segment of your talk, so plan it carefully.

The Body: Now That I Have Your Attention

If your introduction has been effective, it sets the stage for the body of your presentation. The body presents your main points, elaborates on them, clarifies, and summarizes so the audience will remember what you've said. The number of main points should be limited to as few as will cover the material adequately. With too many main points your listener's retention will suffer. Psychologist George Miller has studied short-

233

term memory, concluding that it is limited for most people to between five and nine items.[7] To be safe, try to keep main points to four or five.

Organizing Your Main Points

The arrangement of main points will vary depending on your purpose. But before I recommend specific arrangements for different purposes, let us see what options are commonly available.

Direct plan. This arrangement begins with the main idea or the general conclusion of the briefing followed by supporting information. It uses *deductive* logic, that is, a general statement followed by explanatory details. Here is an example:

> The coming year should be our most profitable year since 1973. (main point) In the last 6 months, orders for our solar collectors have increased by 86 percent; costs of raw materials have remained stable and are projected to increase by not more than 2 percent in the coming year; and our recent contract with the union freezes wages and benefits at present levels for the next 18 months. (supporting details)

The direct order may be used to organize details under their main point and/or to arrange the entire body of the presentation. When used in the latter way, the main points should be prioritized so that the most important or dramatic or significant point comes first. The selection of these priorities may be a judgment call for the presenter but it should be based on audience needs and interests.

The direct organization is appropriate for many if not most briefings. It is efficient and hits the high point immediately while the audience's attention level is still high.

Indirect plan. The indirect or *inductive* order starts with details or supporting information and builds up to the main point. Main points, similarly, are arranged in ascending order of importance so that *the big idea* or major conclusion comes last. Here is how the example above would look if arranged inductively:

> Our recent contract with the union freezes wages and benefits at present levels for the next 18 months. Costs of raw materials for our products have remained stable and are projected to increase by not more than 2 percent in the coming year. And, in the last 6 months, orders for our solar collectors have increased by 86 percent. *The coming year will be our most profitable year since 1973.*

The indirect arrangement works best when the speaker sees the need to be persuasive, when the briefing's purpose is to get the listeners to believe or to do something they are not likely to otherwise believe or do. If the conclusion were presented first as in the direct plan, the listener may be defensive or even argumentative, tuning out the evidence that supports that conclusion. The indirect plan avoids this by putting the evidence first, using convincing detail to lead to the general conclusion. Much resistance can be overcome with skillful use of indirect arrangement of ideas.

Problem-solution plan. Another arrangement especially useful in persuasive situations is the problem-solution approach. Here, extensive effort and time is dedicated to the clarification and amplification of some felt need. The objective is to get the listener to recognize and be concerned about the problem in personal terms. Once this point is reached, introduction of your solution is welcomed and acceptance is likely. This approach is used frequently on television advertisements. We tend to identify with the guy who backs his trailer into his neighbor's porch (problem) because we know how difficult steering a trailer can be and we're relieved to hear that his insurance company will pick up the tab for the damage if not the embarrassment (solution). We relate to the headache and stomach ailments of the late night party-goer on a personal level (problem) and sigh with relief at the appearance of "plop, plop, fizz, fizz." This persuasive approach is as common as jogging shoes. But it still works. Here's an example:

> In the past six months our use of long-distance telephone service has increased by 71 percent with no noticeable decrease in the use of letters or teletype. As a result of this increase, our monthly phone bills now exceed $850 a month. Even if the usage could be held at this level, that's $10,200 a year for long distance—as much as we'd spend on an extra, desperately needed clerical employee. While the increase is alarming, the prospect of not being able to put a lid on it is what really bothers me. Without better control, our profit picture and our individual earnings are going to be hurt. (need development and personalization of problem)
>
> There is a way we can deal with this that I think you'll like. The telephone company representative has been talking to me about installing a WATS line. Here are some cost figures. . . . (solution)

Cause-effect plan. This approach simply develops the relationship between two events. By clarifying how one causes the other, the speaker can recommend changes in one to bring about corresponding changes in the other. This arrangement can be useful in either explanatory or informational briefings or, when followed by a call for action, in persuasive presentations. A *chain of events* pattern simply links together a series of cause-and-effect relationships.

Chronological order. This organization plan simply arranges points as they occur in time. A briefing on the company's financial history based on fiscal periods would use this plan.

Topical or spatial order. Points in the presentation dealing with different but related topics or examples are arranged so that each supports the main conclusion, which may be stated either before or following the evidence. Space order typically moves from examples which are near to those far away or vice versa. For example, a progress report on computerization may begin with the local branch and move to outlying branches or to other cities.

Increasing magnitude or difficulty pattern. A briefing on the effects of the economy on a business may develop from relatively local, temporary factors over which the organization maintains some control, to the more complex national or worldwide condition which is beyond its control. For example, a slowdown in sales in a downtown shoe store may be attributed to

- fewer sales made per employee
- increased competition from newer stores in outlying shopping malls
- a higher crime rate in the vicinity of the store
- higher unemployment rate due to a layoff at a major local employer
- delays in getting high-demand shoes from distributors
- a worldwide shortage of quality leather

Each of these points represents increasing difficulty for the local businessman.

This order of arrangement may also be used to instruct listeners. The speaker could begin with something familiar or already known by the listener and move to the unknown or more complex. For example, training on the use of a new machine could begin by first reviewing the operation of an already familiar machine, then pointing out basic similarities of the steps in using the unfamiliar new machine.

Order of importance plan. Particularly useful in the progress report, this arrangement presents the most significant or noteworthy point first, with other developments following in descending order of importance. For example, main ideas may be

- The wind tunnel test of the missile tail assembly was successful.
- The electronic malfunction problem in the sensing device has been narrowed down to two possible causes.
- The engineers are considering the use of a different coating which will be more resistant to wear.

Figure 7-4 summarizes the ways of arranging the body of your oral presentation.

Developing and Supporting Main Points

Most main points take the form of simple declarative statements. Few of these can stand alone. Support, elaboration, clarification, and proof can shore up these themes and result in audience acceptance and agreement. Several types of support are discussed below.

Specific details or explanation of the main point are probably the most common though not always most effective way to build support. Here we simply explain in other words what we have asserted. This support may be prefaced by remarks such as "Let me explain why I've said that" or "Another way to say this might be. . . ." In my experience, speakers rely too heavily on this type of support when other, more interesting approaches could be used, some of which are discussed below.

Comparisons or analogies often result in strong support. Frequently these take the form of a narrative. Here is a recent example overheard at a convention. A young professor asked an older, well-established author how long it took him to complete his recent book. The author responded with a narrative about a wartime experience in Europe in 1945. The author, who was then a soldier in recently liberated Paris, approached a sidewalk artist whom he had observed painting. He asked if the painting was for sale and the artist responded, "Yes." When informed of the price, the soldier replied, "But it only took you an hour to paint that!" The artist responded indignantly, "But I have prepared all my life." The young professor got the point of the analogy and felt a bit embarrassed for even asking the question. Think about what a different impact this narrative had. It communicated very clearly and went far beyond anything else that

Type Briefing	General Objective	Organization of Body
Persuasive	Get audience to accept ideas and/or do something ("sell" them something)	Inductive pattern: Show several specific cases or lines of reasoning which lead up to general conclusion/action step. (Use when audience resistance to your key idea is expected to be strong.)
		Problem-solution pattern: Describe a problem vividly and in a way that your audience feels the need. Then offer your solution/action step
		Cause-effect pattern: Develop relation between two events and show how a change in one will affect the other
Explanatory or instructional	Inform audience (teach them something)	Deductive pattern: Present the conclusion and explain how it was arrived at. [May also be used in persuasive talks when the key idea is not likely to turn off your listeners.]
		Chronological pattern: Show how events developed over time.
		Topical or spatial pattern: Give examples from different places or categories which relate to the topic.
		Increasing difficulty pattern: Starting from something already known, add to it to explain more complex or unusual concepts.
		Chain of events pattern: Show how different steps or procedures lead to a certain conclusion.
Progress report	Inform or update knowledge	Chronological or chain of events pattern: (as above)
		Order of importance: Present the most significant developments first.

Figure 7-4 Arranging the body of a presentation

could have been said in a direct response to the question. The parables taught by Jesus are, of course, analogies told in narrative form. They provide long-lasting and thought-provoking support to His teachings.

Examples, especially those of a personal nature, add support to main points and also lend credibility to the speaker. Some speakers are unduly hesitant about using personal experiences. These provide support of a firsthand nature and can be very convincing. Be certain that your example is typical of and pertinent to the point being supported. An isolated incident or fluke occurrence will be obvious to your audience and should not be presented as illustrative of a general condition. For example, if our main point is: "Morale in the plant is low," we do not sufficiently support it with a single example of one employee's complaints about working conditions. If, however, we string together a series of isolated examples, we develop support for our theme:

> *Main point:* Employee morale is low.
>
> *Supporting examples:* Six different workers have complained about the excessive heat in the plant.
> Absenteeism is up 20% over last month.
> Three workers quit, citing unbearable shop conditions.
> Four grievances have been filed with the union.

Statistics provide support when they are used ethically. There are many well-known ways to distort information using statistics but, of course, there are many ways to lie, period. The problem is that some speakers don't really understand how statistics are derived or what they have when they get them.

There are two general types of statistics: descriptive and inferential. *Descriptive* statistics can take a large quantity of numbers and make another, much smaller set of numbers out of it with the essential information remaining intact. In other words, they condense or describe the original mass of data to make it more intelligible. *Inferential* statistics predict conclusions based on evidence provided by samples and mathematically calculate probabilities that a given conclusion is so.

Sometimes statistics confuse more than they clarify or support. In briefings, the speaker should determine what level of statistical expertise his audience has before relying heavily on the more sophisticated statistics. Most people can readily grasp descriptive statistics but are rather confused by probabilities. I recently heard a speaker misusing actuarial data compiled by an insurance company to project life span based on health habits. He told his audience such things as "If you smoke more than two packs of cigarettes a day, subtract 8 years from your life; if you live in the country, add 2 years to your life." By the time he finished, half his audience figured they'd live forever and the other half wondered why they weren't already dead. The point is that actuarial data on life expectancies are very complex statistics. If you don't thoroughly understand the implications of their use, don't use them.

Three things will help you develop an idea by statistics.

1. Round out large numbers so your listeners can digest them.
2. Interpret the numbers in some meaningful way. Percentages seem to be the easiest for most of us to cope with.
3. Be sure to compare "apples to apples." I recently heard a speaker express relief that our unemployment rate was only six or seven percent, whereas in Israel, "one person in 18 is unemployed!" That, of course, is virtually the same percentage.

Use statistics sparingly. They should not be considered the only type of support but should be part of an assortment of developmental approaches.

Formal quotations are less frequently used in business briefings than in public speeches. But they can be effective if we choose to quote an authority who is

1. a recognized expert
2. in a position to know about the specific point we are trying to support
3. in general agreement with other authorities on the subject
4. free from prejudice which would distort his or her view

The person quoted need not be a world-renowned expert; he or she may well be someone within the organization with considerable experience or training in the area being discussed. In deciding whether an authority is free of prejudice, consider what the person quoted may stand to gain or lose. You would probably not quote a TV advertising salesman's views on the relative merits of newspaper versus broadcast promotions.

Audiovisual aids may be used in conjunction with several other types of support. There is an increasing awareness of the importance of supplementing the spoken word with another medium. Many employees in organizations have been raised in the "television age" and have been conditioned to audio and visual communication techniques. As was mentioned in Chapter 4, frequently communication effectiveness is enhanced by use of more than one medium. Visuals can range from a simple chalkboard or flip chart to the highly sophisticated multimedia productions involving slides, movies, special lighting effects, and elaborate sound systems. In most business presentations we can often use a wide variety of devices such as charts, graphs, overhead projectors, slides, movies or videotape, tape recordings and models. Often our creativity is our only limitation. I'll discuss audiovisual aids in more detail later in this chapter.

Conveying Your Credibility

One more factor crucial to your effectiveness in supporting main points must be considered. Although this is not a specific technique nor is it something you use only in the body of the briefing, it is probably the single most important factor in determining overall effectiveness. I am speaking of your *credibility*.

Aristotle's treatise, *The Rhetoric*, was probably the first book on communication theory. In it, he explains three types of arguments one may use to convince an audience: logical appeals (*logos*), emotional appeals (*pathos*), and ethical appeals (*ethos*). And of these three, *ethos* is the strongest.

Over time the concept of ethos has come to refer to the *credibility* of the message source. People who are held in high esteem because of perceived intelligence or ethical standards are far more likely to be effective communicators.

Credibility is an ongoing personality characteristic which permeates all our interactions with others. In organizations where we are likely to have repeated communication opportunities with the same people, what we said or did yesterday or last month may well have bearing on our credibility today.

Most of the considerable research into what determines credibility has concluded that there are four factors which determine our perceived credibility in a given situation:

(1) *Expertise.* How well informed we are about a given topic affects credibility. The highly credible source is likely to be one who has experience and/or training relevant to the topic *and* who effectively conveys this competence to the audience. Demonstration of understanding of the issues discussed and use of firsthand experience or personal examples is one way to build this expertise factor.

(2) *Trustworthiness.* When a speaker is seen as being sincere and unbiased, credibility will be enhanced. One way to convey such an impression is by using facts and reasoning carefully and usually avoiding overuse of emotionalism in language. Also, recognizing and presenting opposing points of view can demonstrate the propensity to weigh alternatives carefully and examine issues judiciously. Of course, the absence of

secret motives such as personal gain or special advantages for the individual's work group will also strengthen trust in the speaker.

(3) *Composure.* Whether a person is seen as poised, relaxed, and confident as opposed to nervous, tense, or uncomfortable affects credibility. These perceptions arise from our audience's awareness of cues, most of which are nonverbal. Appearance, posture, mannerisms, and purposefulness of movements combine to create an impression of personal composure. There is, of course, such a thing as being *too* composed. The meticulously groomed, carefully rehearsed, and precisely choreographed presentation might be a bit suspect. Being too perfect may cause others to question your trustworthiness. The image created by looking sharp and acting confidently—with an added dash of humility—seems to be the kind most of us prefer.

(4) *Dynamism.* A fourth factor believed to affect source credibility is a sense of personal dynamism: the tendency to be active, outgoing, talkative, or bold. The very introverted, shy, or apprehensive individual is usually seen as less credible. But, as with composure, this can be carried too far. The stereotyped hotshot used car salesman or the loud-mouthed jokester may be dynamic but not credible. In many situations, the soft-spoken voice of quiet reasoning is welcomed. Research showing a relationship between dynamism and high credibility has been less convincing than that relating high credibility to expertise, trust, and composure.

Credibility permeates all the activities of a communicator. In many cases, it arrives before you do in the form of others' past impressions. The speaker whose credibility is not yet established must make a conscious effort to demonstrate these characteristics to the audience. The speaker who is already high in credibility must reinforce that view. And the speaker with low credibility must expend considerable effort to create more favorable images. These changes in attitudes toward the low credibility speaker take time and usually repeated demonstrations of change.

The organization of a presentation can do much to build credibility as well as improve audience comprehension and retention. Studies have shown that the speaker who is well organized in his or her presentation is regarded as a more credible source than a speaker who is disorganized. This was determined by measuring audience attitudes toward the speaker after presenting essentially the same speech in either organized or disorganized fashion.[8]

Transitions, Summaries, and Conclusions

Transitions are statements or questions which help provide coherence in the talk by bridging together separate thoughts or parts of the presentation. Typically they remind the listener of what was just said and then preview what's coming up next. Frequently they also serve as internal summaries and thus add repetition which helps the audience remember what has been said on that point. Here is an example of a transition: "I have just suggested that transitions bridge together parts of a talk and often double as summaries. Let's look more closely at the function of the general summary which leads into a conclusion."

A general summary should be presented near the end of the briefing to tie together the whole presentation. The functions of a final summary are to review and remind the audience of the major points you have presented and to emphasize particular points *this audience* should take with them. A good summary is brief, hits the high spots, and *does not introduce new material.*

An effective summary leads naturally into a conclusion. Everything you have done to develop this presentation comes to a climax at the conclusion. So a most important question goes back to your preliminary planning—what was your specific intent? Picture yourself as a listener and ask that tough question: "What does all this mean to me?" Your talk should have provided a clear answer.

Action steps are appropriate for all kinds of briefings. Your audience has a right to expect and receive guidance from all your research and preparation. And if you don't provide such guidance in the form of a clear, action-oriented conclusion, you have probably let your listeners down. The actions you advocate should, of course, be ones you can realistically request from your listeners.

Use of Audiovisual Aids

Virtually any oral presentation will be reinforced by the use of some sort of audiovisual materials. Clearer understanding and retention of ideas results from use of several media in combination.

When developing your preliminary plan, you should think about audiovisual support. The most common approach is to develop graphic illustrations such as posters or flip charts, overhead transparencies, or slides. Here are a few thoughts to keep in mind when using such illustrations.

(1) Each aid should be planned to drive home a *single* point. The quickest way to lose the effectiveness of an audiovisual aid is to overcomplicate it or try to convey too much information. This is especially true with charts or illustrations. Keep them simple and concise. Never display a chart or graph that your audience cannot comprehend in 30 seconds. You can accomplish this by sticking to one key point and removing any superfluous materials.

(2) Be sure you know exactly *when* to present your illustration so it coincides with your oral briefing. Keep the chart or illustration covered until you are ready to present it. Otherwise it will distract your audience's attention.

(3) If you use slides or overhead transparencies that require dimming the lights, keep in mind that you are losing some important speaker-to-audience variables. Marketing consultant Deane Haerer recommends against the general use of slides for this reason. Physical presence has a great deal to do with psychological motivation. When the lights go out, you lose eye contact with your audience. You become an impersonal voice in the dark—at best a mere narrator.[9]

(4) Be sure you know how to work any equipment you may use. Slide projectors, tape recorders, videotape playback units, and the like all have their own idiosyncracies. For example, the first time I used a videotape playback I was unaware that each time I hit the "stop" button, the tape

would rewind several feet. When the tape was started again there was a distinct sense of *déjà vu,* the illusion of having previously had a given experience. I soon learned to use the "pause" control instead.

By and large, the flip chart or poster is the simplest type of visual aid to use and gives good value for the money. An added benefit is that either can be easily transformed into a printed handout and given to your audience after the presentation.

Prepare Your Body and Voice

No matter how well you've planned and prepared the presentation, your success will still depend in large part on the delivery. Delivery is a combination of many factors which collectively produce a total impression upon your audience. We've discussed a few of these in the section on speaker credibility. Here are some others:

Eye contact. Never trust a person who won't look you in the eye. It is a cultural expectation for most of us that when we communicate we look into the eyes of our receiver. When addressing a large group this can become a problem. The best bet seems to be to look at one individual for a few seconds and then move on to another. Don't just scan over the crowd—really look *at* individuals. Be sure you get to almost everyone in the room at some point. Be aware of tendencies to look too much at one particularly attractive person while ignoring the ugly guy in the back of the room.

Gestures and movement. Our sense of personal dynamism or self-confidence come across via such body language as gestures, posture, and mannerisms. Gestures can be useful to punctuate what is being said. They should be spontaneous and natural, yet used purposefully. We all have different tendencies to use or avoid gestures. For some, it feels uncomfortable to point or raise hands in exclamation. For others it may be said that if you tied their hands they'd be speechless.

There are several common mistakes people make with gestures. (1) They fail to use them where they can be very useful for emphasis. (2) They use the same gesture over and over to the point that it becomes monotonous or even distracting. (3) They use gestures that cannot be seen clearly; a hand motion hidden from audience view by a podium is of no value.

Body movement is another important way to bring life to a talk. Pausing between points in the briefing and physically moving to another place in the room help your audience to know that you have completed one

point and are now ready to address another. This pause helps your listeners follow your logical development. If you cannot freely move around because you must speak into the microphone, you may still use the pause and a shift in position, or a change in the direction you're looking, to indicate the same things. Physical movement is the preferred approach. Whenever possible, avoid the speaker-behind-the-podium format. If a mike is needed, a portable microphone around the neck will allow you more freedom of movement.

Pronunciation. Being careful not to mispronounce words may be more important than you may think. As with other distractions, such goofs may not seriously change meaning but will reflect on your credibility. One audience at a large university was appalled to hear a renowned expert in library science pronounce the word library as "liberry." A dead silence fell over the room as the audience reassessed this speaker's expertise. I have heard data processing people mispronounce "satistics" and supervisors explain "pacific" examples. Just today a professor was commenting about the unusually rainy weather we've been having. He hoped that the "moon-san" season was soon to end. I think he meant *monsoon*. While at an air force training school I was surprised to hear that "humid air" is responsible for a large number of plane crashes. Finally I saw this culprit described in writing. It was "human error."

Voice. A speaker's voice reflects his or her personality. A clear, strong voice increases the probability of audience understanding. Clear articulation of the language is important, but other voice characteristics such as variation in pitch, loudness, and rate of speech have as much or more impact. The range of pitch one uses may be wide, allowing for effective vocal emphasis, or very narrow, resulting in what is commonly called monotone. Over time, a committed monotone can, as the sleeping aid commercial says, "Help you relax, feel drowsy so you can fall asleep."

The key word to keeping listener attention is *variation*. From my experience in coaching speakers, I have seen two common voice variation problems come up over and over again. For male speakers, there is seldom enough variation in pitch. Men seem to think that it sounds macho to talk only in a deep tone and they do so continuously. Tremendous emphasis can be made by raising and lowering the pitch, yet many speakers don't want to "risk" it. Some female speakers tend to have a different problem; they tend to lose the conversational tone in their voice when addressing a group. Their voice sounds theatrical and artificial. Occasionally this comes out sing-songy.

This latter problem results from habitual pitch change patterns that become monotonous and distracting. It also arises from overdoing voice *intensity*, perhaps in an effort to sound assertive. We've all encountered people who are overly loud as well as some who are so soft-spoken we want to ask them to "speak up!" Most business presentations can be made at a conversational level although additional emphasis can be achieved by variation. Don't assume always that a louder voice commands more attention. Often that "still small voice"—the one we have to lean toward and work to hear—is the most powerful.

Verbalized Pauses. Few things can drive your audience up the wall like the liberal use of "ah," "um," "uh," and (the popular favorite) "ya know." I have heard intelligent and apparently rational men and women salt their every utterance with these expressions till I want to scream at them, ya know?

The human talker abhors a vacuum. And when the detested monster, silence, raises its ugly head, we beat it to death with ah, uh, um, or ya knows. Do yourself a favor; ask others you speak with to point out when you are drifting into this habit. Rid yourself of the fear of silence.

Emphasis. Putting more stress on certain words can have interesting effects on meaning. Think of the different inflections you could give the question "What do you mean by that?"

   What do you mean by that?

   What *do* you mean by that?

   What do *you* mean by that?

   What do you *mean* by that?

   What do you mean by *that*?

Professional communicators are very sensitive to these kinds of differences. Listen carefully to the words emphasized by the radio announcer. *"Big Jim wants* to sell you a car" is likely to come across quite differently than, "Big Jim wants to sell *you* a car" or, better yet, "Big Jim wants to sell you a *car*." The last of these three examples focuses your attention on the product while the first one focuses on what Big Jim wants. Who cares what Big Jim wants?

After the Briefing:
Handling the Question and Answer Session

In preliminary planning a speaker must decide how much audience give-and-take will be useful to his or her purpose. For most business presentations there is a considerable amount, often in the form of a question and answer session following the talk. Sometimes a great deal of meaningful information is exchanged in such sessions. When, however, the audience is very large or your topic is unusually controversial and you don't want to risk undermining your presentation, you may want to avoid the question and answer session altogether. If you do accept questions from the audience, keep in mind that the two fundamentals of handling questions are simply (1) be prepared to handle them and (2) keep control of yourself and control the audience.

Preparing for questions should not be a serious problem if the briefing is well planned. In each step of preliminary plan and content development, you should put yourself in the shoes of your listeners and anticipate likely questions or reactions. Many anticipated responses will, of course, be addressed as a logical development of the briefing. There may, however, be other issues or sticky questions that you've chosen not to discuss in the talk. These are the kinds of questions you need to be prepared to handle. Brainstorm all such possible objections with the help of others, and work out the best possible answers. Then have an associate fire the tough questions at you and practice your response.

Keeping control of the situation requires some effort when you face hostile or surprising questions. First, let's not get paranoid about the questions asked. What may at first sound like a real zinger may simply be a listener's way of testing you under fire or even confirming his *agreement* with your view. If you don't know the answer, say so. Don't try to fake it. Remember how important trustworthiness is to your credibility.

When hostile or loaded questions arise, take them in stride and don't heckle back—maintain your dignity and good appearance.

"Retortmanship" by Chandler Washburne (p. 251) points out that we have three options when we are presented with audience questions. We can (1) not answer at all, (2) manage the question, or (3) manage the questioner. Although Washburne's article is intended to be somewhat tongue-in-cheek, it offers a number of useful tips.

Diagnosing Your Briefings and Oral Presentations

After-the-fact feedback from a trusted associate is probably the best way of diagnosing your presentational speaking skills.

Be sure that both you and your critic are in agreement about what is important. Review this chapter together so that you will both be using the same language in evaluating and diagnosing the presentation. It is exceptionally helpful to videotape yourself (at least in a practice session) for later critique. If this is not possible, an audio tape recording is probably the next best thing.

The critique form which follows focuses on the ideas presented in this chapter. A useful critique goes beyond simply filling out a form, however. Be sure those critiquing you are leveling with you. And, of course, be willing to accept their criticism and act upon it when appropriate.

Evaluation of an Oral Presentation

SPEAKER: _____ CRITIC:_____

DATE: _____ OCCASION: _____

    1. The speaker's specific topic was _____

    2. The speaker's intent was to _____

    3. What type of introduction was used? How effective was it?

    4. Did the speaker preview for the audience the order of arrangement she or he would use? _____ What order was used? ____ How appropriate was this? _____

    5. What were the speaker's main points? Were these clearly distinguishable from one another?

    6. What types of support were offered for each main point? Was the support adequate?

    7. Did the speaker use periodic summaries and effective transitions?

8. Did the speaker effectively use visual aids to make points clear? _____ Were they readable? _____ Easy to grasp? _____ Presented only at appropriate times? _____ Comments about visual support materials:

9. Did the speaker conclude with finality? _____ Was a clear action step presented for the audience? _____ What was the final conclusion/action step (in your own words)?

10. Was there a question and answer session? _____ Did the speaker seem to listen carefully to questions and answer them completely? _____ Were the answers well organized? _____ Comments about the question and answers:

11. Was the speaker's delivery comfortable and natural? _____ What distracting mannerisms or vocal characteristics were noticeable? Be specific.

12. Was the speaker's voice clear? _____ Enthusiastic? _____ Free of excessive verbalized pauses? _____ Comments about voice:

Some Other Thoughts About Speaking Before Groups: READINGS FOR CHAPTER 7

**Retortmanship:
How to Avoid
Answering Questions**[10]

Chandler Washburne

At the risk of being considered somewhat Machiavellian, I would like to deal with some practical methods in use today to defend man from the omnipresent question. Our age, in addition to being atomic, contains further dangers to the individual—in that he is continually bombarded with questions. Atomic bombardment is viewed as evil, whereas we have come to accept the deluge of questions, prying into every aspect of our lives, as a natural event. In a democracy this trend is particularly strong. The idea of equality allows anyone, as an equal, to presume to question you and makes you feel compelled to answer. A clear demonstration of this is seen in politics. Even the President is continually subjected to questioning by newsmen. He cannot revert to a position of superiority, from which he could resist being questioned or not feel the need to give answers, as a dictator might.

All this means that various defenses must be built against the question: methods must be developed by which we can keep the questioner from feeling that his question has not been answered. In other words, we appear to cooperate in answering the question; yet somehow he fails to secure the information which we do not wish revealed—without his being fully aware of it, as this would only lead to another question. (Washington, D.C. would be the world's greatest laboratory.) We leave him (1) satisfied or (2) in a position where he is restrained by politeness from further imposition or (3) in a state of confusion, which prevents him from formulating another query.

A further limitation which has been placed on the methods used here is that the reply should be within the limits of truth. The outright lie is not dealt with here. Distraction and misunderstandings may be exploited, but using the methods that follow should prevent one from being faced later with contradictory "facts." This is because these methods are really ways of not responding to what the question is asking about—primarily by throwing roadblocks in the questioner's way, which hinder his progress or get him off on other roads.

There are two aspects of the subject of questions which we have to look at before we begin to think about the answer that is not an answer.

First, we must determine as closely as possible what meaning the question has for the questioner. This is where people frequently make their first mistake. In psychological terms, they project their own meaning into the question, rather than holding it to the meaning of the person who asked it. "What did you do last night?" is not an attempt to find out about the crime you committed then. The answer can very well be a statement about the delightful supper which preceded the act. We do not have to avoid answering, in many cases, if we interpret the question properly.

The second principle in regard to the question grows out of the first. It is limitation of the question to certain restricted meanings—associated with the intent of the questioner. We often lead others just to the area we don't want them to investigate by responding as if their questions were directed to this area. The neurotic person may feel that all questions are focused on his guilty secret and then is constantly on the defensive. Heavily defended areas are likely to draw fire. We thus do not let our opponent—if I may call him that—know what area we are defending; or, even better, we do not let him know that we are defending any area and that he is our opponent.

If we look at the questioner's meaning and limit the question to this, we may find it harmless to answer. If not, we must then proceed in one of several ways to avoid answering the question.

There are three basic methods of solving the problem of not answering: (1) not answering at all; (2) managing the question; (3) managing the questioner. There is a certain amount of interrelationship among them; but, for the purposes of study, let us look at them separately.

Perhaps it should be pointed out that the methods don't have to be used in a particular order. Feel free to work them in any combination, depending upon circumstances and inclination. Remember that retortmanship is an art; to perfect it, practice the ones that are not familiar.

Not Answering at All

Some questions can get along in life very well without a mate. Let us not suppose that every question demands an answer. Many people have burned themselves by picking up a hot question which they might well have left lying. Even if the question seems to demand an answer, there are ways of avoiding making any response at all. The simplest is to ignore or apparently not hear the question. This can be done in some circumstances without impoliteness. Sometimes it is best to wait and see if your interrogator is going to force the question into your awareness.

Or you may cope with the question by means of *distraction*. The commonest tactic is related to the use of cigarettes. You may let time lapse—and the more time, the better—by lighting a cigarette, inhaling, removing ashes, coughing, and choking. If the situation has still not changed, at least you have had time to plan a defense. Pipe smokers have excellent props for delaying action for several minutes. Occasionally one can try things along the line of spilling a glass of water (preferably over the questioner), or the smoker may drop his cigarette into the depths of the sofa. But what if we get beyond all this, into the dangerous quicksands of the evasive answer?

Managing the Question

A method that can be used occasionally is *misunderstanding* the question. Although we have carried out the first step of probing the meaning of the question, we lead the questioner to think that we have misunderstood it. If he asks about Tuesday night, start in by saying: "Well, Monday we had gone. . . ." He waits, thinking you will go to Tuesday, but you never do. It helps if the misunderstanding is not immediately detected and therefore subject to correction. The example starts as if laying background, so you are not stopped. If the questioner asks you to go back to Tuesday after you finish, he seems to be imposing. One can generally count on a question not being repeated, but if it is, additional techniques can be used.

Limitation is closely connected with misunderstandings. Limitation does not call for confirming the question to the interrogator's intent; it requires artfully constructing it to the desired meaning. "How did you like my play?" is answered with, "I particularly noticed the storekeeper's role; it must be extremely difficult." Or, "What did you do Tuesday night?" can be answered with, "We started off with a wonderful dinner. The soup, you can't imagine! It was made of. . . ." Then you discuss foods for half an hour. You have limited the field twice, first to the dinner situation, then to the foods, and you have moved the question into neutral territory.

Another method related to misunderstanding is the *non sequitur.* The politician, when asked about food prices, may end up talking about red-blooded Americans, motherhood, and the Fourth of July. The answer is not logically related to the question. Some when asked a question they can make neither head nor tail of—or do not care to answer—give a five-minute history of aviation or some such thing. In this case, you should usually start in by saying, "As I understand that, it would include . . ." or "I think I can best answer by drawing a parallel example," or "This whole thing seems closely related to. . . ."

In using the non sequitur, it often is advisable to respond with things that have emotional appeal to the questioner. The politician refers to motherhood and we are drawn up in the associated emotions and forget the question. It helps if the answer is fairly long and wide-ranging, so that the questioner can read his own answer into the material you present.

Another method most useful to the professor, politician, or lecturer, but well adapted to everyday usage, is *restatement.* One takes the question and then, apparently in the interests of clarity, restates it before starting to answer. This is the opportunity to convert the question into one that is easy to answer. The politician may be asked, "Are we going into a depression?" He says, "As I understand your question, you are really asking about the present state of the business cycle. Business income is the highest in history. . . ." He has restated the question and thus secured permission in advance to answer his own version of the question. The questioner is seldom alert enough to notice the skirting of his question when we use restatement and begin by saying, "What you are really asking is. . . ."

A method similar to restatement is that of the *more fundamental question.* When asked, "Are you a socialist?" you can respond that we must first consider a more fundamental question: "What is socialism?" This gives you the opportunity not to answer until you resolve the fundamental issue, and you can avoid this by arguing over the definition. Don't think that what you claim as more fundamental must be so; almost any sort of question can be thrown in as a roadblock, just so you make it seem necessary to deal with the second point before answering the original question.

The *hypothetical answer* or the use of *objectivity* is a method widely used by intellectuals. When asked a question, you answer, "Well, now, I would like to respond to that. Supposing you were in this position, then you might feel this; or again, in another position, you might feel that." A senator might be asked, "Should Red China be admitted to the U.N.?" An answer might be, "Let us look at this objectively. There are a number of courses open to the United States. . . . And, of course, is the United States in a position to prevent Red China from entering?" The essence of the method lies in presenting various alternatives without committing yourself to any specific position.

One of the most interesting operations is the approach I call: *Is this really a question?* Using this method, you proceed to destroy the question. You show that it really consists of three or four questions, or that it sets up a false situation or uses false premises, or that the terms have no fixed meaning. On the question about admitting Red China to the U.N., one answers, "That is really several questions: What is the purpose of the U.N.? What government represents China? What do U.N. members feel?" Take the question, "Do you believe in evolution?" You answer, "It is not really a question of belief, but of the meaning of certain pieces of evidence. . . ." After you break the question down into three or four others, from the various parts you select one you want to expand upon, and you keep from having the question put back together again.

A somewhat similar method is the *moot* question approach. Whether the question is answerable or not, you assert that it is really a point that can't be answered. Taking the Red China question, we answer: "One should not really speculate upon a question of that type, because of the imponderable elements. We cannot know what the future will bring or what position we will be in, and crossing bridges before we come to them is foolhardy."

The *assertion-of-nothing* is often most satisfactory in answering. The proud mother asks what you think of her ugly baby, and you answer, "That *is* a baby!" (But not: "*That* is a baby?") A display of strong feeling and emphasis is necessary to carry this method off, as you seem to be saying something so strongly the questioner feels you must be answering.

Managing the Questioner

This is the counterattack approach. Not recommended generally is putting the original questioner on the defensive, so that he becomes engaged in defending himself. You can point out what profound ignorance such a question reveals, or you can say you feel sorry for anyone who does not understand these things. This is likely to silence him in regard to further questions, but it will also make him angry and vengeful. This technique can be most effective when a friendly manner is used—for example, "You probably didn't mean to ask that, what you would really like to know is. . . ."

Another typical form of counterattack is to answer with *another question.* Question: "What do you think of the Republicans?" Answer: "First we should look at political parties; what do you think of them?" Question: "What did you do Tuesday night?" Answer: "I never do much. You probably had a much more interesting time; what did you do?" Any good evasive technique should always end with a question. As long as you are talking, you are safe. When stopping, pick the topic for the other person in safe territory.

Already in the preceding example we are moving on to an excellent and very subtle counterattack. This is the method of *compliment.* Question: "What do you feel about Marie?" Answer: "How penetrating that you should ask such a question. You seem to have a wonderful understanding of what people are feeling. How did you ever develop this ability?" (Or: "I have long wanted your opinion of her.") Praise is one of the most disarming of methods. That is why the questioner, unless he is particularly alert, is likely to be so absorbed in feelings of gratification that it will be difficult for him to recognize a smokescreen for operations of another kind.

You are now on your own. You will discover many subtle variations and combinations as you work on this. The future of this much-needed science is in your hands.

Notes

1. Frederick C. Dyer, *Executive's Guide to Effective Speaking and Writing* (Englewood Cliffs, N.J.: Prentice-Hall, 1962), p. 36.
2. Adapted from Harold P. Zelko and Frank E. X. Dance, *Business and Professional Speech Communication,* 2nd ed. (New York: Holt, Rinehart & Winston, 1978), pp. 77–79.
3. Ibid., p. 78.
4. George L. Morrisey, *Effective Business and Technical Presentations,* 2nd. ed. (Reading, Mass.: Addison-Wesley, 1975), p. 23–24.
5. Myron Cohen, *More Laughing Out Loud* (Secaucus, N.J.: Citadel Press, 1960), pp. 169–170. By permission of the Citadel Press © 1960.
6. Edward S. Strother and Alan W. Huckleberry, *The Effective Speaker* (Boston: Houghton Mifflin, 1968), p. 167.
7. George A. Miller, "The Magical Number Seven, Plus-or-Minus Two: Some Limits on Our Capacity for Processing Information," *Psychological Review* 63, No. 2 (March 1956), pp. 81–97.
8. Larry L. Barker, *Communication* (Englewood Cliffs, N.J.: Prentice-Hall, 1978), p. 241.
9. Deane Haerer, "How to Plan Your Visual Presentations," *Public Relations Journal* 34 (March 1978), p. 25.
10. From *ETC: A Review of General Semantics,* 26 (1969), 69–75. Reprinted by permission of the International Society for General Semantics.

Recommended Readings

Dyer, Frederick C. *Executive's Guide to Effective Speaking and Writing.* Englewood Cliffs, N.J.: Prentice-Hall, 1962. Although this book has been around for some time, it remains one of the most functional texts I have seen. Geared clearly to the business person, it provides a step-by-step method for improving effectiveness in expression.

Another book with a similar, how-to approach is George L. Morrisey, *Effective Business and Technical Presentations* (2nd ed.). Reading, Mass.: Addison-Wesley, 1975. The book is especially strong in concisely presenting step-by-step preplanning ideas.

Another book dealing with oral communication in business is Harold P. Zelko, and Frank E. X. Dance, *Business and Professional Speech Communication* (2nd ed.). New York: Holt, Rinehart & Winston, 1978. The book is current, and well written by well-known communication scholars.

Finally, there are several books on speech communication which, although focused more on public speaking, can be of value to the presentational speaker in an organization. Two of the best are Larry L. Barker, *Communication.* Englewood Cliffs, N.J.: Prentice-Hall, 1978; and Donald C. Bryant, and Karl R. Wallace, *Oral Communication* (4th ed.). Englewood Cliffs, N.J.: Prentice-Hall, 1976.

CHAPTER 8

LISTENING
Getting More Than
Your Ears On*

There's Nothing Wrong with My Hearing!

Criticize someone's listening skills and they immediately respond by quoting you the latest medical report from their ear, nose, and throat specialist. They have perfect hearing, so you and your criticisms must be out to lunch. Many of us confuse hearing and listening. They are two different things.

Hearing is a physiological process that involves changing energy from one form to another. In oral communication, three forms of energy are employed: acoustical, mechanical, and electrochemical. Acoustic energy is the patterning of sound waves in the air; mechanical energy refers to the vibration of one of the physical structures of the ear, much the same as the cone on a speaker; and electrochemical energy is the patterning of responses in the fluid within the middle ear. The process referred to as "hearing" is simply the changing of energy outside the body (acoustical) into energy sources within the body, mechanical and electrochemical, that the brain can act on. All of this has little to do with listening.

Listening refers to the psychological processes which allow us to attach meaning to the patterns of energy we "hear."

*The author wishes to acknowledge the assistance of Dr. Elliott A. Pood of the University of North Carolina at Greensboro in the development of this chapter.

The "cocktail party effect" provides a good example of the difference between hearing and listening. At a cocktail party there are usually several conversations going on simultaneously in the same room. Everyone present at the party is aware of these conversations in that they can be heard. On the other hand, we usually have to make a conscious effort to *listen* to any one of these conversations. We are physically capable of changing all or most of the acoustic energy in the room into electrochemical energy. We are much less capable of attaching meanings to all the electrochemical impulses.

What Contributes to Listening?

Before we can begin to improve our listening skills, we need to understand the demands placed upon our listening capacities. These demands fall into three categories or elements of the listening process.

Internal Elements

As we just noted, listening involves attaching meanings to words or sounds we hear. There are two preconditions that must be met. First, the words or other sounds used by the message source must be *received* by the hearer. Second, the listener must possess a set of meanings or *referents* for these sounds. Overhearing someone speaking a strange foreign language is an obvious example of a breakdown in this second step. If the sounds have no referent, we cannot understand. Listening is the way we put sounds and their meanings together to create understanding. I'll deal more with this process of assigning meanings to words and other symbols in Chapter 11. For now, let us simply recognize internal factors as one set of elements in the overall listening process.

Environmental Elements

The second set of elements involved in the listening process includes the factors of the communication environment which determine what we are able to listen to and what we cannot. These factors include our individual listening capacity, the presence of noise, and the use or misuse of gatekeepers.

There are two ways our listening capacity can be overburdened: it can be overloaded with too much information, or it can be underutilized with too little. In both cases, listening tends to break down.

Examples of listening breakdowns caused by an exceeded listening capacity can be found in our everyday experiences. Only so many messages can be heard and responded to in any given day; only so many phone calls can be answered at one time. Once our capacity to accomplish these tasks has been reached, we develop defensive mechanisms for coping. We develop psychological strategies for selecting what we will attend to and what we will tune out. These selection mechanisms, although often unconscious, are normally based on our individual needs, which, of course, change from time to time. The point is that when our capacity for paying attention to incoming information is exceeded, the impact on our listening behavior is difficult to predict. Only one thing is for sure: we are likely to miss some messages.

The problem is magnified for the organization as a whole. As discussed in Chapter 3, in many organizations the information load for certain people is so great that a situation of overload is created. The results can only be detrimental to organizational functioning.

The opposite problem, where environmental demands cause us to underutilize our listening capacity, is also widespread. Most people speak at the rate of about 120 words per minute, (except for auctioneers or disc jockeys) yet our normal capacity for listening—assigning meanings to words—is about 500 words per minute. The problem, of course, is that we listen faster than anyone can talk to us, providing ample time for our minds to wander far afield. Listening to others becomes a tedious task, forcing us to slow down our thinking to stay synchronized with those speaking to us.

The presence of noise is another environmental element affecting listening. Noise refers to those sounds which are irrelevant to the conversation. It is important to note that noise may be either environmental (the sound of machinery, other conversations, buzzers, bells) or internal (a headache, our dislike of the person to whom we are listening, preoccupation with a meeting with the boss later in the day). Whatever the source, noise distracts us from the business of listening.

One way managers deal with the problems of exceeded listening capacity and excessive noise is through *gatekeepers*. The term gatekeeper is used in organizational communication literature to refer to one who previews incoming information to determine if it is appropriate to the needs of the organization or an individual manager. If messages appear irrelevant, they are withheld from the system. In this sense a gatekeeper is a person whose job it is to do some of our listening for us. Almost every manager has at least one. This person may be a secretary, administrative assistant, or any other person we turn to for organizational information. In many instances, these individuals determine what needs our attention and what doesn't.

While gatekeeping has its benefits, it also poses an important problem. When we finally do get the information it has been through at least two sets of interpretations, our gatekeeper's and ours. There is no guarantee that we are listening to the message as originally intended. The serial transmission problem (as discussed in Chapter 3) may become acute.

Interactional Elements

In contrast to the environmental elements of the listening process, the interactional elements concern internal psychological processes which are not as easily identified. Two such psychological elements deserve careful consideration: *self-centeredness* and *self-protectiveness*.

Self-centeredness arises frequently in listening. Especially in situations where there is a lack of agreement between speakers and listeners, people develop some degree of "vested interest" in their own position. It isn't hard to understand why this occurs. When we have taken the time to formulate an idea, we usually believe that idea is a good one. We feel obliged to defend it when we have verbalized that idea in the presence of others. In essence, we have made a public commitment to that position and it becomes embarrassing for us to change. At the same time, the people we are interacting with have also publicly committed themselves to their opinions. Since listening is a psychological process, based in our individual needs, we think and listen from a self-centered orientation. As a result, we don't listen to *what* the other person is saying; we listen instead to how their views affect our position. In other words, we are "listening" through a predetermined set of biases, looking for flaws in our "opponent's" views rather than seeking common understanding. We develop a mind like a steel trap—closed.

Here's an example of the effects of self-centeredness on listening. In a recent training session and workshop for personnel managers, a group was split into a number of male-female pairs. Each pair was given a different conflict situation to discuss and solve.

In one discussion problem, the pair was asked to role-play the following situation as husband and wife: "The husband has a very good job in his chosen profession in the city where the couple resides. The wife has just completed her master's degree and received only one job offer in her chosen profession, but it would require the couple to move to a distant city. Although the husband has tried, he has been unable to find a job in that new city."

An analysis of the resulting interaction revealed the self-centeredness concept in action. Both participants made a valiant effort to appear to understand the other's position; however, the communication revealed that neither was as interested in listening to the other for the sake of gathering conflict-reducing information as much as to find a means of convincing the other person of their own viewpoint. Few of the participants developed a genuine understanding or a satisfactory solution.

The listening behaviors here are not unique. In many instances in our daily interactions we can find ourselves listening to another person solely for the purpose of finding the weaknesses in their position so that we can formulate a convincing response.

Another example of the self-centeredness problem arises when we listen to the other person only long enough to key an answer in our own minds. At that point we stop listening and begin to plan what we'll say in response. The other person is still talking and we still hear them but we are no longer listening.

Self-centered listening has direct impact on the amount of information we receive. Since research indicates that the more information we have, the better decisions we are able to make, such blocking out of relevant information cannot help but lower the quality of our managerial decisions.

A second interactional element affecting the listening process is *self-protectiveness*. This involves the process of playing out the communication interaction in our own minds before the real interaction ever occurs to make sure we don't get caught saying something stupid. In essence, then, we are practicing by listening to ourselves listen to others.

One example of this occurred in the office of a state agency which employed five secretaries. Four of the women had been with the agency for several years, the fifth had recently been hired. All five secretaries were very efficient and produced superior work.

One day, one of the four veteran women came to see the supervisor. The gist of her conversation was that all four of the women who had been there for a number of years were unhappy with the new secretary's appearance. They didn't have any complaints about her work; they merely objected to the fact that she didn't wear a bra. The supervisor was told that unless he spoke to this woman and convinced her to wear a bra to work, the other four secretaries would quit.

The manager's behavior is a classic example of self-protectiveness in listening. Since he valued the services of all five of the secretaries and didn't want to lose any of them, he spent the next few weeks trying to find a way to *tactfully* discuss the problem with the new girl. He began seeing their discussion in his mind, anticipating what he would say, how she would react and practicing how he would respond to her reaction. Each time he played this scene in his mind, he would change his approach slightly to compensate for her anticipated reactions.

He finally believed he had the right way to talk with her and proceeded to do so. In their conversation he used very abstract terms, mentioning the effect of personal appearance on other people in the office and, without any reference to the embarrassing situation of bralessness, asked her to emulate her peers in the office. In this manner, she would feel more a part of the social atmosphere and be readily accepted by the other secretaries.

The young woman said she understood and promptly quit, stating that she wasn't about to replace her wardrobe of slacks with dresses just to please the other women.

The point the manager was trying to make completely eluded this employee because, in his effort to avoid offending her, the manager had not said what really needed to be said. His message was formulated in response to what he *anticipated* her reaction would be. He adjusted his communication behavior prior to establishing a need for that adjustment, and consequently, mishandled the problem.

How does this illustrate self-protectiveness? The answer to that lies in examining the manager's motives for behaving as he did. He had played the scene in his mind and adjusted his communication behavior *not* because of his fear of hurting her feelings, although that may have been the apparent motive. In reality, he had done so because of his fear of being hurt or embarrassed himself; he was being self-protective. He was really concerned with the way she would feel *about him* if he were to say something objectionable to her.

A serious listening problem arises when we engage in conjecture by listening to ourselves listen to others, by anticipating what might be said and reacting to that instead of the actual situation.

Both of these interactional elements—self-centeredness and self-protectiveness—affect the listening process in that they tend to orient our listening behavior toward biased interpretations of messages and away from the extraction of the maximum amount of available information.

These three elements of the listening process—internal, environmental, and interactional—pose potential problems for the listener. Overcoming these problems requires *active* effort. Listening must be recognized as more than something we sit back and do to kill time when we're not talking. As communication scholar Harold Janis has said, "Listening . . . is not merely hearing; it is a state of receptivity that permits understanding of what is heard and grants the listener full partnership in the communication process."[1]

What can we do to improve our listening skills? Here are a few suggestions.

Steps to Improved Listening

Break old habits of poor listening. Most of us didn't become poor listeners overnight; we learned how. Here are several habits that do no good.

Faking attention in an attempt to be polite results in what someone called the "wide asleep listener." This is usually accomplished by looking directly at the speaker when in reality we are thinking about something else, nodding responses which are automatic, or even saying "yes" and

WOULD YOU MIND REPEATING YOUR SUGGESTION...
I MUST HAVE DOZED OFF.

"uh huh" to conversations we have mentally tuned out. When you have agreed to listen to someone, commit yourself to expending the needed effort to listen and give that conversation your undivided attention.

A second bad habit to avoid is changing channels in the middle of a conversation. When something appears to be too dull, or too hard to comprehend, or too time consuming, the poor listener will tune out a conversation. Since we know there is plenty of thinking time between the speaker's thoughts, we figure that we can switch back and forth between several conversations without losing any information. This assumption is often incorrect.

One other habit to avoid is listening only for facts. Much of what people communicate is feelings, impressions, emotions. Factual messages are often wrapped up in these. Here's a personal example.

A student came to my office recently and in the course of our conversation, she appeared very upset about something. When she explained to me that her husband had just been terminated from his job, I expressed what I thought was appropriate concern and soon changed the subject. Shortly after, she abruptly left my office, apparently angry with me. I had listened to the facts of what she'd said, but completely missed her meaning.

From my perspective, these were the facts:

a. Her husband had just lost his job.
b. Her husband, I knew, was a very capable young executive who was unhappy with his present employer and had been looking around for another company.
c. This couple was young, had no children and few financial burdens.
d. Her husband had recently been offered another comparable position which he turned down because it paid about the same as he was now making.

In my listening process, I associated the new fact (a) with facts I already knew (b, c, and d) and concluded that there was no real serious problem. He'd find a new and probably better job soon.

So why did she storm out of my office? We later talked about it. I had listened only to the facts while she wanted to talk about feelings, concerns she had. She wanted me to listen to what she was *not* saying. What she needed was someone to share these thoughts with, and perhaps get some comfort from. Many conversations convey an emotional as well as an informational dimension. Listening only for the factual data is seldom enough.

Avoid response behaviors that turn off others. The communication behaviors we use while listening to others can cause those speaking to us to shut off or modify their message. Here are some examples of counterproductive responses:

"Spanish Inquisitioning" involves the repeated use of questions, one after another, but without ever dealing with the answers you receive. "What do you mean?" "Why do you say that?" "What do you mean by that remark?"

"Cold shouldering" is the elimination of a person from the conversation by your physical actions. For example, if you don't agree with something that has been said you might turn away from that person, or you might close your eyes, or even begin staring out the window.

"Buttinskying" involves never letting the sender of a message finish his or her thought. The minute you think you know what the other person is going to say, you interrupt.

"Stonewalling" is the use of nonverbal behaviors to convey a response to the sender. For example, many people have at one time or another said something of a sensitive nature and before they have finished they receive the "later, you louse" look or a semiconcealed head shake from the listener. In this case the listener is stonewalling. Cold shouldering can also be a form of stonewalling.

"Wet blanketing" is still another counterproductive response—or, more accurately, *lack* of response. To dampen enthusiasm or enjoyment for the speaker, we simply withhold all responses, verbal or nonverbal. The effect is to extinguish the behavior, as we discussed in Chapter 6. The no-response may be the most devastating turnoff of all.

Be patient. Because we can listen faster than a person can speak, we sometimes use some of this excess listening time to evaluate messages before they are completed. The result is that we are evaluating incomplete messages. Demonstrate some patience with the speaker by waiting until he or she is finished before you begin trying to interpret the message. Don't feel compelled to avoid silences in conversations by interpreting messages too quickly and responding immediately.

Minimize the number of gatekeepers. As I noted before, gatekeepers result in our listening to someone else's version of the message. Whenever possible, avoid sending an intermediary to get the story from the source and then reporting back to you. Avoid requesting that someone tell their story to your secretary or administrative assistant and then let that person synthesize the information for you. Avoid channeling through someone else something which will eventually end up in your office.

You'll notice I prefaced this recommendation with "whenever possible." Obviously, no manager can listen to everything everyone wants to say. To reduce the probability of information overload, managers should develop a clear policy on which information needs their direct personal attention and which can be satisfactorily handled by others in the organization. Problems that can be handled at lower levels in the organization, should be. A message requiring a decision should go only as far as the lowest ranking person authorized to make such a decision. Although the policy should not be overly rigid, it should be specified in advance and widely understood.

Solicit clarification. As a listener, one of the most dangerous things we can do is recognize that we don't understand the message and then fail to make that recognition clear to the sender. We do this because (a) we are afraid to appear ignorant, (b) we believe we can figure it out on our own, or (c) we don't want to take the time or expend the effort to make sure we have the message right.

By failing to solicit clarification from the sender, we force ourselves to rely too heavily on our own perceptions for help in interpreting messages. When you ask questions about the meaning of a message, any implication that you lack knowledge will be more than compensated by the recognition of your sincere desire to understand. This is flattering to others. It conveys a regard for that person's worth.

Use counterattitudinal advocacy. Counterattitudinal advocacy is a big term for a simple process. It means "take the other guy's position." In any situation in which there is disagreement, the ultimate goal of communication is to improve the understanding of all parties involved. By doing so, it is hoped that all parties will receive new information which will result in a better overall decision.

The objective here is to reduce the degree to which a listener listens through his or her own biases. Counterattitudinal advocacy forces the listener to objectively listen and understand, rather than to listen only until a response is cued. Here is how it works: you, as a listener, simply make a commitment to restate and defend the position which is "counter to your attitude," that is, opposite to your position. We can implement this by honestly trying to restate to others exactly what we hear them expressing. This, of course, includes both the factual utterances and the emotions you think are being conveyed. You use your own words rather than the speaker's.

What happens, essentially, is this: by committing yourself to restate and defend someone else's position, you must listen more effectively to that position in order to understand what you are defending.

There are additional implications that can be especially useful in conflict management situations. By defending a position counter to your own, you create a mental set different from your personal biases and force yourself to consider information which you avoided when advancing your own position. Because of your involvement in the arguments for the contrary position, you become ego-involved in that position. You have forced yourself to listen to ideas through someone else's biases. The end result is a better understanding of the entire situation, rather than just your position.

This process does not obligate you to cave in to the views of others when you honestly disagree. It simply provides one way of better understanding where those you disagree with "are coming from." In some cases disagreements evaporate when we clarify each other's position. We recognize that we don't really disagree in principle; we were simply expressing similar ideas in unfamiliar or confusing ways. The meanings we attached to the words used by others are a frequent source of communication problems which I'll discuss in more depth in Chapter 11.

The Motivation to Listen Better

Most thoughtful managers recognize the need for careful listening. We spend more time in listening than any other communication activity. As Phil Lewis has said, "Of all the sources of information a manager has . . . listening is the most important; no tool rivals skilled and sympathetic listening. If managers were more cognizant of the needs for effective listening, they could actually increase substantially—even double—their success by controlling their tongues and really listening."[2]

How do we motivate others to listen? A cartoon I once saw suggested a way. It showed the boss talking to employees at a meeting saying: "Now pay careful attention. I'll let you know at the end of the meeting who will write up the minutes." When everyone in the organization begins to listen as though they were going to have to write up the minutes, understanding will advance in a quantum leap. But listening improvement starts at home, starts with ourselves.

Diagnosing Your Listening Skills

It takes at least two people to diagnose listening skills. Only by comparing what we heard against what message was sent can we determine the degree of listening accuracy. For this reason, training teams work best. The following simple exercises are designed to be used in training sessions to help managers diagnose potential listening problems.

Exercise 1

In any size of group, have one person stand up and talk for at least three minutes on a topic where opinions may be expressed. Typical topics may be.

1. The three greatest problems confronting this organization are _____?
2. I believe that recent union demands are (are not) bad for the economy of this country because _____.
3. Affirmative action programs are (are not) a good way to rectify past discrimination because _____.

After the person has completed the talk ask a second person to stand and explain to the group what the first person has just said. Emphasize accurate reporting. When person number two is finished have person number one and the remainder of the group evaluate how effectively person number two listened and reported what was originally said. Repeat as many times as necessary for each group member to have a chance.

Exercise 2

Select five group members and ask two to remain in the room while the other three leave. Ask one of the remaining people to write out some instructions to be given to the other remaining person orally. When the second person has been told the instructions, invite one of the other three people back into the room and have the message receiver repeat the instructions he or she has just heard. This continues until each person has heard and told the instructions to another. The last person to enter the room should repeat the instructions to the entire group after hearing it.

Check this against the written original version and discuss the changes that have occurred as the information has passed from one person to another. In addition, you might point out the way the listener reacts to information that is unclear or makes no sense.

In selecting the original instructions, be careful that the procedure described is neither too complicated nor too simple. The most effective ones will have five to seven separate steps. Here are some possible examples:

- How to make tacos.

- How to preflight check an aircraft.

- How to get somewhere (a distant city or someplace in town).

- Directions for a series of errands you want the person to accomplish (include addresses and details).

- Qualities you seek in an employee (teacher, spouse, friend, etc.).

Exercise 3

Divide into three-person groups. Person A and B should discuss a topic or issue on which they suspect they disagree. Person C will act as an observer. After each interaction between A and B, the partner who received the message should paraphrase and repeat back what she or he heard to the speaker. This may have to be repeated until the paraphrase is acceptable to the original speaker. Here is an example.

> *Person A:* "I think the company's affirmative action program unfairly forces the company to lower the quality of our employees."
>
> *Person B:* "*What I heard you say* is that people hired under affirmative action programs are always of lower quality than others."
>
> *Person A:* "I will not accept your paraphrase."

The process should continue until B provides a paraphrase of A's comment that is acceptable to Person A. In paraphrasing, the listener should seek to use different words from those of the speaker. After 15 or 20 minutes, Person C should offer his or her observations of what has happened. Did these people really seem to communicate—did they understand each other's views when they were finished?[3]

Some Other Thoughts About Listening:
READING FOR CHAPTER 8

Lend Me Your Ears[4]

Charles R. McConnell

When I gave my eleven-year-old permission to visit a girl-friend I warned her against the last-minute call asking to bring her friend home for the night. We had guests coming and it was no time for an extra youngster. Nevertheless, minutes before I was to go after her she telephoned and rapidly and urgently asked if Shelly could please, please, please come home with her.

I got angry, and talking over a frantic torrent of tearful words I abruptly squashed her plea. After all, I'm the parent so I win automatically—right? When I got to Shelly's door I was met by two glum girls and one patient mother who asked if *my* girl could stay *there* for the night. I said she could.

My daughter's eyebrows popped upward at my ready consent. "But, Dad," she said, "that was the second thing I asked and you said 'absolutely no'!"

Taken aback, I apologized for not listening well. After a few thoughtful seconds she said, "It's okay, Dad. I guess you were just too busy saying 'no' to listen to what I was saying."

This prompted some serious I-ought-to-know-better thinking. I write about communication and teach effective listening classes, yet I was undeniably guilty of hearing without listening. I didn't doubt I'd *heard* most of her words, but if I'd been *listening* I would have correctly received my daughter's altered request.

Listening is the toughest of the communication skills. As the one which ought to consume the largest part of our communication time, it's the skill for which the least amount of solid help is available. And it's the one most often taken for granted.

Let's first consider why we're likely to take our listening abilities for granted. Then we'll look at the common barriers to effective listening and suggest some ways of overcoming them.

Using words—audible and visible symbols that stand for things—we send out information by speaking and writing. In two other ways, reading and listening, we receive information from others.

Imagine you're a radio with four settings. You can be switched to writing, reading, speaking, or listening. When you're tuned to one of the first three you can still hear, so spreading over your other settings is this one ability you can't turn off. When you're not writing, reading, or speaking, you're in what we can call a *Listening Mode*.

I have a little sign saying: Please Engage Brain Before Putting Mouth in Gear. Regardless of whether your brain is fully engaged, you *do* have to put your mouth "in gear." You need to perform certain voluntary actions to form the words and get them out. Likewise, writing and reading require some physical effort.

We can· say that writing, reading, and speaking are *active* physically. We can't say the same about listening or the capacity to listen. Providing your ears are in working order, you don't have to do anything to "turn on" your receiver.

Close your mouth and you've stifled your ability to speak. Shut your eyes and you can't read, and if you sit on your hands you'll find writing is out of the question. But there's no way short of outside force—ear plugs?—to close down your audio circuits.

Because this listening mode—the simple state of hearing—is passive, we tend to take it for granted. We don't realize that listening, when properly done, requires *more* conscious effort than writing, reading, or speaking— effort that must be completely self-applied between the ears.

Consider the importance of listening in our daily lives. We spend the least amount of our communication time writing and the second least, reading. The next to the greatest part is spent speaking, and listening commands—or ought to command—most of our communication time. This suggests we could profit by sharpening our listening skills.

There's a sign on the wall of a quaint restaurant:

How Come It Takes Two Years to Learn to Talk and 60 to 70 to Learn to Be Quiet?

The sign's lesson is simple: when you're talking, you're not listening. The conscious effort listening requires can't be applied while you're busy generating speech. Neither can you truly listen while you're reading or writing. When you try to deal with different things using different skills at the same time, something's bound to suffer. (This could be why that book report Junior dashed off in front of the TV last night is something less than his best work.)

The first step toward effective listening is giving the incoming message your undivided attention. Only then will you be able to apply all your mental energy to the listening process. Next you need to become aware of the common barriers to effective listening and learn how to overcome them.

One of the greatest barriers is found in the failure to separate talker from topic. This is especially likely if the person speaking is one you don't get along well with, or someone whose manner you find annoying. Maybe the tone is preachy or patronizing; perhaps the voice is a dreary monotone.

These and other things can be listening turn-offs, and even though you're reacting to the talker you're blocking out the message.

There are many things about a speaker—in either a lecture setting or face-to-face situation—that can hamper listening if you let them. That's the key: *If you let them.* It sometimes requires supreme effort to focus on the topic in the face of all else, but it can be done.

Another common fault is trying to listen for specific information, for "facts." We should rather be listening for ideas and whole thoughts, usually more important than specifics. Most of us aren't able to retain more than a few of a number of facts coming our way in a short time, but we can recall ideas and express them in our own words. Facts themselves are not nearly as important as the ideas that bind them together.

Situation: you're nose to nose with your spouse in an important discussion. Something that's said rubs you wrong; you think it's incorrect and certainly unfair. Words are still coming your way, but your mind is racing ahead shaping your response. You can hardly wait for your better half to pause for breath so you can leap in. You're guilty of premature reaction.

Save your reactions. Whatever the cost in self-control—bite your tongue, stuff a hand in your mouth, whatever—keep quiet and hear the talker out. Most of the thoughts you have while another person is speaking won't desert you, and you'll find many of them aren't pertinent once you've taken in the entire message. Remember the old advice: It's better to remain silent and be thought a fool than to speak up and remove all doubt.

Strongly related to reaction-rushing are the listening roadblocks placed by emotion. We all have our sore spots, little emotional triggers causing us to feel anger, injury, or defensiveness when touched. You've probably had the experience of being rubbed the wrong way by something someone said. You were feeling resentment or other negative things, yet the other party rattled on as though nothing happened.

Maybe you've also had the experience of realizing—after the fact—that you had apparently offended someone but had no idea what damaging thing you said. You blundered, but in innocence.

These two sides of the same coin lead us to one important conclusion: your blunder was innocent, and chances are the other party's jab was also unintended. Do your best to always extend the benefit of the doubt. You'll probably never be fully aware of all your own little sore spots, let alone second-guess everyone else's, so be quick to forgive.

When you react emotionally you're forming possible responses—excuses, complaints, accusations, and so on. And you're not getting the rest of the message. Even if you intend to remain silent, nurturing injury or resentment can be fully as damaging to your listening capacity. Generally, as your level of emotion rises your ability to listen effectively lessens.

Another listening obstacle is found in our natural ability to think about four times faster than we can talk. When someone else is talking you can take in and tuck away all the words and still have most of your thinking time open. Unfortunately, it's easy to be led astray during this open time.

Let's say your conversation partner uses the word "cleaner." You suddenly remember you need to have your best outfit cleaned by Friday. This means you should get it to the cleaner today, and you know they close at . . .

When you get back to the talker you find some added words have zipped through your head without hitting anything. You weren't there; you were at the cleaner's. You may have most of your thinking time open, but it occurs in such brief chunks that any tangent thought you chase causes you to miss something.

Use your open thinking time so it works for you. As you take in more words and thoughts, roll them into what's already been said and do some summarizing. Or if possible—if the message is logically delivered—anticipate what might be said. Not second-guessing or jumping to conclusions, but honest anticipation of what *might* follow based on what you've already heard. But whether summarizing or anticipating, stay with talker and topic the whole time.

Routine distractions such as other conversations and external noise can cut into your listening ability. You may be able to control these distractions in a private conversation and you probably do so at times. If you're discussing yesterday's ball game with Uncle Joe you might do it well in a people-filled room. However, if you're trying to hammer out some serious personal differences you'll want to go where it's quiet.

If you're part of a listening group you may not be able to control distractions—the chatterers behind you, the brawl in the next room, the speaker's annoying habit of saying uuuuuhh! every five words. You can't control these things, but you can reduce their effects with deliberate concentration.

One last listening barrier is outlined for people who find it helpful to take notes at times. The problem lies in the tendency to try to listen with the paper. I got caught by this time and again in school. The professor would say we were about to hear the seven great pearls of wisdom, and we'd better know them cold. Next week's test, you know.

I'd try to catch everything only to find I was still frantically scrawling pearl number two and the professor was already voicing number five. I'd leap to number five, catch a piece of number six, then quickly try to fill in the gaps. By the time I looked up from my page of erratic chicken tracks, I'd discover the speaker was two new topics down the road.

If you must take notes, keep them brief. Remember the suggestion to listen for ideas and whole thoughts? Do this, and catch each in a two or three word phrase or a single key word. Later you can use these words and phrases as mental triggers when you begin to rework and expand upon your notes.

Through all of these words about listening the notion of concentration has popped up several times. Concentration—deliberate focusing of mental effort—will give you the best start on becoming a better listener. To this concentration add your determination to separate talker from topic, listen for ideas instead of facts, avoid rushing reactions, control your emotions, and fight distractions. Then you'll be ready to begin building improved listening habits.

It's been said that man is the only animal who can talk his way into trouble. Most of us slip once in a while; I have days when I feel like I only open my mouth to change feet. Take heart; listening is not only more valuable than speaking, it's also safer. As Calvin Coolidge said, "Nobody ever listened himself out of a job."

To be an effective listener, keep your mouth closed and your mind open (*don't* get these turned around). In the words of Wilson Mizner: "A good listener is not only popular everywhere, after a while he knows something."

Notes

1. J. Harold Janis, *Writing and Communicating in Business*, 3rd Ed. (New York: Macmillan, 1978), p. 492.
2. Phillip V. Lewis, *Organizational Communication: The Essence of Effective Management* (Columbus, Ohio: Grid, 1975), p. 91.
3. Adapted from Larry L. Barker, *Communication* (Englewood Cliffs, N.J.: Prentice-Hall, 1978), p. 67.
4. Charles R. McConnell, "Lend Me Your Ears," *The Elks Magazine*, August 1977. Reprinted by permission of Charles R. McConnell.

Recommended Readings

Rogers, Carl R. and Richard E. Farson, "Active Listening," in *Readings in Interpersonal and Organizational Communication*, (3rd ed.) eds. Richard C. Huseman et al. Boston: Holbrook Press, 1977, pp. 561–576. This outstanding article stressing the importance of expending effort to meet our responsibilities as listeners gives examples from business and industrial contexts.

Another "classic" article on listening is Ralph G. Nichols, "Listening Is a 10 Part Skill," *Nation's Business*, 45 (July 1957), pp. 56–60. Nichols begins by citing that 40 percent of a manager's work day is spent listening to others and goes on to prescribe ten ways to improve listening skills.

Barker, Larry L., *Communication* (Englewood Cliffs, N.J.: Prentice-Hall, 1978), Chapter 3. Aimed at student readers, this book clearly explains principles of effective listening and feedback. Additional exercises and thought questions are offered.

PART

WRITTEN
COMMUNICATION
ACTIVITIES

CHAPTER 9

LETTERS AND MEMOS
Write Right
or Don't Write at All

The difference between literature and business writing is like the difference between culture and agriculture. In business we're concerned with the yield.

Back in Chapter 4 we discussed the costs of letters. You'll recall that American business spends almost $90 billion a year on original business letters sent through the mail. These costs include (1) the labor time of the executive who composes and dictates or produces a rough draft (this is the highest single cost); (2) the time of secretaries, mailroom employees, file clerks and anyone else who processes the letter; (3) materials costs, postage, and fixed charges such as depreciation or rental on typewriters, duplicators, and file cabinets; and (4) the costs of the office space utilized by letter processing activities. Every file cabinet takes up office space which is usually rented by the square foot. The same goes for the space set aside for the mailroom. When we consider all these things, the conservatively estimated average cost per letter of $4 to $5 begins to make sense.

Ironically, the dollar figure calculated this way still leaves out what may be the single highest cost: the cost of the *ineffective* letter which requires follow-up, clarification, or an unnecessary exchange of more messages. The ultimate cost may be the irate reader who reacts to a poorly written letter by becoming a *former* customer or collaborator. These costs are incalculable, but I suspect they may make the other figures look like small change.

If some way could be found to reduce letter expenses by only 10 percent, businesses in the United States could devote $8.8 billion to other productive uses. That's the equivalent of saving about $41 for each man, woman, and child in America every year.

The key to cost cutting lies in the answers to three questions every business person should ask each time a letter is generated:

1. Is this letter really necessary?
2. Is this letter efficient?
3. Is this letter effective?

Is This Letter Necessary?

The major advantages of the letter medium are its permanent record, relative formality, and capability of conveying fairly complex data. Disadvantages include high cost, low speed, and lack of immediate feedback. If a given communication situation is likely to require an extensive two-way exchange of information in order to create understanding, don't write. Call or visit. There are times when flying across the country for a face-to-face conversation can be "cheaper" than a letter. Such trips would be worthwhile to save a major customer or to influence legislation affecting your business. If, however, you do need to convey fairly complex but not highly emotional information (say, a list of costs and serial numbers of parts for example) or if it is important to have a permanent record of what was said (like a proposal for services with prices quoted) or if a somewhat formal message would be useful to convey a contractual agreement, go with a letter. Just remember the $4 or $5 cost as you take pen in hand.

Even when we conclude that a written response is called for, there are still several more economical options to dictating (or writing a rough draft) and typing a formal letter. We could handwrite a note, send a form or preprinted document, or, when responding to someone else's written message, simply write a brief reply on the original letter and return it, keeping a photocopy for our own records. This latter alternative to the formal letter has become more widely used in recent years. An example is shown in Figure 9-1.

There are, of course, many business situations in which an original letter is more appropriate. When we answer the question, "Is this letter necessary?" in the affirmative, we should ask a second question.

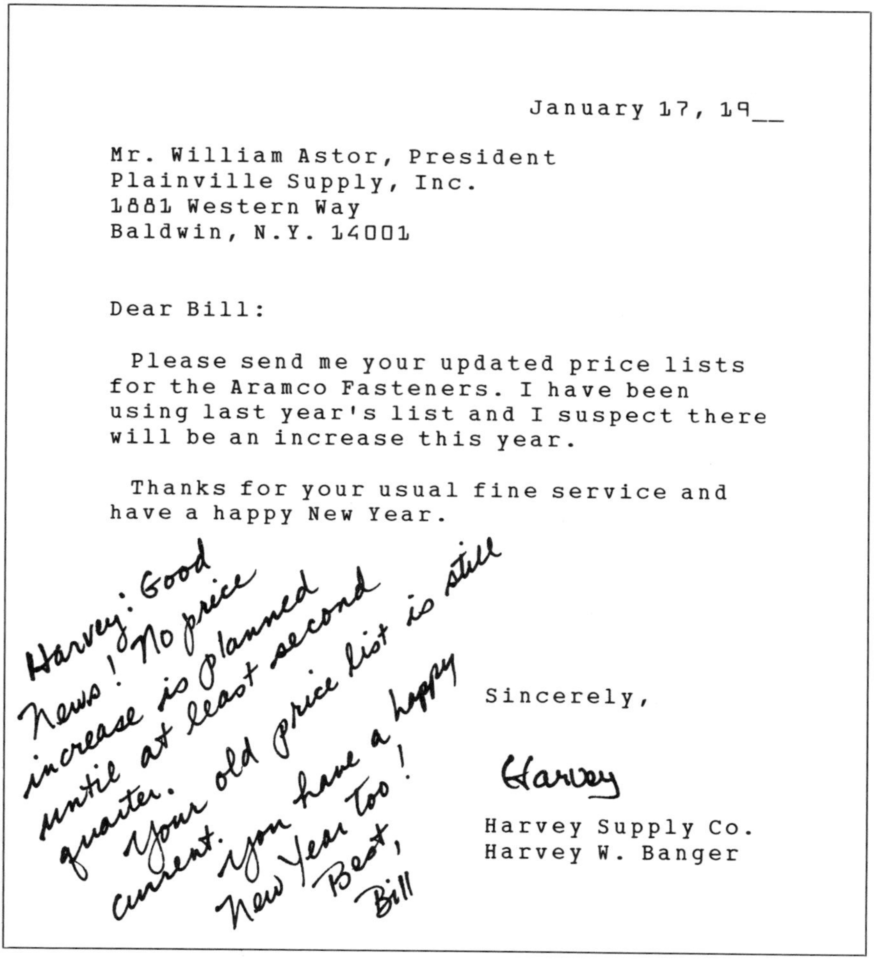

January 17, 19__

Mr. William Astor, President
Plainville Supply, Inc.
1881 Western Way
Baldwin, N.Y. 14001

Dear Bill:

   Please send me your updated price lists
for the Aramco Fasteners. I have been
using last year's list and I suspect there
will be an increase this year.

   Thanks for your usual fine service and
have a happy New Year.

*Harvey: Good
News! No price
increase is planned
until at least second
quarter. Your old price list is still
current. You have a happy
New Year too!
Best,
Bill*

                                    Sincerely,

                                    Harvey

                                    Harvey Supply Co.
                                    Harvey W. Banger

Figure 9-1 Quick reply format

Is This Letter Efficient?

There are two factors of efficiency in a letter—economy of language and
organization of the message. Most letter writers would agree with this
statement in principle, but when they sit down to write, something very
wordy and ill-arranged too often materializes on that blank sheet. But
how can writers improve efficiency? Here are some ideas.

Economy of Language

Many of the phrases that appear in business letters are there because "we've always done it that way." Typically, inexperienced letter writers check the correspondence files to see how others have written in the past. And they end up using phrases like the ones in the rhyme below:

> We beg to advise you and wish to state
> That yours has arrived of recent date.
> We have it before us; its contents noted.
> Herewith enclosed are the prices we quoted.
> Attached you will find, as per your request,
> The forms you wanted, and we would suggest,
> Regarding the matter and due to the fact
> That up to this moment your order we've lacked,
> We hope that you will not delay it unduly.
> We beg to remain, yours very truly.[1]

Although an exaggeration, this poem illustrates how the meat of a very simple message can get buried under these overworked expressions.

The most economical language results when we write pretty much the way we would talk in a planned, purposeful conversation. It is unlikely that, upon handing an envelope to a coworker in our office, we would say, "Enclosed herewith please find the report I've written." In conversation we'd be more likely to say "Here's the report I prepared on . . ." So why not write that way? It gets to the point and conveys your message efficiently. The trend in written communication is to the less formal, more conversational tone.

A few weeks after I taught a writing workshop for a group of manufacturers' representatives, to whom I preached this point about informality in tone, the following "letter" was sent to me with the question "How's this?" attached:

```
Hey Julian, remember when you asked me for a
clean price list for organics? Well, here that
sucker is. Hope it will get the job done.
Hang in there buddy.

                                              Don
```

Seldom does a teacher find his or her exhortations followed so literally. Of course, even informality has its proper limits.

Most of us can make a dramatic improvement in letter efficiency and tone by concentrating on word selection and consciously breaking stuffy habits of usage. Here are some useful rules to encourage a conversational and a more economical style.

Use simple wording. Often a common word can do the job of a multisyllable jawbreaker. There is a clear correlation between the number of syllables in a word and its difficulty in reading. Lots of big words slow down both the writer and the reader, and they usually don't communicate any more effectively despite the increased effort. In the examples below, listen to how much easier the short version is to express.

Long and Heavy Wording	Short and Simple Wording
Our *analysis* of the *situation* suggests needed *experiential* training to *optimize* job performance.	We think our people need more job training.
John *acceded* to the demands for *additional compensation*.	John agreed to pay them more.
My investment recommendations were *predicated* on *anticipations* of additional *monetary funds* being made available.	My investment recommendations were based on an expected increase in money available.
Ramifications of our *performance shortfall* included *program discontinuation*.	Since we didn't reach our goal, the program was discontinued.

Use familiar, conversational words. Everyday language inevitably helps your reader understand what you are saying. Many business writers feel they must use technical or very formal language to convey the appropriate *image*. The fallacy in this is that the most intelligent business person is one who wants to *serve* those he or she communicates with. You serve only your illusions of status with language so technical and stilted that it loses meaning, or at least a sense of warmth for your receiver. Overuse of "status words" mixed with frequent clichés makes your letter sound stuffy. Talk in terms your reader is sure to understand.

Unfamiliar, Stilted Words	Everyday, Conversational Words
ascertain	find out
terminate	end
endeavor	try
with all due dispatch	quickly
forthwith	soon

monetary transaction   sale or purchase
occupational position   job
financial obligations   debts
disproportionate   unfair

Use words with punch. Words have personality. Some are dull, weak, or rather mushy in meaning. Others are hard-hitting, precise, and vigorous. Skilled writers develop a sensitivity to words and search for those that produce just the right effect. They give their writing punch by avoiding overuse of adjectives or adverbs that soften or qualify the noun or verb they are attached to. Figurative language also adds vitality to writing. Here are some examples.

Dull Words	Vigorous Words
a good sales representative	an *aggressive* sales rep
She was a real leader in that group.	She was the *sparkplug* in that group.
He told some interesting stories about . . .	He told some *hair-raising* tales . . . or he had us *spellbound* with his stories.
Houston is enjoying considerable prosperity.	Houston is *booming*.
The loss of that account was very disappointing.	The loss of that account was a *crushing* disappointment.
a nice personality	a *vivacious* personality

Avoid technical jargon. Every field and every organization develops its own jargon which becomes part of the everyday vocabulary of the people who use it. Since it is so common, we often make the mistake of assuming others outside the field know what we mean. Sometimes such jargon includes dull, heavy-sounding words (*infrastructure*), acronyms, (words made up from letters, like BOA for business office accessibility, or SCORE for Service Core of Retired Executives), or terms used in a specialized sense (like the photocopier industry's term *duplexing* to mean copying on both sides of a sheet of paper). When you have any doubt that your reader may misunderstand your specialized term, use a layman's version.

Technical Terms or Jargon	Layperson's Version
accounts receivable	how much is owed the company
cerebral vascular accident	stroke

HVI bonus	extra pay for selling high volume machines
easement for ingress and egress	agreement allowing passage in and out
maturity date	final payment date
SAT score	Scholastic Aptitude Test score

Use concrete words. Concrete words not only improve efficiency but also hold your reader's interest by creating a vivid and sharp image. Often these are short, familiar terms. Sometimes the concrete term takes a little longer to phrase, but the precision tends to stay with your reader longer. The well-known advertising campaign claiming that Ivory soap is "99 44/100 percent pure" sticks in our mind. If they had said simply "Ivory is very pure," few would have been impressed.[2]

Abstract	**Concrete**
the leading student	top student in a class of 80
most of our people	87 percent of our people
in the near future	by noon Wednesday
lower cost than . . .	$43 less than . . .
very accurate	pinpoint accuracy
a sizable increase in sales	doubled in sales
low energy consumption	uses no more power than a 60-watt lightbulb
the cost would be enormous	. . . would cost every taxpayer $86 per year
the computer can produce form letters very quickly	the computer types 1000 personalized letters per hour

Use active verbs. Just as concreteness improves nouns and modifiers, use of the active voice adds impact to verbs. The grammatical term *voice* refers to whether the subject of a sentence acts or is acted upon. If it is *acted upon*, passive voice is used; if it *does the acting*, active voice is used. Active verbs make your sentences more:

1. *Specific.* "The Board of Directors decided" is more explicit than "A decision has been made."

2. *Personal.* "You will note" is both personal and specific; "It will be noted" is impersonal.

3. *Concise.* The passive requires more words and thus slows down both the writing and reading. Compare "Figures show" with "It is shown by figures."

4. *Emphatic.* Passive verbs dull action. Compare "The child ran a mile" with "A mile was run by the child."[3]

The clearer relationship between subject and verb in active voice adds force and momentum to your writing. By closely associating the *actor* (noun) and the *action* (verb), we help our reader visualize more clearly what is happening. There are, of course, cases where the writer may intentionally want to deemphasize this association (or remove the actor entirely) by using passive voice. For example,

I just ran over your cat. (active)

Your cat has been run over. (passive)

The changes in emphasis caused by the selection of active or passive voice can be quite dramatic. For most business writing, the active voice is preferred because it adds vitality.

Passive	Active
Each tire *was inspected* by a mechanic.	A mechanic *inspected* each tire.
A gain of 41 percent *was recorded* for paper product sales.	Paper products sales *gained* 41 percent.
A full report *will be* sent to you by the supervisor.	The supervisor *will send* . . . or, You *will receive* a full report from the supervisor.
All figures in the report *are checked* by accounting.	The accounting department *checks* all figures in the report.

Avoid unnecessary repetition. Although repeating an idea can be an effective teaching device (especially in oral communication), redundancy—unnecessary repetition—distracts the letter reader.

Needless Repetition	Repetition Eliminated
The *provisions* of the contract *provide* for a union shop.	The contract provides for a union shop.
The new rule will affect *each and every* employee.	The new rule will affect every employee.
In my opinion I think the plan is reasonable.	I think the plan is reasonable.

The factory is *completely surrounded* by chain link fence.	The factory is surrounded by chain link fence.
Try to eliminate *unnecessary* and *repetitive redundancy.*	Try to eliminate redundancy.

Avoid surplus words and cluttered phrases. Words that add nothing to the meaning of the sentence should be dropped. Phrases that can be replaced by a single word or shorter expression should be changed. Here are some examples:

Cluttered	**More Concise**
I would like to say how much I enjoyed visiting with you.	I enjoyed visiting with you.
In the event that payment is not received . . .	If payment is not . . .
The report is *in regard to the matter of* our long-term obligations . . .	The report is about . . .
I have just received your letter and wanted to respond quickly.	I wanted to respond quickly to your letter.
The quality of his art work is so good that *it permitted us to* offer him a long-term contract.	His work was so good that we offered him a long-term contract.

Organizing the Message

Efficiency can be further improved by adopting a few suggestions for arranging words into sentences, paragraphs, and entire letters. The key seems to be to keep it *short* and *simple.* A detailed discussion of grammar would be out of place in this book so I have recommended several good handbooks at the end of the chapter. If you have problems with basic grammar or syntax (word arrangement) you should get in the habit of referring to such reference materials. Keep in mind that rules of grammar are simply statements of logical relationships between words. We need not be slaves to grammatical correctness. But when our logic is fuzzy the message is likely to be less clear, the image of the writer may well be tarnished, and the letter will doubtless be less efficient.

Building sentences. The factors that make written messages hard to read are (1) the heavy use of polysyllabic words, (2) use of technical, repetitious, or cluttered phrases, and (3) the heavy use of long sentences.

Many readers tend to silently vocalize the words as they read. Longer words with three, four, or even five syllables simply take longer to say and drag down our reading efficiency. Similarly, the complex or compound sentence with several related clauses makes for slow going. The remedy: short words and short sentences. The drawback: if we carry this too far our letters sound like the Dick and Jane reader and we risk insulting our reader and/or sounding foolish. There is, of course, a happy medium. The choppiness of short simple sentences can be broken up with a few compound or complex sentences. Sentences should convey bite-size pieces of information that can be digested by your reader one piece at a time. The rule of thumb is that for most adult American readers, sentences should *average* about 16 to 18 words in length. Of course, some sentences may have only 2 or 3 words while others can run to 30 or more.

One other consideration in dealing with sentence length: different lengths have different effects on readers. Short sentences have punch. They emphasize. They hit hard. Longer sentences, on the other hand, can be useful in deemphasizing information which may be objectionable or unpleasant for your reader. They can also be used to subordinate less important information which you do not want to dwell upon but which is necessary for understanding.

Building paragraphs. Paragraphs should usually be short unless further deemphasis is desired. People prefer to read information presented in manageable bits. When I receive a letter with very long paragraphs, I usually anticipate a hard-to-read format. Even before reading the first words, your letter recipient makes some quick judgments about the message, based on nonverbal cues such as quality and appearance of the paper, typeface, letterhead design, and countless other things. The amount of "white space" between paragraphs is one such cue. In the illustration in Figure 9-2, which letter would you prefer to read?

Most paragraphs should have a topic sentence which expresses the "big" idea. The rest of the paragraph provides support, elaboration, or clarification of that idea. The main idea may be at the beginning, in the middle, or at the end of the paragraph, depending on the writer's purpose. If it is at the beginning or the very end, it'll carry more emphasis than if it is buried in the middle. I'll talk more about positions of emphasis later in this chapter.

So far I've suggested that your letter's efficiency arises from your choice of words and phrases and the way these are organized into sentences and paragraphs. The arrangement of the total letter also affects efficiency. But before we go into formats for different types of messages, let's consider the third question we should ask when we use the letter medium:

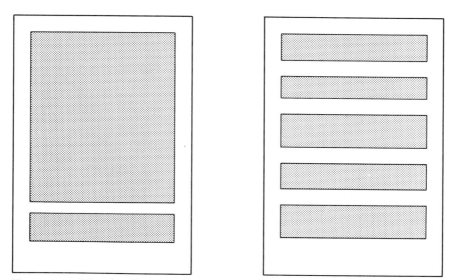

Figure 9-2 Visual effect of long versus short paragraphs

Is This Letter Effective?

Every letter does two jobs. It attempts to *convey a message* and it *projects an image* of its writer. Sometimes one task is relatively more important than the other. Figure 9-3 illustrates how these functions could be plotted on a grid. As with the more famous "managerial grid," let's assume that each axis is calculated between 1 and 9 (low to high), with the vertical axis reflecting the degree of reader understanding—the *accuracy* with which the message has been received—and the horizontal axis reflecting favorableness of the impression created by the writer—his or her *image*. The ideal business letter would be a 9-9 (high accuracy, high image), while the total waste of paper and money would be a 1-1 (low accuracy, low image) letter. We may, however, get by with a 9-1 letter if the overriding task of the letter is to convey accurate information with minimal concern for image projected. A military directive or routine transmittal of some data may be efficient and fairly harmless as a 9-1. At the other end of the grid, a 1-9 letter, one whose message content is less than precise may be well received when it's the "thought that counts." Inadequate but thoughtful expressions of sympathy or cheerful but rather vague notes of congratulations may be 1-9s.

This letter grid serves as a reminder of the two dimensions of effectiveness.

A friend of mine received a note of congratulations from his banker that could be classified as a 1-9:

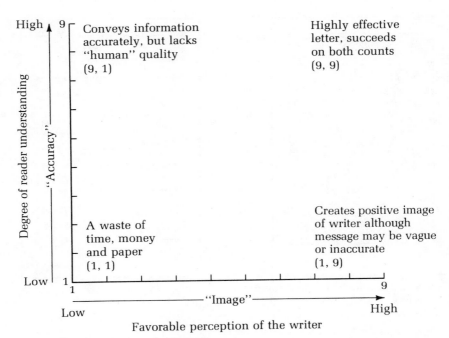

Figure 9-3 The effective letter grid

```
Dear Pete:

    Congratulations on your promotion last month to
VP! We're proud of you. Best wishes for continued
success.

                                            Cordially,
```

Although Pete had been promoted to *senior* vice president and the promotion was to be effective *next* month, the note was still well received and reflected positively on the sender.

A 9–1 letter is accurate but without charm; it has a mechanical tone to it:

```
Dear Mr. Braswell:

    The parts list requested is enclosed. In addition,
this is to inform you that shipment of all orders
from the Atlanta Warehouse must be prepaid.

                                        Yours truly,



                                    Jordan Automotive
```

We should normally be concerned with both information sharing and image building in our letters. Going back to our earlier discussion of word choices, the lawyer or stockbroker who insists upon using professional jargon in an attempt to feed her sense of professionalism may convey a learned image but will soon turn off the reader who can't figure out what she is saying. Such "impressive" sounding letters may stroke the writer's ego but only frustrate the reader. Conversely, the writer who spits out cold, heartless, but fact-filled sentences with great precision may seem like a well-programmed android. Good business letters are more than pure information transfer. They also involve impressions and expressions of humanity. Even when mass printed by a computer, professional letters can sound like a chat over the back fence with your neighbor. Perhaps a classic example is the advertising letter you recently received from *Reader's Digest* or the solicitation from a political candidate you once supported. Letter effectiveness arises from both the informational and "human" content of the message.

Building the Total Letter

About 90 percent of the letters written in a typical organization convey some sort of routine information. We send letters to report, to confirm, and to request information. These messages are factual, generally unemotional communications which generate predictable responses.

There are, however, situations in which the reader of our letter is likely to get much more emotionally involved with the message we write. To be effective in such situations we need to be aware of psychological factors at work in our communication attempts. In a word, we need to be more reader-sensitive.

Most business communication writers agree that there are only a few basic letter types. The easy ones convey routine, nonemotional messages or good news for the reader. The trickier ones deal with the reader's emotions by conveying disappointment, refusal of a request, or by trying to get the reader to do something she or he would not normally do (e.g., buy something, pay an overdue bill). A fourth letter type is the goodwill letter in which image is often more important than content.

Routine or Good-News Letters

Be direct. There is little a writer can do to destroy the effectiveness of a good-news letter. The intent is to tell the reader something he or she is glad to hear, or, at worst, is neutral toward. Efficiency of communication should be an important consideration here. These letters are generally brief, although not curt, and to the point. A direct order of presentation should normally be used. This means that the central point of the letter should come first. If you are writing to order 200 Disco-trimmers, start your letter with "Please send me 200 Disco-trimmers. . . ."

The big idea of the letter may then be followed by other relevant subordinate information which clarifies details such as "I am enclosing a check for $1000" and "Please ship them parcel post to our warehouse at. . . ."

This may seem like a ridiculously simple issue, but many routine letters fail to get directly to the point. They might begin, "We are impressed with your advertisements for the amazing Disco-trimmer" or "We are interested in exploring the possibility of doing business with you." You simply don't need this stuff. Your reader isn't likely to miss the lack of pleasantries since the main thrust of your letter is good news.

Be complete. Let me hedge slightly on my statement that there is little we can do to louse up this type of letter. I have seen two ways to fail. First, the letter that is incomplete may fail to do the job. I recently received a letter from an insurance agent in a distant city I was about to move to. He invited me to purchase my homeowner's insurance from him, stressing that he could give me good coverage at low cost. The letter was pleasant enough but one detail was missing: There was an incomplete return address and no phone number!

Murphy and Peck tell this horror story about a company's direct mail sales campaign: A sales letter, personalized with a typed inside address and personal salutation, was to be sent to 100,000 potential customers. The letter ended with the instructions that the reader "could take advantage of the offer" by simply initialing the letter and returning it in the prepaid envelope.

> However, to save the expense of having typists insert the 100,000 inside addresses and personal salutations, a budget-minded official requested that the entire message be printed and that all inside addresses be omitted. And the salutation was changed to the general, printed, "Dear Customer." The result was that the company received over 11,000 of the letters back, but no one had had the slightest idea whom the 11,000 initials . . . belonged to![4]

Don't be overly assumptive. The second example of a good-news letter that flops is illustrated by one received from the president of a university where a friend of mine had applied for a job. The opening statement read: "You are hereby appointed Associate Professor . . ." The letter sounded more like a coronation than an offer of employment. While my friend was pleased to be offered the position, the tone clearly assumed that he would jump at the opportunity. Instead, the presumptuous sound of the letter turned him off. He declined the job. Even in good news letters, some sensitivity to tone is necessary.

Bad-News Letters

There are some business letters that convey information the reader is not anxious to hear. Occasionally we need to refuse a request or give some other type of bad news. When this is the case, another cost decision must be made. Is maintaining goodwill with that reader important enough that you are willing to expend some *extra* effort in writing to him? The alternative is to simply blurt out the bad news and let the public relations chips fall where they may. This decision isn't always easy to make. A tactful, carefully arranged bad-news letter costs more to produce but is likely to at least soften any negative impressions your reader has toward you or your organization. The payoff in maintaining goodwill may or may not be worth the effort.

These are the options: (1) be blunt and organize your bad-news letter in the same direct manner as a routine letter, or (2) apply a pattern of organization which attempts to psychologically soothe or at least create understanding of your viewpoint in the reader. If you decide on option 2, here is a way of going about it.

The organization of the bad-news letter includes four distinct ingredients. These are:

1 • A buffer

2 • Presentation of reasoning

3 • The actual refusal or bad news

4 • An optimistic close

The buffer sentences or paragraph presents neutral or positive information the reader is not likely to disagree with. Often we thank the reader for his or her interest in the organization. We may also make a general, rather abstract statement which anyone would be likely to agree with. This buffer is designed to get the reader into the rest of the letter—to avoid a premature turnoff before you've had a chance to explain the reasoning behind your refusal. It should cushion the blow. One caution: the buffer should not sound so encouraging that the reader is led to expect a favorable message. Keep it neutral or vaguely positive.

Next, there should be a natural flow from the buffer into the reasoning. Any refusal should be based in reasoning that makes sense to the manager writing the letter and, it is hoped, to the reader. The task of this type of letter is in large part to convey that reasoning to the reader so he or she will either agree with the bad news or at least understand *why* you decided as you did. Ideally, the reader will say, "I'm disappointed but I'd probably make the same decision if I were in your shoes."

The reasons presented should be logically and clearly presented. Avoid jargon or elaborate explanations of complexities the reader may not comprehend. Also avoid overuse of negative language or words that have undesirable overtones. These can be a real turnoff to your reader. If your decision was based on prudent reasoning, there is no need to sound arbitrary or judgmental in your tone. Be especially careful to avoid words and phrases that may imply a judgment of your reader. The list below illustrates the kinds of hidden meanings that may be conveyed to your reader.[5]

Words and Phrases Having Undesirable Overtones

If you say:	You imply:
Apparently you are not aware	Not very well informed, are you?
I do not agree with you	What I say is right
Our records show	You can't be telling the truth
Our unassailable position	We are never wrong
We are not inclined to	We do as we wish
We cannot understand your	You don't make yourself clear
We differ from you	We must be right
We do not agree with your	So you are wrong
We object to your	You aren't doing what we want
We question your	You're probably either wrong or lying
We repeated to you	Must we tell you over and over?
When you question our decision	How dare you!
Why didn't you?	You are so stupid, forgetful, negligent
You apparently overlooked	You are careless
You are accountable for	We hold you responsible—we aren't
You are misinformed	Somebody lied to you; it wasn't I
You are wrong	As you usually are
You claim	Not a word of truth in it
You complain	Crybaby!
You contend	Arguing again, are you?
You did not include	Carelessness
You do not realize	Stupid!
You do not understand	How dumb can you be?
You failed to	Not efficient

You forgot to	No memory
You led us to believe	Did you lie to us?
You may be right	But we don't think so
You must do	We order you to
You must realize	Can't you understand anything?
You neglected to	Again, you are careless
You overlooked	And again
You say	But we don't believe you
You state	But we don't believe you
You were ill-advised to	How could you have been so stupid?
You will have to	Do as we say
Your complaint	Crybaby! whiner, griper!
Your contention	Stubborn, aren't you?
Your criticism	How dare you?
Your delay	Late again
Your demand	Don't be bossy
Your disclaimer	So you deny it?
Your dispute	So you want to argue!
Your disregard	Careless
Your dissatisfaction	Won't anything satisfy you?
Your failure to	Inefficient!
Your grievance	Crybaby! whiner, griper!
Your statement was incorrect	See, you were wrong!

Avoid "but" or "however." In addition to choosing words carefully, we should try to avoid the use of "but" or "however" when these mark a direct shift in tone. The abruptness of the change can destroy any goodwill you've salvaged to this point. Here's a letter I received several years ago which classically illustrates how *not* to write a refusal letter. I had written to this individual requesting permission to do some interviewing and to administer questionnaires to employees in his organization. He began his response with a pretty good buffer, but look where he went from there.

```
Dear Paul:

   Thanks for your letter of November 10. Very happy
to hear from you and I'm delighted you are finish-
ing your graduate work.
   I've been giving your proposal to do some re-
search work in the Orlando District a great deal of
thought. Your project sounds interesting and it is
```

```
the kind of thing I've personally been interested
in for several years. However, after having con-
sidered your request, I've decided to decline your
offer.
    I hope you will be able to conduct your research
elsewhere without any difficulty and I wish you
the very best.
                                    Yours very truly,



                                    District Manager
```

Instead of moving from his fairly good buffer into reasoning, this writer shifted gears with the deadly "however." If I had not recognized the value of this letter as a classic bad example to use in my classes, I would have been quite upset.

Be tactful but conclusive. The actual *refusal* or bit of *bad news* should be carefully worded and strategically placed to avoid undue emphasis on it. At the same time it must be clear so that there is no misunderstanding on the part of the reader. He must not see the matter as open to further discussion lest additional correspondence (and cost) be generated. But usually it is a good idea to be explicit. The slightest perception of in-conclusiveness and you may end up with a pen pal.

One technique to soften the blow would be to phrase the bad news in the passive voice ("your request must be denied") versus active voice ("I am denying your request"). Another technique is to position the actual refusal where it naturally receives less emphasis. The positions of strong-est emphasis (which should normally be avoided for bad news) are at the very beginning and the very end of each paragraph and the total letter. Figure 9-4 shows these positions. The top positions are emphasized be-cause they are the first words the reader sees in each paragraph. The end positions are those phrases that tend to linger in his mind and are thus emphasized.

The same principle applies to the individual sentences—emphasis is achieved best in the first and last words—but the effect on the reader is less pronounced than the positioning in paragraphs or the arrangement of the whole letter. The two strongest emphasis positions in the whole letter are the first and the very last phrase written. Your refusal or bad-news phrase would be best positioned toward the *middle* of the letter for deemphasis.

XXXXXXXXXXXXX _____
_____
_____
XXXXXXXXXXXX _____
XXXXXXXXXXXXXXXX _____
_____
_____
_____
_____
_____ XXXXXXXXXXX. _____
XXXXXXXXXX XXXXX _____
_____
_____ XXXXX XXX. _____
XXX XXXXXX XX XXXXX _____
_____
_____
_____ XXXXX XXXX XXXXX. _____

Figure 9-4 Emphasis positions in a letter

Offer a lesser alternative. Often it is appropriate to offer the reader an alternative to the original request. The alternative should be explained in a positive tone conveying the assumption that it will be accepted. The letter below illustrates such an effective refusal.

                                          September 20, 1972

Mr. Bob Gambrell, President
Young Businessmen's Federation
119 North Central
Hamburg, N.C. 28104

Dear Mr. Gambrell:

    We are highly complimented by your interest in
the kinds of employee motivation programs we are
developing here at SYNECTIC-SYSTEMS. Your request
that I speak to your group in November is personally flattering and has been considered carefully.
    After checking my travel schedule for the re-
mainder of the year, I find I have a conflict with
the November 19 date you mentioned. I will be at-

```
tending a conference in New York and will not
return until November 22. May I suggest an
alternative?
     Dr. Elliott Anderson has recently joined our or-
ganization. He brings excellent academic back-
ground and seven years' industrial psychology
experience with a major manufacturing organiza-
tion on the West coast. He is anxious to know more
people in the area and has indicated a willingness
to talk with your group on November 19.
     Elliott is an excellent speaker and I'm sure
you'll enjoy his presentation. He will be calling
you to confirm this early next week.
     Again, we appreciate the opportunity to speak to
your fine group.
                                   Cordially,

                          SYNECTIC SYSTEMS
                          George
                          George Bell
```

One final point about offering an alternative: make it easy for the reader to accept. I've seen dozens of letters that simply toss the ball back to the reader. Here is an example of the refusal-alternative section of such a letter:

```
     After checking my travel schedule for the re-
mainder of the year, I find I will be out of town on
the date you wanted me to visit your group.
     If some other date would be acceptable or if an-
other person from our company could be of help,
please write to me again.
```

A letter such as this one fails to achieve closure—the problem remains unresolved. If your letter must refuse a request, do so in explicit terms so there is no misunderstanding. But if you offer an alternative, follow through on the new idea. Don't just give the problem back to the reader and start the whole letter-response cycle over again. Offering a lesser alternative should not be used as a way to cop out on saying no. It should only be used when you genuinely want to offer an option to the reader.

Don't hide behind policy. If you sincerely want to spare your reader's feelings, explain your reasoning as vividly as possible. One quick way to aggravate your reader is to cite "company policy" as the reason for a refusal. Policy is, or should be, based on *reasons*. To cite simply "policy" without getting into the underlying reasons for that policy is like simply saying "because" when asked "why?"—not a very satisfactory answer.

Once the refusal has been clearly and tactfully conveyed, an *optimistic close*, which is similar in function to the buffer, should be written. Here we are interested in further repairing any damage to goodwill that may have occurred. Expressing confidence that a good business relationship will continue is one approach. It is important to *not apologize.* If, in fact, your decision has been based on sound, adult reasoning, there is no need to apologize. In fact, the effusive apology may cause your reader to question the reasoning. "The lady doth protest too much" implies underlying guilt for some imagined misdeed. Instead, confidently express a desire to maintain a favorable relationship with the reader.

As you can see, the bad-news letter requires more thought and effort than the routine informational letter. Its payoff lies in projecting a favorable, caring image to the reader.

While this bad-news letter format is widely regarded as an effective way to deal with potentially sticky situations, there are some who disagree that it's worth the effort. One communication consultant, responding to an article which recommended careful use of this bad-news pattern when refusing job applicants, advocated "directness in 'no' letters—not rude bluntness, but straight-to-the-pointness." He went on to say, "I believe we patronize an unsuccessful applicant when, from whatever motivation, we lead him through a circuitous route to the core of our message." His alternative is to say something like this: "Dear Mr. Applicant: If it disappoints you to learn that we have selected another candidate to fill the position for which you applied, we want you to know that this reflects no unfavorable assessment of you or your excellent qualifications."[6]

This individual's view was primarily critical of the bad-news letter that sounds overly optimistic in the buffer section only to shift gears with the deadly "however" paragraph. Although I agree that the transition from buffer to refusal is sometimes too abrupt, I do not advocate throwing out this time-tested pattern in favor of the more direct one. I will concede, however, that some mature people could accept the more direct format without being offended. But many could not. Stick with the bad-news format to be safe.

Persuasive Requests

The persuasive business letter, like the persuasive oral presentation, is *action*-oriented. It seeks to get the reader to *do* something he or she normally would not do without some prodding. The letter's effectiveness can often be judged by the action that results. The effective sales letter sells. The effective collection letter collects. By their fruits shall they be evaluated.

Persuasive communication situations presuppose some resistance to your proposals in the mind of your reader. Your message calls for action and action implies change. Change requires effort, and expending effort is something most of us would just as soon avoid. It's the writer's job to motivate the reader to expend the effort to change in the desired direction. To do so, we need to make some guesses about our readers' needs, wants, and motives.

Letters which persuade people normally require a slow, deliberate approach. They need to be phrased in terms of *the reader's* interests, not the writer's. They need to employ vivid language that conveys clear images. The underlying theme of the entire letter should be one of explaining the benefits of your proposal to your reader. And the letter should follow a systematic arrangement which leads the reader inevitably to the desired action. There are three phases to the persuasive letter: the attention getter, the explanation of the proposal, and the action getter.

Getting the reader's attention. Just as in the persuasive oral presentation, it is crucial that we grab the message receiver's attention immediately. Remember, the very first line is a position of emphasis in your letter—so use it wisely. Lead with your strongest motivator and don't waste any words.

Attention getters can take several forms but all should appeal to the reader, not necessarily the writer. Joel Bowman and Bernadine Branchaw suggest four categories of appeals we can make to gain reader attention. We can appeal to the reader's needs for *health, wealth, pleasure,* and to his or her *curiosity.*[7] In the organization we might add appeals to the need for *success, power* or *status enhancement,* and *self-satisfaction.* Such attention-getting appeals may be phrased positively or negatively. Positive appeals focus on what the reader stands to gain, while negative appeals accentuate what the reader might lose if he or she does not pay attention to your message. Examples of such appeals are presented in Figure 9-5.

Often the attention getter combines interest-creating information with a description of a problem. Television commercials typically follow this pattern, presenting an unpleasant situation in such a way that we can identify with the victim of, say "ring around the collar" or indigestion or "the heartbreak of psoriasis." The intent is to create a problem which can be solved by the product they want you to buy. Although TV spots are exaggerations, the persuasive pattern of attention, need development and need solution, is often an effective one. In this letter excerpt the persuasive intent is to get the reader to contribute to the university radio station. Here is the opening need-development phase:

```
With the recent change of WBCY-FM to a rock music
format, those of us who enjoy easy listening
stereo radio are stuck. There remains only one
```

such station in our community. And because of this no-competition situation, that station has increased its advertising time and reduced the amount of beautiful music.

I still like the soft sounds of our one remaining station, WEZC-FM, and I suspect you do too. But it seems absurd that a city this size cannot offer more than one high quality station. What would we do if WEZC would follow their competitor into the lucrative rock radio market? We'd all suffer the loss. Charlotte needs another FM station to play the kind of music discriminating adults enjoy.

Now you and I can play a part in filling that need and guaranteeing the continuation of our kind of music. The State legislature has pledged $70,000 in matching funds to WFAE-FM, the university radio station, if we can raise only $20,000.

Explaining the proposal in terms of the reader. Once the opening appeal has succeeded in gaining the reader's interest, the writer's job is to explain how the need aroused can be satisfied. You need to show the reader what's in it for him.

Success	Power and Status Enhancement	Self-Satisfaction	Curiosity
Positive Appeals			
Acting will lead to the reader's success in accomplishing goals. *Example:* "You can break into the million-dollar sales club . . ."	Acting will improve the reader's power and status. *Example:* "Want to get others to perk up and listen when you have something to say?"	Acting will lead to a sense of satisfaction for the reader. *Example:* "How would you like to be your own boss?"	Acting will answer questions the reader would like answered. *Example:* "How would you like to know your competitor's exact pricing tables?"
Negative Appeals			
Not acting will lead to the reader's failure to accomplish goals. *Example:* "Can you be satisfied with another *average* sales year?"	Not acting will cost the reader in loss of power or status. *Example:* "Are other young executives passing you by?"	Not acting will lead to dissatisfaction or missed opportunity for the reader. *Example:* "How much longer can you take the drudgery of your 8 to 5 job?"	Not acting will leave important questions unanswered. *Example:* "Is what you don't know about the competition killing you?"

Figure 9-5 Some possible attention-getting appeals

Many persuasive requests run afoul when the writer forgets the "you" attitude. The letter below illustrates what I mean. This letter was used by a political candidate to raise money for his campaign. It was printed on letterhead paper, personally signed, and was a generally attractive document. But let's consider the content:

```
                         $15,279.47

    The figure above is the amount which I must raise
in order to win election to the North Carolina
House of Representatives.
    You are one of 700 friends I feel that I can count
on. I'm asking for your financial support in the
amount of $21.83!!!
    July 25th is the date we must have all money on
hand!!!
    Please make checks payable to: Alan Jones for
N.C. House and forward to: John S. Fredericks,
Treasurer, 2011 Doughton Road, Charlotte, N.C.
28207.

Thank you for your consideration.

                                      Sincerely,


                                      Alan Jones
```

Obviously the tone is "I"-oriented. The use of the dollar figure at the top of the page is fairly effective—it does spark curiosity in the reader. The use of exclamation points and underlining for emphasis seem out of place. Exclamation points give us the image of a circus barker.

Suppose you were working on this candidate's campaign. How would you rewrite this message to create a "you" orientation?" First, consider what the reader potentially has to gain by doing the desired action (sending in $21.83). We may want to appeal to the reader's need or desire to have good people elected to public office, assuming, of course, that they perceive this candidate to be a good person. But more specifically, most people are likely to feel a sense of status enhancement in having a friend they supported get elected to office. A positive appeal may imply that their contribution will result in the candidate's election and that his election will give them some special influence in the legislature. Thinking along these lines, we might rework this letter, adding a "you" orientation, like this:

$15,279.47

The figure above is what it will cost to put your representative in the North Carolina House.
You are one of 700 friends I value deeply. Your past friendship and support have led me to believe that we share similar concerns for our state government and that I can effectively represent your interests in Raleigh. To bring this about, I'm asking for your financial help. Your contribution of only $21.83 puts us in a position where we can, and will, win the election on November 7.
To meet our campaign expenses, the money needs to be in the hands of John Fredericks, my Campaign Treasurer, by July 25. With your help, your voice will be heard in the upcoming legislative session.

Cordially,

Alan Jones

Explaining your proposal to the reader calls for action verbs and concrete nouns to create the vivid images people respond to. Often this calls for a longer letter, but without such detail, the persuasive appeal will fail. As we explain our proposal, we should seek to gain the reader's *interest* and create *desire*; a useful way to accomplish this is to clearly understand the distinction between the *features* of your product or proposal and the *benefits* to the reader. The skillful sales representative alludes to the product's features only as they relate to the customer's benefits. The feature is some attribute of the thing you are selling. The benefit is what the feature means to the customer.

I used to work with sales representatives for a large office products manufacturer. The copying machines we sold had lots of impressive features. They had capabilities to copy on both sides of the sheet of paper automatically, to reproduce from light originals, to reduce the original onto a sheet half the size, etc. These, at the time, were features unique to our products. Time after time I heard sales reps sell these *features* but fail to sell the product. The successful persuader was the one who tied features to benefits: "This machine copies on both sides of a sheet (feature). And what this means to you, Mr. Customer, is that you can cut your paper costs significantly, reduce postage costs, perhaps even reduce the need for additional filing cabinets. This feature can save you a lot of money (benefits)."

Let's apply this feature-benefit distinction to a persuasive request made to another department. The example below is an effort to persuade one manager that the suggestion of another manager is good enough that he should pay for it.

April 19, 1979

Jackson Gray, Manager
Installations and Repair
Central Telephone
Piedmont, Ohio 45701

Dear Jack:

Would you like to know why almost 15 percent of our orders are being worked later than the time agreed upon with the customer? And why both your service index and mine are among the lowest in the Division? I'd like to find out before we get a lot more heat from the Area manager.

Jack, we've talked about this ongoing problem for several months and neither of us seems to be able to pinpoint the problem. Here's an idea I'd like to share with you.

My District Manager has just hired a management trainee named Gail Engles. Gail is a recent Ohio State graduate with a major in operations management. That means she's had good training in business systems—exactly where we seem to be having problems. We could turn her loose with a stopwatch and some checksheets to see where our operations are fouling up. She could trace sample orders through the whole system.

Since Gail hasn't yet been assigned permanent duties, the only cost to us is that she'd have to be paid out of our temporary help or overtime budget. And we'd be obligated to use her only as long as she's needed. I think we should take advantage of this.

I'd appreciate it if you'd do two things. First check to see if you can swing one-half her salary costs for two or three weeks. Her base salary is $14,200. I'll pay the other half. Second, go with me to the DM's office to make the request. I think he'll be glad to see our interdepartmental cooperation on this.

I'll call next Monday the 23rd to confirm all this. I really think this will improve our customer service and help us avoid some future grief from the Area people.

Sincerely,

Helen

Helen Baker, Manager
Commercial Operations

Helen is translating the features of her idea to the benefits by explaining "What this means to you. . . ."

Features	What This Means to You
Gail majored in operations management.	Her training can be usefully applied to our problem.
has been trained in business systems	She can trace orders through the system to pinpoint problems.
is not yet permanently assigned	We can pay her out of our temporary budget and use her only as long as needed.

Getting the reader's action. The third phase of the persuasive letter is specifying for the reader what action you'd like to see occur. In the example just cited, the writer requested two things: check the budget and go to the district manager's office with the writer. Often this action step is accompanied by a reminder of reader benefits to be gained, a form of re-selling the idea.

In addition to clearly stating what should be done and reminding the reader why, the action step should set a deadline or provide some other incentive to act soon. The promise of a follow-up call in the above example does this. The action step should also make it easy for the reader to comply. Often a mailback reply card, a phone number or promise of a follow-up call or visit alleviates some of the burden for the reader.

The tone of the action step should be assumptive. Assume that your reader has understood and agreed with your reasoning and now simply needs to be pushed a bit to obtain the benefits you promise. There is no need to be hesitant. Remember, what you're telling your reader to do is for his/her own benefit.

There is, of course, much more that can be said about the persuasive letter. Many of the points I discussed in Chapter 7 on presentations and briefings apply equally well to the written persuasive effort. Several of the books listed in the recommended readings section at the end of this chapter are good sources of further details on persuasive letter writing.

Goodwill Letters

A goodwill letter is one you write even though you don't have to. Many managers, by failing to send goodwill letters, overlook an excellent opportunity to promote good feelings in their organization. Few things make an employee feel better than to receive from the boss a brief letter of appreciation, congratulations, sympathy, or concern. It only takes a minute, yet it can get a lot of mileage in good employee relations.

As a manager for a telephone company, I used to make it a point to send short letters to the homes of employees whose work was exemplary. The payoff for such a simple action is that (1) the employee knows you recognize and appreciate their good work; (2) by sending it home, you allow the employee's family to share in the praise; (3) the letter can become a part of the employee's personnel file; and (4) by noting that copies have been sent to higher levels of management, the employee knows he or she is getting additional attention.

Opportunities for goodwill notes come up almost daily. Besides on-the-job performance, personal and family accomplishments can be acknowledged. A daughter's wedding, an impressive bowling score, and recognition for church or community service can all be opportunities to show you care.

Differences Between Letters and Memos

Everything I've said about effective and efficient letters also applies to memos. A memorandum is essentially an "inside" letter. It serves to convey written messages *within* the organization. Because of this, it may differ slightly from a letter in that (1) it is less formal; (2) its writer is probably already known to the receiver, so there may be less emphasis on creating favorable image; (3) it normally conveys only one theme and is organized in a direct format; and (4) it frequently employs shortcuts which streamline the message, such as subject lines and enumeration of key ideas (often using incomplete sentences).

Subject lines. A memo has two main parts, a *heading* and a *body*. The heading consists of four pieces of information at the top of the page: (1) the name(s) of the intended receiver(s) (the *To:* line), (2) the name or title of the writer (*From:*), (3) the date, and (4) the subject of the message. The subject line can be particularly useful in speeding the flow of information. There are two types of subject lines commonly used, *topic* and *informative*. The topic subject line describes in a word or two the general subject matter of the memo. Although this has some value, especially as a guide for filing, I strongly recommend using an *informative subject line* instead. The informative subject line actually states the main point of the memo. Since most memos convey routine, nonemotional information, placing the big idea in an informative subject line makes a great deal of sense. Your reader can grasp the main point immediately. If you need to get an idea to a busy executive who may only scan memos, this will improve your chances of success. Below is a list of topic and informative subject lines. Note how much more information is immediately presented in the informative style.

Topic	Informative
Guest Speaker	Bob Dole will be guest speaker at Kiwanis Luncheon.
Air Travel on Expense Account	Reimbursement for business travel will be tourist class fare only.
Advanced Management Program	You have been selected to participate in the Advanced Management Program on May 28.
New Policy on Rental Car Insurance	Don't buy the dollar-per-day supplemental insurance when renting a car.
Staff Meeting	The entire staff will meet April 26 at 2 P.M.

Enumeration or itemization. In memo format, itemizing a series of points is a common way to streamline the message. Compare the two memos below—one with itemization, one without. Which communicates more efficiently?

```
                                                      Date:

To: Jean Kovatz, Assistant Supervisor

From: Pat Reynolds, Manager

Subject: Manager's Conference


   Please contact the people at the Hilton in Green-
ville to arrange for our upcoming conference. We
will need rooms for 30 managers (singles) for the
nights of July 13, 14, and 15. Also arrange for a
buffet dinner on the 13th, a "happy hour" the eve-
ning of the 15th and the conference room with
tables and seating for 30 people from 9 a.m. to 5
p.m. all three days. "Breakout rooms" for groups
of 6 or 7 near the conference room will be needed
for the afternoon of the 14th. Be sure they have a
35 mm movie projector, overhead projector, and
flip charts. We should also have them bring in cof-
fee, juice, and doughnuts in the morning (about
10) each day and soft drinks about 3 each
afternoon.
   Thanks for taking care of this.
```

Here is the same memo using an informative subject line and itemization. Notice how much easier it is to grasp the details. This memo could also serve as a checklist for those making the arrangements.

```
                                               Date:

To: Jean Kovatz, Assistant Manager

From: Pat Reynolds, Manager

Subject: ROOMS, SERVICES, AND EQUIPMENT NEEDED FOR
         THE MANAGER'S MEETING, JULY 13, 14, and
         15.

   Please arrange the following with the people at
the Hilton in Greenville.

ROOMS:

30 single rooms for the nights of July 13, 14, and
15
Conference room with tables and seating for 30
   from 9 a.m. to 5 p.m. on all three days
Five "breakout" rooms for the afternoon of the
   14th (six people per room)

FOOD SERVICE:

Buffet dinner the evening of the 13th
"Happy hour" bar and snacks the evening of the 15th
Coffee, juice and doughnuts each morning at 10
Soft drinks each afternoon about 3

EQUIPMENT:
35 mm movie projector (all three days)
Overhead projector for transparencies
Screen
Flip chart—tripod with paper

   Thank you for taking care of this.
```

Some Additional Thoughts on Letters and Memos

If you were to analyze the letters and memos produced in your organization—and I'll show you a systematic way to do that at the end of the chapter—you would be likely to find some effective letters and some that missed opportunities to create understanding and project a favorable image. Here are some common reasons letters flop.

Noise in the Message

Anything that distracts the reader from the message can be considered "noise." Among the most common sources of noise are unattractive paper or letterhead, smeared type, strikeovers, margins too narrow, and coffee stains or finger smudges on the letter. In addition, misspellings and obvious grammatical errors create distractions, and reflect on the credibility of the writer. Below is a replica of a letter a friend of mine received from his bank: a classic noisy note. He no longer banks there.

```
Dear Mr. Prewitt,

    Since Milton Anderson insist on keeping a copy of
the deposit ticket that he sends us maybe if you
would give him these deposit that we have send you.
Please tell him to keep only one pink copy and send
us añd of the other copies to us.
    He has been tearing off the white copy which we
need to prpcees to the deposit.

                                            Sincerely,


                                            Norwood Office
```

Letters That Sound Like a Machine Wrote Them

Most people resent getting a mechanical sounding message. I recently received this message from my mortgage company:

```
IMPORTANT COMMUNICATION NOTICE TO ALL MORTGAGORS

WE ARE PLEASED TO ANNOUNCE THAT WE HAVE RECENTLY
COMPLETED A MAJOR CHANGE IN OUR ACCOUNTING PRO-
CEDURES. WE FELT THIS CHANGE TO COMPUTER PROCESS-
ING WAS NECESSARY IN ORDER TO PROVIDE ADDITIONAL
SERVICES TO YOU IN RESPONSE TO MANY REQUESTS RELA-
TIVE TO ESCROW AND LOAN ACCOUNTING INFORMATION.
HOWEVER, IN ORDER TO FACILITATE PROMPT RESPONSES
TO YOUR INQUIRIES WHICH WE DESIRE TO RENDER AS SER-
```

```
VICER OF YOUR MORTGAGE AND TO ASSURE PROMPT CREDIT
OF PAYMENTS TO YOUR MORTGAGE, WE REQUEST THAT YOU
PLACE YOUR ACCOUNT NUMBER ON ALL CORRESPONDENCE
AND CHECKS OR MONEY ORDERS COMMENCING JUNE 1.
          YOUR ACCOUNT NUMBER IS 01976328
WE APPRECIATE YOUR USUAL FINE COOPERATION AND SUP-
PORT IN OUR ENDEAVOR TO FURNISH ADDITIONAL
SERVICES AND INFORMATION FOR YOU.
```

Not only does this message sound machinelike, but it is terribly wordy and uses an indirect approach to convey a simple message: "Put your account number on all correspondence or checks." It's bad enough to get a letter from a machine—but when it talks *down to you*, it's downright maddening.

Failure to Conceal Irritation

We all receive letters occasionally that are, frankly, a pain in the neck. The question we face is should we answer at all, and if so, how much effort should we exert? Is the potential goodwill created worth the cost? One of my colleagues once wrote to a professional football team asking for information about their organization structure for a research paper she was doing. Two executives answered her request. Their replies show a marked contrast in concern for goodwill. Here is the response from a vice president of the organization:

```
Dear M. McFarland:

   In answer to your letter, I would be happy to dis-
cuss in general terms the subject matter whenever
it might be convenient to you.
   It is a little too complex to answer in letter
form as you suggested.
   We appreciate your interest.

                                        Sincerely,
```

Here is the response from the president:

```
Dear Carol:

   Thank you for your interest in the Buffalo Bills
and in our organization.
```

Generally, pro football organizations are of two
types: one with a head coach/general manager and
the other with separate coach and general manager.
Ours is the latter form with our general manager
supervising our public relations, stadium operations, ticket and marketing departments. The Head
Coach supervises his assistant coaches and works
closely with the head of our player personnel
(scouting) department.
    The team physician is an independent contractor
with a medical practice outside of his services to
the Bills, while the trainers are employees of the
Bills.
    I appreciate your interest in our organizational
set-up and your support.
    With kind regards.

                                            Sincerely,

                                            BUFFALO BILLS

For a few additional moments of thought, this writer satisfied, at least
in a general sense, the reader's request and conveyed a sense of goodwill.

Failure to Use Creativity

Many business writers feel bound to the traditional business letter format.
For some reason we hesitate to set up the letter differently. The following
is an example of one who dared to be different. This letter, from a manager of an insurance agency, cleverly encourages the reader to respond—
to establish a dialogue.

There are two sides to every question--one half of
this letter is for your side.

THIS HALF IS MINE   THIS HALF IS YOURS

You have been a valued
policyholder for some
time, but recently you
neglected to pay your
premium. There must be a
reason for this, and I

```
am writing you because I
am sincerely interested
in knowing that reason
and wondering if we
could be of assistance.
Will you please use your
half of this letter to
tell me WHY? I can as-
sure you that it will
receive my personal
attention.

Sincerely,



Manager

P.S. If you have already
made arrangements to re-
instate your policy,
disregard this letter
and accept our thanks.
If you now wish to rein-
state, please complete
the attached form and
return it with your re-
mittance of $231.67.

Thank you.
```

Failure to Give Your Letter Clout

One way to give a business letter clout is to let the reader know that others are also reading the letter. This can be done by simply "copying in" others. For example, suppose you are writing to another division about a problem in receiving parts from them. By copying in an executive with authority over both divisions, you serve notice that others are being made aware of the problem. A simple "cc: John Robinson, Division Manager" adds clout. Consumer advocates have long recognized the added power that comes from a complaint letter to, say, a local auto dealership, when the automaker's regional manager or even corporate president is copied in.

By the same token, a goodwill letter of congratulations to an employee means more when others are copied in. And, of course, a notation indicating that the letter will go into the employee's personnel file also makes the recipient feel good.

Writing While Angry

A final reason letters flop—or in this case, bomb—is that people write when they are hot under the collar. Many a blistering memo has haunted the normally thoughtful manager. I once wrote a devastating reply to a message received from the personnel department which had advised me that some medical expenses I'd incurred were not covered under our group insurance. I also expressed my conviction that the people working on my case were inept, unconcerned, and generally not too bright. No sooner had I mailed my missile, than the personnel manager called to explain that they had after considerable research effort found a loophole under which I was covered. One large crow was eaten.

Very few letters require an *immediate* response. When I get a maddening letter now, I go ahead and write the response, but I then file it for a few days' cooling-off period. Just be sure your secretary doesn't mail it for you before you've reworked it.

Marvin Swift's article, "Clear Writing Means Clear Thinking Means ..." (p. 315), reviews many of the points made in this chapter. It also points out the importance of frequent and often repeated revisions of our writing efforts to sharpen communication skills.

Diagnosing Your Letters and Memos

Gather a random sample of copies of letters and memos produced in your organization. Analyze these in the following ways:

1. Determine the central purpose of each letter or memo. What was the writer trying to do? What response(s) does the writer want from the reader?
2. Based on these questions, place the letters in four stacks: (a) routine information or good-news messages, (b) refusal or bad-news messages, (c) persuasive requests, and (d) goodwill messages. If it is unclear what the letter's central purpose is, place it aside.
3. Based on the table presented in Figure 9-6, evaluate each message.
4. Make a list of discrepancies found between what your letters do and what they should do. Determine any patterns of repeated discrepancies.
5. Make a list of five or six specific things that could be done to improve letters and memos in your organization. Set objectives for overcoming weak areas, plan repeated analyses, and chart the number of errors found over time.
6. Plan training or awareness sessions as appropriate.

Should this letter/memo be sent at all?
Is it the best medium for the situation?
Is it worth at least $4 or $5? (or)
Is there an intangible benefit to be accrued?

Is the physical appearance attractive?
Is the extra effort to salve the reader's emotions worth it?

For Routine Information or Good-News Messages LOOK FOR:	*For Disappointing Messages (refusals or other bad news)* LOOK FOR:	*For Persuasive Requests* LOOK FOR:	*For Goodwill Messages* LOOK FOR:
Organization	*Organization*	*Organization*	*Organization*
Big idea first	Buffer	"You"-oriented attention getter	Varies with purpose
Subordinate details follow	Reasoning/explanation	Clear need development	
Use informative subject lines and enumeration	The refusal stated or clearly implied	Clear solution and amplification	
	Neutral or hopeful close	Specific action step	
	Offer alternative if feasible		
Style	*Style*	*Style*	*Style*
Conversational language	Use vivid language	Use vivid, "you"-oriented language	Sincere tone
Mostly short sentences and paragraphs	More elaborate explanations	Phrase in second person	
Conciseness	Deemphasize the refusal through wording and positioning	Relate features to benefits ("What this means to you . . .")	
AVOID	*AVOID*	*AVOID*	*AVOID*
Curt tone	Using "policy" as reason for the refusal	Overused or inappropriate attention gimmicks	Condescending tone
Omission of needed details	A positive tone buffer followed by "however"	Unsubstantiated superlatives	
Presumptuous tone	Failure to close the matter	Presenting "solution" before you've explained the problem	
	Use of negative tone that implies a judgment of the reader	Presumptuous tone	

Figure 9-6 Checking your organization's letters and memos

Some Other Thoughts About Letters and Memos:
READINGS FOR CHAPTER 9

Clear Writing Means Clear Thinking Means . . .[8]

Marvin H. Swift

If you are a manager, you constantly face the problem of putting words on paper. If you are like most managers, this is not the sort of problem you enjoy. It is hard to do, and time consuming; and the task is doubly difficult when, as is usually the case, your words must be designed to change the behavior of others in the organization.

But the chore is there and must be done. How? Let's take a specific case.

Let's suppose that everyone at X Corporation, from the janitor on up to the chairman of the board, is using the office copiers for personal matters; income tax forms, church programs, children's term papers, and God knows what else are being duplicated by the gross. This minor piracy costs the company a pretty penny, both directly and in employee time, and the general manager—let's call him Sam Edwards—decides the time has come to lower the boom.

Sam lets fly by dictating the following memo to his secretary:

To: All Employees

From: Samuel Edwards, General Manager

Subject: Abuse of Copiers

It has recently been brought to my attention that many of the people who are employed by this company have taken advantage of their positions by availing themselves of the copiers. More specifically, these machines are being used for other than company business.

Obviously, such practice is contrary to company policy and must cease and desist immediately. I wish therefore to inform all concerned — those who have abused policy or will be abusing it — that their behavior cannot and will not be tolerated. Accordingly, anyone in the future who is unable to control himself will have his employment terminated.

If there are any questions about company policy, please feel free to contact this office.

Now the memo is on his desk for his signature. He looks it over; and the more he looks, the worse it reads. In fact, it's lousy. So he revises it three times, until it finally is in the form that follows:

```
To: All Employees

From: Samuel Edwards, General Manager

Subject: Use of Copiers

We are revamping our policy on the use of copiers
for personal matters. In the past we have not en-
couraged personnel to use them for such purposes
because of the costs involved. But we also recog-
nize, perhaps belatedly, that we can solve the
problem if each of us pays for what he takes.

We are therefore putting these copiers on a pay-
as-you-go basis. The details are simple
enough....
```

This time Sam thinks the memo looks good, and it *is* good. Not only is the writing much improved, but the problem should now be solved. He therefore signs the memo, turns it over to his secretary for distribution, and goes back to other things.

From Verbiage to Intent

I can only speculate on what occurs in a writer's mind as he moves from a poor draft to a good revision, but it is clear that Sam went through several specific steps, mentally as well as physically, before he had created his end product:

- He eliminated wordiness.
- He modulated the tone of the memo.
- He revised the policy it stated.

Let's retrace his thinking through each of these processes.

Eliminating wordiness. Sam's basic message is that employees are not to use the copiers for their own affairs at company expense. As he looks over his first draft, however, it seems so long that this simple message has become diffused. With the idea of trimming the memo down, he takes another look at his first paragraph:

> It has recently been brought to my attention that many of the people who are employed by this company have taken advantage of their positions by availing themselves of the copiers. More specifically, these machines are being used for other than company business.

He edits it like this:

Item: "recently"
Comment to himself: Of course; else why write about the problem? So delete the word.

Item: "It has been brought to my attention"
Comment: Naturally. Delete it.

Item: "the people who are employed by this company"
Comment: Assumed. Why not just "employees"?

Item: "by availing themselves" and "for other than company business"
Comment: Since the second sentence repeats the first, why not coalesce?

And he comes up with this:

> Employees have been using the copiers for personal matters.

He proceeds to the second paragraph. More confident of himself, he moves in broader swoops, so that the deletion process looks like this:

> Obviously, such practice is contrary to company policy and ~~must cease and desist immediately. I wish therefore to inform all concerned — those who have abused policy or will be abusing it — that their behavior cannot and will not be tolerated.~~

~~Accordingly, anyone in the future who is unable to control himself will have his employment terminated.~~
will result in dismissal.

The final paragraph, apart from "company policy" and "feel free," looks all right, so the total memo now reads as follows:

To: All Employees

From: Samuel Edwards, General Manager

Subject: Abuse of Copiers

Employees have been using the copiers for personal matters. Obviously, such practice is contrary to company policy and will result in dismissal.

If there are any questions, please contact this office.

Sam now examines his efforts by putting these questions to himself:

Question: Is the memo free of deadwood?
Answer: Very much so. In fact, it's good, tight prose.

Question: Is the policy stated?
Answer: Yes—sharp and clear.

Question: Will the memo achieve its intended purpose?
Answer: Yes. But it sounds foolish.

Question: Why?
Answer: The wording is too harsh; I'm not going to fire anybody over this.

Question: How should I tone the thing down?

To answer this last question, Sam takes another look at the memo.

Correcting the tone.   What strikes his eye as he looks it over? Perhaps these three words:

- Abuse . . .

- Obviously . . .

- . . . dismissal . . .

The first one is easy enough to correct: he substitutes "use" for "abuse." But "obviously" poses a problem and calls for reflection. If the policy is obvious, why are the copiers being used? Is it that people are outrightly dishonest? Probably not. But that implies the policy isn't obvious; and whose fault is this? Who neglected to clarify policy? And why "dismissal" for something never publicized?

These questions impel him to revise the memo once again:

```
To: All Employees

From: Samuel Edwards, General Manager

Subject: Use of Copiers

Copiers are not to be used for personal matters.
If there are any questions, please contact this
office.
```

Revising the policy itself.   The memo now seems courteous enough—at least it is not discourteous—but it is just a blank, perhaps overly simple, statement of policy. Has he really thought through the policy itself?

Reflecting on this, Sam realizes that some people will continue to use the copiers for personal business anyhow. If he seriously intends to enforce the basic policy (first sentence), he will have to police the equipment, and that raises the question of costs all over again.

Also, the memo states that he will maintain an open-door policy (second sentence)—and surely there will be some, probably a good many, who will stroll in and offer to pay for what they use. His secretary has enough to do without keeping track of affairs of that kind.

Finally, the first and second sentences are at odds with each other. The first says that personal copying is out, and the second implies that it can be arranged.

The facts of organizational life thus force Sam to clarify in his own mind exactly what his position on the use of copiers is going to be. As he sees the problem now, what he really wants to do is put the copiers on a pay-as-you-go basis. After making that decision, he begins anew:

```
To: All Employees

From: Samuel Edwards, General Manager

Subject: Use of copiers

We are revamping our policy on the use of
copiers....
```

This is the draft that goes into distribution and now allows him to turn his attention to other problems.

The Chicken or the Egg?

What are we to make of all this? It seems a rather lengthy and tedious report of what, after all, is a routine writing task created by a problem of minor importance. In making this kind of analysis, have I simply labored the obvious?

To answer this question, let's drop back to the original draft. If you read it over, you will see that Sam began with this kind of thinking:

- "The employees are taking advantage of the company."

- "I'm a nice guy, but now I'm going to play Dutch uncle."

- ∴ "I'll write them a memo that tells them to shape up or ship out."

In his final version, however, his thinking is quite different:

- "Actually, the employees are pretty mature, responsible people. They're capable of understanding a problem."

- "Company policy itself has never been crystallized. In fact, this is the first memo on the subject."

- "I don't want to overdo this thing—any employee can make an error in judgment."

- ∴ "I'll set a reasonable policy and write a memo that explains how it ought to operate."

Sam obviously gained a lot of ground between the first draft and the final version, and this implies two things. First, if a manager is to write effectively, he needs to isolate and define, as fully as possible, all the critical variables in the writing process and scrutinize what he writes for its clarity, simplicity, tone, and the rest. Second, after he has clarified his thoughts on paper, he may find that what he has written is not what has to be said. In this sense, writing is feedback and a way for the manager to discover himself. What are his real attitudes toward that amorphous, undifferentiated gray mass of employees "out there"? Writing is a way of finding out. By objectifying his thoughts in the medium of language, he gets a chance to see what is going on in his mind.

In other words, *if the manager writes well, he will think well*. Equally, the more clearly he has thought out his message before he starts to dictate, the more likely he is to get it right on paper the first time round. In other words, *if he thinks well, he will write well.*

Hence we have a chicken-and-the-egg situation: writing and thinking go hand in hand; and when one is good, the other is likely to be good.

Revision sharpens thinking.   More particularly, rewriting is the key to improved thinking. It demands a real openmindedness and objectivity. It demands a willingness to cull verbiage so that ideas stand out clearly. And it demands a willingness to meet logical contradictions head on and trace them to the premises that have created them. In short, it forces a writer to get up his courage and expose his thinking process to his own intelligence.

Obviously, revising is hard work. It demands that you put yourself through the wringer, intellectually and emotionally, to squeeze out the best you can offer. Is it worth the effort? Yes, it is—if you believe you have a responsibility to think and communicate effectively.

Will American Way Be Buried under a Pile of Memos?[9]

Nickie McWhirter

The disintegration of the American system of free enterprise will not come about because of our inability to cope with runaway inflation, dependence on Arab oil or the capacity of the wily Japanese to glut our marketplace with cheap, zingy little cars with AM-FM stereo standard. No, ma'am and sir. These are but warts on our economic carcass at the very muscle and bone of American business and industry.

The clear and present threat to our way of life is the photocopying machine. It's that simple. The unrestrained proliferation of these contraptions in the offices and hallways of American business is going to do us all in, and soon, unless we take immediate action. I can't understand why Eliot Janeway or Paul McCracken haven't sounded the alarm before now. No matter. I am happy to serve.

The photocopier has been hailed as a boon to paper flow and everybody knows that paper is the lifeblood of commerce and industry. Unfortunately, the channels designed to accommodate this flow are finite in capacity. So is the mind of Man and Woman. Too much paper moving from office to office and piling up on desks demanding attention overloads all the systems, animate and inanimate. This results in which I call industrial infarction or occupational occlusion. These are serious ailments. *close or block*

Disregarding the praise heaped on the photocopier by the folks at Xerox,

IBM, et al., it is obvious how the copying machine is sapping the strength of the economy.

Businesses run on memoranda. Memos used to mean something. Not many years ago it was necessary for a secretary to interleaf six sheets of paper with five sheets of carbon paper and type a memo From: The Boss, To: Department Heads, Re: Getting to work on time. This took time and turned the secretary's fingers blue. It resulted in only six copies anyway.

The mimeograph machine was worse. It turned the secretary's fingers black and you couldn't read the copies.

Bosses thought pretty hard about how many memos they ought to send, how often, without risking a surly secretary.

All this effectively cut down the flow of memos and restricted them to people who (1) had secretaries and were, therefore, bona fide bosses; (2) had something important enough to communicate to a few other people. That all makes sense.

The photocopier has changed everything. Now any jerk with access to a machine can send out 100 copies of anything. And everybody does.

The mailroom clerk zaps off a request that everyone remember not to seal inter-office mail envelopes. (The mailroom clerk reads all the inter-office mail.) The janitor leaves a memo reminding that the sight of half-eaten salami submarines in the waste baskets gives him hives. He threatens to file a complaint with OSHA. The chief copywriter cranks out 30 copies of his greatest hits and sends them to all the junior copywriters to "file for future reference and divine guidance." And every joker in the house turns out a zillion copies of his or her favorite jokes, recipes, maps to the weekend orgy and notes of praise received from the boss. These are circulated to corporate friends and enemies, all marked "Confidential."

Which brings up the marking system now necessary for this blizzard of paper. There is so much trivia and superfluous information circulating through the business tubes that people have had to develop attention-getting devices for their own memos.

By now a plain interoffice mail envelope can sit ignored in anybody's "in" basket for days or even weeks. It's invisible in the mess.

A couple of years ago, clever folks started writing or stamping "Confidential" or "Urgent" on envelopes in an effort to have their missives rise to the top of the daily pile. That worked until everything, including the reminder to sign up for the picnic, was marked confidential or urgent. Then, "Personal and Confidential," preferably marked in red ink, was effective briefly. That hardly works anymore.

An envelope which has "Office of the President" stamped somewhere on its face still gets attention, but even this is likely to be ignored occasionally. Too often such envelopes contain a note from the second assistant administrative assistant to the president, asking all employees to remember to turn out the lights when they leave the office for the night.

No, none of it works because of the clutter of paper made possible by the copying machine. All the bosses and secretaries and administrative assistants and executives junior grade are so busy getting and sending copies of copies of junk that nobody can get a bona fide message of importance through the system or get it read once it arrives. I see this as a definite threat to capitalism as we have come to know and love it.

Questions for Further Thought

1. Do an analysis of your own letter effectiveness using the procedures suggested under Diagnosing Your Letters and Memos, p. 313.

2. How do you feel about the question of directness in the bad-news letter? How would you personally react to the more straightforward refusal? Is the recommended approach worth the extra effort? In what cases might it not be?

3. Collect a series of letters you receive from organizations trying to sell you something. Analyze these to determine why they are constructed as they are. What kinds of attention getters are used? How is the need creation or solution explained? Can you find examples of the feature-benefit relationship as discussed in this chapter?

Notes

1. P. D. Hemphill, *Business Communications,* © 1976, p. 27. Reprinted by permission of Prentice-Hall, Inc.
2. Raymond V. Lesikar, *Report Writing for Business,* 5th ed. (Homewood, Ill.: Richard D. Irwin, 1977), p. 143.
3. Herta A. Murphy and Charles E. Peck, *Effective Business Communication,* 2nd ed. (New York: McGraw-Hill, 1976), p. 83.
4. Ibid., p. 80.
5. Robert M. Archer, Ruth Pearson Ames, BASIC BUSINESS COMMUNICATIONS, © 1971, pp. 391–392. Reprinted by permission of Prentice-Hall, Inc., Englewood Cliffs, New Jersey.
6. Frederick W. Harbaugh in a letter to the editor of *The ABCA Bulletin,* September 1977, p. 28.
7. Joel P. Bowman and Bernadine P. Branchaw, *Effective Business Communication* (San Francisco: Canfield Press, 1979), p. 149.
8. Marvin H. Swift, "Clear Writing Means Clear Thinking Means . . . ," Harvard Business Review, January–February 1973, Copyright © 1972 by the President and Fellows of Harvard College; all rights reserved.
9. Reprinted by permission of the Knight-Ridder Newspapers, © 1978.

Recommended Readings

There are many books which deal with effective business letters and memos. The list below includes those which I am familiar with and which would be of considerable value to the practicing manager.

Bowman, Joel P. and Bernadine P. Branchaw, *Effective Business Communication*. San Francisco: Canfield Press, 1979.

Hatch, Richard, *Communicating In Business*. Chicago: Science Research Associates, 1977.

Hemphill, P. D., *Business Communications*. Englewood Cliffs, N.J.: Prentice-Hall, 1976.

Himstreet, William C. and Wayne Murlin Baty, *Business Communications* (5th ed.). Belmont, Calif.: Wadsworth, 1977.

Janis, Harold, *Writing and Communicating in Business* (3rd ed.). New York: Macmillan, 1978.

Lesikar, Raymond V., *Business Communication: Theory and Application* (3rd ed.). Homewood, Ill.: Richard D. Irwin, 1976.

Murphy, Herta A. and Charles E. Peck, *Effective Business Communication* (2nd ed.). New York: McGraw-Hill, 1976.

Sigband, Norman B., *Communication for Management and Business* (2nd ed.). Glenview, Ill.: Scott, Foresman, 1976.

CHAPTER 10

SEND ME A REPORT ON THAT

The title of this chapter is a frequently heard request in most organizations. Virtually every aspect of the manager's job revolves around having sufficient factual data. Reports of various types, ranging anywhere from the fourth carbon copy of a computer printout to an extensive printed analysis numbering hundreds of pages, provide such data. In this chapter we'll be concerned with people-generated reports which gather a variety of types of information into a digestible format for managerial action. These reports may be *routine*, such as those which provide production figures, membership data, and sales results or *special* reports which deal with specific organizational problems or issues and generally include more than just raw data.

When a report project is assigned, the person or group doing the work should be told their specific purpose—the extent and nature of their information-gathering task. Rosenblatt *et al.* see three such purposes: (1) to merely supply data, (2) to make some analysis or interpretation of the data, or (3) to go a little further and specify some action. The end product would then be an informational, interpretive, or analytical report.[1]

Give Me What I Need to Know

Regardless of the type and extent of the report, its emphasis should be on the comunication of ideas that will help solve organizational problems and keep the company on track, working toward its objectives. The style of the report is far less important than its content. In terms of the letter grid idea I suggested in Chapter 9, reports may be "9-1" and still be effective.

Business communication professor Ray Lesikar defines a business report as "an orderly and objective communication of factual information which serves some business purpose."[2] We've already talked about purposes, but there are two other key terms in that definition which deserve emphasis. First, a report is orderly; it has been carefully prepared so that its contents are arranged in a predetermined fashion. There is generally more emphasis placed on care in preparation of the written report than on other, less formal media. A second key term is objective. A report should report, not opinionate. Special emphasis is placed on facts with considerable care in minimizing opinions or inconclusive inference. When opinions, guesses, hunches, or predictions are made, they are clearly labeled as such so the reader will not mistakenly assume they are facts. Objectivity requires such clarification. It also demands that all relevant data or evidence be presented in such a way that we do not "stack the deck" in favor of or in opposition to a particular viewpoint.

In thinking more deeply about report writing, it may be useful to look at these key terms more carefully. Reports are purposeful, objective (factual), and orderly.

Purposeful Preplanning

Reports involve research and research involves planned inquiry. One of the most important and time-saving steps in report preparation is to think through the research project along general lines before you dig in. Ten or fifteen minutes of concentrated thought may save hours of wheel-spinning effort later. This "thinking through" process should focus on several questions:

- Why is this report being prepared?
- How will I know when the purpose has been achieved?
- Who will be reading this?
- Where can I get the best possible information?

The first three questions above address concerns we considered in earlier chapters of this book. In Chapter 6, we discussed the importance of formulating the specific problem or issue before jumping into the solution step. I also suggested in that chapter that a key question for groups working on problems is, "How do we know when we're finished?" My point there, and here, is that a clear definition of the problem being dealt with and a clear specification of reasonable criteria for a good solution must come before the examination of alternatives. Only when this is accomplished will you know when the job has been done, when the best possible outcome has emerged. The third question above, "Who will be reading this?" is a central concern of Chapter 7 where we discussed audience analysis. Determining who they are, what they already know, and what they need to know is another dimension of the report preplanning process that should not be minimized. Know your message receiver.

Finding Out What We Need to Know

Let's consider the fourth preplanning question, "Where can I get the best possible information?" A detailed discussion of research techniques would go far beyond the scope of this book. But it may be useful to consider the four basic ways to find out what we need to know: reading, interviewing, observing, and reasoning.

Reading. Many managers promptly forget where the university library is the day after graduation. Yet libraries exist for the sole purpose of dispensing information. Become familiar with the library resources available in your area. You'll probably be amazed at what modern libraries have.

The term reading is used here in a general sense to include reviews of graphic or printed matter as well as audiovisual materials such as films, tapes, and pictures. Most of what we'll ever need to know has been recorded somewhere at sometime. The problem is in finding the right manuscripts, books, articles, statistical tables, and so forth. Look around and let a librarian help.

Interviewing. Interviewing an expert or source-person regarding particular data is a most valuable way of getting information. Any person who is intimately familiar with a specific problem or issue, who has firsthand knowledge, may legitimately be considered an expert. This means that the assembly line worker, the keypunch operator, or the building maintenance worker may be the person we need to talk with, even though their formal organizational position does not call for decision making. Many organizational problems are solved by going to those who are seldom sought after for managerial advice. Getting data from the interview requires the kinds of skills discussed in Chapter 5. When we have the opportunity to go to people involved, we should use it. This is the strongest data-gathering approach for many problems.

Observing. When we can't find exactly what we need to know in print or via interviews with reliable experts, we must sometimes observe for ourselves. Direct observation should not be casual observation—the observations should be planned and scheduled to reduce the probability that atypical events or processes are taken as commonplace. If we simply go into an organization, look around, and draw conclusions from one or two observations, we run the likelihood of getting "contaminated" data—a distorted picture. Exactly *what* is to be observed and precisely *when* it is to be observed should be planned in advance. A reasonable number of different observations should be made and, where possible, the reliability of these observations should be established. Reliability is simply the likelihood that, upon subsequent observation, essentially the same things will be observed. Using multiple observations and/or multiple observers helps improve reliability. In short, don't jump to conclusions based on one or two casual observations.

Planning exactly what you are looking for, and how you know when you've found it, also helps improve reliability by reducing the amount of personal bias. Usually it is helpful to design a data-gathering form or tally sheet to categorize events witnessed. The more thorough the preparation of such a form, the clearer your categories and the better your information. Several observational techniques for gathering data about communication behaviors have been presented in the diagnosis sections of earlier chapters.

4 **Reasoning.** The fourth general research approach is *reasoning from what we have learned.* Drawing conclusions based upon evidence gathered may be the most risky step in the research process. Our conclusions can only be as good as our evidence and our reasoning. There is no foolproof way to eliminate our personal biases from this process since our use of logic is an innate characteristic of our personality. Organizational decisions are based on reasoning from the known (i.e., the information gathered) to the unknown (the predicted results of a course of action). If the reasoning processes are valid, and the decision implemented, it should be an effective decision; this is the final test.

These, then, are the four major ways to find out what we want to know for a written report: reading, interviewing experts, observation, and reasoning.

5 *Be Realistic about Purpose, Time, and Cost*

Virtually any topic can be researched to death. Anyone who has written a master's thesis, Ph.D. dissertation, or an extensive term paper under the direction of an exasperatingly rigorous professor knows what I mean. At some point, of course, the cost of new tidbits of additional insight becomes prohibitive. Commonsense limits need to be placed on the expenditure of resources and effort. It would be insane to spend $50,000 on research that will solve a hundred-dollar problem. The magnitude of the problem's effects on the organization provides the key. A decision on what hours to open the cafeteria calls for a quickie report at the most. An analysis of a problem on which the future of the organization hangs, say, the possible depletion of a needed raw material, would be a no-holds-barred research effort. Any expenditure would be justified.

Estimating report costs. For purposes of budgeting time and energy, a common unit of measurement is the page of typed material. Although pages differ greatly in amount of information, ease or difficulty of preparation, and so forth, they tend to average out over the long haul. One average 8½-by-11-inch sheet, double-spaced with attractively wide margins, contains about 250 words of pica type or 300 words of elite type.

How much can a person write in an hour or a day? It depends upon the complexity of the material being written, the depth of analysis, the familiarity the writer has with the material, and the writer's ability, motivation, alertness, and energy level. Analyses of these kinds of factors reveal that the professional writer *averages* from one to three hours of actual writing a day. Some writers can go for 10 hours a day for a week but then "run dry" for a month.

How much can be written in one to three hours? The manager of a large technical writing department in a major corporation responded to that question by saying that he requires his engineering writers to produce at least 3000 words a week and he expects them to accomplish at least one page a day. The "one page" includes research, rough drafts, planning of illustrations, final drafts, and proofreading. That 3000 words a week amounts to approximately 10 typewritten pages of "raw production"—which in turn might convert into five final pages of original, creative writing per day. This is an average production level for professional writers.

Creative editing or the arranging of work contributed by several participating writers into a final report can take as long as original writing. So a team-written report of 30 pages would take about a month to prepare.[3] The mechanics of preparing also take time. Secretarial typing time will average at least 10 minutes per page, with duplicating and proofreading adding at least that much again.

So you can see that reports do cost. Nevertheless, there are times when there is no good substitute for a written report to meet information needs of an organization. As discussed in Chapter 4, there are several significant advantages to the use of this medium, including the capability of conveying complex information in an orderly fashion, the presence of a "hard" copy for future reference, and the relative formality a report affords to important matters. A report can be used efficiently, read when most convenient and when the reader is particularly alert or motivated. The manager need not be called away from his office as with meetings, or interrupted as with telephone or face-to-face conversations. The well-written report can be an invaluable tool to the manager.

The Short Report:
An Extended Memo

In Chapter 9 I recommended that memos cover only one main point, be organized in a direct order (i.e., start with the "big idea" followed by supplemental, clarifying information) and that they use an informational subject line as opposed to a topic subject line. Many reports simply extend the logic of the well-prepared memo—or of a series of memos. In the short report, the informational subject lines become informational headings. By visualizing the report this way, we are likely to make frequent use of headings and to keep explanatory texts brief and clear—a useful approach for almost every business report. In the memo report shown below, the conclusion of the report is offered in the subject line, applying a direct presentation. The reasoning is presented under additional informational headings, making the whole message very efficient to read.

```
                    INTEROFFICE MEMORANDUM

     To: Mac Cartin,                    Date: March 1, 19____
         Office Manager

     From: Pat Garrett, Accounting Supervisor

     Subject: Discontinue Purchase of Supplemental In-
              surance on Rental Cars


     $2000 per Year Saving Possible
     ─────────────────────────────

        Rising costs are a problem in all divisions of
     the company. Because of inflationary pressures, we
     must continually reassess even those expenditures
     that have been routine in the past. A recent audit
     of expenditures for rental cars reveals an oppor-
     tunity to save approximately $2000 per year by not
     purchasing supplemental collision insurance on
     rental cars.

     Excellent Driving Record Makes Supplemental In-
     surance Uneconomical
     ────────────────────

        Rental car agencies insure their cars against
     collision damage with a $100 deductible coverage.
     The renter of an auto involved in an accident would
```

have to pay the first $100 of damages. For an additional charge of $1.00 per day, full coverage including the first $100 can be purchased. Our employees have been routinely paying this extra dollar per day for full coverage. This additional coverage cost has averaged $2700 per year for the past four years.

During this same time period, our people's driving record has been excellent. There have been only four incidents of minor damage to rental cars. The average cost to our company for this damage has been less than $500 per year.

Based on our performance over the past four years with a total of more than 10,000 days of rental car use, the company could save over $2000 per year by discontinuing the dollar-per-day supplemental insurance.

Notify Employees to Discontinue Such Insurance
_____

It is recommended that the company notify all employees who use company-authorized rental cars to discontinue purchase of the supplemental collision coverage. The first $100 of any accident claim will instead be paid directly by our disbursement office as necessary. Employees should be advised that they will not be personally liable for any additional costs.

You'll note that the short report contains three basic parts: (1) an *introduction* which gets the reader's attention by showing a benefit (save $2000 per year), (2) *data* which supports the claim of cost savings, and (3) an ending which advocates specific action (notify the employees).

While this direct, concise format is often useful, we may want to change to an indirect approach when the reader is likely to resist the recommendation offered. An indirect order presents the reasoning first and leads up to the conclusion/recommendation in the same way that a persuasive letter does.

Longer Reports:
The Proposal First

The preparation of a major business report is usually preceded by a written proposal which serves as a working plan. This is important for several reasons. First, the proposal crystallizes the writer's thinking and lets the reader, often the one who contracts for the project, know precisely what

can be expected from the final report. Typically it includes a clear statement of the problem or issue to be dealt with, a description of what research steps will be taken to arrive at a conclusion, and, in many cases, an
estimate of the cost of preparing the report.

The proposal is helpful for the researcher because it permits him or
her to (1) "think out loud" about the research steps to be taken, thereby (2)
providing an opportunity to discover a possible error or faulty thinking
early in the project where it's less likely to do serious damage. The proposal also (3) serves as a guide throughout the investigation.

In addition, the carefully prepared proposal will include material for
writing the introductory section in the final report.[4]

The report proposal should be addressed to the person(s) who will formally authorize the research project. Typically it is presented in elaborated memo format and seldom runs longer than two or three pages. The
major parts of the proposal are discussed below.

Background

Before an expenditure of time, effort, and money is likely to be made, the
decision maker should understand the conditions that gave rise to the
problem or issue to be researched. This section puts the project into context and paves the way for a more specific definition of the immediate
problem the writer will study. Although the background section may tell
the reader things he or she already knows, it also demonstrates that the
researcher understands underlying assumptions about the organization
and conditions affecting it.

Statement of the Problem

Clearly defining the research problem is crucial to the ultimate success of
your project. This section needs to include more than a one-sentence definition. Remember that your reader is likely to view the nature of any
given problem a little differently than you do—our past experiences and
unique predispositions make that inevitable. So in addition to stating your
view of the problem, you'll need to explain *why* you see it that way. You
also must convince your reader that this is a viable view and definition of
the issue.

Be careful of emotional language that may convey your biases. An objective, unemotional statement should be your goal. The examples below
illustrate this.

Too Emotional or Judgmental	More Objective
First-line supervisors are incapable of writing good performance reviews for personnel files.	Most first-line supervisors are writing performance reviews which do not meet company standards.

The company cannot decide where to locate its new store.

The company lacks sufficient information necessary to make a store location decision between three alternatives.

A common error made in preparing this part of a proposal is to state the problem in terms that are too broad. When the problem is too grandiose or unusually wide in scope, the report loses focus. Here are examples:

Too Broad or Unfocused	**More Appropriate**
This report will study the effects of foreign competition on our business.	This report will study the marketing strategy of the three foreign competitors which are having the most impact on our share of the market in color television: Sony, Panasonic, and Mitsubishi.
This report will examine safety problems in our manufacturing operations.	This report reviews lost-time accidents reported in the past 12 months in our manufacturing plant and corrective actions taken to prevent recurrence.

The Goal of the Project

Be sure the statement of your goal or objective fits the statement of the problem. The reader of your proposal should understand from this section exactly what he or she will be getting. You should state this in concrete, specific language. This section may include a list of goals rather than a single one. If a list is used, cite first the most significant goal vis-à-vis the statement of the key problem. Supplementary objectives may then follow. Avoid vague generalities.

Too Vague	**More Specific**
This report will suggest some ideas for changes to cope with rising labor costs.	This report will recommend a systematic approach to offset rising labor costs in the assembly plant via
	1. upgrading machinery
	2. supervisory training
	3. changes in worker incentive plans

Sometimes a report project deals with one major issue but may also recommend wider suggestions. I recently worked with a group whose charge was to evaluate our undergraduate course curriculum and determine which new courses, if any, should be offered. The committee report provided the required recommendation but also offered additional insights not requested. In our final report we presented a list of criteria to be used for future decision making about course additions or deletions. The goals of our project shifted and expanded as another need became evident. The final objectives became: (1) to evaluate undergraduate course offerings in the College of Business and select additional courses from those proposed to the curriculum committee, and (2) to recommend a list of criteria for making future decisions about new course offerings in the College.

The Research Procedures

In this section of the proposal, your methods for gathering and processing information should be spelled out. Since no research project is completely new, you may begin by citing previous work in the area that has been acomplished by others. As anyone who has ever written a major term paper will attest, this "literature search" is often tedious but it does provide a sound foundation for the recommendations offered by the project. Your public or university library will be a starting point for many research projects.

What your reader needs to know is how you are going to find the information needed to solve the problem posed. Your choice of methods is, of course, limited by available resources (time and money, for example).

The Cost of the Project

The final section of the proposal tells your reader what all this will cost so that he or she can decide if it is worth the expenditure. If the writer is on the organization's payroll, it will usually be sufficient to simply estimate the number of work hours needed and other material expenses such as computer time, printing, and postage. If the proposal is prepared by an outside consultant, a charge for professional services will also be included.

Although all this sounds like a great deal of information, the final version of the report proposal is seldom more than a few pages. Here is an example of such a proposal:

September 27, 1978

To: William A. Lasser, Director of Employee
    Relations

From: Kathy Sanders, Employee Communication
      Supervisor

Subject: Proposal for an Analysis of Business
         Periodicals as Possible Gifts for
         Administrators

Background

  Advanced Industries, Inc. is a widely diversi-
fied company dealing in the manufacturing and
marketing of textile products. Each member of the
administrative staff deals with a somewhat different set of management problems although all are
involved on a daily basis with the leadership of
people. Despite continuing mechanization of plant
procedures, overall productivity has failed to increase significantly. Absenteeism and employee
turnover are higher than at any time in the past
six years. There has also been a marked increase in
the efforts of the textile worker unions to organize at several plant locations.

  All of these factors have played a part in management's decisions to increase the amount of
training made available to supervisory employees
throughout the organization. As a supplement to
the training workshops which are now held regu-
larly, it has been proposed that a business
publication which would reinforce ideas presented
in training sessions be given as a Christmas gift
to each member of the administrative staff.

Statement of the Problem

  The problem is that the company lacks the information necessary to make an intelligent comparison
between the many business publications available.
Information is needed to compare the content,
costs, and potential usefulness of these publications in light of the needs of Advanced Industries, Inc.

Goal of the Project

  The goal of this project is to narrow the field of
alternatives to three publications which will be
most useful to company administrators. Background
information will be gathered to support the selec-
tions. These three will also be ranked from most
appropriate to least appropriate based on findings
of the research. A final recommendation will be
made.

The Research Procedures

The information presented in this report will be gathered from three main areas. First, directories and indexes of publications located in the public and university libraries which list management periodicals will be reviewed. These include descriptions detailing the type of information conveyed in each publication. Second, persons in management positions will be asked to suggest specific periodicals which they have either used or have heard favorable comments on. And third, after a publication has been recommended by a directory or by someone familiar with it, the actual publication will be systematically examined to determine its suitability to the needs of Advanced Industries, Inc.

Interviews of managers will be confined to those in local textile-related industries. No travel is anticipated in this study.

The Cost of the Project

Since this project is being done as part of my normal job responsibilities, no special costs are anticipated. It is estimated that the study will take approximately 42 hours to complete. The following is a tentative breakdown of that time:

Preliminary planning of library search procedures	2 hrs.
Review of indexes of publications	2 hrs.
Interviews of managers	10 hrs.
Systematic analysis of selected publications	10 hrs.
Preparation of final report	15 hrs.
Presentation of report findings to Advanced Industries, Inc.	3 hrs.
	42 hrs.

Costs of secretarial services, paper, materials, photocopying, etc. will be absorbed by the Employee Communication Department.

Many organizations have developed standard arrangements and even detailed style manuals which prescribe acceptable formats for reports. In addition, there are many good books available to the working manager which describe the content and layout of formal reports. Several of these are described in the recommended readings at the end of this chapter. There are, however, some techniques for report writing I'd like to share with you. The most common communication problem for most people is the considerable chore of getting the thoughts and ideas from the writer's mind onto that ominous blank sheet of paper. But, as with most tasks, there are shortcuts and tricks of the trade that can greatly streamline the effort and improve the finished product. In the next section I'll describe such a procedure which I modestly call Timm's Miracle Method.

Timm's Miracle Method of Report Writing

There was a time when I figured it would take a miracle for me to get through college. That unexpected blessing came in the form of a bit of serendipity—a chance discovery. Upon returning to college after a tour in the army, I enrolled in a speed-reading class. One day the instructor, who seemed to be an endless source of "tricks of the trade" for students, began discussing clever approaches to organizing term papers and written reports. In a half hour, my unimpressive academic career had been turned around. I applied the technique, amplified it, and gave it the name of Timm's Miracle Method. I would have named it after that instructor, but her name has long since eluded me. At any rate, I'll guarantee this approach for well-organized and often even sensible written reports.

There are nine steps to Timm's Miracle Method.

(1) Think and Grow Clear. It makes no sense to jump into writing your report until you fully understand what's to be done. Be certain that you are on the same wavelength with the person who has authorized or requested the report. The proposal, of course, is designed to do just that. Your planning stage must include at least these three phases described by Richard Hatch:

> First, the problem upon which the report will focus must be clearly defined, and the question to which the report will address itself should be specified. Second, the criteria that the decision makers will use to make a final decision must be spelled out; in other words, the factors that will decide the issue must be identified. Finally, sources of information and evidence must be identified and methods of gathering the information selected. All these decisions have to be made before a proposal can be submitted.[5]

If your report is not extensive or formal enough to warrant a proposal, you may go directly to data gathering once the plan is clarified.

(2) Gather Preliminary Information. Even the most carefully planned research project involves a period of "groping in the dark" for useful data.

Often this takes the form of leafing through books and periodicals or conducting some loosely structured interviews with people familiar with the report topic. A common mistake for many is that we fail to write down or record this information because we're not sure it will fit into our final report. It makes sense to gather a little too much information rather than not enough—at least at the early stages of the project. Don't be overly selective at this stage. Reconcile yourself to the fact that you will not use every tidbit of information you gather. But it is important to get on paper anything that may prove useful.

There is a trick to how you get it on paper too. If you are handwriting preliminary notes, record them on one side of a sheet only and leave lots of room between notes. I prefer to use unlined, legal size sheets. Some students conserve by writing on discarded computer sheets—there are always plenty of these at the computer center. If you are dictating your notes, be sure to instruct the transcriber to at least double-space them (some people prefer triple-spacing) and leave wide margins. The reason for recording your preliminary notes this way will become clear in a moment.

One final point about your early note gathering: be sure to identify each quoted or paraphrased source. You will be taking three types of notes: direct quotes, paraphrased quotes, or your own ideas. For each type, the source can be identified in parentheses following the note. If you copy down a direct quote, use quotation marks and ellipses and brackets as necessary. When you omit words in quoted materials, you should use a series of three spaced periods—called ellipses points—to indicate the omission. It is important that the omission does not detract from or alter the essential meaning of the sentence. Brackets are used to insert a word or phrase of your own to clarify the context of the quote for the reader.

An example of the use of ellipses follows:

> Technical material distributed for promotional use is sometimes charged for, particularly in high-volume distribution to educational institutions, although prices for these publications are not uniformly based on the cost of developing them. (without omission)
>
> Technical material distributed for promotional use is sometimes charged for . . . although prices for these publications are not uniformly based on the cost of developing them. (with omission)[6]

An example of the use of brackets:

> Those who learn to write better reports tend to become more demanding in what they expect of the reports they receive. "When 800 people took my course at Standard of Ohio," says [Albert] Joseph [president of the Industrial Writing Institute], "they began to ridicule the reports that still were written in the old style. The environment has changed."[7]

Without brackets we would not know who Joseph is. He was introduced earlier in the article.

Paraphrased material should convey the same thought as the original author, although in different words. Do not put quotation marks around such notes, but do cite the source of the idea.

One final type of preliminary note is often overlooked by researchers: your *own thoughts*. As you read and gather data, ideas are going to be triggered in your own mind. Don't let these get away. Jot them down immediately and simply identify them as your own by putting your initials in parentheses at the end of the note.

Here are examples of each type of note:

> *Direct quote:* "And unfortunately, the beginning report writer tends to put very little energy into the preparation stage, sometimes even ignoring it completely, preferring to get into the more active job of gathering information." (Hatch, 1977, p. 245.)

> *Paraphrased quote:* Beginning report writers tend to overlook the preparation stage, preferring to get directly into information gathering. (Hatch, 1977, p. 245.)

> *Own idea:* One problem leading to our poor quality reports may be that less experienced writers are not spending enough time in preparation before they gather data. (PT)

I'll explain what the notations in the parentheses following each quote refer to in step three.

(3) *Build a Source Bank.* Prepare a reference card for articles, interviews, or other sources you've made notes from. Do this *immediately*. I normally use 3-by-5-inch cards and record the information in correct bibliographic format. Here are examples of the quotes I cited a moment ago:

```
Hatch, Richard. Communicating In Business
(Chicago: Science Research Associates, 1977),
p. 245.


"Teaching the Boss to Write," Business Week,
October 25, 1976, pp. 57-58.
```

There are variations of bibliographic format covered in detail in writers' style manuals. Note cards for interviews may simply say: "Interview with (name, title, organization) conducted on (date)."

Being careful to provide all publication data on the card at this stage can save hours of aggravation spent in trying to locate a lost source later. Don't forget: one card for each source.

(4) *Review Materials and Create Preliminary Outline.* This step calls
for creativity. Keeping in mind your objectives, develop an outline showing a logical arrangement. Often it is useful to do this on a large blank
sheet, in pencil, or even on a blackboard. Remember the different patterns of arrangement discussed in Chapter 7. Get something down in writing and then rearrange it freely until each piece fits. Be sure to include
the problem definition and decision criteria. Based on your gathering of
preliminary information, several issues and concerns should emerge.
Let's say, for example, your report examines the feasibility of renovating
an older shoe store in your city's downtown shopping district. Your preliminary research shows:

- Fewer *shoppers* use downtown stores than 5 years ago, but there
  has been a slight uptrend in the past 2 years.

- *Tax incentives* are available to companies that expand or locate
  new facilities downtown.

- Renovation of old stores is *less expensive* than a move to a new
  location.

- The Downtown Business Association is supporting a *redevelop-
  ment program* for the downtown area by recognizing the civic
  pride of companies who stay.

- *Shoppers* who do use downtown stores *spend less* than those who
  use our suburban mall stores.

- The *state legislature* is considering a bill to provide *low cost loans*
  to businesses that renovate or relocate in urban areas.

- Many downtown *shoppers are elderly* and cannot travel to suburban stores.

How could this information be arranged? There are essentially three
classes of information presented here:

1. Information about shoppers and potential profits
   a. fewer than in past but improving
   b. spend less than in suburbs
   c. many are elderly
2. Information about costs
   a. less expensive to renovate
   b. tax incentives available
   c. possible low cost loans in future
3. Information about public relations benefits

a. Downtown Business Association recognition
b. demonstrates service to elderly by renovation
c. shows civic pride

Once these areas have been identified and numbered, each note or bit of data gathered should be examined to see where it best fits and a corresponding number written next to it.

(5) *Cut and Sort Notes.* The overall project now becomes far more manageable. Cut out all the notes identified with 1-a and put them in a stack. Do the same for 1-b, 1-c, 2-a, etc. until each segment of the outline is covered. Now you can see why it's important to write only on one side of the sheet of paper and leave ample margins.

(6) *Tape and Transitions.* Beginning with one stack of notes, physically cut and tape them to a larger sheet of paper. Write in introductory comments and transition statements to make the message flow. Don't worry if it doesn't sound exactly right—you'll edit it several more times later. Just get the basic ideas down and tied together. Be sure to use the kind of transparent tape you can write over. Repeat the process for each stack of notes. What you now have is a preliminary draft of the final report.

(7) *Edit and Reedit.* It helps to set aside the preliminary draft for a day or two before editing. This helps you get a fresh perspective. For most reports, two or three thorough edits should be done. This includes cutting and retaping where necessary, as well as stylistic changes such as cutting out deadwood language, improving syntax, and correcting spelling and punctuation.

One tip I find helpful is to use a different color of pencil or pen for each edit. That way you'll know just how many times a section has been reviewed.

Your product now is a mess of typing, tape, and handwritten changes. This is normal. You should have seen the original draft of this book!

(8) *Assemble the Bibliography.* One final step before typing is to go back to your 3-by-5 cards with citations on them and arrange them in alphabetical order. These can simply be handed to the typist for final bibliography preparation.

The citations following each note should remain in the final report (except those which identified your own thoughts). These will tell the reader where the information came from. To locate a source marked (Smith, 1979, p. 3) the reader must simply look at the bibliography sheet under Smith and find the source printed in 1979.

(9) *Type and Proof the Final Version.* The last step is a mechanical one: typing and proofreading. Typing from a "cut and tape" draft should

not be difficult if the material is not crowded and if instructions are clear. It often pays to go through the draft one last time, putting yourself in the position of the typist, and looking for anything that may be confusing.

Voila! Your finished report.

We could summarize Timm's Miracle Method by listing a series of don'ts:

Don't

- be overly selective in preliminary data gathering

- write on both sides of a sheet or crowd your notes

- forget to identify each source used and prepare a reference card for each

- hesitate to be creative in developing your outline

- feel uncomfortable about frequent cutting and taping

- forget to edit several times when your mind is fresh

The Trend in Reports: War on Gobbledygook

Reprinted by permission of the Chicago Tribune-New York News Syndicate, Inc.

The evidence is clear that reports—especially those that go outside the organization—are getting more readable. Or at least most folks are trying. A recent article in *U.S. News and World Report* opened with this statement:

> Stung by complaints from a baffled public, Government agencies and a host of firms that serve consumers are working to remove wordy, legalistic phrases that pervade documents ranging from application forms to insurance policies.[8]

The article goes on to cite examples where the public demand for simpler language is being heeded. Among them—

> With presidential backing, several federal agencies are revising commonly used rules and forms to reduce confusion about their meaning.
> Many banks and insurance companies have acted on their own to make documents less complex by removing outdated terms and explaining procedures better to customers.
> To force action by firms resisting the trend, four states this year ordered insurance firms to make their policies more readable, and New York legislators passed a similar law applicable to all consumer transactions.[9]

In another article, *Business Week* reports that:

> Report-writing courses are being treated with a new seriousness in industry. Companies are having to learn to cope not only with supervisors and first-line managers who have trouble communicating, but also with senior research scientists, B-school graduates, and otherwise bright top executives who cannot turn out a clearly written, logically organized interoffice memo—and often do not realize it.[10]

Major corporations and government agencies are spending a lot of money to train their people in more concise report writing. Why? Because report-writing effectiveness means communication effectiveness which means management effectiveness. More specifically, in one large corporation it was found that, with training, managers could learn to trim the size of their reports by half. The time required to produce the report is significantly reduced and reading time shrinks as well.[11] The impact on efficiency can be considerable.

In the past two chapters we have looked at some ways to get more mileage from our words, logically arrange the parts of a document for maximum impact, and streamline the overall preparation process. The objective of all this is, of course, to optimize communication—the creation of understanding—so that the organization can function efficiently. The keys to good reports lie in high quality information, sensibly arranged and presented in readable form. The diagnostic section of this chapter deals with a way to measure the readability of reports.

Diagnosing Your Reports

A readability formula provides a method for looking at one's writing more objectively. They will not make you, or anyone else, write great literature, but they will help you write more clearly.

There are several ways such a formula—which I'll explain in a moment—can be used. First, it can provide an objective way to check the level of your own writing. Different audiences can deal with different levels of reading difficulty. This technique can help determine if you are "on target" with your audience's ability.

A second use of a readability formula is in helping critique the writing of others. It can come in handy when you run into a sticky case of author's pride or when you know there is something wrong with a piece of writing but are not sure exactly what it is. Frederick Dyer explains,

> When you tell an author, "Your writings are hard to read," he may get his back up and claim that his style is wonderful and the readers are stupid—or are not willing to read what is good for them. He may challenge you to point out the parts which are not composed in clear, beautiful prose, and you may find yourself bogged down in endless discussions of the meanings of words, clauses, and punctuation. However, if you can apply a formula that indicates his work *is* hard to read you put him in the position of not arguing solely against you, but against a host of well-known experts.[12]

Perhaps the most popular and easy way to use readability measure is the *Gunning Fog Index*. The score calculated is easy to interpret since it is in grade level of education. For example, an index of 8 means that the material tested is easy reading for one with an eighth-grade education. An index of 12 indicates high school graduate level of readability while a 16 indicates the level of a college graduate. *Love Story*, the popular novel of several years ago, had a Fog index of about 7. Quality news magazines score around 12 to 14, while a highly technical report may be a 17. One recent application of the Fog Index dramatically illustrated a problem of government documents. The eligibility requirements section for the Food Stamp Program scored a Fog Index of more than 26![13] Normal business letters and reports should be in the 10 to 13 range. Here is how to compute the Fog Index.

(1) *Select a sample of writing.* This should normally be text material (not listings or tables, etc.) with at least 100 words in it. The larger the sample, the more reliable the figure computed, but computation time may

be excessive. For long reports, it would be wise to select several samples at random throughout the work. Be sure your sample ends at the end of a complete sentence.

(2) *Determine the average number of words per sentence.* Divide the total number of words in the sample by the total number of sentences. Independent clauses (i.e., clauses separated by semicolons) are counted as separate sentences.

(3) *Determine the percentage of hard words.* To do this, count all words in the sample that have three or more syllables *except* (a) proper nouns; words that are capitalized; (b) words that are made up of two or more short, easy words like *manpower*, or *bookkeeper*; and (c) verbs which become three syllables by adding -es or -ed such as *repeated* or *finishes*. Divide this total by the number of words in the sample.

(4) *Add these two calculations and multiply by 0.4.* The product is your Fog Index score—the minimum grade level at which the sample could be easily read.

Let's say that your writing sample has 129 words and an average sentence length of 13 words. Twenty-six of the words in the sample are hard words. Your Fog Index would be computed:

Average sentence length	13
Percentage of hard words	20
Total	33
Multiply by	0.4
Grade level of readership	13.2

Some Other Thoughts About Reports: READING FOR CHAPTER 10

An Unsuccessful Report[14]

Charles R. McConnell

Would you like a sure-fire formula for generating unsuccessful written reports at will? Guaranteed to work, or double your errors back?

Seek no further; an infallible method is available in these paragraphs. And it's not the product of just a single mind. In fact, it combines the best of the worst of nearly forty managers, engineers, and other professionals.

This dramatic advance came about after a large organization actively so-licited cost-reduction project ideas from its employees. Forty investigative projects were assigned, representing the most promising of over two hun-dred ideas submitted.

The project investigators were given a recommended report outline. Each was told to create a report with this question in mind: If I were the decision-maker, would this report give me enough information for a reasonable decision?

The forty projects had one thing in common—all had plenty of savings potential. And with two or three exceptions, the reports submitted also had one thing in common: they could *not* be used as decision-making instruments.

Most of the reports bombed out. A wealth of improvement potential lay in a tangle of language and paper, uncommunicated or only partially communi-cated to the persons in positions of action.

The errors committed throughout the thirty-some-odd impotent reports were extracted and condensed into the following guidelines suggesting *"How to Write an Unsuccessful Report."*

1. Don't restrict yourself with a *Standard Report Format.*

Rules or guidelines can be as restrictive as laws, and we all know we have enough of those without asking for more. The free spirit within you should permit words, thoughts, sentences, and even whole sections to tumble from your mind in a stream of consciousness. After all, it's your report and it should really be you. *Formats tend to guide and shape,* and these forces restrict the free spirit.

Forget the availability of a frequently-*Recommended Report Format* con-sisting of: Introduction, Summary, Body or Discussion, Conclusions, Recom-mendations, and Appendices. This isn't for you; your situation is different.

There's widespread practice to back up your decision to follow no partic-ular format. Consider the many management consultants who conclude their labors by giving the client lengthy, wordy, disorganized reports before van-ishing from the scene probably never to return. Of course, a management consultant usually doesn't have to remain and live with the impact of his report. Yet one might wonder if these rambling reports have anything to do with why so many consultants are, indeed, never to return.

2. Use as many words as you can possibly pack into each sentence, and stuff each paragraph with as many sentences as possible. Never *place dif-ferent thoughts in separate paragraphs*; the reader may get the idea you're capable of thinking only one thought at a time. Stick to the popular belief that the more words you use the better the writing. William Faulkner once used a sentence over 150 words long to open one of his novels. With a little imagination you can match or surpass that. What was good enough for Faulkner should be good enough for you.

There are other sound reasons for using many words. If you say the same thing five or six different ways in as many places, your reader is far more likely to get the message. Ignore the unsupported claim that *most written material received in business contains from 25% to 100% more words than are necessary, and that each unneeded word contributes another opportunity for misinterpretation and misunderstanding.*

Stay with the many roundabout phrases we've become accustomed to using in our writing. They're far more impressive than everyday spoken English. Things like "conference in regard to" rather than "meeting about," or "in view of the fact that" rather than "because," are good examples.

3. Use plenty of white space along with your many words. Have your report typed with extra-wide margins and leave large spaces between paragraphs. This will help you spread your report over the maximum possible pages. You will be consistent with the apparent belief of many report writers that quantity equals quality—if it's long it must have required lots of thought and effort.

4. Don't *be specific*. When referring to quantities use well-accepted words such as "sufficient," "enough," or "adequate" rather than amounts. It's not fair for critics to say that failure to identify specific quantities may mean the writer doesn't know them. In using non-specific terms you're actually being honest with yourself and kind to your reader. You're admitting things are constantly changing, and you want to turn out a report which is applicable over a wide range of conditions. And you're allowing your reader to give your words their most convenient interpretation or the one he finds easiest to live with.

5. Scatter humor throughout your report by using certain similar words interchangeably. For instance, say "than" when you mean "then," "affect" when you mean "effect," or "except" when you mean "accept." Your reader deserves a few chuckles as he winds his way through your report. Avoid the use of *desk references of commonly misused words.* They spoil the fun.

6. Keep your conclusions and recommendations well hidden, preferably buried somewhere in the last one-fourth of the report. Many top managers read mysteries for relaxation. What could present more of a mystery to your boss than making him read to the middle of page 43 to find your conclusions? Never *state conclusions early in the report.*

7. Use few, if any, charts, graphs, and illustrations. If it's really true that *"A Picture Is Worth A Thousand Words,"* then one illustration could do you out of a thousand words of report length. This word loss means the loss of three or four pages (maybe five or six, if you make sensible use of white space) in your final report.

8. Put calculations, mathematical formulas, and tabulations right where they're first mentioned. By no means should you *organize all supporting ma-*

terial in an Appendix. This assumes a reader at a given organizational level may be able to get enough information by reading only the narrative portion of your report, while the technical information is evaluated by others. Remember, you want to make every reader of your report read every last word and symbol in it.

9. Keep your overall theme as broad as possible. The more subtopics a report pulls in, the more valuable it will be. Ideally, you should handle several topics simultaneously, leaping from one to another in your narrative as similarities, differences, and variations occur to you. This displays your flexibility as well as your broad knowledge. Set up straw problems and knock them down. Work into your narrative several "what-if-this-happens" situations for which you already know the answers. If you want to tell your audience of your extensive knowledge, you should never *limit yourself to a single topic.*

10. Write your report so it can be read by everyone in the organization from the junior janitor to the Chairman of the Board. Every writer desires— and deserves—as wide a readership as possible. What's the point of writing for only one or two persons? Concepts such as *Primary Audience, The Principal Recipient of the Report,* and *Secondary Audience, Others Who May Read and Act on Parts of the Report,* are unimportant. Popular practice is on your side; had these concepts any real value, would they be so universally ignored?

11. Never *edit or rewrite.* This destroys the spontaneity of your work and makes it something less than "you". Re-writing and editing take time and usually result in a shorter report. Who ever heard of spending more to get less? Regard with suspicion bits of so-called wisdom such as the statement made by Blaise Pascal: "I have made this letter rather long because I have not had time to make it shorter."

12. When giving information, advice, or instructions always provide at least two options for everything, preferably conflicting alternatives. This, like Number 4, is also done out of honesty to yourself and consideration for your reader. Nobody wants to be pinned down; we all need room to maneuver. Stick faithfully to W. C. Fields' oft-quoted advice: "Never mind what I told you—do as I tell you."

Through conscientious application of these guides you can consistently generate lengthy, rambling, complex, contradictory, confusing, unsuccessful reports. With practice you will someday be able to write reports which fail on all counts.

But if you refuse to bow to tradition and popular practice and choose to align yourself with a minority of mavericks and oddballs, consider the italicized portions of the foregoing paragraphs, get a good report-writing text, and start cranking out successful reports.

Maybe—just maybe—there's truth in the old adage: "The person who cannot communicate an idea is as fully limited as the individual who cannot conceive one."

Questions for Further Thought

1. Calculate the Fog Index for several samples from your recent writings. Compare your score with others. Jot down the level of readership your writing is appropriate for. Are you on target with your audience? Schedule additional Fog Index calculations at regular intervals. Record your results.

2. What are the major advantages of using a direct order of presentation in a report? What disadvantages? When would a nondirect arrangement be more appropriate?

3. Review some reports you've received recently. Copy down just the headings used. Does the arrangement make sense? Are the headings informative or simply topical? If topic headings were used, change them to informative. How does this affect the report's readability?

4. Use Timm's Miracle Method to prepare a report. Critique it as a method. What were its strengths and weaknesses? How can you improve on it to make it work better for you?

Notes

1. S. Bernard Rosenblatt, T. Richard Cheatham, and James T. Watt, *Communication in Business* (Englewood Cliffs, N.J.: Prentice-Hall, 1977), p. 292.
2. Raymond V. Lesikar, *Report Writing for Business*, 5th ed. (Homewood, Ill.: Richard D. Irwin, 1977), p. 1.
3. Adopted from Frederick C. Dyer, *Executive's Guide to Effective Speaking and Writing* (Englewood Cliffs, N.J.: Prentice-Hall, 1962), p. 112.
4. Phillip V. Lewis and William H. Baker, *Business Report Writing* (Columbus, Ohio: Grid, 1978), p. 51.
5. Richard Hatch, *Communicating in Business* (Chicago: Science Research Associates, 1977), p. 245.
6. Charles T. Brusaw, Gerald J. Alred, and Walter E. Oliu, *The Business Writer's Handbook* (New York: St. Martin's Press, 1976), p. 153.
7. "Teaching the Boss to Write," *Business Week*, October 25, 1976, p. 58.
8. "Government, Business Try Plain English for a Change," in *U.S. News & World Report*, November 7, 1977, p. 46.
9. *Ibid.*
10. "Teaching the Boss . . . ," p. 56.
11. *Ibid.*, p. 58.
12. Dyer, *op. cit.*, p. 200.
13. Warren S. Blumenfeld, Esther R. Blumenfeld, and James M. Higgins, "Readability of Current and Proposed OFCC Materials Regarding the Development of Affirmative Action Programs." Paper presented at the Southern Academy of Management Meetings, Atlanta, October 1977.
14. Reprinted from the November/December 1977 issue by permission of *Manage* and The National Management Association, Dayton, Ohio. © 1977.

Recommended Readings

To the materials recommended at the end of Chapter 9, I would add the following:

Lesikar, Raymond V., *Report Writing for Business* (5th ed.). Homewood, Ill.: Richard D. Irwin, 1977.

Lewis, Philip V., and William H. Baker, *Business Report Writing.* Columbus, Ohio: Grid, 1978.

Pearsall, Thomas E., and Donald H. Cunningham, *How to Write for the World of Work.* New York: Holt, Rinehart & Winston, 1978.

For further information on developing training programs for writing improvement, see Joseph Baim, "In-House Training in Report Writing: A Collaborative Approach," *The ABCA Bulletin,* December 1977, pp. 5–8. (This is a publication of the American Business Communication Association, 911 South Sixth St., Champaign, Illinois 61820.)

An excellent source of answers to questions of grammar, word usage, format, and writing procedures, is Charles T. Brusaw, Gerald J. Alred, and Walter E. Oliu, *The Business Writer's Handbook.* New York: St. Martin's Press, 1976.

PART **IV**

OUR PERSONAL COMMUNICATION STYLES

CHAPTER 11

OUR PERSONAL STYLE
The Way We Word

I've suggested in the beginning of this book that communication is an attempt to "make common." The degree to which the message sender and receiver have a common understanding after the message is received is the measure of effectiveness. Although we take this whole process pretty much for granted, the way our language behavior works is not well understood by most people. Communication scholar Lee Thayer has said that the way we talk about things determines the social conditions we live with. Our language affects us as well as affecting those we talk to. This chapter will point out some problems and pratfalls in the way we word.

It may strike you as ironic that language—the very essence of what many view to be communication—poses one of the most pervasive sources of misunderstandings and of failures to make meanings common.

We have all developed our own ways of processing and arranging the words and symbols which we use to describe reality. This system becomes our personal language structure. Our sensory experiences, our perceptions from the physical world, can be likened to data cards for a computer. And in these terms, our structure is analogous to a system program which tells the computer what to do with the new data.

Communication failures often arise between people either because of differences in how they relate words to experiences or because of the way they process the words they speak or hear.

Language Structures:
Is That Any Way to Talk?

There are two general ways to improve verbal communication skills: (1) increase the vocabulary so that more precise "data cards" can be produced, or (2) improve the match between language structures and objective reality. Increasing someone's vocabulary will usually be a far less fruitful approach than working on structures. Only in situations where there is seriously inadequate vocabulary—such as in learning a new language—would the emphasis on improved vocabulary be significantly valuable. Clarifying language structures by examing our logic and showing discrepancies between the way we process words and the way the real world behaves is a far more valuable approach.

Let's look at several assumptions about word use that may be causing common problems in the ways we process language.

Fact versus Assumption

Often miscommunication arises when the way we structure our language does not distinguish between that which has been experienced and that which is assumed. To presume that people—including ourselves—know an absolute fact when they see one is a dangerous presumption.

In truth, the vast majority of information we receive is inference or opinion. Something we personally observe or experience can be regarded as a fact—at least for us. But just about anything else is an inference or opinion. We run into misunderstanding and disagreement when we state inferences or opinions as though they were facts. The language we normally use does not automatically make the distinction clear. So we must make an extra effort to do so.

Under normal circumstances, we can state direct observations—"I saw Tom leave the plant at 5 o'clock"—as facts. But if we take the fact about Tom and elaborate upon it, what we say becomes an inference. For example, when we say, "I saw Tom leaving the plant *to go home*," we are now adding a new dimension to the message which may or may not be true, in fact. That Tom left the plant can be easily verified by observation. That he went home (assuming that his home is somewhere out of our sight) is merely inferential on our part.

An inference is a conclusion based upon incomplete information, and much of what we talk about is based on inference. By necessity, we communicate inferences all the time. The problems arise when listeners are unclear as to whether we are inferring or speaking of fact. Our language often tends to muddy this distinction, so inferences have a way of coming out sounding awfully factual.

354

Again, let me restate. There is nothing inherently wrong with drawing inferences—they are necessary for people to make day-to-day sense out of the world. We seldom have the luxury of having *all* available data at our disposal before we draw conclusions. The important thing is that we (1) recognize inferences as such, and (2) that we word them in ways that will help us and our listeners avoid confusing them with facts. Failure to do so can often lead to confusion and arguments.

For example, if you like the sales manager's dress, and you say, "Hey, I like that dress," fine. That's a fact. You are clearly expressing a factual, as-it-relates-to-me statement. You like the dress and there's little room for misunderstanding. If, however, you say "That's a nice dress you're wearing," you're stating an opinion which sounds like a fact and there's more room for interpreting what you really mean. Do you like the fact that the sales manager is wearing a dress instead of her customary vested pant suit which you think is too masculine? Do you like the fact that you can now get a better look at her legs? Are you being sarcastic and not really complimentary? There's more room for interpretation in an opinion. (Of course, nonverbal dimensions such as tone of voice and facial expression can clarify the point you are trying to make.)

Nobody can argue about what you like. If you say, "I didn't like that movie," that's your right and other people will respect it. But if you say, "That was a rotten movie," then others may be put on the defensive, especially if they liked the movie.

When an opinion is not identified as such, the receiver of the message has to make a decision on how to respond—whether to be "nice" and agree with you or to be true to his or her feelings and say it was not a "rotten" movie, and run the risk of starting an argument.

Here is another example. If we state the opinion that "Frank is stupid," it may appear on the surface that stupidity is some inherent characteristic of Frank. But what, in fact, I am saying is that:

- My personal experience has supplied me with a meaning for the word *stupid*.

- I have perceived Frank's behavior as fitting my view of the concept of *stupidity*.

- Therefore, I have concluded that Frank is stupid.

Notice that the words *I* and *me* enter into this analysis throughout. When I conclude that Frank is stupid, I am really talking about something *I've* done—*I've* related these two things, Frank and stupidity. *I* have related them in my world of words. Whether or not they are related in the "real world" of objective reality remains unclear.

So, in essence, every opinion we offer is a statement about ourselves. This is so because:

- We can never say all there is to say about any topic. It would take too long. Therefore . . .

- Those things we do choose to talk about and those that we choose to ignore involve a selection process on our part, based on our past experiences. Whereas . . .

- Each of us has had totally unique experiences and no two people have experienced the same things, and since . . .

- We have each created our own unique way of attaching words or labels to our world of experiences. Therefore . . .

- When we combine several of these labels into a message, we are saying little about objective reality and instead are describing something that is of great importance to us *personally*.

Thus to conclude that, "Frank is stupid," is to report on some word associations we have made. This statement doesn't really say much about Frank, but it does say some very interesting things about us.

A simple remedy for this problem of expression is to make clear the fact that you recognize this process. You can do so by converting these opinions into facts. "*I think that* Frank is stupid," is a fact. Or, "I've observed Frank doing things *I consider stupid*," is a fact.

Although this changing of terms often results in additional effort and longer messages, the tradeoff results in greater accuracy and clarity of expression. Failure to so clarify our messages can lead to considerable embarrassment, incorrect conclusions, and serious potential harm to our credibility. I suspect this potential breakdown was clearly in S. I. Hayakawa's mind when he said that general semantics—that is, the study of language and its behavioral effects—could be more accurately described as the study of "how not to be a damn fool."

Another common problem in the way we structure language is the tendency to oversimplify the categories into which we mentally sort things. We deal with our life experiences in egg-carton fashion, neatly fitting each experience into one of several compartments.

The Either-Or Temptation

Some people rely too heavily on polar terms, terms that force us to choose between extremes—like good or bad, weak or strong, big or little—and which tend to oversimplify and confuse the issues we are discussing. In reality, most things we encounter in life are more accurately described in terms of probabilities or fine variations among events or experiences than by an either-or categorization. In other words, our experiences represent some shade of gray rather than black or white differentiations. To illustrate, simply ask yourself, and others, questions such as these:

- Are you rich or poor?
- Are you big or little?
- Are you handsome or ugly?
- Are you conservative or liberal?

The appropriate response, of course, to questions like these would be, "As compared to whom (or what)?" It can be very helpful to our communicative abilities to train our thinking away from oversimplified categorization, although it does take active intellectual effort to talk in terms of degrees or comparisons.

In an industrial organization, this process may mean avoiding the tendency to classify workers as "industrious or lazy" or "productive or unproductive." In one company, a sales manager actually had a big chart on his office wall with the names of all his salesmen boldly displayed under the headings "Heroes" and "Bums."

The problem with this tendency is that when our language and thinking utilize such either-or logic, other possibilities are overlooked. If we only classify a manager as a "good leader" or "bad leader," we leave out a lot of other possibilities. Maybe he or she is effective in some dimensions of the job while ineffective in others.

Sales representatives or other persuaders often manipulate this either-or orientation to their advantage. "Would you like to take delivery next Monday or Wednesday?" attempts to preclude the option of not taking delivery at all. It's the old story of the ice cream shop operator who asked each customer whether they wanted one egg or two in their milkshakes. Few people said neither, and he charged extra for each egg, of course.

Our credibility can be seriously damaged when listeners recognize these kinds of oversimplified language structures. While there are legitimately dichotomous categories—such as male-female, present-absent—most things don't fit so neatly into either-or slots. Or sometimes the categories become so broad as to be meaningless. Whenever we hear ourselves or others sending either-or messages, we might be wise to consider:

- Are all the options covered?
- As compared to what (or whom)?

Self-Fulfilling Expectations

The manager who comes to actually see his subordinates as heroes or bums is obviously not relating to reality. It is far more realistic and hopeful to think in terms of ever-changing individuals who can and will change their work performance. Today's hero may have been yesterday's bum if we as managers have been able to avoid the related problem of self-fulfilling prophecies. Because we usually choose what perceptions we will pay attention to, and then mesh these things into our views of reality, there is a strong tendency to look only for the pieces that fit.

Similarly, there are interactive effects between our perceptions and the ways we talk. What we see directly affects what we say. And what we say affects what we see. The filters of our mind develop over time as we label our world of experiences, and these filters determine what we select to perceive. When we can make no sense out of some thing or event—that is, if it doesn't fit our world view—we tend to reject it.

It can be quite disconcerting, for example, to find that the worker we've labeled as "rebellious" is suddenly vigorously defending the status quo. Or to find that "nice, pleasant" receptionist suddenly shouting angrily at a visitor. We'd prefer to reject or explain away such discrepant observations because they just don't jibe with "the way things are" in our mental world. The way we label things leads to expectations of how those things will behave in the future.

Furthermore, expectations have a way of becoming self-fulfilling. The supervisor who labels a subordinate "lazy" will undoubtedly find more and more evidence to support the judgment. And in all likelihood, this supervisor's attitude will be perceived by the worker, thus leading to suspicion and distrust. The overall result: a strong potential for miscommunication. So let's keep our labels somewhat loose. Maintain some flexibility so that unanticipated changes in things, events, and people can fit into our mental worlds without throwing us off balance.

Recognizing Change

In human interaction, people receive feedback which either reinforces or modifies their view of the world. The development of self-image, stereotypes of others, and role expectations all result from this interactive process of communication.

Modern self-help techniques all begin with an important premise: *each individual is unique and capable of change.* But problems of communication arise because, although our world of experiences is dynamic and ever-changing, the world of words is much less flexible. Language tends to change very slowly, leaving us with the problem of trying to describe fluctuating processes with words that stress consistencies.

People are also constantly in a process of change. As George Bernard Shaw has said, "The only man who behaves sensibly is my tailor; he takes my measurements anew each time he sees me, whilst all the rest go on with their old measurements and expect them to fit me."[1] So failure to accept change leads to many communication difficulties. Psychologist Carl Rogers suggests, "If I accept the other person as something fixed, already diagnosed and classified, already shaped by his past, then I am doing my part to confirm this limited hypothesis. If I accept him as a process of becoming, then I am doing what I can to confirm or make real his potentialities."[2] In other words, if I believe that the word labels I've attached to a person are not changeable, I cannot then cope with changes in my world of experiences with regard to that person.

Before I leave this discussion of change, let me clarify one point. Language and word associations *do* change over time, but the changes in these labels are not necessarily logical. We need only look at the different meanings of terms (often slang expressions) in recent years, for examples:

- *Dude* used to mean an inexperienced cowboy; it now more often describes a "street-wise" city dweller.

- *Heavy* is no longer only a measure of physical weight, it can mean good or desirable or a half dozen other things.

- *Coke* isn't just a cola beverage anymore.

- *Righteous* doesn't necessarily mean full of religious virtue.

- For that matter, in some subcultures, *bad* means good.

Need for Clear Thinking

To be credible as a message source, a person must be constantly aware of such things as the pervasiveness of change. In short, we need to think clearly and communicate clearly; when our ways of thinking become too rigid, we move away from paralleling reality.

Words do not have inherent meanings. They are simply labels that we attach in unique and individual ways to our world of experiences. And since labels trigger meanings in others, the degree to which we achieve common understandings when communicating is determined in part by how accurate we are in relating these labels to reality. If we are inaccurate we describe a world that is not there. Carried to the extreme, these inappropriate language structures can affect our mental health. Our psychological and sociological well-being can depend upon our being aware of the important ways in which language reflects and influences the ways we think and communicate.

Maladjusted people typically have language use difficulties like the ones I've been describing in this chapter. Psychologist William Pemberton identifies five tendencies of the maladjusted:[3]

1. They tend to assume that everyone is having the same experiences at the perceptual level as themselves—that there is only one "right" way too look at or feel about anything.
2. They tend to assume that if they talk long enough, loud enough, or "reasonably" enough, they will be able to influence others to their way of thinking.
3. They tend to assume that the characteristic by which something is named, labeled, or judged is *in* the object, that what they say about it is in the "right" characteristic, the "real" name, the "real" meaning.
4. They tend to make generalized conclusions from very few experiences in such a way that new experiences have to fit old conclusions or remain ignored.
5. They tend to shut out further consideration of a problem with, "That's all there is to it."

Many communication problems arise from a lack of awareness of the way we word. When the many pitfalls of language processing are pointed out, it seems amazing that we can communicate at all. *Nevertheless, we muddle along.*

Words Do Not Have Meaning—
People Have Meaning

Many people tend to oversimplify communication by viewing it as the transfer of meanings from one person to others. The use of the term *transfer* is misleading. It conjures up images of simply carrying a package (message) from one point to another. It's not that simple. A sender cannot really transfer meanings but rather the mind of the receiver *creates* meanings. The sender's task is to use symbols which trigger responses that accurately create meanings similar to the sender's. The creation of meaning by the receiver is a function of relating the incoming symbols to his total life experiences up to that point.

Redding cites understanding of this viewpoint as absolutely essential to anyone who communicates in organizations, especially managers, executives, and supervisors.

> The failure to observe the notion that meanings are *created* in people is probably the cause of one of the most pervasive errors in everyday communication. This error has been labeled the *content fallacy*. It is the common

assumption that there must be some way of so wording our message that . . . our ideas will be "transferred" to the minds of the receivers. . . . What happens all too often is that we keep tinkering with the content of the message-sender's message rather than trying to find more ways of making sure that the message-receiver's responses are appropriate. This content fallacy leads us to believe that we are "getting through" to our audience merely because we are getting through to ourselves.[4]

The meanings do not reside in the words themselves but in the minds of the word's users. Associations conjured up cannot always be predicted. An interesting cartoon in the *New Yorker* several years ago showed an alligator reading the novel *Jaws* and laughing so hard that tears ran down his face. Although I'm not willing to make any statements about reptile language behavior, the point is that our messages may create very different associations than we intend.

Emotional Loadings

Many terms carry emotional connotations which can excite, anger, offend, or create other pleasant or unpleasant associations in those who receive them. An obvious example is the profane expletive which, for example, could be extremely embarrassing or offensive to a group of worshippers while being a source of considerable amusement to a group of punk rock fans. The word itself doesn't change, only the receiver's associations and, in this case, the context in which the term is used.

But there are countless other more subtle examples. Words that may connote very positive images to one person may be very negative to another. I can recall a university professor who felt there was no higher praise than to refer to a colleague as a "liberal." Others conjured up very different emotional values for the term.

Stuart Chase once described "purr" words and "slur" words. This was a catchy way of describing *euphemisms* and *dysphemisms*, word descriptions given to things or events which evoke either more pleasant associations or more unpleasant ones. The degree of pleasantness will, of course, depend upon your predispositions. For many terms we have a choice of how to "load" them. Here are some examples based on my perspective:

Euphemism	Neutral	Dysphemism
Emotionally handicapped	Hard-to-manage child	Brat
Luxury automobile	Standard size car	Gas guzzler
Go powder my nose	Go to the restroom	Go to the toilet

Passed away	Died	Croaked
Sizzling steak	Cooked meat	The flesh of a steer

Some very humorous exchanges can arise when we use euphemisms or dysphemisms in unexpected ways. A cartoon I recently saw showed a woman talking to a man who was carefully inspecting his food saying, "That yellow scum on top happens to be Hollandaise sauce." Another illustration of slur words came from one of MacNelly's "Shoe" cartoons:

Newspaper Editor to Writer: Senator Belfry's office is complaining again about our unfair treatment of the distinguished senator in our editorials . . .

Writer: Baloney! I'm never unfair in any of my editorials! Which one are they talking about anyway?

Editor: The one called "Bozo the clown goes to congress."

There is considerable skill involved in anticipating how people will tend to associate meanings. In the advertising business symbols are extremely carefully manipulated to project the best possible associations.

For the manager processing information, the key is to reduce the emotionalism in language when clear, objective decisions and actions are required. A good starting point is to carefully listen to your own language first. Do you tend to use terms that may carry inappropriate associations? Are there certain terms or expressions that seem to result in others "getting their fur up"? Are you sensitive to the possibilities that some expressions you routinely use may be real turn-off terms to others? Getting answers to these questions involves developing sensitivity to feedback from others.   *women's lib*

Understanding What I Mean, Not What I Say

The words we use often don't communicate our "real" message. In the language of Transactional Analysis, these are the *ulterior* transactions. The classic example of the use of ulterior transactions may be when the bachelor says to his date, "Why don't you come up to my place and see my etchings?"

Often we don't say what we really want. The situation may make us feel awkward or we might simply keep our thoughts to ourselves for other reasons. Often we rely on clichés or platitudes, which are usually acceptable to those we interact with even though they convey little or no real information. Consider the following dialogue between a manager who wants to promote a worker and the employee's immediate supervisor who would love to get rid of him.

Manager: Tom, I'm looking at your man Harrison for that foreman's job over in shipping. What do you think of him?

Supervisor: Harrison? Sure, he's quite a guy.

Manager: Do you think he can handle it?

Supervisor: No problem. He's really with the program. He's been one of my heavy-hitters ever since he came here. He has his stuff together.

Manager: Thanks, Tom. I appreciate your being up front with me on this one. I'll push things along and we'll get some action on it real soon.

Supervisor: Right on!

Whatever factual information might have been exchanged here was completely muddled by the clichés. What did these men really say to each other? Not much!

Here's a real-life example of how clichés were misunderstood with a profound effect:

> One instructive account of how clichés distort communication was that given by Senator Thomas Eagleton after the 1972 Democratic presidential nominations. He explained that his only contact with Frank Mankiewicz, a top aide of George McGovern, about the Vice-Presidential nomination "was the thirty-five seconds I spent on the phone with him after Senator McGovern called me to be his running mate. Mankiewicz said, 'No skeletons rattling around in the closet, right?' and I said 'Right!' "
>
> Eagleton interpreted the skeleton-in-the-closet cliché as it is usually understood, meaning concealed gross misconduct. Therefore he answered Mankiewicz' second cliché, "right?" with the cliché that is required: "Right!" Mankiewicz probably did not expect "Wrong" and did not get it. Mankiewicz knew at the time that Eagleton had been hospitalized for mental depression, yet felt "it wasn't a serious problem." When later informed of this, Eagleton said, "They sure didn't let me know about it." If he had known that they were concerned about this as a political liability, he commented, "I would have said, 'That's right. The reports are true. That's the way it is.' " Thus a breakdown in communication was due to the use, or rather misuse, of a cliché.[5]

It is useful for a manager or any other communicator to reexamine his or her speech patterns every now and then. Do you find that clichés repeatedly creep into your talk? I suspect we all do. An open and trusting relationship with others can be a source of feedback regarding your language behavior. Ask for feedback. Encourage it. One acquaintance of mine had recently gotten into the habit of describing complex paradoxical situations as "mind boggling." That was a pretty clever expression a few years ago, but it's gotten stale. When I pointed that out to her, she appreciated the criticism and has now switched to newer clichés. Occasionally she even says, "Very confusing!"

It is interesting to me that television and other mass media seem to produce dozens of new clichés every week. As colorful as these may seem at first, like all clichés they age quickly and lose their strength and vitality.

Functions of Our Words

Gerald I. Nierenberg and Henry H. Calero have written a thoroughly fascinating book called *Meta-Talk: Guide to Hidden Meanings in Conversations*, in which they describe some functions of expressions we use in conversation. I have used their categories and added some examples of my own to assemble a guide to word functions. Verbal responses can often be categorized as softeners, foreboders, continuers, interesters, downers, convincers, strokers, and pleaders. Let's look at some examples of each of these.

Softeners

We often preface remarks with expressions intended to influence the receiver in a positive way—to soften him or her for the "real" message. Here are some examples:

Expression	Purpose or Real Meaning
"You're going to like what I'm about to tell you."	Prepares the receiver for what we believe will be good news for them
"It goes without saying . . ."	Attempts to get agreement by assuming it to be so
"What I'm about to tell you . . ."	Usually indicates that a disclosure that should be handled carefully and involves the receiver is to follow
"I venture to say" or "off the top of my head" or "I'm sticking my neck out" or "at first blush . . ."	The message sender is about to draw a conclusion based on incomplete data.
"Would you be kind enough to . . ."	Flatters receiver so he or she will do what is asked

"I'm sure someone as intelligent as you ..." or "You're very perceptive about ..." or "What is your expert opinion of my ..."	Asks for concurrence; expects the listener (receiver) to indicate agreement; sets up for an exchange of compliments
"You are right but ..."	Attempts to avoid conflict by feigning agreement
Use of acceptance or agreement statements followed by *but, yet, however, still,* etc.	The message sender does not feel the receiver is right but wants to soften the blow of disagreement
"You are right."	Probably a genuine statement of fact.

Foreboders

Often we put our listeners in a negative or anxious frame of mind by using these expressions. They can lead to unpleasant encounters or psychological games.

Expression	**Purpose or Real Meaning**
"Nothing is wrong." (accompanied by a look of anxiety)	There is something wrong but I don't want to talk about it (or) There is something wrong and I want you to show concern and probe further.
"It really doesn't matter."	It matters.
"Don't worry about me."	Please do.
"I have nothing more to say."	I'm about to blow up and argue.
"That is all that can be said."	More could be said but it'll lead to disagreements.
"I'd rather not discuss it."	I want to talk to someone about it but probably not you.
"We've beat this dead horse enough."	There isn't much more any of us can say to improve agreement.

Continuers

These expressions attempt to get the listener to disclose more of his or her thoughts on a matter. These are often viewed as supportive although they can become counterproductive—when the person goes on and on and you really need to shut them up. Here are some examples:

Expression	Purpose or Real Meaning
"What else is new?"	Introduce another topic for conversation.
"Go on" or "That's very good," or "Now you're talking," "I like that."	Please elaborate on your point. I agree with what you say.
The CB radio operator's "come on" at the end of his transmission.	I'm finished talking, now you say something.
"Why don't you go with that line of thought . . ." or "Tell us more about that idea."	You don't make much sense to me yet but this could become productive if you go on.
"If you have any further questions, do not hesitate to call upon me."	This seems like a good line to end my letter with. I sure hope I don't hear from the reader.

Interesters

Statements and questions which attempt to arouse interest or to get the listener to say something to indicate interest are called interesters. Use of these expressions often reveals something about the speaker and his prejudices. In most cases, interesters add nothing to the conversation and can become something of a verbal tic for speakers. They can also annoy your listeners. Here are some examples:

Expression	Purpose or Real Meaning
"And do you know what he said?"	Are you still listening?
"After all I've done for him, do you know what he did?"	Compliments the speaker and seeks support for the position he took.
"Guess what happened?"	The speaker is uncertain that he has anything relevant or interesting to say so he must demand the listener's attention by getting her to say "What?"
"Did you hear the one about . . .?"	Instructs the listener to conceal any knowledge of the joke that will follow. Get ready to laugh.

"What do you think of [some emo-   I hope you'll agree with my stand
tion-loaded term or expression]   on this issue.
...?"

"I could say something about that!"   I don't want to cause trouble but I
will anyway.

Downers

Downers are expressions used intentionally to put the listener in a defensive state of mind. Typically they appear when a speaker sees himself in a win-lose situation and is moving in for the kill. Appropriate vocal tone and facial expression can add considerable power to the downer. Often the tone is sarcastic.

Expression	Purpose or Real Meaning
"Are you happy now?"	You have just humiliated me and caused great anguish and you should feel miserable too.
"Don't make me laugh."	A mean-hearted reaction to another's request or demand.
"Don't be ridiculous."	You have said something I disagree with and I will now attack you as a person.
"Put it to music ..."	I have heard your excuse and I'm not sympathetic.
"That's the way it is, pal."	I am totally unsympathetic to your plight.

Convincers

We each use verbal logic to justify our proof and strengthen our attitudes, preconceived ideas, notions, and assumptions. But sometimes the pure logic breaks down, as illustrated by this excerpt from Nierenberg and Calero.

> A Kentucky judge, after hearing a moonshining case, said to the defendant, "Although you were not caught using it, we found equipment on your premises capable of producing alcohol. We are therefore going to find you guilty." To that the defendant replied, "Now that you mention it, you might as well also convict me of rape. I've got all the equipment for that too."[6]

Convincers are often used as substitutes for logical argument. When a speaker is having trouble making a sensible case for his point of view, convincers can cause his listeners to forget the logical inconsistency. Here are some examples of convincers:

Expression	Purpose or Real Meaning
"That's the *only* way we can do business in this city."	Justification of an unethical or illegal act
"Why, anyone can do it!"	The task is so simple that even a moron could accomplish it (this can also be a downer when the listener has just failed at the task in question).
"Anyone can follow my line of reasoning."	Persuades by intimidation; I find it simple and so should you.
"I think we all agree that . . ."	Appeals for consensus or tries to smooth over conflict.
"Let me make one thing perfectly clear . . ."	Introduces a conscious deception or tries to hammer home a belief.
"Everybody I know agrees . . ."	Therefore, you should agree too; or therefore, it must be true.
"Believe me, . . ."	Please agree with me, I'm desperate for your acceptance.

Strokers

People need verbal reassurance and approval. Sometimes such statements come naturally from others. Often, however, we feel a need to reach out and solicit some verbal approval statements—some positive strokes. We use meta-talk also to give strokes: to tell people that they are special to us and that we are willing to share feelings and information with them.

Expression	Purpose or Real Meaning
"How do you like my new outfit?"	I need reassurance that I look nice.
"What do you think of my plan? I didn't go too far, did I?"	Although I don't want criticism, here is a double-barreled question that invites you to praise and be critical.

"I shouldn't tell you this, but ..." (followed by flattery)

You'll enjoy hearing this gossip and I want to make you happy and strengthen our relationship.

"I heard some really good things about you ..."

Here are some positive strokes; be prepared to be modest.

Pleaders

Pleaders reflect the emotions of the speaker. These emotions may be envy, uncertainty, or discomfort, concealed aggression or expressions of superiority. Here are a few examples:

Expression	Purpose or Real Meaning
"I certainly wouldn't parade around in a revealing dress like that." (envy)	I wish I had a figure like hers.
"He's pretty obnoxious with all his jokes." (envy)	I wish I could be the life of the party.
"I'll do my best." (uncertainty)	My best probably won't be good enough.
A fat man who says, "Watch me break the chair." (discomfort)	By anticipating disaster, I will be relieved of embarrassment if it does happen.
"Do you mind if I ask you ..." [followed by a penetrating or accusing question] (concealed aggression)	Now I've got you; My disdain is now made visible.
"That's nothing, you should see ..." "Don't you know that?" or "It may interest you to know ..." (superiority)	I'm smarter; I'm more in-the-know; I'm better.

One final function of words is to convey our personal image. Often we do not select our language on the basis of what will communicate most clearly, but rather what will impress our audience the most. If we are lawyers, we need to sound like lawyers and use terms like *whereas, pursuant, litigant,* and *plaintiff.* College professors like to talk about *models* and *conceptual paradigms* and other things few people understand. Military men love to use acronyms and jargon unique to their work. Every organization and profession has its jargon which is a form of in-group shorthand.

Why do we use jargon outside our organizational or professional group? One reason is that it sets us apart from others; it provides a subtle way to identify with groups or other individuals. At the same time, it provides a way to assert our superiority in a specialized knowledge. In short, jargon used when talking to those not familiar with it is used to impress, not to communicate.

A sensitivity to the way we use words is crucial to the effective communicator. The hidden meanings conjured up in the minds of our listeners can often override what we are really trying to convey.

But there is more to our personal communication style than just the ways we use language. Let's look now at the realm of communicative symbols that go beyond words.

Louder Than the Way We Word

As important as it is to develop sensitivity and skill in using language, it's important to remember that verbal communication does not take place in a vacuum. There are nonverbal qualities, many of them very subtle, that cannot be separated from the verbal aspects of received messages. Just what is nonverbal communication? It is probably easier to describe what it does *not* include than to specify all that it does. Scholars who study nonverbal communication seem to agree that the term clearly excludes communication using words, numbers, or normal written or oral language. Instead, it focuses on all the other things that cause meanings to be created in people.

Ray Birdwhistell, a pioneer in nonverbal research, is reported to have said that studying nonverbal communication is like studying "noncardiac physiology."[7] To study parts of the body without considering the all-important function of the heart is absurd. Similarly, to examine the functions of isolated words makes little sense. What we say cannot be extracted from the context in which we say it. Nonverbal communication defines that context and seeks to explain its effects on our word messages.

Mark Knapp, who wrote a well-known book in this area, suggested that nonverbal forms of codification can be usefully divided into the following categories:

1. Sign language—substitution of gestures for words, numbers, and punctuation signs
2. Action language—all movements not used exclusively for signals (e.g., walking, drinking, eating)
3. Object language—all intentional and nonintentional display of material things (e.g., implements, machines, art objects, clothing, and the human body itself)[8]

Phillip V. Lewis, in his book on organizational communication, classifies nonverbal communication as:

1. Body motion or kinesic behavior—gestures, facial expressions, movement posture, or body movements
2. Paralanguage—voice qualities, laughing, yawning, etc.
3. Proxemics—human use and perception of physical space
4. Olfaction—sense of smell.
5. Skin sensitivity—stroking, hitting, greetings, and farewells, etc.
6. Artifacts—perfume, clothes, lipstick, eyeglasses, wigs, false lashes, general attractiveness, height, weight, hair color, skin color, etc.[9]

The ways we attach meanings to messages can readily be affected by physical environment and space, physical appearance and dress, physical behavior, expressions of the face and eyes, and vocal cues that accompany spoken words.

Environment and Space

The variables of environment and space can include any of the objects that surround us as we communicate, including size and visual dimensions of the room, furniture, decorations, lighting, and temperature.

From previous studies researchers know that proximity is a potent variable in developing contact with another person. They know that people have a need for defining their own territorial boundaries—their personal bubble—and we define conversational distances among ourselves. Spatial and environmental behaviors can reflect our style of leadership. The arrangement of one's office furniture can create impressions of status differences or openness. The manager who talks to an employee from behind his or her desk comes across differently than the manager who crosses the room to sit next to the employee.

An even more commonplace example of space as a nonverbal communication dimension is found in the ways we position ourselves when speaking to others. Intimate communicators such as lovers, close friends, or conspirators, position themselves up to about 18 inches apart. In personal or normal social conversation we are likely to maintain 2 to 4 feet between us. In more formal business encounters we stay from 4 to 12 feet apart, while in public speaking situations we maintain 12 feet or more between our listeners and us. In normal conversation if a person moves in closer than arm's length, she or he is seen as pushy or aggressive. If a person stands back a bit further than "normal," it conveys a sense of aloofness.

An interesting thing about spatial variables of nonverbal communication is that we all have clear expectations of how much space is appropriate and when that expectation is violated, we tend to be uncomfortable. For example, observe the behavior of people crowded into an elevator. Their normal social distance is suddenly reduced to intimate distance. Most people respond by looking up at the floor indicator or distracting themselves in some similar way.

Different organizational positions affect space expectations. We assume that higher level executives will have more spacious offices. Their space is also more likely to be "protected" via closed doors, reception rooms adjoining their office, and sometimes even their position in the building— they are often on or near the top floor.

While it's perfectly appropriate for the executive to "invade" the work area of a lower ranking organizational member, the opposite would be unheard of.

Physical Appearance and Dress

The effects of physical dress and appearance are a second group of nonverbal properties. These effects include those things which influence the way people respond to us. Physical attractiveness as well as dress appearance can influence one's self-image and one's perceptions of others. If we arrive at a meeting dressed in a business suit and find the other participants in Levi's and cowboy boots, we may feel a bit awkward. The key variable is *appropriateness* to the occasion. And the people we interact with along with the purpose and context of the interaction will determine what is appropriate. An interesting example in changing group dress standards was seen during President Jimmy Carter's first year in Washington. Presidential aides in short sleeves and tieless still seem strange and even disturbing to some people.

Closely related to appearance and dress are the artifacts which people display. The expensive jewelry, elaborate office decorations, or attractive personal belongings "tell" others something about us. The absence of such things may tell us something else. Either way, the impression formed from such nonverbal cues will be in the mind of the observer.

Physical Behaviors

Nonverbal effects of physical behavior include the combined effort of the arms, legs, and posture with verbal output. According to the research of Knapp, "body language" tends to parallel the spoken language. These body movements often communicate unspoken messages such as:

1. like or dislike for another
2. status differences

3. affective states or moods
4. intended and perceived persuasiveness
5. approval seeking
6. quasi-courtship behavior
7. need for inclusion
8. deception
9. interpersonal warmth[10]

Included among these physical behaviors would be nervous manner-isms, shuffling from position to position, frequent looking at one's watch and posture or position when seated.

One type of physical behavior which also ties in with the spatial vari-ables is touching behaviors. While a literal pat on the back or a reassuring handshake is often appreciated, some people get a reputation for being a "touchy-feelie" type. People can feel uncomfortable with excessive touching.

Expressions of the Face and Eyes

Facial expressions and movements of the eyes are especially important ways people convey a variety of emotions ranging from fear or anxiety to happiness, relief, or requests for additional information. Scientists have found that dilation of the pupil may indicate emotional arousal, interest or attentiveness. Extensive research concerning eye behavior is being done in several disciplines.

One of the key obstacles to more effective use of nonverbal commu-nication to create clearer understanding is illustrated by the studies of face and eye expression. Paul Ekman's research in this area concludes that with proper training, one can learn to accurately identify facial ex-pressions with emotions and personality of the subject. He also states that there is strong evidence that there are some constants which transcend different cultures.[11] Other researchers, such as anthropologist Ray Bird-whistell, disagree. Dr. Birdwhistell contends that "there are no universal gestures. As far as we know, there is no single facial expression, stance or body position which conveys the same meaning in all societies."[12]

Vocal Cues Accompanying Spoken Words

We discussed the effective use of voice in Chapter 7, showing how such things as emphasis, diction, rate, pitch, and loudness affect speaker cred-ibility. People stereotype others on the basis of their voices: The fellow with a lisp is a sissy. The lady with slurred speech is assumed to be drunk. The woman with a husky or breathy voice is aggressive or "sexy." Al-though these stereotypes are often unfounded, studies have shown that a person can judge with fair accuracy the age, sex, and status of others from the sound of their voice alone. Also, people make judgments about one's trustworthiness, likability, competency, and dynamism on the basis of voice.[13]

The messages we receive are colored by these and undoubtedly other nonverbal factors, all of which create a total impression.

The Effects of Nonverbal Communication

The sobering reality is that what we *say* is almost always overridden by what we *do*. While the language we use conveys certain objective information, our bodies convey how we *feel* about what we say. Whenever there is a discrepancy between the words we receive and the nonverbal cues we perceive, the nonverbal message is likely to be taken as the "real" meaning. Here is a newsclipping which provides an interesting illustration of such message discrepancies:

When You're Smiling . . .

BUFFALO, N.Y. (AP) — Barbara Coyle, 20, a clerk at a late-nite grocery store in suburban Amherst, thought someone was playing a joke on her the other night.

A man holding what looked like an automatic pistol entered the store Wednesday, his face covered with a black ski mask.

"Put all the money in the bag or I'll shoot you," he commanded.

But when she looked out a window, she saw another man sitting in a car. He was smiling.

Joining what she thought was a game, she simply smiled at the gunman. He threatened her again. She smiled. The man finally turned and walked out.

It wasn't until the man in the car walked into the store to see if anything was amiss that the would-be holdup victim realized the man with the gun had been serious.

The effective manager must be sensitive to nonverbal messages he or she sends off, as well as to those received from others. The recommended readings at the end of this chapter provide additional sources of information about this important dimension of commmunication.

Questions for Further Thought

1. Consider your nonverbal communication and how you come across to others. Make a list of adjectives that describe your image. Ask several associates to make a similar list about you. How do these lists compare?

2. It has been said that language does as much to conceal as to reveal. How would you respond to that idea? Does nonverbal behavior work the same way?

3. Make a list of your favorite euphemisms and dysphemisms. How do they tend to cloud the meaning of terms? When are euphemisms or dysphemisms useful?

4. Try this simple experiment with spatial communication. While in conversation with someone, move in closer than you would normally. What reactions do you get from the other person? Next, try positioning yourself further away than normal. How do others respond?

Notes

1. George Bernard Shaw as quoted in Kenneth G. Johnson, *General Semantics: An Outline Survey* (San Francisco: International Society for General Semantics, 1972), p. 13.
2. Carl Rogers as quoted in Johnson, *op. cit.*
3. William Pemberton, "A Semantic Approach to Counseling," *ETC.: A Review of General Semantics*, 13, 2 (Winter 1955–56), pp. 83–92.
4. W. Charles Redding, *Communication within the Organization* (New York: Industrial Communication Council, 1972), p. 29.
5. Gerald I. Nierenberg and Henry H. Calero, *Meta-Talk: Guide to Hidden Meanings in Conversations* (New York: Trident Press, 1973), pp. 15–16. Reprinted by permission of Simon & Schuster.
6. *Ibid.*, pp. 40–41.
7. Mark L. Knapp, *Nonverbal Communication in Human Interaction*, 2nd ed. (New York: Holt, Rinehart & Winston, 1978), p. 3.
8. *Ibid.*
9. Phillip V. Lewis, *Organizational Communication: The Essence of Effective Management* (Columbus, Ohio: Grid, 1975), p. 153.
10. Knapp, *op. cit.*, p. 113.
11. *Ibid.*, p. 137.
12. Birdwhistell quoted in *New York Times Magazine*, May 1970, pp. 8–9.
13. Knapp, *op. cit.*, p. 173.

Recommended Readings

Language Behavior

Nierenberg, Gerald I. and Henry H. Calero, *Meta-Talk: Guide to Hidden Meanings in Conversations*. New York: Trident Press, 1973. A thoroughly enjoyable book that is hard to put down. The authors' discussion of the functions or real meanings behind common expressions has to make you laugh—and think. The book is loaded with examples.

Haney, William V., *Communication and Interpersonal Relations: Text and Cases*, 4th ed. (Homewood, Ill.: Richard D. Irwin, 1979). This excellent behavioral text is built around general semantics principles. Many interesting case studies of communication and management problems are presented.

Fabun, Don, *Communications: The Transfer of Meaning*. Beverly Hills, Calif.: Glencoe Press, 1968. Fabun was publications editor for Kaiser Aluminum and Chemical Corporation when he produced this 48-page illustrated booklet. Colorful and entertaining, the book explains some basic concepts of language processing very nicely.

Johnson, Kenneth G., *General Semantics: An Outline Survey*. San Francisco: International Society for General Semantics, 1972. This is a concise but thorough outline of general semantics principles with examples.

Eschholz, Paul, Alfred Rosa, and Virginia Clark, eds., *Language Awareness*, 2nd ed. New York: St. Martin's Press, 1978. A fascinating book of articles which foster awareness of some ways language affects our behavior. This is fun reading, an entertaining view of language in many different contexts. Contributing authors include S. I. Hayakawa, H. L. Mencken, Edwin Newman, and Stuart Chase.

Postman, Neil, *Crazy Talk, Stupid Talk*. New York: Delta Books, 1976. The very descriptive subtitle of this book is, "How we defeat ourselves by the way we talk—and what to do about it." This is entertaining reading by a well-known general semanticist.

Hayakawa, S. I. *The Use and Misuse of Language*. New York: Fawcett Premier Books, 1964. Like Eschholz *et al.* above, Hayakawa assembles readings in the field of general semantics. This is one of the best-known books in the field.

Nonverbal Communication

Knapp, Mark L. *Nonverbal Communication in Human Interaction*, 2nd ed. New York: Holt, Rinehart & Winston, 1978. This is probably the most complete survey of empirical research on nonverbal communication available. Its twelve chapters go into considerable depth to explore known nonverbal variables.

For a shorter review of the literature, you may want to consult one of the following texts:

Goldhaber, Gerald M., *Organizational Communication*. 2nd ed. Dubuque, Iowa: Wm. C. Brown, 1979, Chapter 5.

Rosenblatt, S. Bernard, T. Richard Cheatham, and James T. Watt, *Communication in Business*. Englewood Cliffs, N.J.: Prentice-Hall, 1977, Chapter 8.

I've Read the Book. So What Happens Now?

The information and diagnostic techniques presented in this book taken alone will not solve any communication problems. Only we can solve communication problems. Solutions come from changes in the ways we, as individuals and as organizations, create meanings and influence behaviors. As managers we have the responsibility to make what the organizational development specialists call "interventions." An intervention is a managerial action taken to bring about improvement in group functioning. Listed here in ascending order of difficulty are ways managers may intervene in organizational communication behaviors:

1. Increase awareness and sensitivity to the way one is "coming across" to others.
2. Teach principles and standards of appropriate communication behavior.
3. Induce changes in individuals' attitudes toward communication and interpersonal relations.
4. Induce changes in group attitudes toward "the way things should be."

5. Create opportunities for individuals to try on new communication behaviors.
6. Reinforce any improvement in communication behaviors as soon as it occurs.
7. Develop a climate of trust and support conducive to group changes.

This entire book has been about improving communication effectiveness—improving the probability that understanding and appropriate influence will be achieved in your organizations. By applying the principles presented here and by helping others to apply them, most organizations can realize significant improvement.

These eleven chapters do not fully cover the subject and neither would eleven more. No one could ever say all there is to say. But the materials in this book, however incomplete, can make each of us a better manager. Remember, communication is what managers *do*. So let's do it well.

INDEX